WATER RESOURCE MANAGEMENT

By the same author

Frontiers in Migration Analysis (Ed.)
Introductory Methods in Population Analysis (*et al.*)
Land Utilization : Theory and Practice
Patterns of Regional Geography : An International Perspective (Ed.)
Vol. 1 : Conceptual Development
Vol. 2 : Indian Perspective
Vol. 3 : World Regions
Introduction to Rural Settlement (Revised and Enlarged Edition)
Recent Trends and Concepts in Geography (Eds.)
Statistics for Geographers and Social Scientists (Revised and Enlarge)
Systems of Rural Settlements in Developing Countries
Urban Geography : A Text Book

About the Editor

Ram Bahadur Mandal, (*b. 1948*) M.A. (Geography) and Ph.D., is a University Professor in Geography at T.M. Bhagalpur University, Bhagalpur. Earlier, he was a Senior Lecturer in the University of Dar-es-Salam, Tanzania and Reader at R.D. & D.J. College, Munger.

Prof. Mandal has 21 Books and 66 Research papers to his credit. Also, he has completed projects on 'Management of Wetlands in North Bihar' and 'Wasteland Management in the Districts of Munger and Jamui', sponsored by the UGC and ICSSR, respectively. He is life member of Bihar Association of Geographers and National Association of Geographers of India, and is Editor of East-West Geographer, published by Anga Geographical Society, Munger.

WATER RESOURCE MANAGEMENT

Edited By

R.B. Mandal

CONCEPT PUBLISHING COMPANY, NEW DELHI-110059

Cataloging in Publication Data—DK
Courtesy: D.K. Agencies (P) Ltd. <docinfo@dkagencies.com>

Water resource management / edited by R.B. Mandal.
p. cm.
Papers presented at the fifth BAG conference held at Bhagalpur during 18-19 October 2003.
Includes bibliographical references.
Includes index.
ISBN 818069318X

1. Water-supply—India—Management—Congresses. 2. Water-supply—India—Bihar—Management—Congresses. I. Mandal, R. B. (Ram Bahadur), 1948-

DDC 363.610 954 22

ISBN : 81-8069-318-X

First Published 2006

Published and Printed by
Ashok Kumar Mittal
Concept Publishing Company
A/15-16, Commercial Block, Mohan Garden
New Delhi-110059 (India)

Phones : 25351460, 25351794
Fax : +91-11-25357103
Email : publishing@conceptpub.com

Preface

Water is life sustaining resource for several creatures on the earth surface but unfortunately the good quality of water is scarce. The Third World Water Forum (WWF) held in Kyoto, Japan on 16-23 March, 2003 concluded that demand for water in the world has increased three times more in comparison with the growth of population. Hence, the supply of fresh drinking water is the focus of attention to the whole problem which relates to the drinking water and to increase people's awareness over the entire world regarding the judicious use and management of water resource. Therefore, 'wars of the 21st Century will be fought for water only not for oil'.

The Planning Commission, Government of India has warned that India will also face water crisis by the year 2025 A.D. Bihar with about 10 per cent of India's population has just 5 per cent of the country's water resource. But North Bihar has very high potential of underground water resource due to abundance of flood plains and perennial rivers. On the other hand, it has flood prone parts of India where kalazar, malaria and death tolls due to water borne diseases are high. The entire state of Bihar faces non-availability of fresh drinking water problem to the masses all the times and low agricultural productivity due to non-availability of water for irrigation as well.

"The clean drinking water Oh! Where I get it? Everytime walking on foot for several kilometres in the desert, but even a bucket is not full to satisfy the small brother's thirst who have running stomach". The establishment of water treatment plants is quite essential in almost all urban areas and under 'Amrit Drinking Water Scheme' in the entire north-eastern part of Bihar in order to remove iron content, arsenic and lack of iodine in the water.

This book on "Water Resource Management" is an attempt to bring together available research papers at the time of Vth BAG Conference held in the P.G. Department of Geography, T.M. Bhagalpur University, Bhagalpur on 18th and 19th of October, 2003. Almost all the contributions are related with the understanding of water resource in a complex natural environment in which water serves as the unifying thread through almost all the fabric of geographic thought. It is so because the entire nation is in search of increasing the efficiency of water management. It involves a complex interaction among various factors, e.g. the soil, the crop, the climate, the natural environment and others. Most of the contributors focused on the need to view the problem in totality in relation to the area concerned. This book suggests improved methods of water resource development and suitable water management practices. This volume includes water harvesting techniques, sustainability of water resources, problems of water supply in rural and urban areas along with the help rendered by watershed management and remote sensing.

In the completion of this book I am highly thankful to Dr. R.A. Yadav the then Vice Chancellor of T.M. Bhagalpur University. I am highly grateful to Dr. D.P. Yadav Ex-Minister of Culture, Government of India, Sri B.N. Mandal, Member of Parliament, Munger along with honourable colleagues of the Department of Geography Dr. U.P. Singh, HOD Geography, T.M. Bhagalpur University, Dr. R.N. Pandey, Dr. G.N. Singh, HOD Geography, R.D. and D.J. College, Munger and others.

I hope that this book will help to stimulate a new environment in the field of geography, economics, planning and agriculture in the spread of new knowledge of water resource management.

R.B. MANDAL
University Prof. of Geography
R.D. & D.J. College, Munger,
Bihar

Munger
2nd November, 2004

Contents

List of Tables

List of Figures

1

Introduction

R.B. Mandal

All the items used by man is known as resource. Water resource is quite essential for the human society along with the development of other resources as well. Human beings and all other living creatures, plants and trees are made up of 60 per cent water content. Hence, it has been truly said that "nothing will survive in this world without water".

Most of the international confrontations took place for sharing the river water and the development of river valley projects. On the other hand, the availability of safe drinking water becomes a problem throughout the world. Water resource is a saviour of human life. Today due to overwhelming growth of population, about 2 billion population living in 80 countries of the world face the problem of water crises. For this fact, UNO has declared 2003 A.D. as the 'International Year of World Water Conservation' under the auspices of which 'World Water Forum (WWF)' has been established in March 2003 in the city of Kyoto in Japan.

Water is available as solid, liquid and gaseous form in our oceans, rivers, tanks and wetlands. It is a resource which could be seen in Dhuandhar waterfall in Bheraghat on the Narmada river, Jog waterfall on the Sarawati river, in the form of Niagra Geyser in Yellow Stone Park, USA; Artisan well in central Australia, Sweet water of Great Lakes, USA and the mighty river like Ganga in India. The proper use of water brings prosperity whereas misuse brings calamities for the humanity. Now-a-days, water has been utilised from surgical operation of human body upto irrigation, navigation, fishing and industrial uses as well. Today the Developed Nations are working on mega-projects for the search of fresh water resource but we are unable to use even the water of the Ganga for the betterment of humanity and use as prime source of irrigation. A survey indicates that at Kashtharani Ghat in Munger in the Ganga river the BOD has reached in between 3.50 to 5.00 which shows danger point for any future use of the water of Ganga.

For the conservation and increase the value of water resources, one has to consider various parameters in its management. This includes availability of the amount of water, its location, its quality, distribution, climatic conditions of the area, nature of soil, demand for water and socio-economic conditions of locality where it occurs. After considering all these one has to make the best possible use of water either for crop production, running industry and supply of safe drinking water to the people.

The available water needs scientific management for irrigating the dry farm lands, development of profitable agricultural practices and optimum use of available water for hydro-electricity generation, recreation by boating and navigation as well (Johnson, 1966).

Review of Past Studies

India is very rich in water resources specially for irrigation and power generation. These two are the subject matter of special interest of geographers who have studied about the problem of flood, flood control and the river valley projects.

In the 1940s, several research papers were published on different aspects of hydro-electric power. Krishnamurty analysed the Papnasnam Hydro-electric Project. He pointed out the potential of Western Ghat mountain for the development of hydro-electric power in Peninsular India. Majumdar has studied about 'Rivers of the West Bengal Delta'. Banerjee has written about 'an outline of devastation caused by the floods in Damodar Basin and suggested flood control measures. Mukherjee in his paper attempted a survey of the electric installations in pre-independence Bengal. Kuriyan and Nair have examined the development of hydro-electric power in Peninsular India. Later on Kuriyan made a survey of the distribution and development of hydel power in India and suggested planning measures. Sidhiqi's study about 'Potentialities of Tube-well irrigation in Burdwan District' in which regional analysis of irrigation has been attempted.

B.N. Jha studied about the rivers of Bihar and analysed the problems posed by them and the development of schemes and projects. Goirala has studied about flood problems of the Ganga Drainage Basin and suggested methods by the construction of dams for controlling the flood. Jauhari search about the regional distribution of different schemes of electric power generation in North-West India. Raina has analysed about the water power of Jammu and Kashmir State. Chakravarty studied about measures to control floods in the Himalayan rivers of the Ganga Basin.

Banerjee has investigated about the regional pattern of power development with special reference to power resources and requirements of power in different parts of the country. Chaudhuri has divided West Bengal into different power zones as per requirements of power. Jain emphasised that surface and underground water resources of Rajasthan is in deficient quantity. R.P. Sinha discussed the installed capacity of power in Bihar and suggested the construction of thermal and electric power stations in different parts of the state.

Present Situation

Today due to fast increasing population we are in urgent need of fresh, pure, abundant and regular supply of water. The need of fresh water is omnipresent in our day-to-day life. A monsoon laden with rain gives us cheer but false sense of security due to encoming of flood. The world's fresh water resource is 2.5 per cent and it is depleting so fast that it may be problematic for the future generation. This fresh water is concentrated in rivers, ground water, snow cover and in the form of ice and snow and the rest 97.5 per cent is salty water in the ocean. Out of this, only one per cent is fit for our use which has been affected by the hydrological cycle, seasonal variations and over exploitation by the human being.

Water is life sustaining resource for several creatures on the earth but unfortunately the good quality of water is scarce. The Third World Water Forum (WWF) held in Kyoto, Japan on 16-23 March, 2003 concluded that demand for water in the world has increased three times more in comparison with the growth of population. Hence, the supply of fresh drinking water is the focus of attention to the whole problem which relates to the drinking water and to increase people's awareness over the entire world regarding the judicious use and management of water resource. Therefore, 'wars of the 21st century will be fought for water only, not for oil.'

The Planning Commission, Government of India has warned that India will also face water crisis by the year 2025 AD. Bihar with about 10 per cent of India's population has just 5 per cent of the country's water resources. But North Bihar has very high potential of underground water resource due to abundance of flood plainns and perenial rivers. On the other hand, it has flood prone parts of India where kalazar, malaria and death tolls due to water borne diseases are high. The entire State of Bihar faces non-availability of fresh drinking water problem to the masses all the times and low agricultural productivity due to non-availability of water for irrigation as well. North-eastern Bihar is almost floating on the vast sea of underground water but unfortunately here the water suffers from presence of excessive iron content. In 2001 Mrs. Rabri Devi, the Chief Minister of Bihar announced in her public meeting for the establishment of *Amrit Paijal Yojna* for the people of this area but as yet no work has been done in this regard. Thus the programme based on community based water harvesting and watershed management for overall development of the area is a far cry. In this regard the Sukhmajari Experiences of Haryana, Tarun Bharat Sangh Experience of Rajasthan, Pani Panchayats of Maharashtra and Seva Irrigation Cooperatives of Gujarat are laudable.

Today, due to rapid population growth, there is misuse of the precious resource in India. Per captia this scarce resource has declined from 5177 cu.m. 1951 to 1820 cu.m. in 2001 and it be just 1440 cu.m. in the year 2050. Hence, urgent action needs to be taken.

The Government of India has declared 2003 as the year of freshwater in accordance with the United Nations Resolution in declaring 2003 as 'International Freshwater Year'. Our Water Resource Ministry has chalked out four objectives for implementation of this scheme as :

(a) Awarness created regarding the scarcity of freshwater.
(b) Its conservation and effective use.
(c) Preservation of its quality and ecosystem.
(d) Community participation is essential for augmentation of freshwater.

For the implementation of these objectives the Ministry is targeting students and teachers of different stages, educating women for domestic use, health issues, farmers for irragation and policy-makers of the society.

Fig. 1.1 : Accumulation of Water from Mountain to the Ocean

Some of the Aspects of Water Resource

- Necessary to reduce drought.
- Control the problem of flood.
- To save the drying crops.
- To reduce the death of livestock wealth.
- To check the torture of human being.
- Contagious disease related to water.
- Lack of safe drinking water.
- Change in the courses of river.
- Availability of Arsenic, Fluoride and Iron content in the water.
- To get rid of polluted water.

Accumulation of Water

Most of the water on the earth is concentrated in the mountainous and plateau regions of equatorial and the frizid zone of polar areas. In relation to this most of the population is concentrated on mid-latitudinal belt of the earth but in terms of water this has been considered as less privileged zone. Similarly, there is no dearth of water in North Bihar due to flood whereas South Bihar is facing with the problem of drought each and every year.

Two piper Chiene Aeroplane helps in giving artificial rain with the spray of Hygroscopic salt on cloud. In the Vidarbha region of

Maharashtra at Baramati and Shagaon two Radars have been established by the Meteorological Department for the purpose.

Conservation of Water

The following measures may be adopted for the conservation of water :

- By the construction of embankment.
- By the inter-linking of rivers, ponds and lakes.
- With the help of afforestation.
- Dredging of courses of the river.
- By the construction of high dam.
- By the fitting of shower and water pipe in the houses.
- Taking of water to far away places with the help of canal and pipe.
- With the establishment of water treatment plant.
- With water harvesting technique.
- Irrigation with pipe and springs.
- Water tax should be taken and audit of water consumption should be made.
- Purification of polluted water should be done.
- Use of low cost technology should be adopted.
- Don't through refuge of the houses and unburnt carcasses into the river.
- Quality of water should be improved with the help of chemical treatment.
- Waterbody should be saved from the pouring of night-soil and polluted materials.
- Bleaching power and lime should be used for cleaning the water.
- Proper use of water site should be made by the establishment of tourist spot and the construction of dam and canal.
- Water is a useful resource but it is not available sufficiently as safe drinking water.
- The flow of water should be regular, water reservoir of fixed capacity should be made and with the construction of embankment along the rivers is essential for flood protection.
- With the collection of water its proper conservation is quite essential.

- The extraction of too much of water from the ground keep its water layer low and this makes the tubewell and well dry especially during the summer season.
- Purification is also a way to conserve water. For long the sewage disposal and the pouring of poisonous water from gas plant, leather works and mills into the rivers and lakes make it difficult to get clean water.
- Afforestation is essential in order to keep the water level high. It has also been helped by natural rain. Hence, the coexistence of the availability of water and plant has been considered essential.

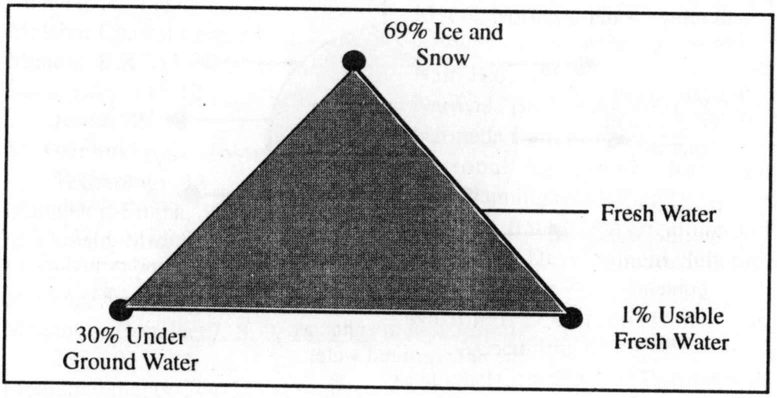

Fig. 1.2 : Fresh Water

Activities Related to Conservation of Water

It is essential because human being wants to use clean water. The availability of clean water is either most irregular or its supply is meagre.

Most of the industries in the entire world is either situated along the river, lake, pond or the sea coast. Unfortunately the industry make them polluted due to pouring of industrial refuse. In the surroundings of Jamshedpur industrial sector which keeps the sources of water black. In this regard UNO has said that "The clean drinking water Oh! Where I get it, everytime walking on foot for miles in the desert but even a bucket is not full to satisfy the small brother's who have running stomach."

Amrit Drinking Water Project of Kosi Belt

In north eastern Bihar the district of Purnea, Araria, Kishanganj, Katihar, Madhepura, Saharsa and Supaul in order to get rid of the problem of iron mixed water the government has announced Amrit Drinking Water Project for this region. The plan was to start with 18 iron-extraction machinery along with 10,000 hand pumps for the purpose in 1998. At present there are 7.78 lakh hand pumps in the State of Bihar out of which about one lakh is out of order.

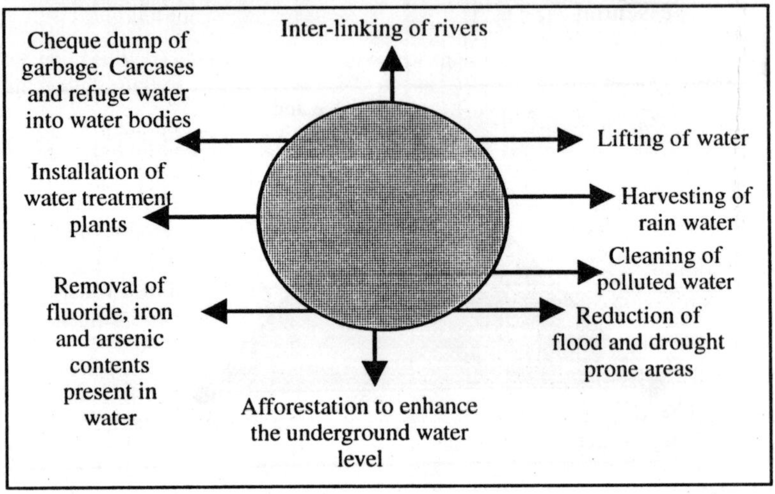

Fig. 1.3 : Collection of Water

Table 1.1 : Our Need of Water *(Billion cubic metres)*

Use	*Year 2000*	*Year 2010*	*Year 2025*
Domestic	30	56	910
Irrigation	501	688	910
Industry	20	12	23
Energy	20	5	15
Others	34	52	73

Collection of Water

In West Bengal the Institute of Wetland Management and Ecological Design has been given a grant of Rs. 307200 to Birbhum-Purulia region for the cleaning of arsenic and fluoride content found in the water. In this regard the work done by several associations for water collection and purification are laudable.

The Fulani tribe of Nigeria maximises the use of water by its wider distribution through tank to save the life of animals in the desert (Fig. 1.4).

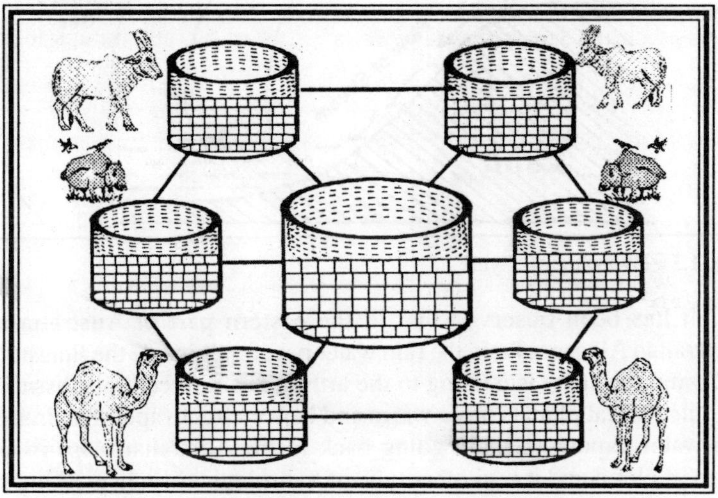

Fig. 1.4 : Use of Water by Fulani tribe of Nigeria in the Desert

In the 1980s the Government of India proposed the Ganga-Cauveri link 1600 kms long by lifting water from the Ganga river west of Patna and lifting it at 12 places in Jharkhand State in order to irrigate the drought affected peninsular India each and every year. At present China has proposed the similar gigantic scheme of 3500kms long canal by lifting the water of Hawangho and Yangtzekiang river to the drier west.

The Hydrological Cycle

The evaporation of oceanic or waterlogged areas from the land into the atmosphere in the form of cloud and again rains back on the ground and its movement back to the ocean in a cyclic fashion is known as "hydrological cycle". The cycle is operating most efficiently in coastal areas of the ocean and lakes (Fig. 1.5). This process helps in natural recharge of groundwater (Kathpalia, 1972).

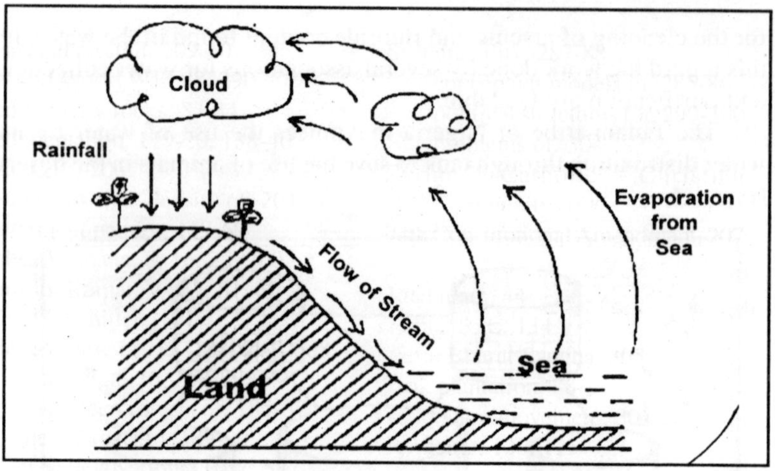

Fig. 1.5 : Hydrological Cycle

It has been observed that in the eastern part of Australia on Australian Alps mountain the rain water penetrates inside the limestone rock and the same is coming to the artisan basin of central Australia. As this central plain is more warm and hence after evapotranspiration the water vapour is again going back to the Australian Alps in the form of cloud and it is another type of hydrological cycle working on the earth surface (Fig. 1.6).

Hence, solar radiation evaporates oceanic water into the atmosphere. The column of water vapour rises and get condensed in the form of cloud. Later on with slightest of cold wind in the upper sky the cloud gives various forms of precipitation, e.g. rain, hail, sleet and snowfall on the earth surface and again all these move down according to the gravity of slope through the porous rock of limestone.

Linkage of Rivers

It is a Herculean task with immense potential to alleviate the sufferings of people in drought affected and water scarcity regions of the country. This National Water Grid, has been proposed by the Ministry of Water Resources, Government of India. This scheme originates due to unequal distribution of rainfall in different parts of India. During the rainy season the north Indian rivers overflow as the flood condition prevails while the entire southern, central and western parts of the

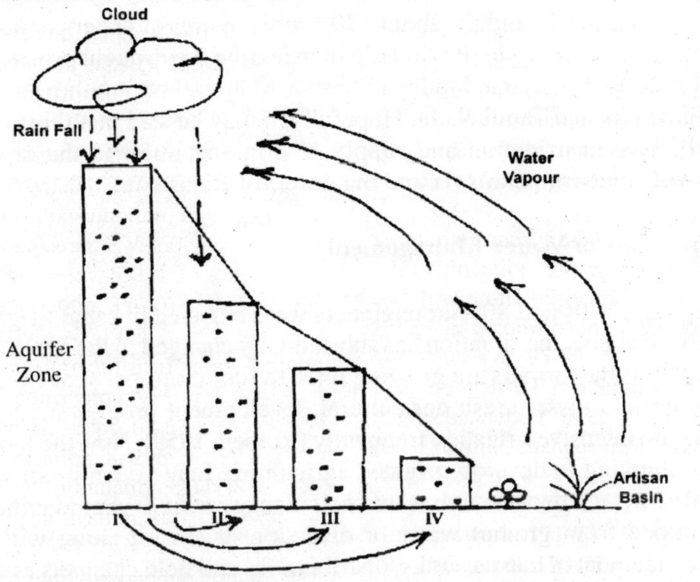

Water Moves from highland to lowland inside the earth and back on the mountain tops in the form of cloud as plain land in more drier.

Fig. 1.6 : Local Hydrological Cycle

country are reeling under sufferings of drought as all these areas receive low amount of rainfall.

The proposed linkages of river systems will follow the components as given below :

1. The Ganga-Cauvery link which connects the Son, the Narmada, the Tapti, the Godavari, the Krishna and the Pennar rivers.
2. The Brahamputra-Ganga Link.
3. The Narmada to Luni and Mahi Link.
4. The Chambal to Ajmer Link.
5. The Mahanadi with Damodar and the Krishna Link.

Among all these the Ganga-Cauvery link is most important which lift the water of river Ganga near Patna in Bihar to upper Anicut on the banks of river Cauvery in Tamil Nadu. Its length will be

2660 kilometres and lift about 1700 cubic metres of water per second from the Ganga river. It will help in irrigating the drought prone areas of Rajasthan, Gujarat, Madhya Pradesh, Maharashtra, Andhra Pradesh, Karnataka and Tamil Nadu. Hopefully, it may be said that this project will help in irrigation and supply of drinking water to the drought prone southern peninsula and the desert of Rajasthan.

Problems of Water Management

During 1970s and 80s our engineers were engaged in canal irrigation only. But now the situation has substantially changed in the agriculture sector as the farmers are growing three to four crops per year from the same field under crash agricultural development programme which require intensive irrigation frequently (Russell, 1959). Now the farmers are thinking to develop irrigated agriculture. Large quantity of water harvest is needed through watershed management. It should either be pumped from ground water or diversion of stream along with the management of canals, tanks, distributaries and field channels as well. It has been learnt that unscientific use of water for irrigation leads to heavy loss of water resource through seepage and percolation in the root zone of plants. In some areas waterlogging and accumulation of salt pans on the ground is harmful for the standing rice crops as the author has observed near Jankinagar branch canal of the Kosi and near Tribeni canal of East Champaran district. Quite often this has happened due to faulty planning of irrigation. The integrated development of water resource is the only method for its efficient management and carrying water upto the field for irrigation.

Water Resource Regions of India

On the basis of river basin water resource regions could be analysed as they are the natural unit in the form of watershed boundary and in one river basin the level and quality of underground water is of the same nature. The management of water resource is not possible without knowing the quantity, quality and distribution of water resources along with the demand set by the people in different watersheds as per changing land use pattern and the cropping pattern (Rege, 1972).

One can divide India in the following water resource regions for the purpose of water resource management :

The Indus Basin of North West

Indus river originates from the northern part of Mansarover lake in Himalaya. Its tributaries are the Jhelum, the Chenab, the Ravi, the Beas and the Sutlej rivers. All these rivers originates from Verinag, Lahul Spiti, Kulu, Rohtang pass and Darma Pass of Zanskar range respectively. This watershed has an average rainfall of 60 cm and the total catchment area is 35.40 million hectare. It covers the States of Punjab, Jammu-Kashmir, Haryana and Himachal Pradesh.

The Ganga Basin

It covers an area of 100 million hectares in the States of Uttar Pradesh, Bihar, Madhya Pradesh, Rajasthan and West Bengal. The average yearly rainfall is 125 cm. The confluence of rivers Alaknanda and the Mandakini is at Dev Prayag from where these two become the Ganga. It has long and tortuous routes in the Himalaya and then transverse into the flood plains of north India. Its main tributaries are the Yamuna, the Ramganga, the Gomati, the Ghaghra, the Son, the Gandak, the Budhi Gandak, the Bagmati, the Kosi and the Mahananda.

The Brahamputra Basin of the North East

The red river originates in Tibet Himalaya east of Mansarover lake in the name of Tsangpo river. It makes a deep gorge of 9500 metres deep at Namcha Barua on the southern slope of Himalaya. Its watershed receives more than 200 cm of rainfall annually. It covers the States of Assam, Nagaland, Meghalaya and Sikkim. Its watershed has a catchment area of 51 million hectare.

River Basins of the East Coast

On the eastern coastal plain of Peninsular India the watershed of rivers has an area of 120 million hectares with an average annual rainfall of 115 cm. The Godavari watershed originates from Nasik district of Maharashtra. Besides, it also covers Madhya Pradesh and Andhra Pradesh and has several tributaries like the Indravati, the Sabari, the Pranhita and the Manjra. The Krishna river rises from the Sahyadri mountain and it covers the States of Maharashtra, Karnataka and Andhra Pradesh. Its tributaries are the Tungbhadra, the Bhima and

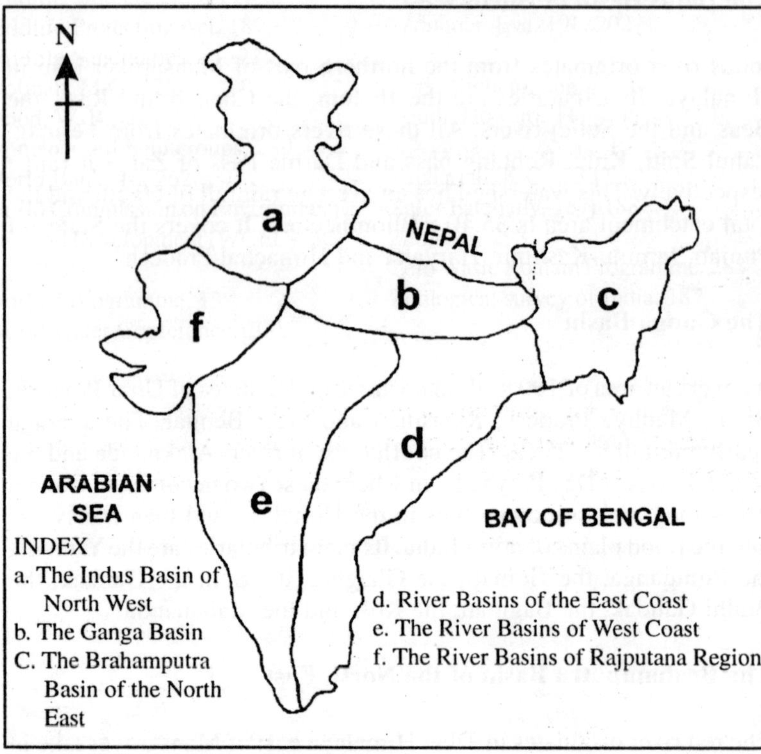

Fig. 1.7 : Water Resource Regions of India

the Koyana. The Mahanadi river has a length of 858 kms. and originates from Sinawa of Madhya Pradesh. It has several tributaries in its watershed, namely the Sheonath, the Hasdeo, the Mand and the Tonk. The Cauvery river originates from Mercara in Coorg district of Karnataka. Its tributaries are the Hemavati, the Lashmantirtha and the Bhavani. This is the single river of India whose water potential has been fully harnessed.

The River Basins of West Coast

It has an area of 49 million hectares with average rainfall of 125 cm. It covers the states of Gujarat, Maharashtra, Karnataka and Kerala. This watershed has 600 rivulets to its credit which fall into the Arabian sea. Most of the rivers are smaller in length and carry 14 per cent water resource of the country.

The River Basin of Rajputana Region

The desert region of Rajasthan has deficient rainfall and hence there is a lack of water resources. The river basins of this watershed has an area of 17 million hectares with an average annual rainfall of 50 centimetres (Fig. 1.7).

Conclusion

In this book most of the papers are associated with water accumulation, conservation, collection and practice of irrigation for better management of our agriculture and societal needs. Some of the papers are also related with GIS and remote sensing along with sustainability and control of pollution of water resources. Floods and droughts are also given due position besides urban water supply as they are the urgent problems of water resource management.

Thus about 90 per cent of the water that flows in rivers of India is a result of monsoonal rainfall between June to September and snowfall in the Himlayan region during short winter season of mid-December to mid-February. Due to unequal distribution of rainfall and its uncertain schedule there are recurring period of floods and drought in different parts of India. There is great need to properly manage our river waters and prevent pollution through proper public awareness programmes and legislation. The industrial units should be prohibited from letting their wastes flow into rivers and lakes.

REFERENCES

Banerjee, K.C., "Regulation of River Floods : The Problem of Damodar River", *Calcutta Geographical Review,* 1943.

Banerjee, R.K., "Power Regions of India", *The Earth,* 1964.

Chakravarty, A.K., "Floods in Himalayan Rivers of Ganga Plain : Causes and Controls", *Calcutta Geographical Review,* 1949.

Chaudhuri, M.R., "Power Resources of West Bengal", *Geographical Review of India,* 1965.

Edward E. Johnson, *Ground Water and Wells,* Saint Paul, Minnesota, USA, 1966, p. 440.

Goirala, S.S., "Flood Problems of the Ganga Drainage Basin", *National Geographical Journal of India,* 1955.

Jain, J.K., "Water Resources of Arid Region of Rajasthan", *Indian Journal of Geography,* 1967.

Jauhari, A.S., "Electric Power Development in North-West India", *National Geographical Journal of India,* 1956.

Jha, B.N., "River Problem of North Bihar". *Calcutta Geographical Review,* 1955.

Kathpalia, G.N., "Water Policy in Agriculture", *Indian Farming*, Vol. XXII, No. 2, 1972, pp. 17-18.

Krishnamurty, N., Papnasnam Hydro-electric Project, *Journal of the Madras Geographical Association,* 1940.

Kuriyan, G. and Nair, V.P.K., *Development of Hydro-electric Power in South India,* 1946.

Kuriyan, G., *Hydro-electric Power in India,* The Indian Geographical Society, Madras, 1948.

Majumdar, S.C., *Rivers of Bengal Delta,* 1943.

Mukherjee, R.G., "Present Position of Electric Power Installations in Bengal", *Calcutta Geographical Review,* 1943.

Raina, A.N., "Water Power Resources of Kashmir State", Proceedings of the International Geographical Seminar, 1956.

Rege, N.D., Soil and Water Management Problems in India; *Indian Farming,* Vol. XXII, No. 2, 1972, pp. 12-16.

Russell, M.B., *Water and its Relation to Soils and Crops;* Acad. Press, New York, 1959.

Sidhiqis, A.H., "Potentialities of Tube-well Irrigation in the Burdwan District", *Indian Geographical Journal,* 1949.

Sinha, R.P., "Power Development in the State of Bihar", Abstracts of the International Geographical Union Cogress, 1968.

2

Water : Its Importance, Uses, Problems and Management

Ashok Kumar Sinha and Tulika Sinha

Introduction

The origin of water on the earth is not clear so far. However, the current presumption is that the primordial earth had no oceans and perhaps very little atmosphere. It is believed that the volatile constituents bound in the earth's crust, oozing the surface through volcanoes, rock, movements, and hot springs, condensed to form the ocean and the atmosphere. This way, perhaps the remarkable combination of hydrogen and oxygen—called water, came into being and eventually become an indispensable component of the earth's environment. (Singh, 1991).

Water moves from the ocean to air to land and back to ocean in a set cyclic pattern called hydrologic cycle. In other words, this cycle represents a continuous process of exchange of water from the earth's surface to the atmosphere and *vice versa* under the influence of solar heat.

It is estimated that of the total available water, 97.3 per cent is contained in the oceans and out of remaining 2.7 per cent is in solid form. The amount of water actually available in the atmosphere is a very minute fraction and estimated to be only 1×10^{-5} of the world's total water.

The factors which control the process of evaporation and evapotranspiration include temperature, humidity and wind. It is a continuous process going on day and night from the ocean surface, ground surface, inland waters (like lakes and streams), plant and animal surfaces. Rising in the atmosphere this water forms clouds that float around in gaseous or driplet form. The atmosphere above the earth up to varying heights of 10 to 17km (depending upon latitude and season) is called the troposphere up to which the clouds float and in which all weather changes take place. Water returns to the earth in the form of precipitation, most of which takes place over the ocean and a little on the land surface. Rainfall on the land surface may have following fates : it may percolate through the soil and become a part of ground water regime; accumulate in a pond, lake or reservoir as inland surface water; flow down to the ocean in the form of stream; taken up by plants and animals; or evaporate (Trivedi *et al.,* 1994).

Importance, Requirements and Uses of Water

Goethe rightly said that, "Everything originated in the water, and everything is sustained by water". Water is needed to fulfil diverse requirements in so many diverse ways. It is vital for life and all physiological activities of plants and is essential for animals as well. On an average it constitutes 80 per cent of protoplasm ranging from 8 per cent in dry dormant seeds to 95 per cent jelly fish. It serves not only to quench the thirst but also to meet the food requirements because it is an essential raw material in the process of photosynthesis through which green plants make food that is used by all trophic levels directly or indirectly. Ambient humidity which is indeed the invisible form of water that surrounds us is necessary to prevent desiccation of terrestrial life forms. Thus, it can be said that water is biologically essential and it serves as milieu internal as well as milieu external.

Flood plains of rivers have been the cradle of civilization and centres of population since ancient times. The reason being their high fertility, an easy accessibility to water for various uses like drinking, washing and transport. Egypt was developed on the flood plains of the Nile : Babylon on the flood plains of the Tigris : and north Indian on the flood plains of the Ganges. Even today the Mississippi plain is about the most densely populated area in the USA as flood plains of the Rhine in Europe, and the Yellow river in China (Sharma, 2000).

Besides temperature, water is the other such key factor that influences the global ecology. Covering about 70 per cent of land surface and circulating in hydrologic cycle water influences weather and climate on any region and thus its flora and fauna.

Agriculture is dependent on water, may it be rainfall, or surface or ground water irrigation. It eventually is a more important commodity in a country like India because her largely agrarian economy depends critically on water. Huge amount of protein rich food in the form of fish, shell fish, and prawn is obtained from the inland as well as very potent industry.

The kinetic energy of gravitational flow of water is tapped and transformed into electricity, what is called hydro power. This concept of electricity generation is one of the oldest and cheapest tricks largely used world over. Moreover, it leaves no pollution burden on nature as in case of thermal or nuclear power generation.

Hardly any industry can do without water. It has multifarious application in industrial processes, *viz.* a raw material, solvent, chemical reactant, coolant, and cleaning agent.

"Water, water energy where not any drop to drink is the situation not only found amidst sea but also at places where industrial and domestic refuse make the benevolent water sources so severely contaminated with pathogens and/or toxins that they are left impotable. Being the best dilution medium it is frequently used as the cheapest and convenient way for liquid and solid waste disposal. Further, it was practically impossible to maintain sanitary conditions without water for it is needed in all common cleaning and washing practices.

Water at many places serves as a very convenient means of navigation. Besides, it adds to the aesthetic value of the landscape and provides opportunities for recreation and sport.

Water being unevenly distributed over the land, influences interstate and international relations and thus is the cause of what is known as hydro-politics.

It can, therefore, be said that while water is essential for life it is significantly linked with social, economic, political and ecological intricacies.

Problems and Management of Water

Management of water implies making the best use of available water resources for human benefit while not only preventing and controlling its depletion and degradation but also developing it in view of the present and future needs. Water, like forest, is a multipurpose resource and it is important to see that its various uses should not conflict with each other and it can be enjoyed in its totality by man and others. Thus, its right allocation, and quantitative and qualitative conservation are the primary tasks before water managers.

Floods, droughts, improper use, pollution and disease transmission are the important problems related to water. Because usable inland water resources constitute a very minute fraction of the world's total water and because man largely depends upon this minute fraction of water for his various activities. It is important to make efficient use of available water and at the same time prevent abuse of it. This has to be considered not only in giant irrigation projects of industrial and municipal processes but also in everyday life. Taps running unpurposefully, leaking water supply pipes, using filtered water for gardens and building construction are a few instances of inefficient and misuse of water in daily life.

Water being the best and convenient dilution medium is the worst affected resource by pollution. To a common man pollution of water means only the drainage of industrial effluents or domestic sewage in natural waters. It may astonish a layman that even pure distilled water when release in sea may act as a pollutant since it alters the normal salinity of sea water which adversely affects the marine life. Besides chemical alterations, changes in physical condition of water also have grave effects on the biota of system as during thermal pollution caused by the discharge of heated effluents in a body of water. Pathogens, chiefly entering natural waters through municipal wastes rich in excreta and other organic filth, also render the water unsuitable for human use.

In fact, it is not only the man who has to use the water resources by these are equally important to land animals and more to fish and other aquatic animals who live in it. Thus pollution of a body of water does prove detrimental not only to the human society but also to regional ecology and the ecology of very aquatic ecosystem. It is, therefore, essential that the water should not be treated as a simple repository of waste disposal, and if inevitable, the wastes only after proper treatment should be released in it under strict ecological consideration.

The qualitative degradation of water is also in a way quantitative depletion of usable resources. Therefore, recycling of waste water after due treatment would relieve the water scarcity to a great extent especially in regions marred by water shortage.

Future Needs and Alternate Sources of Water

The demand for usable water, like any other resource, is increasing fast with the continuous increase in world population and continuous increase in per capita demand linked with more of sewage disposal and transport prolific use of water-using gadgets (like air cooling and conditioning devices, washing machines etc.) and increased recreational activities. According to an estimate, the daily per capita demand for water of an American was 600 gallons in 1890 which increased to 1,500 gallons in 1960 and it has further increased upto 2,700 gallons by 2005. The fact is no different in developing world. Thus, the question is where will the water needed for fulfilling increasing demands come from? The answer is not so simple and can only be found through long term planning. Possible means of meeting out the pending water deficit problem include : (i) reclamation of sewage and waste water, (ii) development of ground water sources and surface storage, (iii) long range forecasting of rain; (iv) rain making; (v) transfer of surface water, (vi) desalination of sea water, and (vii) rain water harvesting etc.

REFERENCES

Sharma, P.D. (2000) : *Ecology and Environment,* Pub. Rastogi Publications, Meerut.

Singh, Savindra (1991) *Environmental Geography.* Pub. Prayag Pustak Bhawan, Allahabad.

Trivedi, Priya Ranjan, Singh, Uttam Kumar, Sudarshan, K' Cherry, Tuteja, Tripat Kaur (1994) : *International Encyclopaedia of Ecology and Environment,* Vol. 5, Pub. Indian Institute of Ecology and Environment, New Delhi.

3

Use of GIS and Remote Sensing in Water Resource Development in India

SUMIT DHANUKA

Introduction

GIS and Remote Sensing are the modern tools of geographic survey, analysis and decision-making. They are very effective in understanding the complex and dynamic features occurring around the earth surface. This approach is increasingly being used in the field of hydrology and water resource development. Realising the challenges of water resource development and management in India, attention has been given to use GIS and Remote Sensing capabilities. Programmes in this direction are being implemented at macro and micro levels involving a number of agencies. Several organisations are providing the required data and other facilities compatible with this task. Application of hydrological models and other such studies in different regions are quite successful with the help of GIS and Remote Sensing. These techniques have been found to be very helpful in discovering, monitoring, analysis, evaluation and management of various aspects of water resource in the country.

GIS is a computer-based system that records, stores and analyses information about the features that make up the earth's surface. In other words, it is data handling and analysis system in which data sets have some kind of spatial relationship. GIS involves 5 key components : hardware, software, data, people and methodology (Jagadeesha, 1999).

Remote Sensing implies acquisition of information about the objects of earth by using radiant energy. It includes both, air-photos and satellite imagery. Satellite remote sensing is more useful with its unique capabilities of synoptic coverage, repetitively and capturing

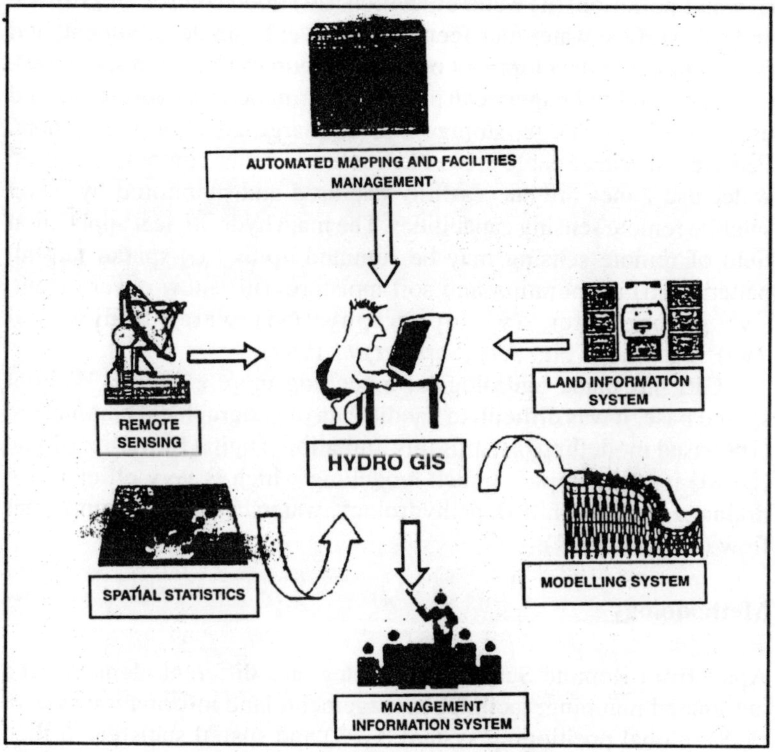

Fig. 3.1 : A conceptual structure for GIS applications in Hydrology

features of inaccessible areas. Being a basic survey methodology providing resource related spatial data, Remote Sensing is regarded as a layer in the GIS (Grover, 1999).

The integrated approach of GIS and Remote Sensing is recognized as a highly effective technology in evaluation, management and monitoring of natural resources and environment. To study various phenomena occurring on the earth surface is not an easy task as these phenomena are very complex and dynamic. But, with its high speed, accuracy, storage and versatility, GIS provides a promising solution (Seth, 1999).

GIS approach is playing a rapidly increasing role in the field of hydrology and water resource development. It has helped in the preparation of hydrological modelling in spatial and temporal domains. These models have proved to be helpful in solving various issues like

(i) water pollution, (ii) water utilization, (iii) flood control, (iv) surface and sub-surface water management, (v) river basin development, and (vi) sustainable development of water resources (Navalawala, 2002).

The satellite imagery can provide information on hydrologic land use, run off, recharge, storage and discharge areas besides others. Features of inaccessible areas like reservoir water contours and crop water use zones are successfully captured and monitored by using satellite remote sensing capabilities. The main hydrological application field of remote sensing may be summed up as : (i) spatial rainfall patterns, (ii) evaporation and soil moisture, (iii) snow cover extent, (iv) groundwater, (v) topography, (vi) water bodies and (vii) vegetation (Fig. 3.1) (Saraf *et al.,* 1997).

GIS has made hydrological modelling more effective. Without spatial base, it was difficult to handle data of geographical parameters. GIS based modelling discards this limitation. Digital Elevation Model (DEM) is an example of such modelling which is very efficient for drainage analysis, hill slope hydrology, watersheds and groundwater flow (Sankar, 2001).

Methodology

Apart from Remote Sensing, GIS integrates different elements like automated mapping, facilities management, land information system (LIS), global positioning system (GPS) and spatial statistics. It then serves to management information systems and modelling systems in the research domain (Paik, 2000).

Basic steps in GIS include :

— Setting up the aim and objective
— Collection of required data
— Automation of the map
— Conversion of the map to real world coordinates
— Error correction
— Topology building
— Addition of attribute data
— Spatial queries
— Map composition
— Final reproduction

The first step is with regard to the project for which GIS has to be used. The required data are both spatial and non-spatial. Automation means digitization of the map. Real world coordinates implies assigning of latitudes and longitudes to the map. Editing is done as there may be errors such as double digitizing, undershoots etc.

Topology is an important aspect of GIS. It denotes spatial relationship of geographical data (point, line and polygon) based on their relative locations. Attributes are added to designate the different types of features. Queries are done to obtain data in required condition. On this basis maps are composed and then plotted. Map displays can be supplemented with reports, tables, 3-D views and photographic images.

Indian Scenario

In India, present policies of water resource development and management stress on the use of integrated approach of GIS. Various governmental and non-governmental agencies are doing their job in this perspective. International organizations are also assisting in preparation of hydrological data set in GIS environment.

The National Water Policy regards water as 'a prime natural resource, a basic human need and a precious national asset'. Realizing the ongoing issues and challenges, the (Revised) National Water Policy (adopted on April 1, 2002) appreciates the use of data available with remote sensing and its advanced analysis applying GIS.

India's Remote Sensing programme started with the launching of IRS-1A in 1988. Presently India has the largest constellation of remote sensing satellites. High resolution imagery from IRS series are very important regarding surface water. National Remote Sensing Agency (NRSA), Hyderabad provides the satellite data.

Survey of India (SOI), Dehradun supplies topographical sheets on various scales. These sheets have been used as base map for GIS application. Now, SOI has undertaken creation of Digital Cartographic Data Base of its topographical maps. Besides, National Resources Information System (NRIS) under Department of Space provides the spatial data in digital format. These maps include themes that are used by water resource scientists and modellers (India 2003).

The Natural Resource Data Management Programme is being implemented at district level. As a part of this programme, spatial and non-spatial databases are being generated and updated at the state and district GIS centres. The programme also envisages developing and demonstrating the use of GIS techology for the identified sectors that include water conservation, water management and hydrology of small watersheds.

The Central Ground Water Board responsible for subsurface hydrological investigation; and National Institute of Hydrology (Roorkie) for promotion of systematic works in hydrology are using the GIS and Remote Sensing capabilities in their respective jobs.

The National Perspective Plan of the Government envisages interlinking between Peninsular rivers and Himalayan rivers for transfer of water from water surplus regions to water deficit areas. To firm up this link scheme, National Water Development Agency is formed. The agency is engaged in data collection, water balance studies, toposheet studies and preparation of feasibility reports. All these jobs fall under GIS compatibility.

Regional Approach

Different areas of the country are being studied by using remote sensing and GIS capabilities with reference to water resource development and management. A few of them are illustrated here to have a glance of the situation.

Hilly Hydro Project

The Ministry of Non-Conventional Energy Sources had led Hilly Hydro Project (HPP) under UNDP. Its purpose was to identify the real potential available for Small Hydro Power (SHP) in Indian Himalayas. It acquired latest information from the analysis of remote sensing data and managed all thematic information on a GIS platform. Basically, it used Survey of India (SOI) toposheets of 1:50,000 scale. The project identified 1700 potential small hydro sites. In order to get clusters of these sites, it used SOI 1: 10,00,000 scale map and applied Nearest Neighbour Analysis method.

The above project also used GIS for alternate site selection. Example is given from Rungsung Khola catchment in Darjeeling tea estate area. Contour information was captured using SOI 1 : 50,000 topographical maps. These contours were then overlaid on the Digital Elevation Model (DEM). Some proposed channels were also overlaid. This procedure provided information about slope and available headwater. Applying certain constrains four alternate SHP sites were selected for Rungsung Khola catchment.

The Topmodel and the SHE Model

The Topmodel and the Systeme Hydrologique Europeen (SHE) model are the models used for hydrological studies. These have been applied successfully for river basins in India.

The Topmodel is a variable contributing area conceptual model. It was applied to Malaprabha catchment (Karnataka) to simulate the daily flows at Khanapur. The model used topographic index for the formation of runoff. For this, it developed a Digital Elevation Model (DEM) by interpolating the contours in the basin. It was found to be quite efficient in terms of model calibration and validation.

The SHE model is a physically based model organised on a typical GIS format. It was applied to six sub-basins of river Narmada, namely Kolar, Bama, Sher, Ganjal, Hiren and Narmada up to Manot. This model was successful for modelling the rainfall and runoff process in these sub-basins.

Groundwater Potential in Agnigundala (Andhra Pradesh)

GIS was used to identify the groundwater potential sites in Agnigundala mineralised belt of Andhra Pradesh. The Remote Sensing data from IRS 1B and Spot were used. Their visual interpretation showed conformity with the field observation. The field data were further integrated with spatial data through GIS. This improved the output for quantitative analysis and assessment.

The groundwater potentials were evaluated for the individual geomorphic units. After then a complete hydrological picture of the area was obtained.

The study found out that hydrologically majority of the wells were confined in north-eastern, eastern and southern parts of the region. It also showed the state of watertable (Shallow/moderate/deep) in different areas of the region. Thus it was helpful for groundwater exploration in the region.

Saraswati : The Lost River

Saraswati, once the mighty river of north-western India, disappeared due to changes in physical conditions. A part of the river now exists as Ghaggar in Haryana.

Attempts are being made to trace the river Saraswati through numerous signatures of palaeochannels identified by the tonal variation in the satellite imagery. It has been inferred that its initial course flowed close to the Aravalli and the successive stages took west and north-westerly shifts. (Fig. 3.2)

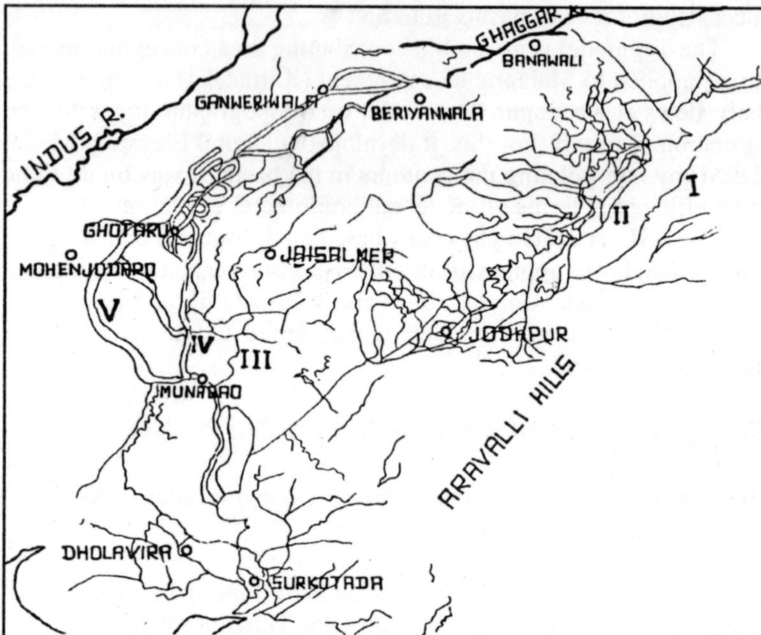

IV : Stages of Shift of Course by River Saraswati
Courtesy : RRSSC, ISRO : Jodhpur

Fig. 3.2 : River Saraswati Channels

Digital enhancement studies of IRS 1C and ERS ½ data, have recognised the palaeochannels beneath the sands of Thar Desert. These palaeochannels are associated with wetness (presence of water). Bhaba Atomic Research Centre, Mumbai and Physical Research Laboratory, Ahmedabad are attempting to 'unearth' the Saraswati. This can be a boon for the people living in the desert belt of Rajasthan, thanks to GIS and remote sensing.

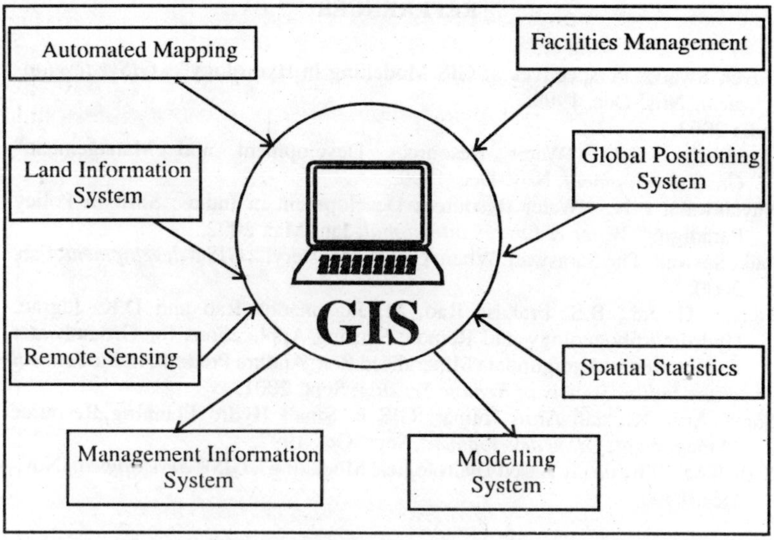

Fig. 3.3 : GIS as an Integrating System

The Government of India has launched Hydrology Project (commenced in September, 1995) with the help of World Bank for 9 peninsular states. These states are Andhra Pradesh, Chhattisgarh, Gujarat, Karnataka, Kerala, Madhya Pradesh, Maharashtra, Orissa and Tamil Nadu. The objective is preparation of hydrological data sets for water resource evaluation, planning and management. The project also helps in the development of interactive computerised data banks for the concerning states. GIS is playing its role in the execution of this project (Fig. 3.3).

Conclusion

The study of resource (be it water or any other resource) has been an integral part of geography. Moreover, they to all GIS is the fundamental map base, the base which is more concerned with geographers than people of other backgrounds. Hence, the work of resource management using GIS can't be left only for scientists, engineers and IT professionals. It is but the ignorance and neglecting attitudes of geographers due to which they have no significant and active involvement in the gamut of GIS.

REFERENCES

Gover, Swati, "Perspectives of GIS Modelling in Hydrology", *GIS@development;* Nov.-Dec. 1999.

India 2003.

Jagadessha, C.J., "Water Resources Development and Management." *GIS@development*; Nov.-Dec. 1999.

Navalawala, B.N., "Water Resources Development in India : Shift in Policy Paradigm;" *Water & Energy intentional*; Jan.-Mar. 2002.

Paik, Saswati, The Saraswati, Where Lies the Mysteryl", *GIS@development*; Feb. 2000.

Sankar, G. Jai., B.S. Prakasa Rao, M. Jagannadha Rao and D.K. Jugran; Hydromorphogeology and Remote Sensing Applications for Groundwater Exploration in Agnigundala Mineralised Belt, Andhra Pradesh, India: *Journal of the Indian Society of Remote Sensing*; Sept. 2001.

Saraf, Arun K., and Arun Kumar; GIS in Small Hydro Planning Resource Management; *GIS@development*, Sept.-Oct. 1997.

Seth, S.M., "Physically Based Hydrological Modelling", *GIS@development*; Nov.-Dec. 1999.

4

Application of Remote Sensing in Groundwater Investigations

DEEPAK KUMAR

Introduction

Groundwater cannot be seen as it lies inside the earth's surface. A variety of techniques can provide information concerning its occurrence and its quality from above surface locations. Surface investigations are partially successful. Geologic methods involving interpretation of geologic data and field reconnaisance represent the first step in groundwater investigation. In the scientific era of today the technique of remote sensing has gained momentum and dramatically enhanced man's capability of resource exploration, mapping and monitoring of various natural phenomena. Remote sensing from aircraft or satellite has become an increasing valuable tool for understanding sub-surface water condition (Grover, 1999).

Remote sensing technique has many advantages, which cannot be achieved from different geological investigations like electric resistivity survey, geophysical techniques etc. In remote sensing technology satellite, aircraft with sensors are used for collecting information about the earth surface and sub-surface. We can get the satellite imageries of those areas also where we cannot reach due to mountainous terrain or dense forest, swampy areas etc. After interpretation of data received by the imageries we can interpret the prospects of groundwater in those areas (Jagadeesha, 1999).

Remote Sensing Technique

Photograph of the earth taken from aircraft or satellite at various electromagnetic wavelength ranges can provide useful information regarding groundwater conditions. The technology of remote sensing has developed rapidly in recent years. The imageries of different areas received from remote sensing satellite help us in knowing the groundwater conditions of the area. Stereoscopic examination of black and white aerial photograph has joined steadily its importance. Observable patterns, colours and relief of different imageries received from satellites make it possible to know about the surface as well as groundwater conditions of the area.

Groundwater Investigations Using Aerial Photographs

Remote sensing technology is helpful in the visible infrared and microwave regions of the solar radiation to collect information about various objects of the earth surface. The region of spectrum is very important in remote sensing for vegetation and soil moisture. Photogeology can differentiate between rock and soil types and indicate their permeability and area distribution. The most commonly seen false colour images display the very near infrared region as red, red as green and green as blue. In satellite imageries the healthy vegetation look red, clear water appears dark blue to black, silty water light blue, moist ground shows different tone and building appear blue (Mandal, 1979).

On the false colour longest (F.C.E.) we can also locate the area of recharge and discharge. On the basis of satellite imageries we can classify the area of good discharge, average discharge, areas of harder rock terrain where there are minimum fracture and fissure zone along which discharge is minimum. In this way, aerial photograph plays an important role in the investigation of groundwater.

Good aquifers have good porosity and good permeability. The principal source of groundwater recharge and precipitation and stream flow and those of discharge include effluent seepage into rivers and lakes, springs, evaporation and pumping. Remote sensing of water can be done by a number of techniques. Most of them utilize the interaction between electromagnetic radiation of water, water vapour, ice and snow, water bodies usually appear in the satellite imageries as dark regions, because they emit comparatively less amount of thermal radiation as compared to other characteristics of groundwater occurrence.

Aerial photograph also reveals fracture pattern in rocks, which can related to porosity, permeability and ultimately well yield. Springs and marshy areas indicate relatively shallow depth of groundwater. Xerophytes desert plants subsisting on minimum water, suggest a considerable dispatch to the water table.

Important indicators of groundwater on remote sensing data products help in evaluating groundwater condition.

(After Healt trainer)

First Order or Direct Indicator

1. Features associated with recharge zones.
   River, Canals, Lakes, Ponds etc.
2. Geologic landforms likely to contain relatively Permeable strata.
3. Features associated with discharge zones—springs and other seepage.
4. Vegetation.

Second Order or Direct Indicator

1. Drainage density.
2. Hard and soft rock areas.
3. Fracture and system in harder rock areas.
4. Porosity and permeability of rocks.
5. Folding, faulting and shear zones.
6. Moist depressions and seepage.
7. Springs.

Other non-visible portions of electromagnetic spectrum could not be traced by aerial photographs. Remote sensing techniques are very much helpful in knowing the groundwater conditions of areas of harder rock terrain like Giridih. Infrared imageries which records differences in apparent surface temperature enables information on groundwater circulation, waterfalls etc. One of the most interesting results of infrared aerial imaging has been mapping the coastal submarine springs. Radar imagery can provide information of the presence of moisture on shallow depth below ground surface with low frequency electro-magnetic aerial surveys have outlined buried channels and zones of sea water intrusions. The various fluvial geomorphic features such as alluvial plains, natural levees can also be recognized on the satellite imageries. These are potential zones of groundwater.

Need of Artifical Recharge

Giridih region represents mostly a hilly tract with extremely rugged topography. There is no perennial source of water in this region and it falls in the shadow zone. The annual rainfall is always below average. The result is that despite the vast mineral resources and agricultural potentialities available in this region it is not possible to work on them. Besides, there is also acute scarcity of drinking water supply in several parts of the region. Therefore, artificial recharge is essential for the area.

Rain is the only perennial source of fresh water. The distribution of total water availability in world is as below :

Saline water in oceans	97.2 %
Ice Caps and glaciers	2.16%
Groundwater	0.16%
Surface water	0.0009%
Soil moisture	0.005%

When rain falls on the ground, some of it seeps into the soil and rest flows off as surface run off. The rainfall which infilterates through soil, after saturating the moisture of soil, percolates further down and gets stored in the unsaturated pore spaces of the aquifer. The rain water infilterating and joining the aquifers forms the water table. The aquifer may be sufficiently defined as of water residue in the pores and cracks of the rock which are drained by digging wells and tube wells.

The groundwater resources has been categorised into two components, viz.

(i) Dynamic resource, and
(ii) Static resource.

The dynamic resource is that component of groundwater, which is annually replenishable. The main source of replenishment is from rainfall. The static groundwater resource is that component of resource, which have built up over the years and is of presently a part of hydrologic cycle. Presently, there is no fine demarcation line to separate the dynamic source from the static source.

Barakar river which is one of the main rivers of Giridih region is the tributary of Damodar. Both the Barakar and Damodar rivers have great importance after Ganges. The Barakar river covers the maximum area of Giridih district. The Barakar is a tributary of Damodar river bifurcates in the north-eastern part of Hazaribagh. This river has been named Barakar because it flows through the coalfields. The river Usri, however, retains the fine open space with crumbling peaks scattered over the area.

Khandoli the peculiar saddle shaped hill made up of granitoid gneiss dominates the landscape near Giridih, the well known mica splitting centre. The peak of Khandoli hill is like a volcanic cone and the great saddle attached to it consists of massive boulders.

The rivers of Giridih are alike that they are fed by surface precipitation of rain water. This is the reason that most of the borings are sunk at a deep level for water. Giridih falls in harder rock terrain that is why there is scarcity of groundwater in Gondwana region as well as in pre-Cambrian region. There is maximum fluctuation of water table in the pre-Cambrian region of harder rock terrain. The different rivers affect the movement of aquifers are quartzite, amphibolite, Grit, Granite, Gneiss, Scheists etc. Dugwell and tubewell which are dug in quartzite and amphibolite go dry during the summer, because in these rocks there are minimum fractures which obstruct the movement of water in aquifers.

The principal source of groundwater of Giridih is mainly from precipitation. Recharge, also takes place through springs in spate, by return seepage from irrigation and lateral inflow from adjacent areas. The metamorphic rocks of the area are weathered at places and extensively jointed at the surface. These are covered with thin mantle of residual soil in lowlying areas. Groundwater occurs in fine interstices of weathered granites and joint planes of hard rocks which occurs in fine interstices of weathered granites and joint planes of hard rocks. The availability of groundwater is well depends on the number of such planes of weakness exposed in the inner part of the well.

Artificial recharge means recharge of the groundwater by artificial methods. In course of natural recharge the groundwater is recharged by the natural process like rainfall in order to increase the natural supply of groundwater. People do artificial recharge of groundwater basin. Artificial recharge of groundwater is very essential in harder rock terrain like Giridih.

Our agriculture is totally dependent on the rainfall and in different parts of Jharkhand specially Giridih experiences lesser rainfall, which is not sufficient for the recharge of groundwater when we see the graph of annual rainfall of different districts of Jharkhand. We find except few all districts are having rainfall lower than required to recharge the groundwater. The government is also not so much serious in conserving the rainwater and other surface water to recharge the groundwater. In agrarian society like ours, assured irrigation is a prerequisite to sustain the growth of agricultural production to match the food production, to match the food requirements of over growing population. It has been observed that exploitation of groundwater by and large is essential for providing assured irrigation and drinking water supply. But the fluctuation of groundwater, level of Giridih is so much that during summer season many wells and tubewells go dry. As the water level goes down and the fluctuation is nearly 3-5 mts. Therefore, in Jharkhand region specially North Chotanagpur artificial recharge through different techniques is very essential to maintain the groundwater level. It is essential that groundwater resource is conserved as far as possible and replenishment is artificial, for sustainable development.

Recent studies have shown that groundwater table is depleting fast in different parts of Jharkhand. Excess exploitation of groundwater and presence of harder rock of terrain is the main cause of depletion of groundwater table. Increasing demand of drinking water and irrigation water has led to over-exploitation of available groundwater resources. Therefore, different methods of artificial recharge is essential for maintaining the proper groundwater table.

REFERENCES

Grover, S., Perspectives of GIS Modelling in Hydrology; *GIS@development,* Nov.-Dec., 1999.

Jagadeesha, C.J., Water Resource Development and Management. *GIS@development*, Nov.-Dec. 1999.

Mandal, R.B., *Land Utilization : Theory and Practice;* Concept Publishing Company, New Delhi, 1979.

5

Water Resources Utilisation and Management of Munger Division

PRAKHAR PRAKASH

Introduction

Munger Division comes under east central part of Bihar. The Division of Munger has good system of water resource. Munger division is fortunate in having several large and small rivers, springs, lakes and ponds. Rivers constitute an extremely important water resource as they form the basis of irrigation, domestic, industrial, water supply, hydro-power generation and inland water transport (Fig. 5.1). In addition they provide fish and variety of other animals. Water resource is the key both, for increasing cropping intensity and permitting new technologies.

Rivers such as the Ganga, the Gandak, the Bagmati, the Tilguja, the Kiul, the Barnar, the Alai, the Kamla, the Harohar, the Kosi, the Anjan, the Ajai, the Amrasarai flow in Munger Division. Besides these, there are also a number of smaller streams, which come down from hills during the rainy season (Fig. 5.2).

The water from well is lifted for irrigation through Persian wheel, mote, lever, pumping set, tube well, rahat pump, *ahars*, *ditch*, *latha* and *koori* in Munger Division.

Water resource usage is in domestic irrigation, industry and power sector. But our consumption of water is growing due to rapid increase in population, industrialization, and food production in Munger Division. Industries consume substantial quantity of water.

There are three terrain units—the hills, the Tal land and the Diara lands found in Munger division. The hilly areas located near Jamalpur are full of quarries of quartzite rocks. The forest cutting is destroying the ecology of this hilly terrain.

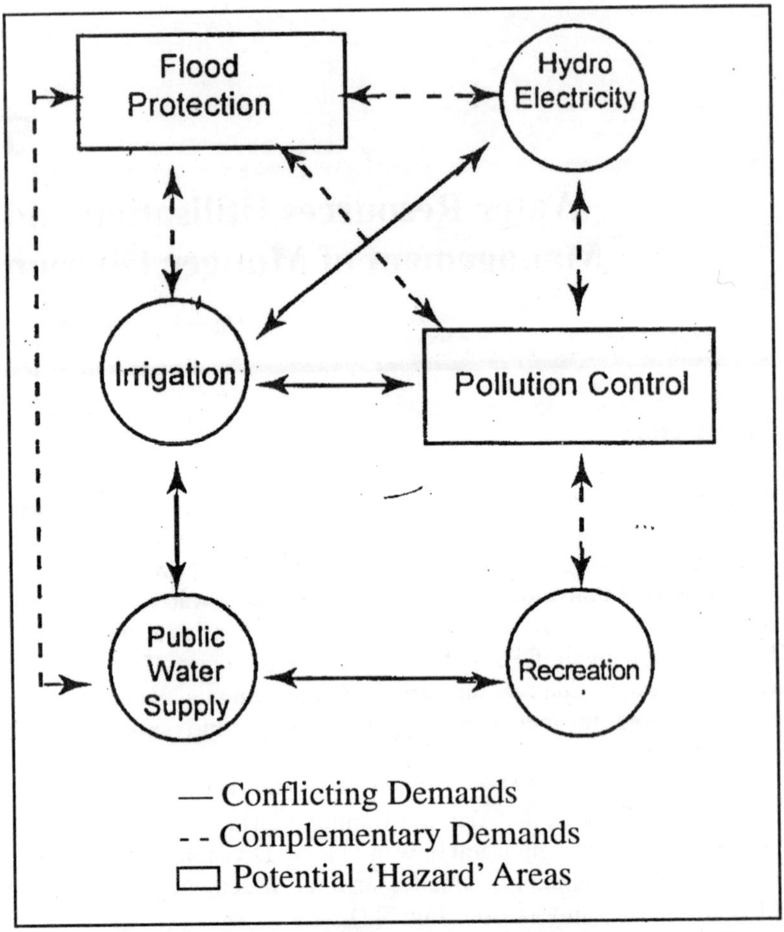

Fig. 5.1 : Multi-purpose water demands

The Tal and Diara tracts have no scarcity of water resource. Both surface and sub-surface water are available in plenty. But they have different problems to be solved. During rainy season most of the tal lands are flooded. During two decades the planning for utilization of the Ganga water by Dakra Nala Pump Canal has failed. The main channel of the Ganga has shifted northwards and so very little water is available for pumping into the canal. Again the poor supply of electricity is another problem. If the energy is not available how the pumps of Dakra Nala will work? Digging of channel to bring the

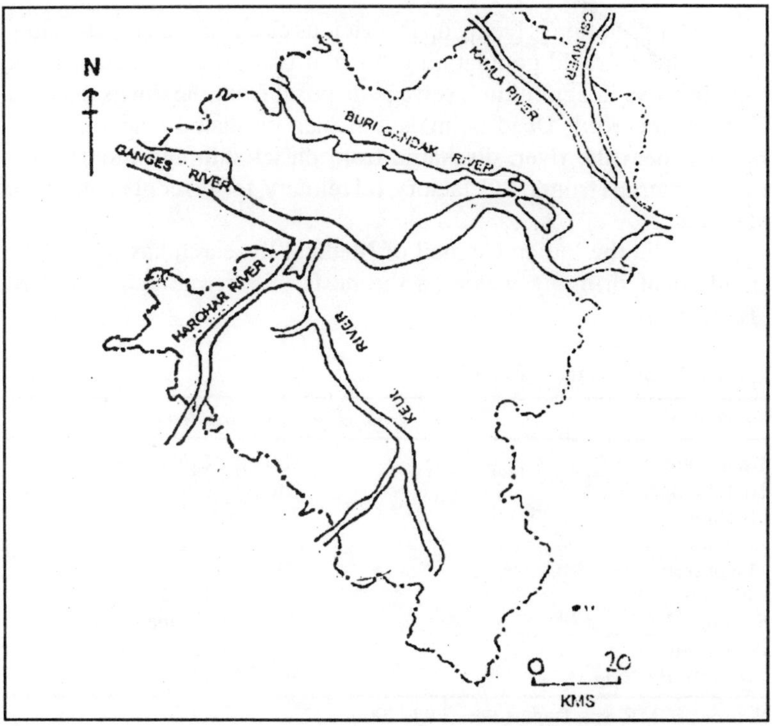

Fig. 5.2 : Drainage Lines in Munger Division

water of Ganga from midstream and then pumping into the canal is a costly affair, but this is the only way out. Boring in Tal and Diara tracts during dry period and getting underground water is the only probable solution left. By this method the yield of Rabi crops on both Tal and Diara tracts, and growing of vegetables in the Diara areas will definitely improve the economy of the area.

The National Water Policy of 1987 has defined water allocation priorities broadly for supply of water for drinking, irrigation, hydropower, ecology, agro and non-agro-industries, navigation and other usages. Various processes like sedimentation; filtration, post chlorination etc. are tend to produce the quality of water desired.

The unabated and indiscriminate exploitation of water resource is confounding the problem of water availability, pretending ill for the very survival of the mankind. In short the vital development process is in jeopardy.

Water pollution is facing up in a vicious circle in Munger Division. This is due to rapid population growth, urbanization, pesticides and chemical use in agriculture, sewage disposal from the towns near the Ganges, the Kiul. Dead animals and men cremated near the river, worship near the river, discharge from diesel ship and motor boat, waste materials from I.T.C. factory, oil refinery, fertilizer plant, thermal plant etc.

In India the Indian Council of Medical Research has set out the standard of drinking water on the basis of international standard (Table 5.1).

Table 5.1 : Standards of Water Quality

Substance	*Highest Desirable Level*
Total Solids	500 mg / Litre
Total hardness	2 m Eg / Litre
pH Range	7.0 — 8.5
Calcium	75 mg / Litre
Magnesium	30 mg / Litre
Chloride	200 mg / Litre
Sodium	500 — 1000 mg / Litre
Potassium	500 — 1000 mg / Litre
Coliform Bacteria	10 / 100 ml.

Source : ICMR Spl. Report Series 94, 2000.

Tube wells, wells, hand pumps, rivers and tanks are the sources of domestic water supply in Munger Division which is far from the desirable standards set by ICMR.

The chemical and bacterial indicators reveal that the water which being used in the division is highly polluted. This has led to prevalence of a number of water borne diseases all over Munger Division. The problem is more acute in the slum areas of Munger Division.

The diseases which are spread as a result of microbial contamination of water include those caused by enteric bacteria and virus like cholera, acute gastro-enteritis, diahorea, jaundice, dysentery, typhoid, Viral hepatitis A, B, E and Poliomyelitis in Munger Division.

Water available for daily use contain suspended impurities, dissolved poisonous salts, COD, BOD, Hg^{++}, Pb^{++} F^-, Cl^-, SO_4, HCO_3^-, CO_3^- etc, which cause bacterial and viral diseases.

In India about 80 per cent of the diseases are believed to be water-related and the World Health Organisation has estimated that merely 5 million human deaths occur every year from polluted drinking water.

This problem could be solved by adopting two fold strategy. The sincere efforts must be made for the supply of clean water in one hand and people should be educated about the general hygiene and the harm caused by the use of polluted water on the other.

The Ganga Action Plan has failed in Munger Division. Several scientific studies have calculated that the Ganga river water has lost its credibility as pure and has turned into the most contaminated one. At several places the water of Ganga is suitable neither for drinking nor bathing.

Various processes like sedimentation, filtration, post-chlorination, etc. are tuned to produce the quality of desired water. Groundwater plays significant role in meeting the requirement of people of the area, be it a drinking water or water for irrigation and for other uses. For the identification of the groundwater the hydrological variables like geology, geomorphology, lineament, drainage density, rain water, land data and pump test analysis are used. The use of remote sensing data for hydro geomorphological mapping, zoning of the area into groundwater prospects and evaluation of zones by using well discharge data located in the area of Munger Division. It has been observed that structured and weathered rocks are more potential in ground water discharge.

Fluoride is often called a "two edge sword". It helps in mineralization of bones. Presence of small quantities of fluorides, less than one part per million in drinking water prevents dental decay and helps enamel formation. However, fluoride, when consumed more than one mg/l can cause several kinds of health problem, viz., skeletal fluorosis, dental fluorosis, osteofluorosis and get-fluorosis (Table 5.2).

Table 5.2 : Effect of Fluoride on Human Health

Amount of fluoride in ground water (ppm)	*Adverse effect on Human health*
0	Adverse effect on pregnancy power and can also damage a foetus.
0.5–1.5	Helps in teeth-enamel formation
1.5–4.0	Dental Fluorosis
4.0–10.0	Dental Fluorosis, Osteo-Fluorosis, Severe pains in joints, back bones and other disorders.

Source : Raijv Gandhi National Drinking Water Mission, New Delhi,

During weathering and circulation of water in rocks and soils, fluoride is leached out and gets dissolved in the ground water.

Several methods of defluoridation of drinking water have been reported and are based on the principle of exchange or absorption employing the use of iron exchange resins, activated carbon, bauxite, lime and alum, bone char, activated alumina and osmosis.

The most important aspect of prevention and control of endemic fluorosis is to create awareness among people. Expectant mothers should not use fluoridated water. We should also promote oral hygiene and more calcium and vitamin C in diet to the people of fluorosis affected areas.

Water indeed is a symbol of life. It is continuously changing from one shape into another, however changing character and is always indestructible.

Absence of water can turn fertile land into desert and can destroy the civilization. It is becoming precious and scarce in recent times. As the consumption increase, shortage occur and equality of water is also affected.

Today growing population, industrialization, transportation, urbanization and faulty agriculture practices are causing threats day by day to this very elixir water. They polluted them and deplete in terms of their quality and quantity. It is imperative to use the life operator water properly through enhanced technique and skilful management (Fig. 5.3).

Therefore, management of water can become a boon for the development of Munger division. Management of water implies making the best use of available water resource for human and environmental benefit while not only preventing and controlling its depletion and degradation but also develop it in view of the present and future needs.

There are several water management agencies at the centre and state level to deal with surface water, groundwater, drinking water, supply and sewage disposal. It is necessary to have an interacted institutionalized mechanism for management of water resources both in terms of quality and quantity. Municipal authorities, NGOs and citizen's organization could be involved in a multimedia campaign to create awareness as the crucial role of the individual in promoting appropriate water management (Fig. 5.4).

Hopefully, we will be able to meet the challenges ahead in ensuring efficient and full utilization of our water resource. There is need for

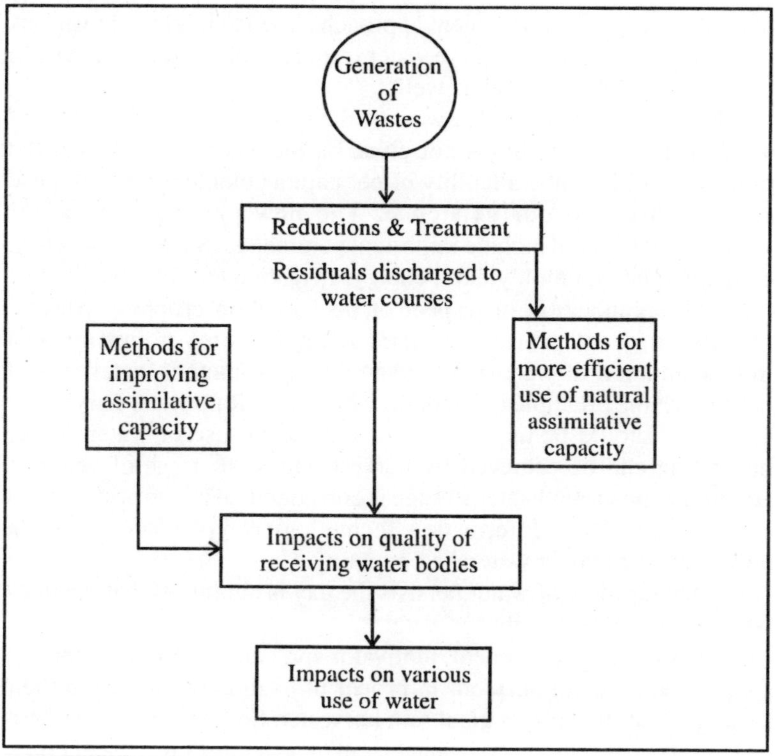

Fig. 5.3 : Systems Management of Water Quality

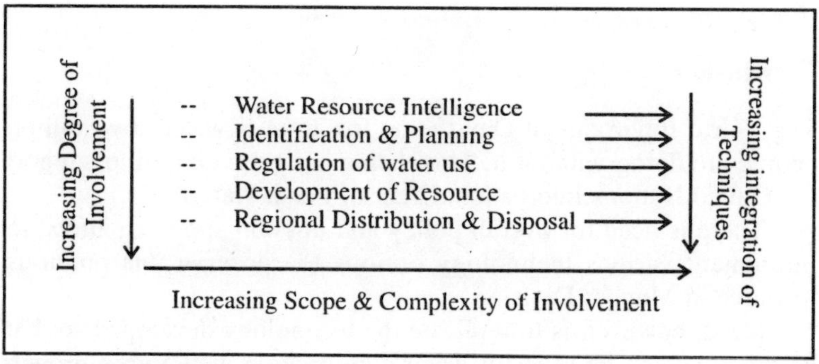

Fig. 5.4 : Techniques available to the Government for influencing water management

overall policy and management approach aimed to implement various technology options to conserve water resource not in Munger Division but in India and the world as well.

People should be made aware of the need of the conservation of water. If proper attention is not given on the water management the rapidly declining of availability of per capita potable water will pose serious threat to our existence. The new paradigm of water management should include important parameters. Such as efficiency, ecology, quality, employment, energy, irrigation etc. Involvement of farmer's organization in respect of decisions on cropping pattern, maintenance of water and irrigation system, planning and implementation of water release should be promoted. Water should be used on the principle of "economy of force". Rain water harvesting technique should be applied to prevent the misuse of water. Water harvesting can be achieved by harvest due to shortage of water in acquifer zone groundwater storage is considered to be the best method of water harvesting. Information Technology can play a Vital role in enforcing systematic watershed planning.

If the problem of water persists the day is not far off that the third world war will be fought for water.

Crux of the environment, motivator and conservator of water, the forest would be our surviour in proper utilization of water and their management. It is also a great rain harvester. So forest comes to help us in proper utilization and management of water resource, water crises is eminent. The most concerned fact is that water is finite natural resource and no technology, till date, has successfully contributed in making or producing water for mass consumption in Munger Division (Fig. 5.5).

Conclusion

The World Environment Day theme for 2003 is water. Two billion people are dying without it. This theme has been chosen to support the United Nations International Year of Fresh Water.

There is need for overall policy and mission approach aimed to implement various technology options to conserve this precious resource in Munger Division.

Need, however, is to replicate the technology developed so that its potential can be used for water conservation, better crop growth and thus better quality of life. Only through such efforts further technology development would be pursued.

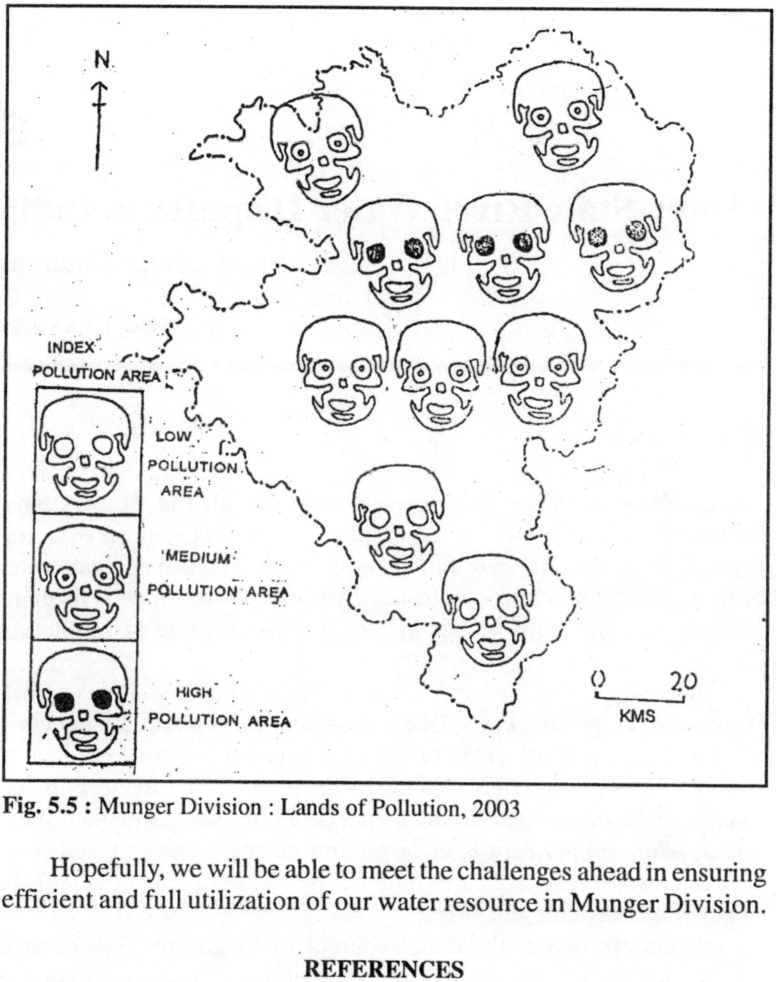

Fig. 5.5 : Munger Division : Lands of Pollution, 2003

Hopefully, we will be able to meet the challenges ahead in ensuring efficient and full utilization of our water resource in Munger Division.

REFERENCES

Gerasimov, I.P., *Man, Society and the Environment,* Progress Publishers, Moscow, 1984.

Goudie, A.S. *The Human Impact, Man's Role in Environmental Change,* Basil Blackwell, Oxford, London.

Mitchell Bruce, *Geography and Resource Analysis,* Longman, Waterloo, Ontario, 1978.

Powell, J.M., *Approaches to Resource Management,* Sorrett Publishing, Australia.

6

Inter-State River Water Disputes in India

Problem and Solutions

RASHMI PRAKASH

Introduction

Water resource is the fundamental base for all the life systems, including human being, on the earth's surface. Water is an essential ingredient in virtually ever-human endeavour. The use of fresh water is so omnipresent in our day-to-day lives that the resource is taken as infinite. But the truth is that the fresh water resource is depleting rapidly.[1]

Basically, 3/4 of the earth is water. The estimated volume of fresh water in river, groundwater, lakes, snow and ice is about 2.5 per cent, the rest being sea/salt water. Of this 2.5 per cent only one per cent is usable freshwater which is affected by the hydrological cycle, climatic change and human exploitation, 69 per cent is ice and permanent snow cover, while 30 per cent is underground resource and soil moisture. Our freshwater resources are finite but by virtue of water cycle fresh water is a renewable resource.[2]

Rivers are one of the major sources of freshwater. Rivers have always deeply influenced the inspiration of men. They seem to be the most enduring features of the earth's surface. There are innumerable ways in which man makes use of river water. It has been used for household consumption and irrigation purposes since times immemorial. There is increasing demand of river water in industries, agriculture and water power used by the people.[3]

Economic prosperity of any country depends upon its natural resources and river water is one of the most important natural resource. River water can be exploited for generating power for irrigation and for industrial processes. Rivers are also one of the cheapest mode of transport. They are also source of aquatic life, i.e. fish, which form an integral part of the ecological food chain. Demand for fresh river water has been increasing with rapid population growth and economic development for various purposes. This has led to greater exploitation of river water. But the supply has been almost constant or in some cases even lowered.[4]

Rivers flow across different state/national boundaries and are thus inter-state or international rivers. The development of river water resource especially of inter-state rivers, involves combined efforts of various agencies under different state governments.

The inter-state river disputes arise over sharing of waters, the submergence of land, sharing of costs etc., among the states through which the river flows because every state claims right over the waters of the river. The upper riparian states always try to derive maximum benefits, while the lower riparian states tend to be apprehensive of the plans of the former. Exploitation of river water in the upper reaches of the river affects the water resource availability of these lower states. The disputes in general may look alike but the basic cause of dispute may differ from one another.[5]

Inter-state river water disputes are historically inevitable. Since early times rivers have been perhaps causes of disputes between states, because the word 'rival' derives its origin from a Latin word 'rivus' meaning 'stream'. There are two legal theories of olden times on the basis of which river disputes were resolved earlier, (1) Riparian Rights and (2) Prior Appropriation Theory.[6]

Riparian Rights

The essence of the Riparian Rights theory is the recognition of equal rights to the use of water by all owners of land abutting a stream as long as it does not interfere with the rights of other riparian owners. Each riparian has a right to have water flow past his lands undiminished in quantity and unimpaired in quality for his ordinary use, i.e. use for household works and for cattle. Any other use of water is considered as not interfering with the rights of other riparian owners if it is for reasonable use and for agricultural purposes. Water in general cannot be included in the subject matter of property. In fact, water must continue flowing by the law of nature. Common law is that all who have the right of access to it may reasonably use it, none can have any right of property on water itself, except on the portion he may choose to abstract from the stream and take into possession. That too only till the time of possession. Riparian rights are founded on the rights of access to the river and a riparian tenement must be in reasonable proximity to the water/river. The common law (in U.K.) principles applicable to riparian rights and the common law rights to riparian owners to abstract water from and to construct on rivers also found place in the Indian Easement Act, 1882.[7]

This theory denies the benefits of modern technological uses of river water resources to non-riparian land owners, as rights go with the course of the river.

Prior Appropriation Theory

This law dates back to Roman times and was adopted in the arid and semi-arid states of U.S.A. in early years. This theory states that water in its natural course is the property of the public and cannot be owned. The right to use the water may be acquired by appropriation and application for beneficial use. The first user established a prior right and subsequent users can only appropriate what is left by the first user. This theory has now become obsolete as states have acquired full or partial ownership of river water. This doctrine is not accepted as law in India.[8]

The common factor in both the theories is that abstraction of water is by the permission of the state or other authorities controlling the use of water. In India river water disputes are not new. Acts were made to resolve many such disputes even before independence and even in ancient India.

Purpose

The paper is an attempt to discuss the history, the causes and the types of inter-state river disputes in India in general. It also refers to the constitutional provisions and methods available in India regarding settlement of such disputes. Effort has been made to suggest certain general principles to be followed in case of settlement of disputes.

Area of Study

India is one of the largest countries of the world covering an area of 3,287,782 km^2. It is divided into a number of states and union territories for administrative purposes. A large network of rivers is found well spread over the country, except in the northwestern part of Rajasthan (Thar desert). These rivers can be grouped in two categories—(a) snowfed perennial rivers of north India (Himalayan river system) and (b) rivers of central and southern India (Peninsular river system).

The Himalayan river system of northern India is comparatively of recent origin and differs from that of peninsular river system. The rivers are eroding, transporting and depositing agents, flowing across the plains. They have built the vast northern plains of India. The Himalayan rivers have large catchment basins spanning over different physiographic and climatic regions. Further, the rivers flow across many states and thus are inter-state rivers. The major rivers, Ganga, Indus and Brahmaputra, have different hydrological conditions and problems in various sections of their courses. The Ganga basin, for example, covers an area of about 861,404 km^2 and the total length of its first order streams flowing throughout India is 7,552 km. These rivers widen considerably during floods. Shifting of courses poses another problem.[9]

The river systems of peninsular India are of great antiquity. Consequently, due to degradation of ages, their channels have approached last stage of river development. The valleys are broad and shallow, characteristic of the regions where vertical erosion has almost ceased. One notable feature in the drainage system is the easterly trend of its main channels, the western ghats being the main watershed. The three major rivers, Godavari, Cauvery, and Krishna are inter-state rivers.

Thus major Indian rivers are inter-state rivers. There are (1) rivers of Indus river basin, in the Punjab, Haryana, Jammu and Kashmir and parts of Himachal Pradesh and even in Pakistan; (2) river Ganga and its tributaries in Himachal Pradesh, Delhi, Haryana, U.P. , Rajasthan, West Bengal, M.P., Bihar, Nepal and Bangladesh; (3) river Mahanadi, Godavari river and its tributaries, the Cauvery river and its tributaries and river Krishna are all inter-state in nature. These rivers have been flowing on the same route since times immemorial but there have been changes in the political boundaries. Some rivers have, thus, become inter-national in character, e.g. Indus and Ganga. Even Brahmaputra is an inter-national river.

There has been development of river water resource for irrigation and hydroelectric power generation in India since independence. Many multi-purpose river valley projects have been completed on inter-state rivers, e.g. the Bhakra Nangal, the Hirakud and the Tungbhadra, the Kosi Valley Project and the Gandak River Valley Project to provide water for irrigation, power generation and to control floods. In many projects the states working in an integrated manner, have cooperated and have derived maximum benefits from rivers. But in many cases there arose disputes over sharing of water and cost etc.

India's economy, for the most part is based on agriculture which, to a large extent, is dependent upon rainfall. Rainfall, however, is very unevenly distributed leading to drought in some areas and floods in others. The average annual rainfall is 115cm but it varies from 8 cm in desert areas to 1250cm in hills of Meghalaya. Irrigation in India is as old as its civilization. Irrigation by river was either by proper channeling of flowing water or by utilization of water from natural dams, i.e. lakes or tanks. Generally, for river irrigation dams are constructed across the river where there is surplus water. Water is then diverted through different canals to areas deficient in water.[10]

Along with the regional disparity India also experiences seasonal variation in rainfall. Rainfall is mainly received during monsoon months from June to September. So there is need of irrigation facilities, for successful agricultural production in one form or another.

Projects were also undertaken to control floods. With these aims dams and canals were constructed in India. Irrigation has helped in increasing agricultural production. Multi-purpose projects have led to a successful green revolution, and increase in food production.

Since independence there has been increase in the demand for hydro-electric power. As hydroelectric power is cheap, non-pollutant and a renewable source of energy, demand for hydel power has increased. With the growth of a large number of industries, India has now became one of the highly industrialised states. So, power has to be generated and supplied to keep these industries working at full capacity. Many electrically operated pumpsets are in demand and in use all over the country.

Rise in the standard of living, has led to demand for consumer goods like, refrigerators, air-conditioners, television sets and other electrically operated gadgets, not only in towns but also in villages. So to meet these demands rivers have to be harnessed to generate as much power as possible.

The development of river water assumes greater significance because the quantum of water available in rivers is much greater than that available in tanks or lakes.

Because of all these factors exploitation of river water for various purposes have begun ever since British rule in India. After independence considerable importance has been given to development of river water resource. There have been high allocations for irrigation and flood control in all the Five Year Plans.

History of Inter-State Water Disputes in India

In India the accepted principle of equitable apportionment of river water was first introduced in 1867. Equitable sharing at that time meant irrigating the largest possible area at the lowest cost, irrespective of state boundaries, because it was thought that governments may change, canals should last for ever.

Another important feature of those times was that water of a river were not to be used by riparian states only, even a non-riparian state could share the water provided. The concerned state was willing to bear the cost of the irrigation project in proportion to the benefit accrued. (Patiala received waters from Sirhind canal on Sutlej river.) The principle adopted was that each state was allotted a fixed proportion of water and was free to use its share.

In India the rights of the co-riparian states were regulated by an agreement even before any precise legal provisions existed. The earliest agreement related to apportionment of waters of river Jhelum in 1873 known as Sirhind Canal Agreement and was between British government and the states of Patiala, Jheend and Nabha. Next agreement was that of Cauvery in 1892 reached between the princely states of Mysore and the Government of Madras.

The agreement over distribution of Indus water could be made only in 1960 by Indus Waters Treaty between India and Pakistan.

In 1953, Anderson Committee submitted its report on the sharing of water. The report was based on "Benthamite Principle" of the greatest good to the greatest numbers in the allocation of water. Another important principle recommended was that no permanent right should be allowed to be acquired over water. The third point was that the agreements should not be permanent but should be reviewed periodically as there are chances of alternative irrigation sources which can be developed.

In India it is an accepted principle that no state can be given entirely free hand in the utilization of a common source of water such as inter-state river. These rivers are for the general welfare of all the states through which they flow irrespective of political boundaries.

Constitutional Provisions and Acts relating to Water Disputes

An earnest attempt was made to resolve water disputes in India in 1935 itself. The Government of India Act, 1935 for the first time provided for the intervention of Governor General in case of any complaint regarding interference of water supplies. The Act specifically describes the powers of Governor General in case of any river water dispute among different states. Under our present Constitution provision exists for settlement of water disputes under Article 262 of the Constitution.

The Constitution of India has made several departures from the provisions of the Government of India Act, 1935. (1) The State's Legislative power was made subject to Parliament's power, (2) The mechanism for resolving water disputes is not written in the Constitution but is to be provided law by the Parliament, (3) The jurisdiction of all courts including the Supreme Court is not excluded by the Constitution but Article 262(2) empowers the Parliament to provide for such exclusion by law.

The Parliament enacted two laws : (1) The River Board Act of 1956 relating to inter-state rivers and river valleys. The Act has remained ineffective as River Boards were never appointed. (2) Inter-state Water Disputes Act of 1956 entitled "An Act to provide for the adjudication of disputes relating to waters of inter-state rivers and river valleys" (*Journal of the Indian Law Institute,* 1978). This Act defines water disputes (section 3 of the Act), describes the complaints (section 3), constitution of Tribunal, the actual jurisdiction of water disputes, and power and tenure of the tribunal etc. in its various sections. According to the Act of 1956 "Water dispute means any dispute or difference between two or more state governments with respect to (a) the use, distribution or control of the water of or in any inter-state river or river valley or (b) the interpretation of the terms of any agreement relating to the use, distribution or control of such water or the implementation of such agreements or (c) the levy of any water rate in contravention of the prohibition contained in section 7 (Inter-State Water Disputes Act, 1956, Section 2, Sub-section 'C').

Right to have a water dispute referred to a tribunal is not absolute but depends upon the opinion of the Central Government. Negotiated settlement has been given preference.

Types of Disputes

Since independence the development of river water resource has been undertaken for beneficial use in both agriculture and industry. All the Five Year Plans in India lay emphasis on harnessing river water. But the development has not been smooth because a majority of Indian rivers are inter-state in nature. Indian states were organised on linguistic characteristics, and not on geographical consideration. As such rivers pass through two or more states and river disputes may arise. The definition of 'Water Disputes' according to Inter-State Water Disputes Act, 1956 itself suggests that the problem of river water disputes can be of various types. The problems of inter-state river water disputes can be classified as follows :

1. The problems relating to the sharing of construction cost and benefits of a project developed jointly by more than one state.
2. Question of compensation to be given to a state which has been prejudicially affected by the implementation of a project in another state.
3. Dispute relating to interpretation of agreements.
4. Complaints regarding excess withdrawals by a state or not releasing sufficient water for lower riparian states.

Majority of the disputes related to sharing of waters by different riparian states, e.g. Karnataka and Andhra Pradesh objected to the diversion of more water of river Krishna to Koyna than was approved by the Planning Commission. Similarly, Andhra Pradesh being a lower riparian state objected to the construction of dams, for irrigation purpose, by Maharashtra and Karnataka. In case of Telugu Ganga Project upper riparian state Karnataka complained against Andhra Pradesh—a lower riparian state—when Andhra Pradesh Government started work on the surplus water flowing to the sea. Karnataka contented that its irrigation projects had not been complete, and so it was not able to use all the waters of Krishna river allocated to it.

Sometimes two or more states agree to develop a river and implement the development project jointly. In such cases problems arise over sharing of costs and benefits among the states involved, e.g. dispute between Karnataka and Andhra Pradesh regarding the Tungbhadra dam.

When a lower riparian state proposes a plan for the development of an inter-state river that may lead to a change in the land use or use of water by upper riparian state many problems may arise. For example, if a state builds a dam and submergence of land takes place in the upper riparian state many problems arise such as the problem of land acquisition, payment of compensation to the displaced persons, their rehabilitation and settlement etc. Monetary compensation cannot be enough. The farmers may demand cultivable land, houses and also money. Large number of villages may be submerged so compensation must be adequate.

Sometimes there can be dispute over withdrawal of too much water or there can be demand, by lower riparian state, for the release of more water especially in the period of bad monsoon.

Methods to Resolve Dispute

Inter-state water disputes present complex social, economic, technical and topographical problems and involve a judicious balancing and adjustment of these factors. These various factors are not necessarily constant but present possibilities of change in future. This makes settlement of disputes more difficult. Further, each river system has peculiarities of its own. Again, in different countries/areas the climatic conditions, especially rainfall characteristics, are different. So different methods are adopted for settling disputes in different conditions. Various methods are available in different legal systems for resolving inter-state river water disputes. Some of these were tried in India and many of them were not suited to Indian conditions.

These methods basically fall into two categories : (1) Political agreement between two or more riparian states, (2) the judicial settlement of the dispute.

Both have their limitations and advantages. Political agreements are between political leaders and when these leaders fall out of power their successor may not accept the agreement in principle although bound to it. Therefore, problems may arise.

In judicial settlements there is no popular acceptance of the judgement because representatives of people are not involved. Further, there are many factors involved in such disputes and the judicial process is accustomed to apply a definite standard or a rule. Therefore, it may not be of much help in such cases.

Because of these limitations Direct Negotiation Method between parties is also one of the means of resolving such disputes. It has the consent of the parties contending, satisfies all and can be implemented without much delay. That is why even under Inter-state Water Disputes Act, 1956 preference is given to negotiated settlement and only when it is not possible the Central Government refers the dispute to the tribunal.

The Central Government of India has adopted Direct Negotiation Method in various cases of inter-state river water agreements and has been successful in many cases. Some such disputes are—

1. Musakhand Project dispute between U.P. and Bihar; .
2. Palar water dispute between Tamil Nadu and Karnataka (settled in 1956);
3. Tungbhadra Project High Level Canal dispute between Karnataka and Andhra Pradesh (settled in 1956);
4. Dispute over utilization of waters of Ravi-Beas rivers among the Punjab, Rajasthan and J&K (settled in 1965);
5. Dispute over sharing of the waters of Swarnrekha river among Bihar, Orissa and West Bengal (settled in 1964);
6. Problem of sharing of costs and benefits of Jamni Dam Project between U.P. and M.P. (settled in 1965); and
7. Exploitation of the water of Mahi river between Gujarat and Rajasthan (settled in 1966).

But certain disputes could not be solved by negotiations. Some of these are :

1. The Krishna-Godavari water dispute among Maharashtra, Karnataka, Andhra Pradesh, Madhya Pradesh and Orissa;
2. The Cauvery water dispute among Tamil Nadu, Kerala and Karanataka;
3. The Narmada water dispute among Gujarat, Rajasthan, M.P. and Maharashtra;
4. The Tungbhadra Project issues other than High Level canal, between Karnataka and M.P.;
5. The Koymani River dispute between Bihar and West Bengal; and
6. The dispute over the Keolari Nadi water between M.P. and U.P.

So far the following tribunals have been appointed to resolve inter-state river water disputes :

1. The Godavari Water Dispute Tribunal,
2. The Krishna Water Dispute Tribunal,
3. The Narmada Water Dispute Tribunal,
4. The Ravi-Beas Water Dispute Tribunal, and
5. The Cauvery Water Dispute Tribunal.

The first three have given their final reports (Ramana, M.V.V., 1992).

Suggestions and Conclusion

To make any settlement more effective and judicious the following facts should be considered :

1. In case of river water disputes, the entire basin of the river should be considered as one unit, not as separate units belonging to different states divided by political/administrative boundaries.
2. A fixed framework to resolve the dispute has to be developed. It is possible because issues are basically the same with only minor variations.
3. A time limit should be fixed for negotiations beyond which the matter has to be referred to the tribunal.
4. A permanent tribunal should be set-up with the powers of the highest court of the land, equipped with technical personnels to assist in technical matters.
5. Time limit should be fixed within which a tribunal has to give its decisions.
6. A period of 50 years or so should be fixed for the validity of a report given by a tribunal and only after the lapse of the period, it can be replaced by a new one.
7. The award given by a tribunal can be reviewed only once or twice.
8. An agreement arrived at between states through negotiations should be given legislative sanction by making it an Act. This will prevent frequent amendments.

9. A detailed survey should be conducted on all the major inter-state rivers to assess the quantity (average) of water available and the way it is being apportioned.
10. A detailed survey of the quantity of water should also be conducted because though till now disputes are not related to quantity of water or water pollution but there is possibility that in future such disputes may arise among riparian states.
11. The economic benefits that accrue to a state must also be taken into account, (Instead of fixed compensation, a perennial compensation, i.e. free electricity or subsidy on agricultural products may be more acceptable).
12. The quantum of water is not always same in a river. Therefore, a variation should be allowed for such an eventuality.

Finally, it can be concluded that the inter-state river water disputes in India are basically linked to the economic aspects. It is related to (i) increase in irrigation facilities and agricultural production, (ii) production of electricity a major industrial input and, (iii) flood control, again an economic aspect related to all kinds of loss.

Therefore, while arriving at a resolution during negotiation the principle of "the fortunate have to sacrifice something for the less fortunate" should be applied. This can be achieved through mutual understanding between riparian states. Crops can be alternated among riparian states. (For example, if upper riparian state switches over from crops like paddy which require more water to crop which requires comparatively less water, more water can be available to the lower riparian states in one year and the same can be done by lower riparian state in the next year.) Thus no one is at disadvantage.

Again, all areas do not require same amount of water for same crop. The climatic conditions and other factors also matter. So all these facts should be considered.

In the end, the most satisfactory settlement of such disputes is by negotiated agreements among parties, by mutual understanding, as if they belong to single community undivided by political/administrative frontiers. If there is no such agreement, rights of different states must be determined by applying the rules of equitable apportionment, each unit getting a fair share of the water of the common river, in the general interest of the community. The geographical factors should be given preference not the political division.

REFERENCES

1. India 2001: A Reference Annual. Ministry of Information and Broadcasting. Govt. of India.
2. Jain, S.N. *et al. Inter-state Water Disputes in India : Suggestions for Reform in Law*. The Indian Law Institute. New Delhi. 1971.
3. Johnson, B.L.C. "India: Resources and Development", Arnold-Heinemann, 1980.
4. *Journal of the Indian Law Institute*. New Delhi. (1970), (1976) & (1978).
5. Nag, P. and Sengupta, S., *Geography of India*, Concept Publishing Company, New Delhi, 1992.
6. Pounds, N.J.G., *Political Geography*, McGraw Hill Inc. U.S.A., 1972.
7. Ramana, M.V.V. *Inter-state River Water Disputes in India*. Orient Longman Ltd., Madras, 1992.
8. Rao, K.L. *India Water Wealth*, Orient Longman Ltd., New Delhi. 1979.
9. II Report of the study team of the Administrative Reforms Commission on the Centre-State Relationships, pp. 126-134.
10. The Inter-state Water Disputes Act, 1956 (Act XXXIII of 1956).

7

Integrated Watershed Programme Strategy

Objectives and Management

A. MISHRA

In hydrologic terms, watershed is an independent identity. It refers to drainage area going at a point into a particular stream as *nallah.* Watershed management is essentially management of rain water, surface water and groundwater resource for ensuring sustainability in production without causing degradation of overall resources of watershed. The scope of watershed management has been made further broad based. It is integrated management of all types of watershed where moisture conservation receives top priority. It includes all activities for total uplift of the masses living in the area (Murty).

Jharkhand, covering an area of 26,800 sq. km, receives an average annual rainfall of 36,700 million cubic metres of rain water, 12,000 MCM returns to the atmosphere as evapotranspiration and 5,000 MCM recharges groundwater. The existing dams capacity is 1500 MCM. The geographical conditions allow further bundling of similar quantities by major and minor irrigation schemes 16,700 MCM of rainwater waste into the seas perennially (Murty).

Any area is a part of some watershed. Rainwater moves different sides of river in every watershed. Rainwater retention management in upper reaches improves soil moisture harvest, overload water and recharges groundwater. Improve moisture conditions with water sources, which grow bitterly greenery. More water is provided for the crops by managing the water movement in a watershed. Thus, the watershed becomes a pragmatical unit for better crop yield. Watershed management is the management of soil moisture in a watershed for growing greens as better crops (Kanwar).

It may be said that watershed management is the management of land, water and energy in the context of socio-economic conditions to improve the soil moisture with watershed (Reddy, 1995).

The Concept for Growing Greens with Better Crops Why Watershed so Important in Rainfed Lands?

In rainfed land, rainwater is the only major source of water where scientific management is crucial for supporting different activities. For efficient management of water resources, information about their magnitudes and dynamicity is essential. Watershed concept helds in assessment of water resources. It helps in modelling the sources and sinks for defining water flow systems and deciding sizes of structures for rainwater management (Singh).

Watershed concept helps in establishing relationship between input which may be rainwater and output like runoff.

Objectives of Watershed Management

The main objectives of watershed management can be described in a symbolic form by the expression; POWER which may be written as :

P = Production of food, milk, fruit, fuel, fire on sustained basis.
- forage
- prevention of flood.
- pollution control.

O = Over-exploitation of resources to be avoided.
- Over-grazing to be controlled.

W = Water storage to be created.
- Wildlife and indigenous species to be protected

E = Erosion control
- eco-system safety
- employment stability

R = Recharge of groundwater
- reduction of drought hazard
- reduction of reservoir siltation
- recreation.

Watershed Management Plans

Most rainfed lands need watershed management and some have to be given more priority, untreated water may be considered to start with watershed selection should be made considering the nature of problems and expected response offer initiation of programme. There should be sizeable units—anything above 500 ha. and upto 500 ha for this, perspective plans should be prepared by state Agricultural Department/ Conservation Department in Cooperation with other departments. Scientists may be consulted at this stage. NGOs working in the area may also be involved for assessing farmers requirements for this purpose.

The perspective plan will depend upon availability of funds and such projects may need some funds from the government.

Year-wise actual action plan may be prepared taking broad guidelines from perspective plans. The farmers and villagers may be consulted at this stage in detail for surveys. The role of NGOs may be important while finalizing such an action plan. They can play effective role in the implementation as motivation of farmers is important and this can be done later through NGOs. Efforts may be made to creat cooperative societies for watersheds. There should be provision of compensation for those making sacrifice for the society. Similarly, persons drawing benefits from development works may be asked to pay something (Mishra).

Field level conservation measures may be decided in consultation with concerned farmers. Due consideration may be made for the structures/measures already available at the site.

There should be provision for maintenance of works and carrying out follow-up programmes. All these need to be spelt out in detail in master plans of watersheds.

Strategy for Implementation and Maintenance of Watershed Measures in Cultivated Lands

In cultivated land hard core measures/hardwares should be implemented in the first two years. There should be follow up by medium softwares in the same year or during the year to follow. Likewise, softwares may be encouraged subsequently in the following years.

Non-arable Lands

Non-agricultural lands may be put to the following uses :

A. Reserve forests

The lands which are away from habitations where minimum bio-interference is expected. These lands may need few moisture conservation measures in addition to few water storage points/ structures.

B. Grasslands

These lands may be of shallow to medium soil depths. Few hard tree species may be allowed in addition to encouraging grasses and legumes. Controlled grazing may be required.

C. Mixed land covers

Such land may be developed in phases to start with social fencing. Few strips at wider spacing may be developed with grasses and legumes in the first phase. Then, some hardy shrubs may be seeded and planted in some-strips. Planting of trees may be taken up in third phase, by this time there may be some retuns from such land as sale of forage on fuel wood.

D. New plantations

Only limited area to be developed with new plantations where full protection is easily assured.

REFERENCES

Kanwar, J.S., "New Dimensions in Water Management," *Technology for Agriculture in India Farming,* 19 (3).

Mishra, A.I., *Dryland Agriculture—A Case Study of Mandu Block,* Ph.D. Thesis, p. 19.

Murty, J.V.S., *Watershed Management in India,* p. 27.

Reddy, Y.V.R., *Economic Evaluation of Watershed Technologies,* ICAR, 1995.

Singh, Y.P., *Forage Production Technologies for Rainfed Areas.*

8

Management and Utilization of Water Resources in Bihar

M.N. Pandey

Introduction

The whole world is under stress for fresh water which is a life sustaining resource, a basic human need and a precious natural assets. According to one estimate water on our Earth in different forms are 146 crore cubic kilometres. Only one per cent of it is fresh water, while 97 per cent is sea water and 2 per cent is in the form of ice.[1] This water scarcity makes it difficult to meet the increasing demand of drinking water, irrigation and industrial use. The demand for water in the world has increased three times more in comparison with the growth of population. At present one *arab* thirty crore people in the world are not getting fresh water.[2] Most of Africa, much of Western U.S.A. and North West Mexico, parts of Chile and Argentina and nearly entire Australia suffer severe water shortages. In many countries ground-water is being depleted. In India also water is being scared in different parts. It will face water crisis by 2025 but Bihar is floating over fresh water resource. It has rich potential of surface water also.[3] Rivers bring enormous water in the region. But on the other hand, Bihar accounts for more than 17 per cent of the flood prone areas of India. The geographical area of the state is 94.16 lakh hectares, out of which 68.8 lakh hectares land is affected with flood, 10 lakh hectares of land in Bihar has an area of permanent waterlogging.[4] The state faces floods every year causing loss to lives and properties, epidemic deaths due to water borne diseases, depicting the non-availability of fresh drinking water to masses all the times and loss of agricultural productivity due to poor utilization of the irrigation potential. Thus this paper is an attempt to focus the proper management and utilization of water resources in Bihar.[5]

Problem There is a great irony that water is not cultivated nor well stored in Bihar. Most of the rain water flows into the sea without being harnessed in the state. When Jharkhand was separated from Bihar on 15th November, 2000, the development is left with no other alternative but to develop through agriculture and its allied activities. Therefore, it will be highly appreciable if water resource of Bihar, is managed properly to develop agriculture and its allied operations. Though the state has plenty of natural resources like land, soil and water but their utilization and management has not been made after independence. A study conducted earlier has revealed that the length of embankments in Bihar has increased from 154 km in 1954 to 3454 km in 1988 but flood prone areas also increased in this period from 2.5 million hectares to 6.46 million hectares. Apart from the disastrous flood the state is confronted with numerous problems like droughts, drainage congestion, shifting river channels, high population, pressure on natural resources, low income, low literacy, low industrialization and urbanisation. Thus the state of Bihar is below the average of other states of India in every sphere of development. So, the paper highlights that the prosperity of Bihar can only be achieved through agriculture and its allied developments which can be possible with proper management and utilization of water resources in Bihar.[6]

Suggestions

To get rid of the problems of water resources and its better management and utilization in Bihar, the multidimensional approaches are required and so, the following steps may be taken on priority basis :

(i) A successful implementation of integrated watershed development programme is required in our state. This will necessarily supply water to every cultivable land and increases the all-round development of the state. In a watershed development programme construction of dams, contour trenching and bunding, gully plugging measures help to conserve water, soil and recharge of water.

(ii) NGOs and people's participation should be highly activated in management and planning of water resource programmes.

(iii) Local water resource planning should be given due

importance so that each rural area may manage its own water needs as far as possible to its optimum use.

(iv) Watershed programme should be effectively launched in dry land regions of Bihar.

(v) An emphasis should be given to suitable agricultural technology for flood prone area.

(vi) Measures should be taken for the construction of protected embankment along the rivers of Bihar.

(vii) Development of detention basin in rivers should be done.

(viii) Rain water is required essentially to be stored to check the depleting groundwater sources.

(ix) Rivers, lakes and wetlands must be properly and promptly cleaned.

(x) Renovation and utilization of tanks, *Pokhras, Aharas* and other local water sources.

(xi) Efforts should be made to construct reservoirs in the upper part of the rivers.

(xii) Efforts should be made to divert flood water into river basin.

(xiii) Inter-connected canals should be opened.

(xiv) Inter river basin transfer of water plan has been initiated taking the interest of Bihar first.

(xv) Chaurs of Bihar should be managed. It should be linked with each other and with the rivers according to slope of the land to develop drainage and canal system for better use.

(xvi) Comparatively deeper portion of chaurs, where raising of crops become difficult should be made more deep to accommodate flood water and after rainy season stored water should be used for agricultural crops, fishes and other water crops.

(xvii) The rivers should be made deeper by digging their beds.

(xviii) Efforts should be made to reduce the meander length by which the river slope increased, which increase the capacity of the river.

(xix) Both Central Government and Bihar Government should take initiatives honestly for proper water management and utilization in the benefit of Bihar first.

(xx) Bihar Government with the help of Union Government should announce an integrated, effective, proper and suitable water policy for the all-round development of Bihar.

Conclusion

Thus management and utilization of water resources are very much essential for the growth of Bihar. It will not only facilitate irrigation, generate electricity, promote industry, maintain environment, eradicate poverty and hunger but will bring Bihar's economy much ahead in the country.

REFERENCES

1. Sharma, B.K. and Kaur, H., *Water Pollution*, Goel Publishing House, Meerut.
2. *Hindustan,* dated 4.7.2002.
3. *Times of India,* Patna 25.8.2002.
4. *Dainik Jagran,* Patna, dated 1.9.2003.
5. *Times News Network,* Environment issues need holistic approach, UN official, *Times of India*, New Delhi, 17.2.2002.
6. Flood Report 1996, Central Flood Control Department, Bihar Government, Patna.

9

Emerging Hazards and Management

Water Crisis

Anil Kumar Gupta

Introduction

Water crisis is imminent. We have no option but to depend on the available sources of water and towards management, we have to save, conserve and strengthen this scarce resources without fail. Their conservation and creating conditions for new sources are the only need of the hour simply because as long as there is life on the earth, need for water is going on constantly increasing.

Prevailing Conditions : Water Crisis

Earth's ninety seven per cent water, which is in the sea, is very expensive to desalinate. Only about one per cent water is readily available for use and the irrigated agriculture consumes over 70 per cent of water used by people. Industry accounts for more than 20 per cent. Households use only 8 per cent. In other words, the domestic water consumption is the only use that is practically minimum. To assure good health, people need a minimum of about 100 litres of water per day for drinking, cooking and washing. In industrialised countries people are using as much as 450 litres a day, while in the developing countries consumption is as low as 20 litres per day. In water scarce places, the water consumption is not even 20 litres a day. The fact is that more than 26 countries are the main water deficient regions of Africa, West Asia, South Asia, North America, South America and Australia have already been experiencing water scarcity. According to an estimate, over three billion people of almost 65 countries will be affected by the water crisis by the year 2025. India will be one among the water scarce countries.[1]

The most concerned and serious fact is that water is a finite natural resource and no technology, till date, has successfully contributed to make or produce water for mass consumption. In India, the poverty stricken regions tend to be in the climatic zones subject to drought and other water problems as they are least able to afford alternative sourcing. The crisis about water resource development and management thus arises because sufficient water is not available for use and secondly, it is characterised by its highly uneven spatial distribution. Environmentalists like Sunderlal Bahuguna are not wrong in saying that the acute scarcity of water may force the powerful nations to wage a new global war to control the depleted sources of water. Such a parallel makes the future picture essentially depressing.[2]

Water is scarce even for drinking purpose, not to talk about its availability for agriculture, industries etc. Our country already faces an alarming situation. Its fragile water resources are stressed and depleting while various sectoral demands are growing rapidly, even as about 200 million people in the country do not have access to safe drinking water and about 1.5 million children under five years of age die each year due to water borne diseases. The drought conditions in several parts of the country like Gujarat, Rajasthan, Orissa and Andhra Pradesh are unfortunately on rise. Disputes over sharing of the water resources are becoming grimmer. India will face a severe water crisis if the available fresh water resources are not managed properly. According to an estimate, by the year 2025, the country will face a severe water shortage leading to serious struggle. Besides, it is also feared that within a few decades availability of water in the country will be about 1700 to 2000 cubic metres per person as against the world average of 5000 to 9000 cubic metres per person.[3]

In one-third of India's agro-climatic regions, there is water scarcity already in terms of per capita demand and supply of water.

Management

During the 21st century, water management must take an innovative course—a course that recognises water as both a basic need and as a scarce resource. It is very simple to know that if there is scarcity of water, the possibility of economic development will be lessened. Therefore, three major issues—availability, equality and access—must be focused.

Water Harvesting

India which constitutes different climates and geographical features has vast areas (about 68 per cent of the land) which are drought prone and have inadequate rainfall.

India has a long standing tradition of water conservation. Even ancient texts, inscriptions and archaeological remains bear witness to this. Over centuries India developed a range of techniques to harvest water in every farm which include rain water, groundwater, stream water, river water and flood water.[4]

Water harvesting can be achieved by harvesting (collection of water in original place), storage of water in acquifers (artifical recharge of groundwater by percolation tanks, checkdams etc.).

Of all, groundwater storage is considered to be the best method of water harvesting. Land development, soil conservation and afforestation help groundwater recharge and suface water storage.

Benefits

These methods are expected to yield benefits like rise in groundwater levels, reduction in flood hazard and soil erosion, assuring sustainability of the groundwater abstraction sources and mitigating the effects of droughts and achieving drought proofing.[5]

Pure Drinking Water from Dew Harvesting

According to Professor Girija Sharan with earth tube heat exchanger and cooling device, it is possible to collect a good 20 litres of pure drinking water everyday on 200sq. metre surface simply by collecting the huge amount of dew that the coastal region of Kutch gets every evening.

He says that "for 60 days we measured the dew that collected on the top of the greenhouse, we have built at Kothara village some 80 km from Bhuj".

The average collection of dew water was about nine litres a day. The highest was in April when we have collected 31 litres of pure distilled water.

When the water was tested at the Physical Research Laboratory and AMC lab, it was found that there was zero per cent dissolved salts. Dr. Sharan is now in the process of developing what he calls a dew harvester.

It is also found that if the 124 sq. m of roof of the greenhouse can give 9 litres of water, a 200 sq. m surface, made of a material that encourages condensation, should give about 20 litres. Plastic for instance cools quickly and would easily gather moisture from the air in the coastal regions. Besides, the farmers of that area experienced that they receive dew for seven months in a year, including summer. This is ideal considering the severe water shortage at that time.[6]

Conclusion

"Water is life. It is a precious gift of nature, and needs judicious utilization of every drop."

REFERENCES

1. Nautiyal, Suresh, "Water Crisis : Agenda for the Century" in *Yojana,* Vol. 46, February, 2002, p.11.
2. *Ibid.*
3. *Ibid.* pp. 11-12.
4. Bhagyalakhmi, J., "Water Harvesting for Drought Prone Areas," in *Yojana*, Vol. 45, July 2001, p. 27.
5. *Ibid.* p. 28. "Greenhouses are frames of inflated structure covered with a transparent material in which crops are grown under controlled enviromental conditions".
6. David, Robin, "Pure drinking water from dew harvest", an extract, *The Times of India,* a daily newspaper, Patna edition, 20 August, 2002, p. 8.

10

Problem of the Ganga Water Pollution in Bihar

A Geographical Discussion

RANA PRATAP

Introduction

The river Ganga is the most important and one of the major rivers of India. It is so closely associated with the day to day life of the teeming millions of people that it has become the lifeline of the country. And hence, she is affectionately called "Mother Ganga" by most of the Indians. This regard given to her has got its genesis. This includes both mythological as well as geographical. Jawaharlal Nehru, the first Prime Minister of India, has mentoned in his book *Will and Testament;* that "Ganga has been a symbol of India's ageold culture and civilization, ever-changing, everflowing, yet the same Ganga." The river has been being worshipped as a Holy River throughout the course since times immemorial. The Ganga water is supposed to be very pious and is used mostly for drinking, bathing and making offering to deities. The last wish of every Hindu has to have a drop of holy water of Ganga in his mouth at the time of death. Therefore, the Ganga is the faith of eternity for millions and is treated as the goddess which has brought by Bhagirath, the legend king of the past, on the earth from the heaven. Geographically, the river originates from the ice-cap of Gaumukh at the top of Gangotri glacier about 4100 metres (13,452 feet) above the mean sea level in the form of various streams, e.g. Bhagirathi, Alaknanda, Mandakini and Jahnavi. Finally, they all combined into one river—the Ganga and criss-crosses through about 200 km of the mountainous terrain, comes down to plain area at Haridwar. From there it traverses a total length of 2525 km through the Indian states like Uttaranchal, Uttar Pradesh, Bihar and West Bengal and finally, merges in the Bay of Bengal at Gangasagar. The river drains about 861,404 sq.km, that consists of about 26.2 per cent of India's total geographical area making a river basin of prominence popularly known as the Ganga Basin—one of the largest basins of the world (Chatterjee, 1982). The basin is densely populated having about 37 per cent of the total population of the country as per the 2001 Census. The mighty Ganga is served by its many tributaries coming from north-west and south-east. The rivers, like Yamuna, Gomati, Ghaghar, Gandak, Burhi Gandak, Kamala, Bagmati, Kosi, Mahanada come from the north and Karmanasa, Son, Punpun, Phalgoo, Kiul and others from the south. The average flow of the river water at Farakka is 45904 crore m^3 (maximum 12,500 cum/sec., and minimum 1568 cum/sec. (Tiwari, 2003).

The river Ganga enters in Bihar near Chausa, Buxar and flows throughout up to Maniharighat in the extreme east covering a stretch of about 450km. The river is perennial and has a broad meandering courses, which passes almost from the middle, divides the state into two parts — North and South Bihar Plains. Thus the river forms the heart line of all the socio-economic and cultural aspects of the state since long. Therefore, the Ganga must be taken on priority to keep it clean and environmentally sustainable.

The Problem Highlighted

The river Ganga, the symbol of purity and inspiration to millions is challenged today, being one of the most polluted rivers of the world (Bilgrami, 1991). The river which has served the people faithfully for ages, watered the agricultural fields, cleaned the dirts and washed the sins with its unique design of self-purification, is now tired and sick and has become a carrier of death and disease (Sharan and Sinha, 1988). This is simply due to the choking of thousands and thousands tons of dangerous chemicals and organic wastes in the form of liquids and solids which are regularly being dumped into the river everyday. On the account of this the Ganga water has lost its credibility as pure and has turned into the most contaminated one. At several places the water of Ganga is suitable for neither drinking nor bathing. The present paper attempts to find out the main factors, which cause the pollution in the Ganga water of Bihar. The purpose of the paper is, however, to demarcate the polluted areas on the basis of BOD/COD factors in the river course between Buxar to Kahalgaon. It has been also discussed the failure of Ganga Action Plan. Finally, a few measures have been suggested for the abatement of the river pollution ratio upto the drinking level. The study has been based on the secondary sources of information. The study has its relevance since it discusses the national problem of water utilization and its management.

Review of the Literature

The study of Ganga pollution is related to the environmental issues. Water constitutes one of the premier requirements for life. Naturally, its preservation and sanctity in its pure form must be regulated for the healthier living of not only for human beings, but also for animals and other organisms. The sustainability of the socio-economic pursuits be consciously taken care of. But unfortunately, the sheer lack of this consciousness on the part of human development, the ecology and environment have been degraded. This degrading process is worsening with passage of time and also with the advancement of science and technology. Air pollution, water pollution, noise pollution and several other pollutions are the results, which have caused the great damages in upsetting the Eco-system. Now the society is worried and is planning to minimise the pollutions and their effects. The study of Ganga water pollution is the part of this human concern to the environment.

The several studies have already been made about the deteriorating quality of the Ganga water, mostly in between 1960 and 1990. But attempts are being taken even today simply because, the pollution problem continues unabatedly. The researches on pollution of Ganga water have been largely carried out by the life-scientists. The Departments of Zoology and Botany of the different Universities of this State have taken the lead. Moreover, Physico-chemistry; biochemistry and chemical analysis of water never lag behind. But the geographer's involvement is very few. The reason behind this may be said that nature of such research is very much laboratory oriented and geographers being the semi-scientists generally refrain from using the high technique in finding out the lab-tested results.

A number of studies have been made to ascertain the various physico-chemical and biological parameters of Ganga water with a purpose to find out the nature of pollution at various places throughout the course. It has been also attempted to know the impacts of pollution on the aquatic life of the river (Lakshminaraya, 1959, Saxena *et al.*,

1966, Pahwa and Mehrotra, 1966, Kumar *et al.*, 1974, Bilgrami and Dutta Munshi, 1985, and Shankar, *et. al,* 1986). Besides, other studies have been made on the effects of domestic waste, sewage and industrial effluents on the quality of river Ganga water (Ray and David, 1966, Agarwal *et al.* 1976, Bilgrami and Dutta Munshi, 1979, Pandey, *et al.*, 1980, Kayastha and Kumar, 1982, Pratap Rana, 1985, 1990, 1993, 1999, Sinha, 1986 and Srivastava 2000). These studies have highlighted the problem of pollution vividly, Moreover, the Patna University under the leadership of Prof. R.K. Sharan of Zoology Department as a venture of interdepartmental collaborations has presented a study report entitled, "Ganga Basin Research Project Buxar-Barh, July 1985 to June 1988". The report highlights the main causes of pollution in Ganga water. Similarly, the Bhagalpur University also undertook the research project on Ganga under the supervision of Professor K.S. Bilgrami who studied the pollution problem of the river Ganga in Bihar from Patna to Kahalgaon. A report on this concern has been prepared which analysed the pollution of river Ganga. In 1982, a report on the studies of the Ganga River Basin in Bihar was prepared by the Centre for Development Studies, Patna University with the help of Bihar State Pollution Control Board (BSPCB), Patna (Sinha and Dayal, 1982).

The Present Position of the Ganga Water

It has been now established through several reasearches already carried out by the different disciplines that the Ganga throughout of its course right from Rishikesh-Haridwar down to Gangasagar is polluted. But this pollution ratio is not the same everywhere. The Ganga water in Uttar Pradesh and West Bengal is comparatively more polluted than water of Bihar (Pratap, 1999). Even in Bihar the pollution ratio differes from place to place. It is actually a misnomer to believe that the water of Ganga never decays. But in true to the sense it has become virtually a gutter at many places like Kanpur, where the organic load and BOD, the population of faecal and streptococci bacteria is very high and the level of DO (dissolved oxygen) is fairly low to support the life of normal flora and fauna. Varanasi, Patna, Mokameh and Kolkota are other black spots (Bilgrami, 1991). Further on, Saxena and others made a systematic survey of the chemical quality of Ganga water at Kanpur. The study concludes that the Bio-chemical Oxygen Demand (BOD) of the water varies from 5.3 ppm. in winter to 16.0 ppm. in summer. Similarly, the Chloride ranges between 9.2 to 12.7 ppm and the river becomes alkaline except in the rainy season. Another research was carried out of the river Ganga in between Kanpur and Rajmahal—a stretch of about 1100 kms. The study finds that the turbidity increases maximum (1100-2170ppm.) during monsoon and minimum 100 ppm. in winter and summer. Moreover, the pH (Hydrogen Ion Concentration) of the river water ranges between 7.45 (minimum) during June to August and 8.30 (maximum) during January to May. The DO varies from 5.0 to 10.5ppm., the maximum values during January and February. At Patna and Bhagalpur the chloride content fluctuates from 4.0 ppm. to 35.4 ppm. The Potassium Sodium (salt) ratio shows a cyclic pattern being higher during the rainy season as compared to the pre and post-monsoon (Bhargava, 1982). "Pesticides are polluting precious Ganga water" is the title of the research paper of Dr. S.K. Sinha, Department of Zoology, Patna University who concludes "fishes drawn from the Ganga in several parts of the state have been found to be contaminated with pesticides. As such they may be hazardous for the health of those who consume them." Moreover, research by Anupama Kumari and R.K. Sinha of the Environmental Biology, Patna University, also confirms the bio-accumulation of organo-chlorine pesticides in fish. This means those who eat fishes from the Ganga in Patna, Mokameh and Bhagalpur are taking risk. This is on account of increase of mercury, lead and DDT (Dichloro Diphenyl Trichloroethane) in the water. Again the concentration of HCH (Hexa Chlorocyclo Hexane) has been found as high as 628.9 ppb. in Rohu and Katla fish caught from Patna, Mokameh and Bhagalpur. Similarly the dying of dolphins—Souns, "the darlings of Ganga" is also due to the water pollution. According to Dr. R.K. Sinha about 2000 dolphins were found in the entire territory of Ganga in India out of which about 1000 were spotted in Bihar alone. But now their number remains limited due to their death and harpooning. The death of dolphins has caused due to the excesses of DDT, HCH, aldrein and other toxic materials already present in the Ganga water only due to heavy pollution (*Hindustan Times,* Patna 2001).

The Measurement of Quality of Ganga Water in Bihar

The above discussion support this view that the water of Ganga is polluted. This is fact that on account of fairly large volume and high

Table 10.1 : Seasonal Variations in Physico-Chemical Characteristics of the Water of River Ganga

Ingredients	*Monsoon (July to Oct.)*					*Winter (Nov. to Feb.)*					*Summer (March to June)*				
	Bu	Ma	Pa	Fa	Ba	Bu	Ma	Pa	Fa	Ba	Bu	Ma	Pa	Fa	Ba
1. Water Temp. ($0^{o}C$)	31.9	31.3	31.0	30.2	30.0	23.5	23.7	24.0	22.9	24.6	29.9	29.7	29.5	29.3	28.0
2. Turbidity (CM)	13.7	12.0	8.0	7.3	11.7	16.3	16.9	23.0	20.2	27.0	27.6	29.5	39.0	26.9	20.0
3. DO (Mg/L)	5.4	5.5	5.7	6.0	6.3	8.1	7.9	7.5	7.1	8.7	8.0	7.9	7.3	6.7	8.0
4. COD 9 (Mg/L)	15.5	15.2	24.8	24.4	24.2	8.4	8.6	11.2	10.1	7.3	7.9	8.0	11.7	10.2	8.9
5. BOD 9 (Mg/L)	8.4	8.3	11.0	9.4	8.0	3.9	4.0	5.7	5.0	4.8	3.5	3.7	6.5	6.0	3.9

DO = Dissolved Oxygen, COD= Chemical Oxygen Demand, BOD=Bio-Chemical Oxygen Demand

Bu = Buxar, Ma= Maner, Pa= Patna, Fa=Fatuha, Ba=Barh.

Source : Based on Ganga Basin Research Project (Buxar-Barh, July 1985—June 1988), Dept. of Zoology, Patna University, p. 17.

flows of the Ganga in between Allahabad to Farakka, this section is comparatively less vulnerable to pollution to the remaining section lying upstream of Allahabad and down stream of Farakka (Singh, 1989). In other words, the Ganga water in Uttar Pradesh and West Bengal is more polluted than the Ganga water in Bihar. This is simply because, the greater volume of water being received from other supporting rivers of the region makes the master stream voluminous to carry out the maximum pollutants out of area. Moreover, these rivers at least once in a year are full of flood and during that the polluted waters of the rivers are driven out of the region. But during winter and summer when the volume of water reduces, the problem of pollution becomes acute especially in the localities where heavy concentration of human population and industries are found (Pratap, 1993).

The five main ingredients have been taken here as model to explain the problem of pollution in Ganga water of Bihar. These are temperature, turbidity, DO, BOD and COD. Table 10.1 gives the seasonal variations in physico-chemical characteristics of the river Ganga water from Buxar to Barh. This explains how pollution in Ganga water increases from Buxar and Maner to Patna and Fatuha and lower downs again to Barh (Sharan and Sinha, 1988). The water temperature shows variation seasonwise. It is witnessed maximum of 35°C during summer and minimum of 18°C during winter. In case the temperature differs beyond it means this variation is caused due to increase of pollution. Again the Ganga water is more transparent during the late winter and early summer. This is due to less turbidity in water. But turbidity increases during rainy season when it goes upto 58.7 cm. This turbidity degrades the quality of Ganga water, which becomes non-potable.

The other ingredients like DO, COD and BOD can be explained in this way. When the oxidized organic matters such as sewage are discharged in the river, these matters are decomposed due to micro-organism—a process which creates Biochemical Oxygen Demand (BOD) in the river water. This BOD consumes the Dissolved Oxygen, (DO) already present in the water and thus deteriorates the water quality and makes aquatic life difficult. Similarly, the organic matter is bio-chemically non-oxidizable and creates Chemical Oxygen Demand (COD). These factors decreases and aquatic life becomes miserable especially of fishes, etc. (Khoshoo, 1986). The BOD and DO relation has been shown in Fig. 10.1. Table 10.1 explains that the

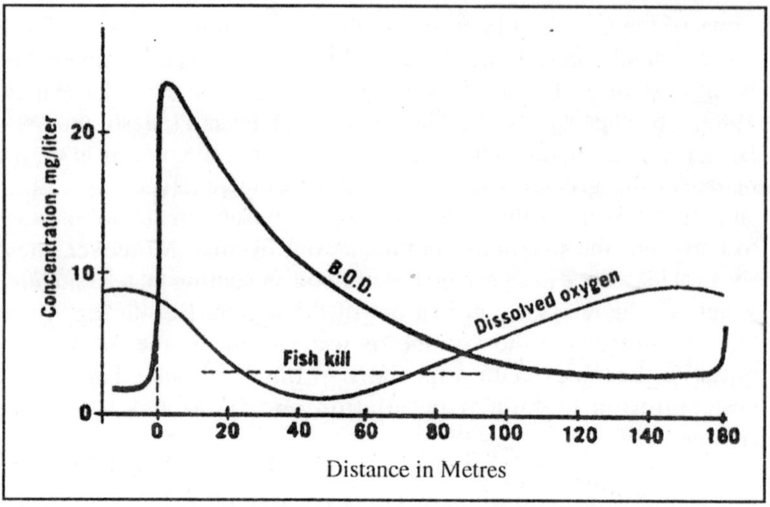

Fig. 10.1 : Increasing BOD and decreasing D.O. from River's Sn. bank to main stream, showing limit of Fishes—A case of Ganga in Patna

Table 10.2 : BOD Discharge in Ganga from three States, 1980

State	*BOD Discharge in kg per day*	
	Domestic	*Industrial*
Uttar Pradesh	371626 (34.1)	718274 (65.9)
Bihar	56172 (52.5)	50828 (47.5)
West Bengal	266076 (70.2)	112924 (29.8)

Note : Figures in brackets are in percentage of the respective State.
Source : Based on Chandhuri's finding (1985).

Ganga water in Bihar is polluted because of BOD and COD being higher in proportion and has reduced the ration of DO. The another study made by Chaudhuri also supports the pollution of Ganga water in terms of BOD dischagre in kg per day, the relative load of the there states— Uttar Pradesh, Bihar and West Bengal has been given in the Table 10.2. It is apparent from the table that maximum load of pollution comes from the domestic sources and here West Bengal leads other states. But Uttar Pradesh contributes pollution from the industrial sources. But Bihar shares in pollution equally from the domestic and industrial sources.

The second aspect of the research of Chaudhari relates to BOD values as indicator of pollution, which has been shown in Table 10.3.

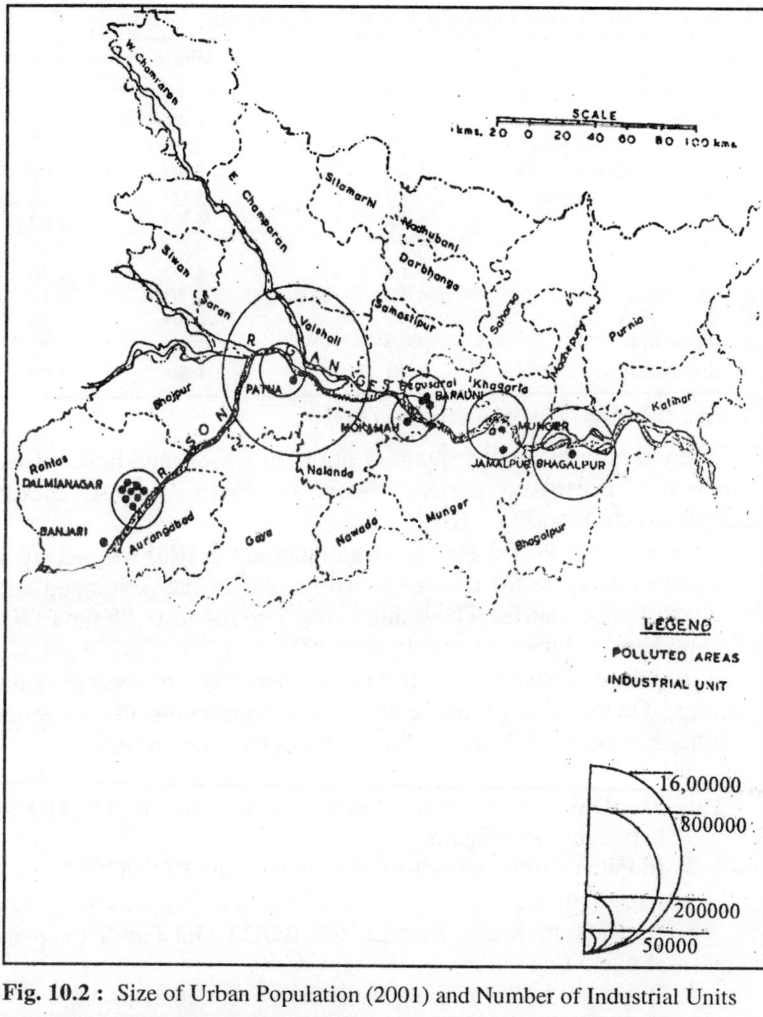

Fig. 10.2 : Size of Urban Population (2001) and Number of Industrial Units

In Bihar important places located on river Ganga have been indicated with their respective BOD value during the monsoon, winter and summer. The table clearly indicates that Patna is a place of high BOD factor in comparison with other followed by Barauni and Bhagalpur. Obviously, these are the larger urban-cum-industrial centres which release maximum urban and industrial wastes and these wastes are finally dumped into the river resulting higher BOD factor. On the other hand, smaller towns like Buxar, Maner, Sultanganj and

Table 10.3 : BOD value as indicator of level of pollution

Places	*Monsoon*	*Winter*	*Summer*
1. Buxar	1.77	1.50	1.70
2. Maner	1.98	1.64	1.71
3. Patna (i) Korji ghat	2.70	2.00	1.90
(ii) Krishnaghat	5.70	3.40	3.00
(iii) Badarghat	6.50	5.00	5.10
4. Fatuha	6.20	4.80	4.82
5. Mokama	3.20	2.61	2.68
6. Barani	5.10	4.60	4.30
7. Munger	4.50	4.20	4.10
8. Sultanganj	1.30	1.60	1.66
9. Bhagalpur	3.90	3.66	3.70
10. Kahalgaon	1.70	1.80	1.92

Source : Based on Chaudhuri's finding (1985).

Kahalgaon release smaller quantity of urban wastes and hence these cause less pollution getting down the ratio of BOD factor comparatively low (Fig. 10.2).

Besides, the World Health Organization (WHO) has set up a standard to measure the quality of river water of the developed and the developing countries. The standard fixed up suggests, "if the BOD/COD present in the river water is up to 3.0 factor, the water is potable or fit for human consumption, if it is 5.0, then it can be used only for bathing." On the basis of this scale of measurement the Ganga water of Bihar has been studied and the result is given accordingly :

1. The Ganga water from Buxar to Maner has BOD/COD in between 3 to 4 factor;
2. In Patna, from Digha/Korjee to Fatuha the BOD/COD factor rises upto 6.5;
3. At Mokameh and Barauni the BOD/COD factor exceeds above 5.0;
4. Bariarpur to Sultanganj, the BOD/COD comes to 3.0;
5. From Nathnagar to Sabour (Bhagalpur) the BOD/COD goes up to 6.0; and lastly,
6. From Kahalgaon to Rajmahal BOD/COD ranges in between 3 to 4 factor, as shown in Table 10.4.

Distribution of Pollution in Ganga Water of Bihar

Table 10.4 displays the distribution pattern of pollution of Ganga water

Table 10.4 : Ratio of BOD/COD available in Ganga ascertaining the Water Quality

Areas	*BOD/COD Factor*	*Catatery*	*Water quality*
1. Buxar to Maner	3-4	C	Fit for drinking and bathing
2. Digha to Fatuha	5-7	E	Not suited even for bathing
3. Barh to Mokameh and Barauni to Maner	4-5	D	May be used for bathing only
4. Bariarpur to Sultanganj	3-4	C	Fit for bathing only
5. Nathnagar to Bhagalpur	5-6	D	Not fit for even bathing
6. Kahalgaon to Rajmahal	3-4	C	Fit for bathing only

Analyses of Results : C = low ratio of pollution
D = moderate
E = high ratio of pollution

in Bihar. It is apparent that the Ganga water in Bihar is polluted throughout of its course. But the pollution ratio is not equal everywhere. This has been measured on the basis of BOD/COD factor and grading of water quality has been ascertained on A, B, C, D, E categories. A and B categories are given to the water which is almost free from pollution. 'C' category means water is slightly polluted and it may be used for bathing and drinking purposes. D and E categories means the water is highly polluted and it is neither suitable for drinking nor bathing.

On this basis, the water of river Ganga in Bihar has been categorized as shown in Table 10.4. The area of water between Buxar and Maner is categorised as 'C' group. The water of river Ganga from Digha to Fatuha has been categorised 'E'. Again 'E' category has been allotted to the water course in between Mokameh, Barauni to Munger. The Ganga water at Bariarpur, Sultanganj, Kahalgaon and Shibganj-Rajmahal comes to 'C' category. It means the Ganga is highly polluted at Patna, Mokameh, Barauni, Munger and Bhagalpur where BOD/COD ranges in between 5 to 7 factor. In comparison with these, Ganga is comparatively less polluted at Buxar, Maner, Barh, Bariarpur, Sultanganj, Kahalgaon and Rajmahal. This is due to the low factor of BOD/COD which is less than 4.0. Here mention may be made that the southern part of the river is more polluted because of heavy concentration of population and industrial activities, except near Barauni where northern portion of the river is more polluted. The middle portion of the river is less polluted as shown in Fig. 10.1.

The study finds that 'A' and 'B' categories of water is totally absent from the river course. River's water at Patna (from Korjee to Fatuha), Mokameh, Barauni and Bhagalpur is highly polluted. At Buxar, Barh and Munger, water is moderately polluted. Again the Ganga water at Maner, Surajgarha, Bariarpur, Sultanganj, Kahalgaon and Rajmahal is the least polluted. Thus, the water quality at Patna, Mokameh, Barauni and Bhagalpur is dangerously polluted and it requires serious attention to be paid by the public and the government. The pollution must be controlled otherwise it would be hazardous.

The Sources of Pollution

The following are the main sources of pollution of the Ganga water which have been identified :

(i) The urban liquid wastes drawn from cities/towns through drains and sewers;
(ii) The urban solid wastes which include domestic and cattle wastes;
(iii) The industrial liquid and solid wastes;
(iv) Surface run-off agricultural fields consisting of chemicals and fertilizers, insecticides, pesticides, etc.;
(v) Throwing animal carcasses, burnt, unburnt and half burnt human dead bodies; and
(vi) Open defecation by the people, washing of dirty clothes by washermen, immersion of idols, etc.

The major source of pollution in Ganga is the urban wastes. There are number of towns and cities developed along the river sides. In Bihar, there are altogether 15 large and small cities/towns having the total urban population more than 30 lakhs (Fig. 10.2). Besides, there are several districts coming in the direct influence of the river Ganga having another 2.5 crores of rural population. This huge population gives pressure directly or indirectly on the river and thus the ecology of river is disturbed. An empirical study has been made through Table 10.5, which shows the important towns and cities located on the either side of the river Ganga. The towns have been given the priority with their status of class and also with their magnitude of population based on the census figures of 1981, 1991 and 2001. It has been manifested the rising trend of urban population with their enhanced urban states. The Table reveals that Patna, the capital city of the state is also the

Table 10.5 : Cities and Towns with Population

Name of the city/town		*Status*	*Urban Population (in number)*		
			1981	*1991*	*2001*
1. Patna (Capital & Largest)	City	Class-I	813963	955889	1376950
2. Bhagalpur	City	Class-I	224062	251993	340349
3. Ara	City	Class-I	125111	156871	203395
4. Munger	City	Class-I	129260	150042	187311
5. Chapra	City	Class-I	111564	136825	178835
6. Hajipur	City	Class-I (as per 2001)	N.A.	82336	119276
7. Barauni+Begusarai	City	Class-I	67995	88216	107203
8. Buxar	Town	Class-II	52922	65000	92975
9. Mokameh	Town	Class-II	54608	51118	56400
10. Barh	Town	Class-II	31890	37614	48405
11. Sultanganj	Town	Class-II	22554	29332	41812
12. Fatuha	Town	Class-II	21183	26617	38362
13. Maner	Town	Class-II	15832	21913	26912
14. Kahalgaon	Town	Class-II	N.A.	N.A.	N.A.

Source : Based on Census of India of 1981, 1991 and 2001.

largest urban centre located on the southern bank of river Ganga. Its urban population exceeds to one million with fast growing trends. Bhagalpur is the second larger urban centre with above 3 lakhs population followed by Ara, Munger, Chapra, Hajipur are others. In this way, there are 7 class I towns, 2 class II and 5 class III towns. However, Ara, Chapra and Hajipur are not located on the Ganga bank but these are located at the confluence sites of Ganga and Son, Ganga and Ghaghara and Ganga and Gandak respectively. Patna is the largest contributor of urban wastes. A huge quantity of sewage water flows into Ganga daily through nine big drains (*Nalas*). It was estimated that about 121 million litres of waste water was going into the river everyday in 1986 (Sharma, 1992). This quantity has increased to 156 million litres in 1996. Again washermen thousand in number wash lakhs of dirty clothes with the help of soda, soap and detergents and make the water polluted. Besides, dirty water from Korjee Holy Family Hospital, Patna Medical College Hospital (PMCH) and several industrial units discharge huge amounts of liquid and solid wastes into the river and add poisons to the water. Table 10.6 indicates the urban wastes discharged in Ganga by different towns/cities of the state.

Bhagalpur is the another city which pollutes the river Ganga by releasing about 32 million litres per day of urban effluents. These are

Table 10.6 : Cities and Towns with Population

Towns/Cities (1996)	*Quantities discharges (in lakh litre per day)*	
	Urban wastes	*Industrial wastes*
1. Patna	156 MLD	12.7 MLD
2. Bhagalpur	32 MLD	8.1 MLD
3. Munger	28 MLD	7.3 MLD
4. Chapra	17 MLD	2.5 MLD
5. Buxar	6.5 MLD	.07 MLD
6. Barauni	3.4 MLD	5.0 MLD

Source : Compiled from different sources.

dumped into the river through 15 big and small nalas. In 1981 the total urban wastes released into the river was 13 MLD per day which was increased to 22 MLD in 1991 and again 32 MLD per day in 2001. It means the pollution problem is gradually increasing which is very serious.

Munger is the third populous urban centre situated on the river bank of Ganga. This class I city has nearly two lakh population. The total urban wastes are produced about 28 MLD per day besides industrial wastes. There are six big nalas through which the urban wastes are discharged into the river. This amount of urban refuses are increasing day by day with the growth of population.

Apart from the urban wastes the industrial effluents are not less responsible for growing the ratio of pollution. There are seven large scaled industrial units located on the river-side. These are mostly in the areas of Mokameh, Barauni and Munger. These units are the Oil Refinery, the Fertilizer and Chemical industries, the large Thermal Plant, dairy plant etc.—all located at Barauni. In fact, Barauni presents a view of industrial complex in the state (Pratap, 2002). The Bata Shoe Company, the McDowel Wine factory along with distillery and Sudha Milk Products at Mokameh are the main units. Moreover, the Indian Tobacco Co. and the Gun Factory although ailing are the industrial units at Munger. All these units discharge their dirty water into the Ganga. Barauni centre is alone responsible for the larger pollution of Ganga water. Its Fertilizer plant alone discharges toxic effluents at the rate of 5600 cubic litres per day in the Ganga. The liquid waste contains a good amount of nitrogenous pollutants with ammonium nitrate, which proves potential hazards for fishes and the human beings. Likewise the Indian Oil Co. discharges several kinds of petrogenous materials, which are released in the river and makes the water contaminated. In 1968, a fire broke out on the river surface from Barauni downward upto 5 km and continued upto two days. This was only due to the excess release of oil-wastes in the water. This caused a great damage to the aquatic life especially of fishes. Likewise the Shoe Factories at Mokameh and Digha in Patna discharge 5500 and 7000 litres of polluted water respectively in the Ganga everyday. Besides, Bhagalpur is the silk producing centre and there are more than thousand silk-weaving houses particularly in Nathnagar. The silk cloths are washed in the Ganga and so a huge amount of bleaching powder, soap and detergent, different colours related to various chemicals, etc. are left in the water polluting it immensely. Moreover, the brick-making industries have been flourished particularly in Maner to Dinapore, Malsalami to Fatuha and to Bakhtirpur along the river side. Thousands of chimneys emit dust and smoke. These dusts are, finally, put into the river making the water silted. Thus air and water both are polluted.

In this way, it becomes apparent from the above discussion that the urban centres and the industrial units developed along the river Ganga are the main sources of pollution. These two contribute to about 80 per cent of pollution in the Ganga water. The rest 20 per cent is added by other factors. These are the agricultural fertilizers, chemicals, insecticides, pesticides, etc., throwing of animal carcasses, burnt and unburnt human dead bodies, open defecation and all dirts related to religious functions. Again almost 60 per cent of the population of area take bath daily in the river and washes clothes using soaps and detergents. Animals like elephants, buffaloes, cow, oxen, horse, dog, are washed in the river. These activities disturb the water quality of the river.

The Preventive Measures Suggested

During eighties the country as a whole was serious on the issue of pollution of the holy river Ganga. The then Prime Minister Smt. Indira Gandhi took the issue on priority. The Planning Commission in 1981 initiated a Research Programme to study the various aspects of the River Ganga. The leading Universities located along the river Ganga were authorised to participate in the scheme, which was called "Integrated Eco-Development Action Oriented Research Programme on the Ganga Basin". Later on, the programme was administered and coordinated by the Ganga Project Directorate. Again in September

1984, Ganga Action Plan (GAP) was formed to prevent the pollution in the Ganga water. Three states, Uttar Pradesh, Bihar and West Bengal, were taken to deal with. The main objective of the Ganga Action Plan was to improve the deteriorated quality of water upto drinking level particularly near the 27 big cities. The first phase started in 1986 under which out of the total schemes of 259 identified, 163 were taken. A total sum of Rs. 169.9 crore was sanctioned.

Ganga Action Plan which was taken on priority and with much enthusiasm was delayed for 2 years. The expenditure was almost doubled. But the result was not very appreciable. Much expenditure was done over the political propaganda. The concerning governments and the related agencies were not very prompt to make it a success. The public of the areas was not taken into consideration. The releasing of urban and industrial wastes in the river was not controlled fully. The flowing of dirty water through drains and sewers were not adequately diverted. The continuing customs of burning of dead bodies, throwing of carcasses, washing of dirty clothes by washermen, immersion of idols and cattle wallowing were not checked. Very little provision of public latrines was made and the open defecation of lakhs of people continued along the riverside. All these made Action Plan a failure. An eminent scientist has remarked about the result of the Ganga Action Plan, which is true, and without any controversy. He may be quoted, "Despite the fact that the implementation period of Ganga Action Plan (Phase I) was extended to almost double of its original time span and a huge amount has already been spent, the objective of bringing Biochemical Oxygen Demand (BOD) and Dissolved Oxygen (DO) levels to desirable norms has not yet been fulfilled" (Agrawal, 1999).

From the above discussions it has been realised that the pollution in Ganga water is due to the many factors. But the principal sources are the domestic wastes, the industrial wastes and the non-point pollution (sources cannot be ascertained) (Singh 2000). The sewage discharged in Ganga from municipal wastes and industrial wastes constitute about 80 per cent pollution and other 13 per cent from agricultural run-off by use of the chemical fertilizers, insecticides and pesticides, etc. If these sources of pollution are controlled and not allowed to release in the Ganges, naturally the major portions of the water of Ganges would be cleaned (Pratap and Pratap, 2003). Hence, it may be suggested that the urban refuse, especially the liquid waste water if treated properly, it may ease several problems. The treated water may be reused in irrigation, industrial and other miscellaneous purposes. It, would surely minimise the water pollution on the one hand and augment the existing fresh water supply on the other.

Moreover, unless and until the general people are involved in the scheme of "making the Ganges clean" through several awakening programmes, the worsening situation of Ganga pollution would continue. It is a happy note already realised that several NGO agencies have taken the pious task in their hands under the banner of "Ganga Bachao Abhiyan". Save the Ganga has been launched by the Patna people. The Patnaits are suggested to refrain from the dirty disposals in the Ganga. Further, proper conservation measures for rearing fishes, turtles and the Gangetic Dolphins must be taken immediately to restore the aquatic quality of water. Lastly, the forceful implementation of Water Prevention and Control of Pollution Act, 1974, and Environment Act of 1986 are very much needed. Moreover, to keep Ganga clean is implemented strongly as the fundamental duty of the citizens of the society.

Conclusion

To sum up in short, the following points are mentioned with a purpose to highlight the issue :

1. The Ganga water is a precious gift of nature, which requires sustenance with care.
2. The river Ganga, one of the largest and longest rivers is grossly polluted unevenly throughout of its course.
3. The 80 per cent pollution of Ganga water is only due to the urban disposals.
4. Faecal discharge, carcasses, sewage and industrial wastes are the sources of pollution.
5. On account of these pollutants the BOD and COD factors have been excessively increased and at the same time have reduced DO in Ganga water leading to ecological disturbances in general and aquatic life in particular.
6. The mother Ganga does not remain holy as it was in the past. Its water cannot be taken as granted. It has been deteriorated to C and D categories and is not fit for drinking and bathing almost everywhere. It has become carrier of disease and death.
7. Taking the pollution of Ganga with great concern and with

objective of abatement of the pollution the massive Ganga Action Plan was launched in 1986 and was partially success.

8. The awakening programmes by the NGOs and others may serve a good deal in making the Ganga water de-polluted.

REFERENCES

Agarwal, A. (1999), *Ganga Action Plan—An Assessment,* Delhi Book Depot, Delhi.

Agarwal, D.K.,Gaur, SD., Tiwari, T.C., Narayanswami, M.S., and Marwah, S.M. (1976), "Physico-Chemical Characteristics of Ganga Water at Varanasi" *Indian Journal of Environment and Health*, Vol. 18, pp. 201-205.

Bhargava, D.S. (1982), "Purification Power of the Ganga Unmatches" *L.S.T Bulletin*, No. 34, pp. 50-56.

Bilgrami, K.S. and Dutta, Munshi J.S. (1979), "Effects of Industrial Water on the Hydrobiological Status of the river Ganges", *The Indian Journal of Zoology*, Vol. 20, No. 2, pp. 95-102.

Bilgrami, K.S. and Dutta, Munshi, J.S. (1985), "Ecology of River Ganga : Impact of human activities and conservation of aquatic biota" Final Report (May 82 to April 85), Post-Graduate Department of Botany, Bhagalpur University.

Bilgrami, K.S. (1991), *The Living Ganga (Ganga Down the Ages)*, Narendra Publishing House, New Delhi, p. 03.

Chatterjee, S.P. (1982), *An Introductory Regional Geography : India*, Orient Lonman Ltd., New Delhi, pp. 34, 35.

Hindustan Times, Patna, 27 May (Sunday), 2001, p. 9.

Kayastha, S.L. and Kumra, V.K. (1982), "Ganga Water Pollution in Kanpur City : A Geographical Analysis", *Transactions Institute of Indian Geographers*, Vol. 4, No. 1, pp. 5-6.

Khoshoo, T.N. (1986), "Environmental Priorities in India and Sustainable Development". Presidential Address, Indian Science Congress Association, New Delhi, pp. 120-127.

Kumar, H.D., Hisria, G.P., Bhandari, L.M., Rana, B.C. and Sharma V. (1974) "Physico-chemical characteristics of Ganga", *The Indian Journal of Environment and Health*, Vol. 16, pp. 247-255.

Laskhminaraya, J. S. S. (1959) *"Phytoplankton of the River Ganga."* Unpublished Ph.D. thesis, B. H. U., Varanasi.

Pahwa, D.V. and Mahrotra, S.N. (1966), "Observation on fluctuation on the abundance of Plankton in relation to certain hydro biological conditions of river Ganga". Proceeding of National Academic, Science of India, Section B, 36 (2), pp. 157-187.

Pandey, G.N., Bharti, A. and Saxena, R.P. (1980), "Role of Microflora in the Assessment of Pollution level of river Ganga at Kanpur", *Journal Inst. Engn., India*, Vol. 61, pp. 27-34.

Pratap, R. (1985), "Water Pollution in Bihar", *Geographical Review of India*, Vol. 47, No. 4, pp. 75-78.

Pratap, R. (1990), "Action Plan and the Control of Pollution in Ganga Water in

Bihar", Paper presented at the Earth System Sciences Section of the 78th ISCA, Calcutta, pp. 1-5.

Pratap, R. (1993), "Pollution in River Ganga in Bihar —A Geographical Analysis", in B. Thakur (ed.) *Research Management in Developing Countries,* Vol. 6 (Water Supply And Quality) Concept Publishing Co., New Delhi (Press).

Pratap, R. (1998), "The Main Pollutants in the Water of River Ganga in and around Patna : A Geographical Study", *Magadh Geographical Review*, Bodh-Gaya, Vol. I, No. 1, pp. 33-38.

Pratap, Rana (2002), "Major Industrial Complexes of Bihar", *In Bihar Resources and Planing* (Prof P. Dayal Felicitation Volume) (eds.), P. Dayal, *Md. Ataullah* and A. Sami, Janaki Prakashan, Patna, pp.213-226.

Pratap, R. and Pratap, D., (2003), "Waste water Management for Controlling the Ganga Pollution : A case study of Patna", Proceedings of Bihar Vigyan Congress, Patna February, 28, p. 25.

Ray, P. and David, A. (1966), "Effects of Industrial Water and Sewage upon the Chemical and biological composition and fisheries of the river Ganga at Kanpur, *Indian Journal of Environment and Health*, Vol. 8, pp. 307-338.

Saxena, K.L., Chakravarty, R.N., Khan, A.Q. and Chattopadhya, S.N. (1966), "Pollution studies of the river Ganges near Kanpur", *Indian Journal of Environment and Health*, Vol. 8, pp. 270-286.

Shanker, V., Sangu, R.S.P., and Joshi, G. C. (1986), "A report on Integrated Study of the Ganga". Dept. of Botany, Gurukul Kangri University, Hardwar.

Sharma, K.M. (1992), "Ganga Action Plan in Bihar", The Institute of Engineers, India (*Souvenir*, All India Council Meet, Patna), pp. 25-29.

Sharan, R.K and Sinha, R.K. (1988), "Ganga Basin Research Project (Buxar-Barh)" Final Technical Report, Dept, of Zoology, Patna University, p. 7.

Singh, R.S. (1989), "An Approach to Ganga Action Plan"; *Water Pollution (Conservation and Management)* A.K. Sinha & others (eds.), Gyanodaya Prakashan, Nanital, pp. 7-12.

Singh, Savindra (2002), *Environmental Geography*, Prayag Pustak Bhawan, Allahabad, pp. 442-448.

Sinha, R.C. and Dayal, P. (1982), "Comprehensive Pollution Survey and Dry Studies of the Ganga River Basin in Bihar", A Project Report, Centre for Development Sudies, Patna University, Patna.

Sinha, U.P. (1986), *Ganga—Pollution and Health Hazard*, Inter-India Publications, New Delhi.

Srivastava, M. (2000), *Pollution of Ganga Water (A Limnological Study at Hardwar)*, Shree Publishers, New Delhi.

Tiwari, R.C. (2003), *Geography of India*, Prayag Pustak Bhawan, Allahabad, p. 101.

11

Growing Challenges of Water Pollution and the Required Remedial Measures

Devendra Kumar

Introduction

Water is the most precious gift of nature, not only to the mankind, but to the whole mosaic of organisms living in different segments of the ecosphere, without which even the imagination of their survival is not possible. The worship of rivers and water bodies in our and many other countries on several occasions is nothing but a glowing tribute and testimony to its vitality. Tanaka Schozo once remarked, "the care of rivers is not a question of rivers but of human heart." (Chaudhary, 1964). Similarly, "it is not until the well runs dry that we know the worth of water" (1991) was the categorical remarks of Benjamin Franklin. These myriads of such observations are the manifestation and acknowledgement of the worth of water.

Availability of Fresh Water

Only a tiny fraction of the planet's abundant water is available as freshwater. About 97 per cent by volume is found in the oceans and is too salty for drinking, irrigation and industry. The remaining 3 per cent is fresh water. About 2.997 per cent of it is locked up in ice caps or glaciers or is burried so deep that it costs too much to extract. Only about 0.003 per cent of the earth's total volume of water is easily available to us as soil moisture, usable groundwater, water vapour, and lakes and streams. If the world's water supply were 100 litres, our usable supply of fresh water would be only one half teaspoon (0.003 litre).

Areas of Surplus and Deficit Supply of Fresh Water

The tiny fraction of fresh water supply is not evenly distributed in the world. Differences in annual precipitation divide the world countries into water haves and have-nots. For example, Canada with only 0.5 per cent of the world's population has 20 per cent of the world's fresh water supply. By contrast, China with 21 per cent of the world's people has only 7 per cent of the world's surplus water supply. This contrast also exists in different segments of a single nation. And it has been rightly predicted that the next world war would be fought for water, which is evident from the water-wars of Middle East and the growing water dispute in several states of India.

Conservation of Water: Need of Hour

The above facts strictly remind us that the entire world humanity is duty bound to conserve and protect this rare gift of nature from pollution which is growing at an alarming rate and posing serious threat to the entire world of organisms, and we have to control the situation before the attainment of the threshold level of pollution.

Natural Purification of Water

Fortunately, the available fresh water amounts to generous supply from nature, that is continuously collected, purified, recycled and distributed in the solar powered hydrological cycle as long as we don't overload it with slowly degraded and non-degraded wastes and withdraw it from underground supplies faster than it is replenished (Singh, 1980).

But, unfortunately we are doing both, causing immense harm to the quality of water and ecological balance, which is emerging as the most challenging vista for the civilised humanity and urgent intervention has become the need of hour.

So, before entering into the remedial measures, it is pertinent to identify and diagnose the various types and sources of pollution that contaminate the surface run off, streams, rivers, lakes, oceans and underground aquifers.

Types and Sources of Pollutants

Disease Causing Pathogens

Bacteria, viruses, protozoa, and parasitic worms come under this category that enter water from domestic sewage and untapped human and animal waste. According to a World Bank study, contaminated water cause about 80 per cent of the diseases in developing countries and kills about 10 million people annually, an average of 27000 premature deaths per day, more than half of them children under age five.

Colonies of coliform bacteria

The average human excretes about 2 billion coliform bacteria per day, thus forming big colonies in short times and contaminating fresh water through sewage.

Oxygen demanding wastes

Large population of aerobic (oxygen requiring) bacteria decomposing oxygen demanding organic wastes can degrade water quality by depleting dissolved oxygen causing harm to fish and other forms of oxygen consuming aquatic life.

Water soluble inorganic chemicals

These include acids, salts, and compounds of toxic metals such as mercury and lead. High level of these chemicals can make water unfit to drink, harm fish and other aquatic life, lower crop yields and accelerate corrosion of metals exposed to such water.

Inorganic plant nutrients

They are water soluble nitrates and phosphates that can cause excessive growth of algae and other aquatic plants, which then die and decay, depleting water of dissolved oxygen and killing fish. Drinking water with excessive level of nitrates lowers the oxygen carrying capacity of blood. This can kill children and infants, those under age 1 year old.

Organic chemicals

These include oil, gasoline, plastics, pesticides, cleaning solvents, detergents and many other chemicals. They threaten human health and harm fish and other aquatic life.

Sediments and suspended matters

These are the biggest class of water pollutants by weight. Insoluble particles of soil and other solids become suspended in water, mostly when soil is eroded from the land. Sediments cloud water and reduce photosynthesis. It also disrupts aquatic food web and carries pesticides, bacteria and other harmful substances. Sediment that settles down destroys feeding and spawning ground of fish, clogs and fills lakes, artificial reservoirs, stream channels and harbours.

Water soluble radioactive isotopes

Water can also be polluted by water-soluble radio-active isotopes. Ionising radiation emitted by such isotopes can cause birth defects, cancer, and genetic damage.

Thermal pollution

Heat absorbed by water used to cool industrial and power plants and the resulting rise in water temperature, called thermal pollution, lowers dissolved oxygen levels and makes aquatic organisms more vulnerable to diseases, parasites and toxic chemicals.

Genetic pollution

Such pollution occurs when aquatic systems are disrupted by the deliberate or accidental introduction of non-native species. Some of these species may crowd out native species, reduce bio-diversity, and cause economic losses. The principal method of introduction of these non-native species into the marine system is through the intake and ballast discharge from ships. When ships take on ballast water at their point of departure, they also take on board thousands of microscopic organisms, as well as the early life stages of large plants and animals.

When this ballast water is emitted at the port of call, these stowaway organisms are discharged as well.

Point and Non-point Sources of Pollution

Point sources discharge pollutants at specific locations, through pipes, ditches, or sewers into bodies of surface water. Examples include factories, sewage treatment plants (which remove some but not all pollutants), active and abandoned underground mines, offshore oil wells and oil tankers. Because point sources are at specific places, they are fairly easy to identify, monitor and regulate. In developed countries many industrial discharges are strictly controlled whereas in most developing countries such discharges are largely uncontrolled.

Non-point sources are those that cannot be traced to any single site of discharge. They are usually land areas or airsheds that pollute water by run off, sub-surface flow, or deposition from the atmosphere. Examples include acid deposition of chemicals into surface water and seepage into the ground from cropland, livestock feedlots, logged forests, streets, lawns and parkinglots. Controlling non-point pollutants is difficult and expensive due to discharges from so many sources.

Stream pollution : Flowing streams and rivers can recover rapidly from degradable, oxygen demanding wastes and excess heat by a combination of dilution and bacterial decay. This natural recovery system works as long as streams are not overloaded with pollutants and as long as their flow is not reduced by drought, damming, or diversion for agriculture or industry. The time and distance required for a stream to recover depends on the water volume, flow rate, temperature, pH level and the volume of incoming degradable wastes.

Most of the streams, particularly of the developing nations are being polluted to the extent of alarming proportion, which are caused by accidental or deliberate, release of toxic inorganic and organic chemicals by industries, manufacturing, sewage treatment plants and non-point run off of pesticides and nutrients (eroded soil, fertilizer and animal waste). Available data indicate that stream pollution from huge discharge of sewage and industrial wastes is a serious and growing problem in most developing countries of the world where waste treatment is particularly non-existent. More than two-thirds of India's water resources are polluted with industrial wastes and sewage.

Prevention and Reduction of Surface Water Pollution

The above facts amply indicate the alarming growth of water pollution which compel us to think about the remedial measures to prevent and reduce the surface water pollution from non-point and point sources before the threshold of pollution is reached.

Nonpoint sources

The leading non-point sources of pollution are agriculture, animal waste and soil erosion. Agricultural practitioners can sharply reduce fertilizer run off into surface waters and leaching into aquifers. They have to adhere to the following suggestions: — using only moderate amount of fertilizers, using not at all on steeply sloping land, using slow release fertilizers, alternating row crops and nitrogen fixing plants to reduce the need of fertilizers, plant buffer zones of permanent vegetation between cultivated fields and nearby surface water, applying pesticides only when needed using biological control or integrated post-management, reduce non-farm uses of inorganic fertilizers and replace it with organic methods.

Pollution from animal wastes can be controlled by checking run off and infiltration of manure from feedlots, managing animal density, not locating feedlots on lands sloping towards surface water, diverting runoff into well designed detention basins, allow this nutrient rich water to be pumped and applied as manures to cropland.

Soil erosion is the major source of pollution, which can be controlled and regulated by reforestation of critical points of erosion and critical watersheds which would reduce the soil erosion and slow the projected global warming and loss of wild life habitat.

Point source

For regulating point source pollution two approaches should be adopted—legal approach and technical approach. Under the legal approach strict legislation should be enacted for making sewage treatment mandatory for each industrial unit big or small and each family.

Under the technical approach any domestic, industrial or urban sewage should not be allowed to enter the surface water directly, but should be diverted towards primary, secondary and advanced sewage treatment plants.

Primary sewage treatment is a mechanical process that uses screens to filter out debris such as sticks, stones and rags. Suspended

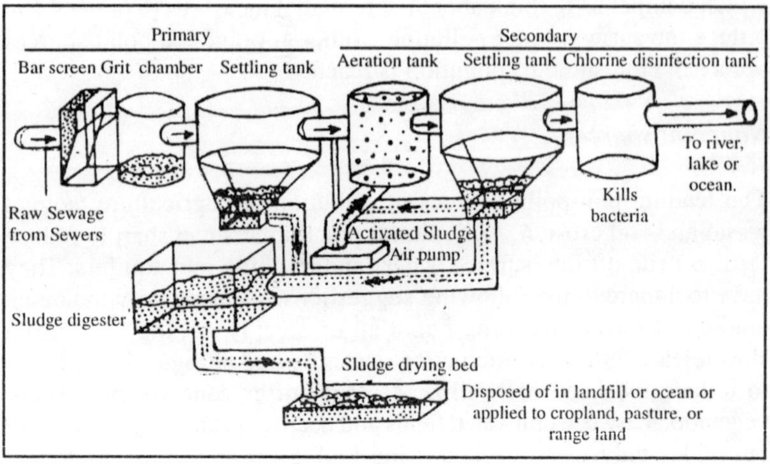

Fig. 11.1 : A Model of Primary and Secondary Sewage Treatment Plants

solids settleout as sludge in a settling tank (Fig. 11.1). Improved primary treatment uses chemically treated polymers to remove suspended solids.

Secondary sewage treatment is a biological process in which aerobic bacteria are used to remove 90 per cent of biodegradable, oxygen demanding wastes. Some plants use trickling filters, in which aerobic bacteria degrade sewage as it seeps through a bed of crushed stones covered with bacteria and protozoa. Others use an activated sludge processes in which the sewage is pumped into a large tank and mixed for several hours with bacteria-rich sludge and air bubbles to facilitate degradation by micro-organisms. The water then goes to a sedimentation tank, where most of the suspended solids and micro-organisms settle out as sludge.

The sludge produced from primary and secondary treatment is broken down in an anaerobic digester and either incinerated, dumped into the ocean or landfill or applied as fertilizer.

Advanced treatment is a series of specialised chemical and physical process that remove specific pollutants left in the primary and secondary treatment. Types of advanced treatment vary according to the specific contamination to be removed. Without advanced treatment, sewage treatment plant effluents contain enough nitrates and phosphates to contribute to accelerate eutrophication of lakes, slow moving streams and coastal waters. Since this treatment involves high cost, its wide application is not possible particularly in the developing countries.

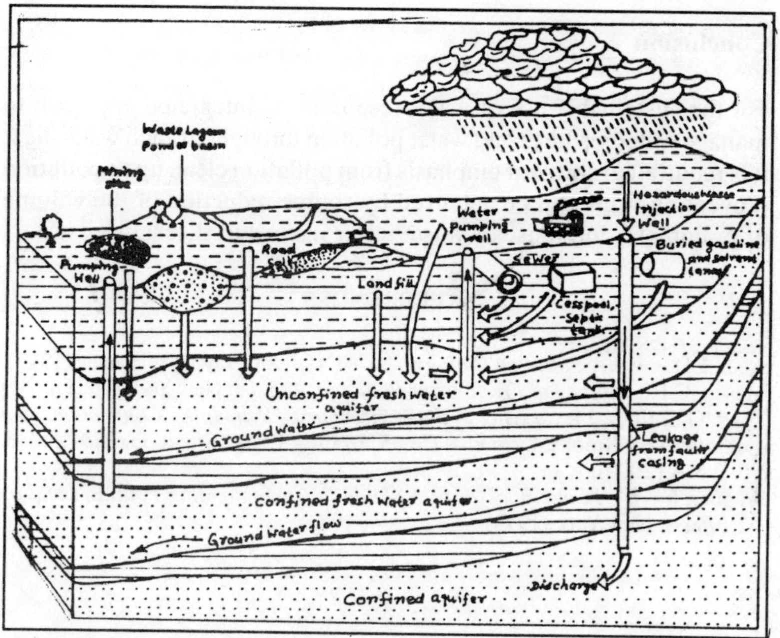

Fig. 11.2 : Some sources of Ground Water Contamination

Groundwater Pollution and Prevention

The groundwater, a prime source of water for drinking and irrigation is easy to deplete and pollute, because it cannot clean itself of degradable waste (as surface water can) as groundwater flows are slow and not turbulent, so, contaminants are not effectively diluted and dispersed. Groundwater also has much smaller population of decomposing bacteria, thus it can take hundreds to thousands of years for contaminated groundwater to clean itself.

Ground water can be contaminated from various sources, such as underground storage tanks, landfills, waste dumps, deep wells to dispose of liquid hazardous wastes, industrial and livestock wastes, storage lagoons located near aquifers.

To prevent the pollution of groundwater by various means is the only effective means of protecting our groundwater resources as cleansing of aquifer is a too costly, difficult and time taking affair.

Conclusion

For the sustainable use of water resources an integrated approach to manage water resource and water pollution throughout each watershed, it is required to shift our emphasis from pollution clean up to pollution prevention. This can be achieved by source reduction of the volume of pollutants, and reuse of waste water instead of discharging it.

REFERENCES

Abel, P.D. : *Water Pollution Biology,* 2nd. ed. London, Taylor & Francis (1997).

Masen, C.F. : *Biology of Fresh Water Pollution,* 2nd, ed. New York (1991).

Tyler, G., Miller, J.R. : *Living in the Environment : Principles, Connections and Solutions,* Brooks, Cole Pub. Co., 511 Forest Lodge Street, Pacific Groove, U.S.A.(2000).

Wagner, Iravis : *In our Backyard : A Guide to Understanding Pollution and its Effects,* New York (1993).

12

Polluted Lakes in the Heart of the City of Darbhanga

ANIL KUMAR CHOUDHARY

Earth has been called the "Water Planet", when seen from outer space. Earth is blue because three fourths of its surface is covered with water. But how much of this resource is really available for our uses?

Estimated amount of fresh water potentially available for human use : Ground water, fresh water, lakes, rivers 0.629 per cent. Human and most land animals and plants cannot survive on a diet of salty water. Hence, knock out the ocean, inland seas and salt lakes, or 97.28 per cent of all water. We need fresh water to sustain us, so we depend on the remaining 2.629 per cent.

Whether all those lie within our reach? Polar ice caps and glaciers are not really usable. The scientist did have a thought of towing an ice berg to their coast and melting it down for drinking water, but the cost was prohibitive. Hence, knocks out 2 per cent there's only 0.629 per cent left for us to use.

We are further reducing this amount through pollution. It is estimated that upto 70 per cent of India's surface water is polluted. You can see that we have a very great responsibility to protect water quality, as well as conserve water and use it wisely.

Table 12.1 : Breakdown of Earth's Water Percentage

Oceans	97.2
All ice caps/Glaciers	2.0
Groundwater	0.62
Fresh Water Lakes	0.009
Inland seas/salt lakes	0.008
Atmosphere	0.001
All rivers	0.001

With the passing of Water Act in 1974 that water pollution work started. The Central Board for the prevention and control of water pollution conducted a survey on waste water collection, treatment and disposal in class I cities (over 100,000 people) and class II towns (50,000–100,000 people) and published the reports.

First of all, it is clear that 41 per cent to 84 per cent of waste water needs to be collected in class I cities and class II towns respectively, and that 63 per cent to 94 per cent of water needs to be treated. Secondly, only 5.6 per cent cities and 1.6 per cent towns have full sewerage and full water treatment facilities and the rest 50.7 per cent to 77.36 per cent have neither sewerage nor have water treatment facilities.

In urban area of Darbhanga as the water resources are not protected from indiscriminate discharges, the polluted water is not only affecting vegetable production but there is also increase in water borne diseases, high medical expenses and loss of public health as well. It has been learnt that in comparison with expense on medical treatment the cost incurred on sewerage disposal and water treatment will be less.

The city of Darbhanga is situated near the river Bagmati between the geographical extent of 26°10′ North latitude and 85°54′ East longitude. Total area of the city is divided into 37 wards under the Darbhanga Municipal Corporation between the geographical area of 204,800 hectares (Chaudhary, 1964). Whole of city lying on the eastern bank of Choti Bagmati river and is located 48.08 metres high above the mean sea level. According to 2001 census the population size of the city is 2,66,834 and the density of the population is about 1470 persons per km^2.

In the city several water bodies are located in the heart of town but only three are major ponds which has been selected for the study, namely Harahi, Dighee and Gangasagar among the main tanks (Areport, 1991) (Fig. 12.1).

1. Harahi is situated near the Railway Station of Darbhanga and have the area of about 1600 feet length and width of the pond is about 1000 feet.
2. Dighee is situated southward direction of Harahi and have length of about 2400 feet and the width of pond is about 1200 feet.
3. The Gangasagar tank is very important in town because it is situated in the middle of Laheriasarai and the city of

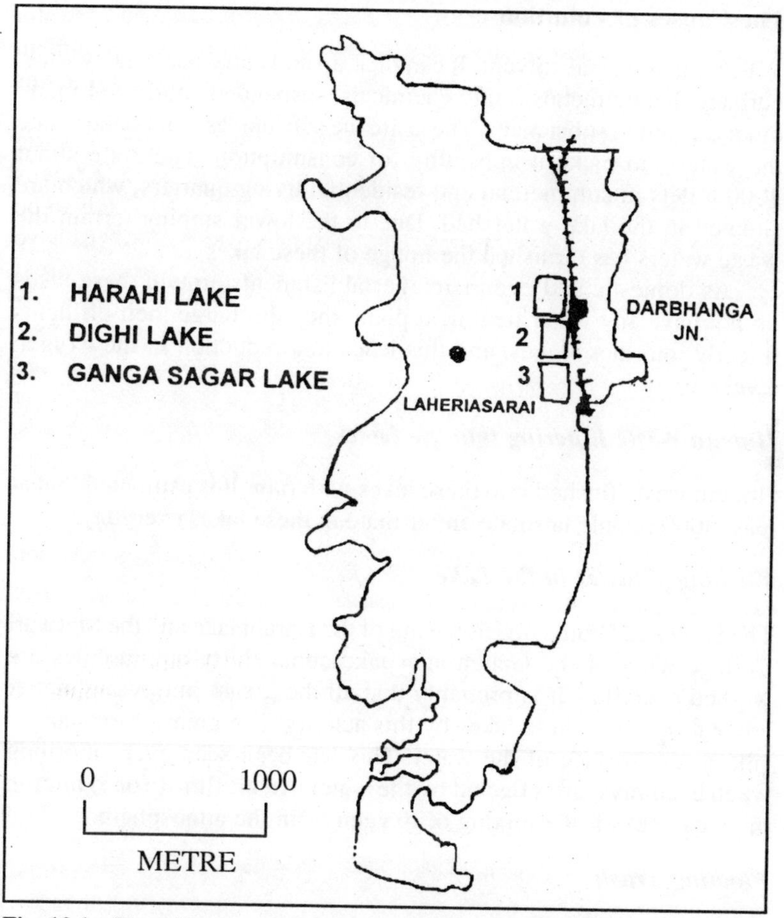

Fig. 12.1 : City of Darbhanga : Centres of Water Pollution

Darbhanga. It has an area of about 2000 feet length and the width of the pond is about 1000 feet. Total number of permanent water reservoirs is 91 in the city, and watershed area is 0.55 per cent of total area of the city.

Harahi, Dighi and Gangasagar are once a prime unspoilt waterbodies of the city of Darbhanga. Today these lakes are highly polluted. Although water quality undergoes, severe changes towards deterioration but human activities are the most common and problematic sources of water contamination. The latter will be our focus.

The Causes of Pollution

Water is a universal solvent. It can pick up and carry bacteria, worms, garbage, heavy metals, toxic chemicals, suspended solids and many other unwanted substances. These are the substances that contaminate the water and make it unhealthy for consumption. There are about 4000 toilets in commercial and residential living quarters, which are situated in the lake watershed. Due to the lower sloping terrain the waste waters has tarnished the image of these lakes.

As domestic and commercial establishments around these lakes do not have any water treatment plant, they discharge their effluents directly into these lakes, and this leads to a reduction in the oxygen level.

Human Waste Entering into the Lakes

Human waste flushed into these lakes with rain. It is estimated that at least 3000 people latrinate and urinate in these lakes everyday.

Washing Vehicles in the Lake

The Song and Drama division wing of the Harahi lake and the Marwari College wing of the Gangasagar lake about thirty automobiles are washed everyday. It is probably that all the grease and waste matter are entering into these lakes by this activity. The grease forms an oil silk on the surface of the water. This has been seen every morning when even rays are reflected by the water. An oil film 1 (one) micron thick can cut-off the mixing of oxygen from the atmosphere.

Floating Trash

These lakes are used as the waste and dustbin by many. Another serious problem is the mal-treatment deaths, either due to accident or due to suicidal instincts (Singh, 1980).

Solutions

Cure of the causes :

1. The odd toilets around the lake watershed should be converted into septic tanks.
2. Washing of cars, trucks, buses and all vehicles around the

lakes or on streams that lead into the lake should be prevented.

3. There is no dustbin or waste collection system around the lake. Refuse dumps with tips should be provided.
4. The commercial establishments must be forced to use their effluent treatment plants and treat the sewage before it is discharged.
5. Public lavatories with septic tanks should be provided and latrinating in the open should be prevented.

Conclusion

For controlling pollution at source the first preference is to generate pollution specific minimal standard. The high concentration of population, congestion of houses, dump of garbage on shores of lakes are the major pollutant along with the use of open space as latrine ground by the local people. There is utter neglect of pollution control measures. Another aspect is the discharge of treated effluents into the municipal sewers. Besides, the sewer systems and the municipal water pipes are damaged and the toxic and hazardous chemicals are poured into the sources of lakes found inside the city. In the city of Darbhanga there are altogether 19 lakes which are so polluted that fowl smell is coming from the lake water. Much attention needs to be paid to this issue by the municipality.

REFERENCES

A Report : District Statistical Office, Darbhanga, 1991.

Choudhary, P.C. Roy; *The District Gazeteer of Darbhanga,* 1964.

Singh, G.P.; *Darbhanga City : A Study in Urban Geography,* Ph.D. Dissertation, L.N.M.U., Darbhanga, 1980.

13

Levels of Water Pollution in the Mahanadi River in Sambalpur-Hirakud-Burla Urban Industrial Complex : A Case Study

Namita Pattnaik

Water pollution is becoming an evil of all industrial and urban development of world. The rapid urbanization with tall growth of population are putting tremendous pressure on natural resources particularly land, water and air. The insatiable needs of urban economy for water leads to its long range exploitation which is one of the prime requirement of life. As Hagget explains that "One of the most acute problem now being faced are disposal of polluted water. The average city of half a million people now produce over 190 million litres of sewage. The disposal of organic sewage poses less difficulty than the disposal of inorganic metallic waste of industry" (Hagget, 1983). The standard for potable water for drinking as recommended that it must be free from pathogenic micro-organism and chemicals which are harmful to human health. But most of our urban population is served by surface water often contaminated with domestic waste and industrial waste that are openly disposed of into the surface water body without treatment (OPCB, 1999).

The River Mahanadi of Orissa is the longest, broadest and deepest of all rivers in the State of Orissa. As stated by Prof. B.N. Sinha—"This river accounts for 30.6 per cent of towns and 54.2 per cent of urban population of Orissa." The river originates from the Amarkantak plateau of Maikal Range and enters Orissa in the north-west. It drains a large part of western Orissa. The present study area is served by this river at western Orissa (Sinha, 1999).

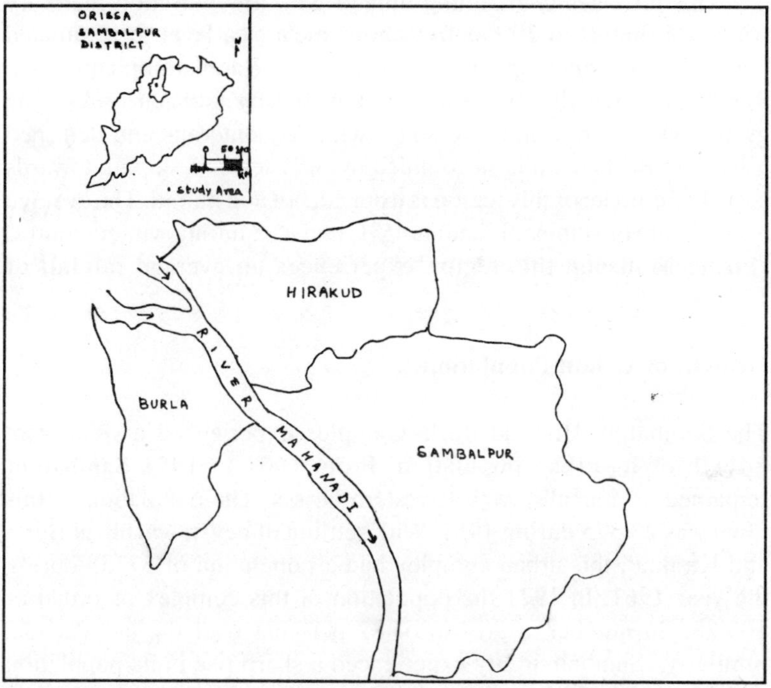

Fig. 13.1 : Sambalpur-Burla-Hirakud Urban Complex

Study Area

The Sambalpur-Hirakud-Burla complex is located in western Orissa along the bank of river Mahanadi between 21°28′ North to 21° 31′ North and 82° 54′ East to 83° 58′ East. The Sambalpur town is the administrative headquarter of Sambalpur district and a principal urban centre covering an area of 46.12 sq.km. The Burla is located on the right bank of the Hirakud dam project and serves as a satellite town of Sambalpur at a distance of 17 kms. in South-East direction. The other town Hirakud is lying about 16 kms. north of Sambalpur town. The Burla town has developed as an institutional town because of location of University, Medical College Hospital, University College of Engineering, Office of Hirakud dam reservoir and Mahanadi Coal Ltd. (MCL). The Hirakud is an industrial town. The Hirakud dam, longest main stream dam in the world is thrown across the turbulent Mahanadi river connecting this town with Burla town (Fig. 13.1).

This area lies over rolling upland with low elevation that vary from 145 metres to 290 metres above mean sea level. It is situated between Jharsuguda upland in the north and Baragarh upland in the South. Geologically entire area is covered by archaen rocks. The ground slopes from north to south with few outcrops and detached hills. The Burla town is surrounded by hilly terrains sloping towards east. The climate of this region is tropical, hot and humid. The average temperature of summer month is 45° C and 8° C during winter months. During Monsoon this region experiences an average rainfall of 155 cm.

Growth of Urban Population

The Sambalpur-Hirakud-Burla Complex experienced a significant growth of its urban population. From 1901 to 1951 Sambalpur remained as a small town of western Orissa. The population of this town was 23,525 during 1951. With settling of new township at Burla and Hirakud, this urban complex had a population of 57738 during the year 1961. In 1971 the population of this complex recorded as 105,285 in number, a growth of 82 per cent over the last decade. Similarly, Sambalpur city experienced a sharp rise in its population which was 74,458 in number and a growth of 91 per cent (Sharma, 1995). The Burla and Hirakud town also registered 52 per cent and 75 per cent growth in their respective population during this period. This high growth rate of population as experienced in this complex was due to rural-urban migration and rehabilitation of people from the drowned area of Hirakud reservoir. Another significant change is noticed regarding the area of Sambalpur city which grew from 20.72 sq.km. to 46.12 sq.km. showing rapid urban growth and conversion of fringe area into urban land-use. During 1981 and 1991 the urban complex registered growth of population by 51 per cent and 19.7 per cent respectively. The population number of this complex during 2001 was recorded as 240,281 and a growth of 24.3 per cent over last decade. The above study reveals the fact that between 1971 to 1991 this area experienced slow population growth followed by a sharp rise in the last decade. This increase in urban population growth was due to rapid expansion of Sambalpur urban area and opening of new Zonal Offices, Commercial centres and regional centres of state

Table 13.1 : Population Growth after Independence

Year	*Sambalpur City*	*Growth in %*	*Burla Town*	*Growth in %*	*Hirakud Town*	*Growth in %*
1951	23,525	–	–	–	–	–
1961	38,915	64.42	10,230	–	8,593	–
1971	74,458	91.83	15,587	52.3	15,040	75.03
1981	1,11,261	51.27	27,882	78.88	21,701	44.29
1991	1,34,824	19.7	34,640	24.39	28,833	19.82
2001	1,63,622	21.3	42,261	22	34,398	19.3

government in last decade. Similarly, Burla town experienced a significant growth of its population due to opening of MCL offices and its residential colonies over there. The better facilities for formal and technical education in this complex also attract temporary migration from nearby rural as well as urban areas. This continuous increase of population in the urban complex is exerting tremendous pressure on water resource of towns because of scope of increase of supply of water of these towns has not yet improved nor there is any facility of treatment of sewage water in this city.

Industrial Units in Urban Complex

This urban complex experiences various growths in industrial units after independence. At present the industries are found concentrated in north of Sambalpur city and at Hirakud. The total number of industries registered in area are found to be 57 out of which 2 are large scale, medium-3 in number and 41 are small scale. INDAL (the smelter unit) and Hirakud power plant are two major industries which are presently generating 1397 kilo litre of waste water everyday which are discharged to River Mahanadi after treatment. The medium scale industries are not water intensive but most of the small scale industries which are found around Sambalpur city such as rice mills, oil mills, automobile service stations etc. are generating waste water which flows to the stream through various nalas untreated.

Use of Fertilizer in the Study Area

The other source of pollution of the river water is the percolation of fertilizer, pesticides and insecticides used in agriculture in Mahanadi Command Area surrounding this urban complex. The land use reveals that agricultural area in master plan of Sambalpur-Burla—Hirakud area covers 82 per cent, 58.62 per cent and 68.09 per cent respectively.

The average consumption of chemical fertilizers in agriculture is constantly increasing in this region. The continuous use of chemical fertilizer and injudicious use of it ultimately pollute the surface water by seepage and percolation.

Table 13.2 : Use of Fertilisers in irrigated area

Year	*Chemical fertilizer kg/hectare*
1995-96	25.2
1996-97	30.6
1997-98	34.93
1998-99	35.51
1999-2000	45.57

Levels of Water Pollution of River Mahandi

The study reveals that river water is constantly getting polluted due to rapid urbanisation and from agricultural and industrial wastes. The State Pollution Control Board in Sambalpur is constantly monitoring the water quality of this river since 1998. It reveals the fact that the down stream of river from Hirakud reservoir at Burla upto Sambalpur city, there has been no proper drainage system and all the municipal waste water and runoff in rainy season are discharged into river at various points by nallahs. There are 12 outlets of sewage to Mahanadi at Sambalpur city. The important nallahs opening to this river are Dhobijor, Durgapalli nallah and Hardjora nallah. The sewage water comprises domestic, hospital and other waste water such as industrial and anthropogenic activities by the people residing nearby area being discharged directly to river Mahanadi without treatment which is really objectionable in respect of health ground. According to municipal reports of towns about 50 per cent latrine drains are directly connected with nallahs and it is the biggest polluting agent of sewage water.

The Central, Pollution Control Board has classified the river Mahanadi as class-'C' river (pH- 6.5-8.5 and BOD 3. Omg/litre) which can be used as a source of drinking water with conventional treatment by deinfection. But the raw water quality at public supply water intake points at present in this urban complex suggest the deterioration of water quality due to heavy pourage of sewage outfall of the towns in upstreams. According to Indian Standard of 2296 on river category, a recent monitor on water quality of this river near this urban complex by Pollution Board reveals the fact that the standard of this river is further deteriorating to 'D' category river. With increasing pH range and BOD value of river water it becomes suitable only for pisciculture (pH 6.5 to 8.6 and other standards above 'C' category).

Table 13.3 : Water Quality of River Mahanadi

Location near river	*pH range*	*Total hardness*	*BOD mg/lit.*
1	2	*3*	*4*
Barabazar	7.2–7.5	86.0	6.2
Kamalibazar	6.2–8.2	79.0	5.9
Balibandha	7.3–8.2	75.0	5.4
Kunjelpada	6.2–7.4	86.0	8.3

Tolerance level of BOD for use is 3mg/lit.
Source : Office of State Pollution Board, Sambalpur.

Effect of Pollution

At this urban complex the quality of water has deteriorated for common man's use for bathing and useful only for pisciculture. The colour of Mahanadi river has turned grey with the presence of various bacterial and micro organisms that are affecting the skin and causing gastroenteritis diseases, amoebic dysentery, diarrhoea and typhoid fever. Although Pollution Control Board has already warned about this fact, still no step has been taken for its treatment.

Conclusion

Mahanadi river is the only biggest source of surface fresh water on which about 2.5 lakh population of this urban complex are directly dependent. The above study reveals that this river is rapidly falling to a deteriorating condition because of heavy carriage of untreated sewage and industrial waste water and becoming unfit for human use. With the steady trend of increasing population of this complex and dependence on this river, government should take immediate steps in setting treatment plants for waste water otherwise this beautiful and big river will remain as the carrier of human borne wastages in future near this urban complex.

REFERENCES

Hagget, P. : *Geography–A Modern Synthesis,* Harper & Row Publisher, New York (1983).

Orissa Pollution Control Board : *Environmental Status of Sambalpur-Burla-Hirakud Complex : A report* (1999).

Sinha, B.N. : *Geography of Orissa,* NBT, India, New Delhi (1999).

Sharma, P.D. : *Ecology and Environment,* Rastogi Pub., New Delhi (1995).

14

River Management of Flood, Drought and Power Shortage in North Bihar

SHARDA NAND CHOUDHARY

Introduction

Flood, drought and power shortage are the most important problems of North Bihar. It is very interesting to hear that North Bihar is the playground of many rivers and rivulets, yet it is suffering from flood and drought year after year. Floods and droughts of North Bihar are synonymous. It consists of the flood plains of rivers descending from the Nepal Himalayas to the Ganga in the south. Its low elevation above sea level, moderate to heavy rainfall concentration within the monsoon months, huge catchments in the Himalayas combine to make the region vulnerable to severe floods, annually (Choudhary, 1993). Floods of 2002 in North Bihar was peculiar in nature. Whole North Bihar was inundated due to heavy down pour for several days in their catchment areas as a result several breaches in the embankments had taken place and many roads were over-topped by flood water. Between Muzaffarpur to Darbhanga, Muzaffarpur to Sitamarhi, Samastipur to Darbhanga, Darbhanga to Sakri were worst affected. During the period 1953 to 2003 the average district damage to Bihar has been 25 per cent of the total damage in the whole country. According to official estimate made in 2002 there is a loss of about 60 to 70 per cent agricultural produce in about 100 blocks of North Bihar due to floods. On the other hand, 20 to 30 per cent loss were due to drought in 20 to 25 blocks. The 1987 flood wrought destruction of assets worth Rs. 1,212 crore. And this was independent of human lives. Other parts of the state have also been hit by flood particularly in 1975 and 2003 when water from Ganga, the Son and the Punpun inundated Patna. For the peasants who inhabit the rich alluvial plains of North Bihar, heavy monsoons ironically is a harbinger for death and devastation. Ravaged by flood every year, with greater degree of devastation in certain years, the poor peasants find themselves totally helpless. A permanent solution ensuring a flood free life has so far eluded them.

Lying south of the lowland Terai of Nepal to North of Ganga and spanning a total geographical area of 58,500 sq. km. North Bihar appears to provide a natural spillover area for the many rivers and their tributaries originating in the upper reaches of the Nepal and flowing into the Ganga.

The Gandak, Kosi, Kamla, Balan, Bagmati and host of seasonal rainfed rivers and their tributaries criss-cross the region before converging into the Ganga (Choudhary, 1993, p. ii). Heavy and concentrated rainfall in the catchment area in Nepal can spell havoc for the inhabitants of North Bihar districts. The aggregate of the catchment area of these rivers, and they enter North Bihar in about three times of the geographical area of the region. Additionally, the average annual rainfall is fairly high varying from 1681 mm in the eastern part to 1070 mm in the western part (Choudhary, 1993, pp. 52-60).

The density of population in North Bihar 888 per sq. km. (2001 census) against the state average 402 per sq. km. and all India average of 216 per km. with agriculture as mainstay of the economy in this part, this implies greater disaster potential of the floods. Weighed in terms of the invisible losses incurred, the restoration to their socio-economic life patterns would be in actual terms turnout to be many times more.

Over the years embankments alongside river banks have been raised to protect people from flood. Such a policy, however, has failed to fulfil the basic objective. Besides, it has also proved to be a costly proposition in terms of maintenance. In 1987, 2002, 2003 when devastation was the most, embankments at 106, 75, 50 respectively places were breached and the canal system severally damaged.

Arbitrarily raising the embankments owing to political consideration has created its own set of problems. A typical example has been found is Kusheswar Asthan bordering Darbhanga and Samastipur districts. Here, the water of practically all the rivers have a free run, rendering the entire fertile belt into a waterlogged area. The area rich for valuable lentils remains under water for as many as nine months in a year. Farming has been replaced by hunting of migratory birds from Siberia. These birds have a ready lucrative upcountry market.

Another most important feature of the rivers of North Bihar, which are aggregative, more floods in this region in the tremendous sweep of their flow has been caused due to the fall from the Himalayan heights. Loads of mud and silt carried from many of the purely muddy Himalayan peaks add intensity to their sweep. Soft alluvial soil in their way is cut into pieces like slices of cake by a sharp knife inundated mud and silt carried by there swift flowing rivers very often block their own course suddenly taking to new course causing dreadful damages and devastation in their wake.

Course Shifting a Regular Feature

During the century itself river Kamla has changed its course thrice. During the end of the nineteenth and beginning of the twentieth century Kamla was flowing through west of the old feudal fort town of Jayanagar on Indo-Nepal border and shared the same bed with river Dhaurs Bagmati for about six miles near Kamtaul on the western border of Madhubani district. During the second quarter of the twentieth century it changed its course through east of Jayanagar mercifully sparing a part of this town, surrounding Madhubani town in the way from three sides. In the beginning of the third quarter of the century it made another east ward jump and occupied the Kosi river bed deserted about 100 years ago and almost completely devoured river Balan, becoming known as Kamla-Balan.

In the beginning of 20th century the Kosi river was flowing through the eastern part of Purnea and Katihar districts. In the beginning of the thirties it had made a big westward jump passing through the border areas of Saharsa. Madhubani, Darbhanga, Samstipur, Khagaria, Madhepura and Katihar districts devouring the Tilyuga, the Bhutahi Balan and several other rivers. Justifying the traditional belief the Kosi and the Kamla-Balan water mixed together presenting an oceanic scenario in the area of the tri-junction of Samastipur, Saharsa and Khagaria districts. During the last decade the Kosi has been attempting an eastward push threatening breaches in eastern embankments (Jha, Bhogendra, 1985, p. 2). River Bagmati also has been changing its course. The last big shift it made just a decade ago when about 32 km. long embankments on both sides had already been constructed and had to be given up because the change of course took place upstream. The Lal Bakaya, Lakhandei, Khirohi, Burhanad, the Dhaurs and the Bagmati rivers merge into the Bagmati at several places turning into only one river to the south of Darbhanga town. This group is known as the Adhawara group of rivers (Choudhary, 1993, p. 26). Thus the Kosi, the Kamla and the Bagmati are not rivers with fixed courses by systems or group of rivers with frequently changing courses, i.e. while travelling east to west and *vice versa* one comes across several dead, semi-dead and living courses and bed of each of these rivers known by the names of Kosi, Kamla and Bagmati. The whole of Mithila region has been the play-ground of these river systems causing endless inundation and destruction of land, villages, towns, palatial buildings, historical monuments, roads and during the last one hundred years of railways too.

Drought

One common feature of all these rivers is that while causing floods all along during the rainy seasons destroying crops, houses, cattle, human lives, roads and rail traffic etc. they do cause droughts too by draining out waters from the fields after only a few rainless weeks. That is why floods and droughts are followed and preceded by each other at very short intervals. Very often they do co-exist at the same time in different parts of the same district or same block and many times on the outer and inner sides of the embankments of the same river. This is the paradox of the tragic situation. Drought is also an annual feature scattered in many districts. But, the scale and magnitude of 1966 and 1967 drought has not been repeated because of good monsoon. (Thakur, B., 2002, presidential address, coping with Natural Hazards a Gegrapher's agenda, NAGI, pp. 17-18).

Management of Rivers

Now this paper deals how this sky-high problem could be tackled. No one can control the flood and drought fully, but it can be minimized to some extent only due to geographical setting of North Bihar.

River management is the term for flood protection scheme. It includes embankment, flood walls, ringbundhs, reservoirs to reduce flood peaks channel improvement (by dredging) cut-offs, detention basin to reduce flood level, watershed management to reduce the rate of run-off river training by spurs or revetments to arrest bank erosion, flood plain zoning, raising level of habitats, advance flood warning and emergency evacuations (Choudhary, S.N., 1993, p. 120). The total length of the embankment have been constructed in North Bihar is about 2,520 km (Rastriya Barh Ayog, 1980, p. 250). Now we are aware that some 3,400 km of embankments have been constructed in the last 35 years at the cost of Rs. 375 crorc but almost Rs. 475 crorc have been spent on their maintenance (CSE, 1991, 1994). Twenty-two schemes for town protection scheme have also been completed. Town protection schemes have been executed for saving important and most vulnerable towns like Chapra, Khagaria, Darbhanga and Muzaffarpur etc. (*Ibid.* p. 121).

Some river improvement schemes have also been undertaken These improvement schemes have been made for improvement of river Khirohi.

No flood detention reservoir (except at Bhim Nagar on the Kosi and at Valmiki Nagar on the Gandak through barrages) river diversion work, village raising (some village raising schemes have been executed) and soil conservation work have so far been undertaken in various river basins of North Bihar.

The Bagmati Master Plan to Perpetuate Flood and Drought

An integrated Bagmati Master Plan was finalized at an estimated cost of Rs. 185 crore with earthen embankments on both sides of the Bagmati, the Lal Bakaya and the Lakhandeyi. Combined with it has a barrage at Ram Nagar on Indo-Nepal Border and canals on both sides of this barrage. This project does not take into its fold the Khirohi. Dhaus and other rivers of Adhwara group which mingle up and become one with river Bagmati to the south of Darbhanga city for which separate embankment scheme are being finalized at an estimated cost of about Rs. 224 crore. Those estimates must have escalated by now.

Realizing the danger of over flooding parts of Terai area in Nepal without any benefit accruing to it from our barrage-cum-embankment schemes. Nepal finalized its own bigger multi-purpose project on the river Bagmati near village Karmaiya 2 km upstream from the east west highway, the proposed dam's height is 244.4 metres. It will also have installed hydel-generating capacity of 140 megawatts. Even though the very location of this Dam will have a few lakh hectores of land further north in Nepal unirrigated and will have less water storage and hydel generating capacity. This Nepalese project will make our Ram Nagar Barrage, canal and embankment all the more redundant. During the lean and needy months there will be no water for our proposed canals. During the floods the water released by Nepal will overflood us making our embankments redundant as explained above. Thus is the Grandois costly Bagmati Master Plan which will in practice, perpetuate both floods and droughts.

The remedies lie in serious and determined efforts for speedy agreement with Nepal for joint harvesting of the Bagmati group of rivers. This can be done through a bigger multi-purpose Dam at Nunthar further north of the proposed Karmaiya Dam. This will secure assured irrigation of larger areas in Nepal as well, almost total trapping of the flood waters of river Bagmati during the peak days and uninterrupted generation of hydel power at larger scale. Absence of the flood waters in the main stream of Bagmati will enable speedy discharge of flood waters from other rivers of this group. In such a situation even earthen embankments on Khirohi, Dhaus etc. with sluice gates at suitable intervals can eliminate both floods and drought from this entire area apart from providing hydel-power. As I heard Nepal had sounded USSR for such a big Dam at Nunthar but concerned officials of India rejected the idea due to Nepal unilaterally approaching the Soviet Union. It is only thereafter that Nepal proceeded with the present site near Karmaiya for a smaller multi-purpose Dam with the assistance of the World Bank at an estimated cost of 47 crores of U.S. dollars. Now, it is late but not too late to speedily strive for and achieve agreement for coordinated control and harnessing of the Bagmati group of rivers.

Kamla Embankments, Canals

The remedy lay and still lies in a multipurpose Dam at Shishapani in Nepal for which preliminary survey had also been made. But in our hunch for flood control and only a bit of irrigation we constructed embankments on both sides of river Kamla. It proved a failure thus if the government with the collaboration with Nepal built multipurpose Dam at Shishapani, that may be appreciated.

The Barahkshetra Multipurpose High Dam

The basis of the Kosi project, the High Dam at the foothills was left out. Shelving of the High Dam project took place not only due to the lack of far-sightedness about lack of market for "huge block of power" and "stored water". It was also due to lack of appreciation of the composite character of all the three-stage of the Kosi project.

Cheap and Abudant Hydel Power

The problem of power shortage is haunting the whole country. Much more so is the case of Bihar where per capita annual power consumption has been around half of the national average. North Bihar's per capita consumption has invariably been about one-fifth of that of the whole of Bihar. Annual per capita consumption of power in North Bihar is 30.02 kilowatts. All-round loss of Bihar due to power famine is, to say the least, really inassessable. None can dare to say now that the huge block of power of high dam won't have market for itself as stated in 1963 by the administrator of the state.

As stated earlier the gravity of flood, drought and shortage of power can be minimized by constructing reservoir in the catchment area as well as in plain itself.

REFERENCES

Bandyopadhya, S., 'Natural environmental hazards and their management,' *Singapur Journal of Tropical Geography* (1997).

Centre for Science and Environment, Floods, Floods plains and Environmental Myths. State of India's Environment : A Citizen Report, No. 3, New Delhi, CSE (1991).

Choudhary, S.N., *"Geography of Floods in North Bihar,* L.N.M.U. Press, Darbhanga (1993).

Jha, Bhogendra, *"Flood Problem"*, speech (1985).

Mishra Harinath, "Some thought of Irrigation Development in Bihar," speech (1984).

Thakur, B., Presidential Address, Coping with Natural Hazards a Geographer's Agenda. (NAGI) (2002).

15

Water Resources : Use and Conservation in North Bihar Plain

VINAY NATH JHA

Introduction

The North Bihar plain is a compact area comprising the whole of Bihar lying North of the Ganga river. It covers an area of 53,788 sq. km. and has total population of over 46.5 millions. The area having a solid block of extremely dense population, the average being 866 persons per sq. km. (2001). A large proportion of nearly 80 per cent of the total land is cultivated and agriculture constitutes the main resource of the region. The morphological characteristics of the region exhibited in its alluvial landscape. Many big streams like the Ghagra, the Gandak, the Burhi Gandak, the Bagmati, the Kamla Balan, the Kosi, the Tilyuga, the Kankhar, the Mahananda and the Adhwara group of rivers are flowing in this region and lastly, fall into the Ganga in the south. Besides rivers there are so many Tals, Ponds, Lakes and watershed like wetlands, chaurs, and other waterlogging areas waiting for proper water resource management and various uses for the area development. North Bihar consists of the flood plains of rivers descending from the Nepal Himalayas to the Ganga in the south. It has been described as the playground of rivers. Its low elevation above sea level, moderate to heavy rainfall concentrated within the monsoon months, huge catchments in the Himalaya combine to make the region vulnerable to severe floods annually. The most important flood producing rivers are the Kosi, the Gaghra, the Gandak, the Budhi Gandak, the Bagmati, the Kamla-Balan and the Adhwara. The Ghagra and the Gandak make a natural barrier between the Eastern Uttar Pradesh and North Bihar. Though the eastern boundary does not coincide with the Mahananda it follows for some distance. The mighty

Ganga forms the southern boundary and the base level for the region (Choudhary, 1992). The water resources, their management and governance in North Bihar presents crucial conditions. Water as a resource is of tremendous importance for the national economy. The increasing use for various purposes is soon going to fall short of our requirements. Water uses vary with time and space. Availability of ground water depends upon factors like porosity, specific yield and permeability of rocks formation. The water resources of the region are mainly utilised for domestic and drinking purposes, irrigation and power production purposes, industrial purposes, and fisheries. Agricultural purposes like Bheint, Makhana, Mothi, Singhara and recreational purposes and so on.

Ground Water

North Bihar is characterized by a monotony of a alluvial deposits the single geological formation spread over the whole study region. It also determines the location of the watersheds. The types of rock also plays a very important role in determining annual and monthly run-off in the rivers. In a catchment with permeable bedrock a much larger storage capacity has to be filled than in the case with impermeable bedrock as a result of streams in such areas respond very slowly and exhibit none of the flashy characteristic of the streams. During the rainy season, the Ganga and its tributaries increase enormously in volume, carrying down vast quantities of silt or mud with the result that they overflow into adjacent country. When the water subsides again the rivers in their retreat, leave some of the silt, which they have brought with them spread over the flooded lands, as a thin deposit. The excessive coarse sediment carried down by rivers, viz. the Kosi, the Gandak, the Kamla, and the Mahananda are to be ascribed to the fact that in their catchment the Himalaya is much more compressed especially in the Kosi. The valleys are narrower, the sides are steeper and there is scarcity of wider basins in the hilly region for the river to spill over their floodwaters and deposit their coarse sediment load. Besides, due to the steep and high sides, frequent slips occur into the rivers and that adds considerably to the coarse sediment load of the rivers.

The availability of groundwater depends upon factors like porosity, specific yield and permeability of rock formation. The water table stage fluctuates continually under the combined influence of a set of forces causing recharge to or discharge from the groundwater reservoir. The rise in groundwater table occurs in rainy season in the area. Table 15.1 shows the districtwise average rainfall in mm^2.

Tables 15.1 : Amount of Rainfall in North Bihar

Name of the District	*June-1989 To Sep-1989*	*Oct-1989 to Dec-1989*	*Jan-1990 to Feb-1990*	*March-1990 to May-1990*	*Rainfall*	*Normal Rainfall*	*Days of Aver. Rainfall*
Saran	1049.8	0.1	4.0	31.7	1085.6	993.3	48.2
Siwan	985.9	6.0	10.1	23.8	1025.8	1171.8	23.9
Gopalganj	1235.0	7.6	32.0	87.3	1361.9	1184.4	65.7
Muzaffarpur	1022.9	2.2	12.0	104.3	1151.4	1180.9	45.5
Sitamarhi	1364.0	0.0	4.9	125.8	1494.7	1266.8	52.7
Vaishali	773.0	2.6	3.2	74.2	853.56	1042.8	54.4
W. Champaran	1337.5	14.6	14.2	102.3	1468.6	1447.6	51.6
E. Champaran	1398.9	25.3	20.1	31.7	1468.0	1356.4	57.8
Darbhanga	1063.0	9.7	7.6	122.2	1101.6	1202.3	59.6
Samastipur	1212.0	13.0	14.5	114.3	1343.8	1168.0	59.5
Madhubani	1143.7	3.2	7.8	122.6	1277.3	1307.3	62.8
Begusarai	1148.1	31.5	13.4	113.9	1306.9	1201.6	55.7
Saharsa	1380.2	13.3	2.1	101.4	1497.0	1391.1	64.4
Madhepura	1560.6	5.6	1.1	84.8	1652.1	1367.5	50.9
Purnea	1911.9	10.2	1.2	162.5	2085.8	1699.0	71.3
Katihar	1377.8	36.4	0.9	118.9	1534.0	1458.1	67.5
N. Bihar	1262.1	27.1	11.8	67.8	1366.8	1211.7	51.2

Source : The Statistical Department 1991 (Bihar Govt.).

Utilisation of Water Resources

Water constitutes one of our most important natural resources. Water as a resource is of tremendous importance for the area as well as the national economy. Water uses vary with time and space. The increasing use of the water for various purposes is soon going to fall short of our requirements, the water resources of the area mainly utilised for (Govt. of Bihar, 1991) :—

1. Domestic purposes like bathing and drinking
2. Irrigation purposes
3. Industrial purposes
4. Navigation purposes
5. Recreational purposes
6. Agricultural purposes

Table 15.2 : Current Basinwise Land-use in North Bihar Plain

Sl. No.	*Name of Basin*	*Geographical Areas in* km^2	*Forest Land*	*Different Trees & Gardens*	*Waste Land*	*Cultivable Wasteland*	*Fallow Land*	*Agricultural Low Land*	*Dry and Permanent Waste Land*	*Non-Agricultural Land*
1A.	Ghaghra-Mahi western Gandak	648,728	–	20195	22314	12434	1983	482423	25620	83809
1B.	Upper Eastern Gandak and upper Burhi Gandak	882,398	91854	39281	36703	9484	5492	547355	11734	140495
1C.	Lower Eastern Baya lower Burhi Gandak	675,666	–	27391	26465	5865	1402	45916	21450	133177
2.	Bagmati–Balan	448,767	–	18279	37173	4971	773	279401	16693	91477
3.	Kamla Balan	1,141,019	3297	34332	90052	31753	7086	709209	79257	186033
4.	Kosi	1,141,019	–	–	–	–	–	–	–	–
5.	Mahananda	615,006	1978	17347	59821	15968	3582	365766	49574	100970
6.	Ganga Stem	– (Diara)	–	–	–	–	–	–	–	–

Source : Bihar Govt., Second Report of Irrigation Commission, Patna, 1999.

Table 15.3 : North Bihar-River Basins and Catchment Area

Sl. No.	Name of the Basin	Name of the River	Length of the River in km	Catchment Area, km^2	Surface water Potential lakh hect. m	Name of the Project of Hydel	Discharge Capacity cusec
1.	Ghaghra Basin	Ghaghra or Sarju	780	131995 Total/2849 in Bihar	6.92	Gandak Project	– –
2.	Gandak Basin	Gandak	420	45843/9540 in Bihar	62.8	Gandak Project	–
3.	Burhi Gandak Basin	Burhi Gandak	320	10150	123	–	2561850
4.	Bagmati & Adhwara	Bagmati, Lalhandai Adhwara, Jamura Sika Burhad Khiroi, Singhia, Murha-Rato	–	139062	969		462
5.	Kamla-Balan	Kamla Balan	150	6720	323		75%
6.	Kosi Basin	Sapt Kosi	390	444	26	Kosi Project	20 MW
7.	Mahananda Basin		240	6300	7.38/3.9 for irrigation		20 MW

Source : Irrigation Deptt. Bihar Govt., 1991.

The most important use of water is its consumption by human beings. Utilisation of water for different purposes in urban and rural areas varies depending upon the nature of requirements. According to determined measures, consumption of water for rural areas is 70 litre per individual per day and for urban area according to classwise towns, the consumption of water is 100 to 140 litre per individual per day. In Bihar total consumption of water should be 2367m cm according to 1991 census. Generally drinking water is used underground water in urban areas. Dug wells are used for drinking purposes (Yadav, 2000).

Table 15.2 shows the basinwise geographical area and the main river flowing under the district catchment area. Among the 2367 mcm drinking water is only 82 mcm available through surface water and 2285 mcm made available from underground water (Kumar, 2000). The surface water resources of the region is about 67% of state total. Out of this only 33 per cent is utilizable. Presently 40.4 per cent of the utilizable resource is being utilised in the region. This part of the state can be divided in seven river basins, viz. the Ghaghra, the Gandak, the Budhi Gandak, the Bagmati and the Adhwara group of rivers, the Kamla, the Kosi and the Mahananda. Summaries of surface water resource potential of the seven basins are presented here.

Table 15.3 reveals that the basin and the catchment area of the rivers flowing in the region :—

1. The Ghaghra that rises in Himalaya crosses the Indian border and joined by the two important tributaries, the Sharda and the Rapti before river drain into the Ganga near Chappra. Basin area get irrigational benefit from the Gandak project.
2. The Gandak basin is located in the Himalaya spreading over the central part of Nepal and Tibet. The Gandak barrage has been constructed few kms below confluence to divert water into channels to irrigate areas in Nepal and North Bihar. The Triveni canal is one of the oldest canal systems of Bihar, which provides irrigation to about 1.65 lakh hectare.
3. The Budhi Gandak basin flowing South Eastern direction and parallel to the river Bagmati which receives spill of river during high flow meets the river Ganga east of Khagaria. The remarkable feature of the basin is chains of lakes like Lal Sarriya, Sugaon, Turkaulia, Motihari, Pipra and Nawada

with depth varying between 1 to 7 metres which collects local runoff. The Southern portion of the basin is composed of recent alluvium with stretches of marshy depression of, "Chaurs."

4. The Bagmati and the Adhwara basin is a complex network of the Bagmati, the Lakhandei, the Adhwara-Jamunia, the Sika-Burhand, the Khirohi, the Singhia, the Marna-rato, the Dhaus and the Thomane group of rivers. During monsoon period all these rivers are generally interlinked and creates flood havoc and spoil all the crops in the region. The main problem of the basin is flood. It is essential to divert extra discharge through old channels and regulate them through bypass channel and by desilting the "*Dhar.*"
5. The Kamla-Balan river at village Bajraha it passes into Bihar plain, presently flowing through the old coarse of Balan, it falls in the Kosi river. The basin is very fertile and is spotted by waterlogged areas called, "Chaurs." Basin has adequate water resource to meet the full irrigation need of the area. For keeping the sub-soil water level low the conjunctive tubewell irrigation has to be put in practice during Rabi and Garma crops.
6. The Kosi is the notorious river for changing its coarse and depositing coarse silt in the flood plain. The Kosi is being confined between embankments and is providing moderate flood protection to the area outside of the embankments which are under constant threat during flood part of water potential of the basin has been utilised to generate 20 megawatt hydro electric power.
7. The Mahananda Basin : Like the Kosi their streams also changes there coarse too often. Surface water potential of the Mahananda is 7.3 lakh hectare out of which about 3.9 lakh hectare can be utilised for irrigation, industrial water supply and hydel pówer generation at suitable sites.

Wetland Status of the Region

The wetlands of the huge region of North Bihar is dependent upon the six major tributaries of the Ganga flowing out from the Central Himalaya in the plain between the Nepal border and the Ganga itself. From the great Gandak river in the west to the Mahananda in the east,

Table 15.4 : Availability of Surface Water Potentiality and Use in North Bihar

Sl.No.	*Name of Basin*	*Total No. of Basins*			*Poten. in Hectare*		*Deep tubewells*	*Total*
		Small wells	*Shallow tubewells*	*Deep tubewells*	*Small well*	*Shallow tubewells*		
1.	Ghaghra Mahi western Gandak	17485	68509	265	31424	306199	25614	363237
2.	Upper Eastern Gandak-upper Burhi-Gandak	84	34974	674	142	102809	80880	183831
	Lower Eastern Gandak-Baya Lower Burhi Gandak	2638	85598	529	6493	277377	63480	347350
	Bagmati and Adhwara Group	258	52030	588	447	182724	66326	249497
	Kamla-Balan	13	21845	311	14	82859	37320	120193
	Kosi	114	78496	472	199	235488	59000	294687
	Mahananda	-	37084	115	-	111252	13800	125052
	Total N. Bihar	20592	378536	2954	38719	1298708	346420	1683847
	Ganga stem Diara	6250	33944	262	12220	106389	31440	150049

Source : Bihar Govt.—Second Report of Irrigation Commission, 1999.

the northern part of the Ganga plain is studied with numerous small fresh water lakes or "Chaurs," the vast majority of which are oxbow lakes marking the historical course of Baya Nadi, the Budhi Gandak, the Kosi and the Mahananda rivers. Chaurs are particularly abundant south east of the region around Kabar Lake which is 22 km. north from Begusarai and 100 km. east of Patna. There are more than 14,000 hectare of these wetlands in Darbhanga district alone. Some of the main Chaurs in Kabar Lake regions are Nagri Jheel, Vikrampur Chaurs, Rajakpur Chaurs, Chalki Chaurs and others. Wetlands are the feeding and breathing grounds for a large range of birds, mammals, amphibians, fishes, insects, crustaceans and reptiles. The very diversity of the services that wetlands offer creates problems as one range of activity is rarely compatible with another and exploitations of the wetlands for one use places constraints on other uses (Jha, 2003).

The industrial use of water is limited to large scale industries such as Fertilizers Corporations of India, Sugar Mills, Distilleries, Jute Mills and other industrial establishments, the perennial streams of the study area like the Ghagra, the Gandak, the Kosi, the Kamla-Balan, and the Mahananda are being used for navigation and other transportation purposes. The use of water for recreational purposes is not very common in North Bihar plains, but the study area uses water for agriculture purposes too. Water burry (Makhana), Bheint, Jute, Mothi, Pater, Singhara, Lilly are common products of major wetlands of the region. Fisheries industry is very much profitable in the study region and about 65 per cent of fishes are exported to West Bengal and other states of India.

Table 15.4 reveals the surface water potentiality of North Bihar plain.

Problems of Water Resources

Water deficiency, flood and water pollution are the main problems of the water resources in the area. Water presents a deceptive index that its importance is less than other natural resources. Water resources prodigious use, and abuse causes many areas too leave on the water bankruptcy. Severe water problems arise because it is not properly distributed for human use. Too much of it creates flood, too little cause droughts or the quality is polluted which causes diseases and ruins crops. Today water problem is part of the national consciousness and we are aware of the fact that future development of the country is intimately related to the wise use of water resources. North Bihar plain that has recorded many devastating floods in one part and droughts in other parts, the proper utilization of surface water resources is much needed requirement of the development processes. Due to heavy discharge of water by tubewells and borings the level of water became very low and surface area water feels affected and crisis started. Scarcity of groundwater, due to irregular monsoon rain, tubewells and dug wells are in spate of drought. Crops and human beings and animal were in short of water crisis in the area (C.S.F. Report, 1991).

Criss-crossed by canals and ponds it is a typical case of scarcity amids plenty, even after flood. Diminution of groundwater and growing demand supply gap have pushed both district towns, namely Banka and Bhagalpur into severe drinking water crisis. Which according to experts is likely to worsen in the coming years. A major factor of the crisis is going down of groundwater level in the past, potable water would be drawn with the help of bore wells from the depth of 8 to 12 metres (Pandey, 1989).

River brings enormous water in the region. The soil is very fertile but on the other hand, this region accounts for more than 17 per cent of the flood prone areas of India. The flood prone area of Bihar has shot up from 2.5 mha to 6.4 mha between 1974 and 1988. In 1987 flood engulfed 33 districts out of 39 districts causing 125 breaches in embankments. Consequently, 30 million people were displaced and 1100 died. According to a report published in *Times of India* dated 11.10.2003, incessant land erosion caused by the Ganga and the Gandak has displaced 4684 families living on the bank of these rivers under different places. The affected areas are Bachawara and Teghra where 439 families and 739 families respectively were engulfed by the changing course of these two rivers during the recent past.

The idea of controlling floods through dams and embankments, is sharp contradiction to the idea of living with floods, came with independence. With embankments failing to solve problem the Bihar Government in reach to see dams being built in Nepal, a highly seismic area. No effort has been made to the presence of wetlands as a cushion against floods. In some cases, even notified natural drainage channels have been used to settle landless people to get their identity.

Some 3400 km of embankment have been constructed in the last 50 years at the cost of Rs. 375 crore but almost Rs. 475 crore have been spent on their maintenance.

Flood control measures includes embankments, flood walls, ring

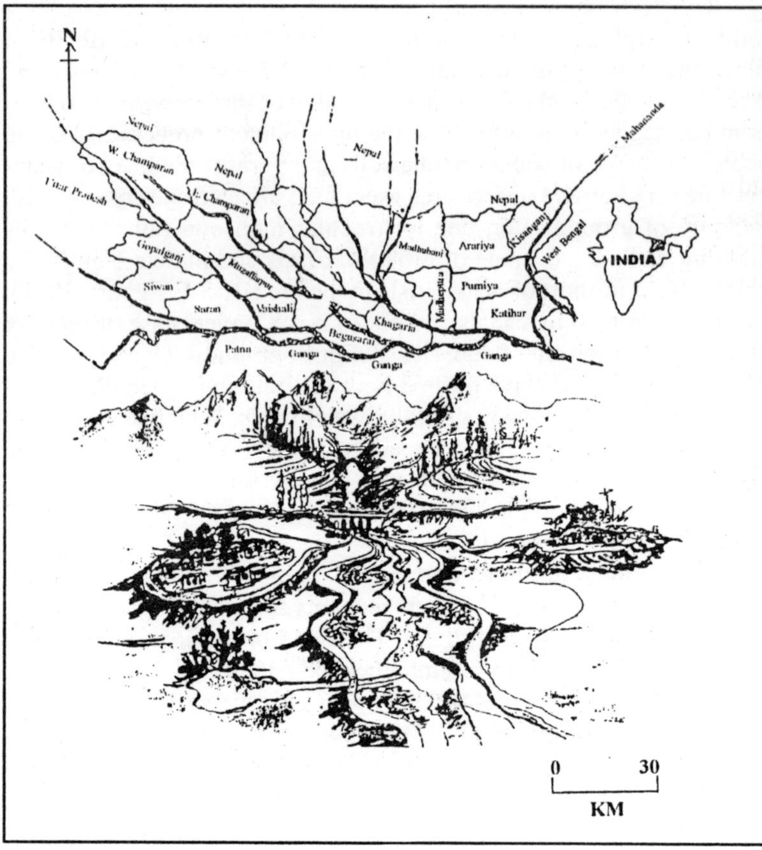

Fig. 15.1 : North Bihar : Flood Affected Areas and Their Management

Bandhs, flood control reservoirs to reduce flood peaks, channel improvement (by dredging) cut offs, dimension basins to reduce flood levels, watershed management started to reduce the rate of runoff, river training by spurs or revetments to arrest bank erosion, flood plain zoning, raising levels of habitats, advance flood warning and emergency evaluations, so far been studied for tackling the problems of flood, drainage and allied problems in the study area.

Population pressure and much other pressures on wetland arise as side effects of activities far removed from the water bodies, fertilizers, pesticides, organic wastes and sediment may be washed down from agricultural laws surface runoff may percolate into aquifers, chemical pollutions, oil, heavy metals and other residues may flow into stream to groundwater or be washed down from the roads. Largely under private ownership and not subject to any known conservation, measures, the use of three wetlands ranges from boating, fishing, water sport, bathing and irrigation to provide final for the human population and fodder for domestic livestock, wetlands play a major role in absorbing the floodwaters. Unfortunately, all of the them are facing a threat to their existence because of human intervention. At present increasing industrial uses pollutes the water of the area. During floods of the entire area looked an island sea. As the sources of drinking water, i.e. wells, tubewells, tanks are submerged by the vast sheet of water, the after effect polluted floodwater resulted into epidemics, which spreads in the adjoining area. These epidemics taken the forms of Malaria, Cholera and other water borne diseases. The conservation of water resources in the area at present is very much important. Flood control eradication of waterlogging areas, purification of polluted water, rational and optimum utilization of water resources are important measures of conservation of the study area (Jha, 2002).

Conclusion

North Bihar is a backward and problem ridden agricultural region in a less developed state of Bihar. The morphological status of the region exhibited in its alluvial landscape. Many big streams are flowing and making a flood ground in the region. I simply described about the use and misuse of water resources in this region. This will lead to forward pragmatic suggestions for well utilization of water resources so that formidable problem of flood devastation may be checked to a great extent (Jha, S.K., 2002). Also measures may be highlighted to develop hydel power, irrigation for agriculture, pure drinking water for rural and urban sectors etc. so that the level of the standard of living of habitat of North Bihar may be raised to satisfactory level. The proper utilization of underground as well as surface water resources will be increasing agricultural production for suitable food security in the study area. Proper utilization and purification of water may help the population healthy and for regional development. Water is precious, we have to conserve it through optimum and rational use.

REFERENCES

Choudhary, S.N., *Geography of Floods in North Bihar,* L.N.M.U. Publication Darbhanga, 1992, p. VIII.

C.S.E. Report, Nightmare in North Bihar, ed. in Report by Centre of Science & Environment, New Delhi, 1991, p. 123.

Govt. of Bihar, *Bihar Through Figures,* Govt. of Bihar Publication, 1991, p. 27.

Jha, S.K., Water Crisis Grisp Silk city, *The Times of India,* Patna Edition, dated 11th October, 2003, p. 6.

Jha, V.N., Agriculture Development : Potential and Strategy (A Case Study of Bihar) in *Geographical Perspective,* Vol. 3, Bihar Association of Geographies, Patna, 2002, p. 20.

Kumar, A., Surface Water Resource of Bihar, *Magadh Geographical Review,* Vol. 2, No. 2 & 3, Bodh Gaya, 2000, p. 23.

Pandey. J.N., Water Resources Use and Conservation in Saryupur Plain, *Uttar Bharat, Bhoogol Patrika,* Vol. 25, No. 2, Gorakhpur, 1989, p. 47.

Yadav, D.P., *Shesh Bihar, Future and Challenge, An Analysis,* Rajendra Prasad Academy, New Delhi, p. 26.

16

Water Crisis and Integration of River Systems in North Bihar

ANURANJAN

Introduction

Water is life. It is an essential natural resource, a basic human need and a precious national asset. The demand for water is increasing rapidly with each passing day due to increase in population. The rapid growth rate of urbanisation, industrialisation and irrigation to farmlands have aggravated the problem of water scarcity. Despite the fact that India is endowed with adequate water resources (4 per cent of the world's water resources) with numerous perennial rivers, and extensive groundwater aquifer, some parts of the country is experiencing scarcity of water. An idea of acute water scarcity can be had from the fact that per capita availability of water per year at the national level has reduced from about 5,177 cubic metre in 1951 to the estimated level of 1829 cubic metres in 2001.

Water Crisis Scenario

The fragile water resources are depleting while various sectoral demands are growing rapidly. Millions of people do not have access to safe drinking water and, therefore, children under age of five years die each year in millions due to water borne diseases. The water withdrawals are very high due to increased consumption all over the world. The surface water supplies are literally shrinking and ground water reserves are being depleted faster than they can be replenished by precipitation. The water is mainly consumed in agriculture, in industry and in households. Agriculture is by far the biggest user of water accounting for over 70 per cent of water followed by industry more than 20 per cent and households to about 8 per cent. Irrigation (by surface water and groundwater is necessary for creating a sound agricultural infrastructure) (Nautiyal, 2002).

The water scarcity has become certainly a serious concern and is most likely to aggravate further in coming years. The projected increase in water demand will occur specially in developing countries, where population growth and industrial and agricultural expansion will be greatest. India already is facing an alarming situation. Though India is blessed with one of the highest annual precipitation (400 m.ha.) in any country of this size (average annual rainfall of 554 mm). But because of its wide space and time variation, India is facing water crisis problem. A highly erratic rainfall distribution in terms of space and time aggravate this problem. Water crisis being a big problem, has become more challenging due to following reasons (Sekar, 2001) :

(a) non-judicious use of existing water resources,
(b) continuously declining potential of reservoirs,
(c) limited scope of expansion of irrigation potential,
(d) greater conveyance losses,
(e) increasing ground-water pollution etc.

The seriousness of water crisis had, not been realised and it was not a major issue even at the International Conference on Water and Environment held in Dublin, or at the U.N. Conference on Environment and Development at Rio de Janeiro, held in 1992. The Stockholm Water Symposium, held annually highlights the importance and relevance of water to the future development. Also its importance to environment conservation has attracted the attention of water professionals around the globe. Now the significance of water crisis has started gaining momentum and is likely to accelerate further in future. Many new institutions like World Water Forum (WWF), Global Water Partnership (GWP), World Commission on Water (WCW), have been established during the last decade. Recently, the third World Water Forum (WWF) held in Kyoto (Japan) on 16-23rd March, 2003 concluded that the picture of water crisis is quite gloomy. Nearly one-sixth (one billion) of the world population lacks access to clean water and nearly one-third (two billion) lacks access to adequate sanitation. The water supplies are falling while the demand is dramatically growing at an unsustaninable rate. In this context we must remember that the next global war if fought will be fought for water resource.

The UN's message is very laud and clear : "Water is a scarce resource to be managed and protected". The year 2003 has been declared by the UN as the "International Year of Fresh Water" (Jha, 1989).

India will face a severe water crisis if the available water resources are not judiously used. Presently six of India's 20 major river basins already fall into water scarce category. It has been reported that by the year 2025, five more river basins of India will face water crisis. The glaciers of the Himalayas (e.g. Gangotari receding at the rate of 10 to 30m/year) are rapidly melting and it is feared that within next 50 to 80 years, most of the glaciers will disappear. The drought conditions in many parts of the country like Orissa, Rajasthan, Gujarat and Andhra Pradesh are unfortunately on rise. The disputes over sharing of water resources are becoming grimmer. The river water disputes and riots over river water are becoming regular features. The distribution and sharing of river water will become one of the most politicised ecological issues in the near future. Therefore, it is proper time to ensure that our finite supply of this valuable natural resource is harnessed and utilized optimally. This can only be done by adopting modern water management practices, and preventing waste caused by uncontrolled runoff. There is a need to initiate steps to prevent loss of seepage, evaporation and runoff into the ocean during excessive rainfall in monsoon season and when rivers get flooded. In this situation the integration of river basins will be helpful in solving the critical problem of uneven distribution of the runoffs and precipitation during monsoon season.

A Crucial Issue

The disastrous flood as well as drought have been the chronic features in Bihar. The catastrophic floods are very common natural phenomenon in North Bihar plain. The rivers which come down from the Himalayas cause devastating floods during the monsoon period almost every year. They destroy crops, break communication lines and devastate the regional infrastructure in the area of their influence. In case of North Bihar the integration of river systems, based on the principle of transfer of surplus water to deficit river basins will solve the flood problems of the region and will provide extra water to South Bihar to fight drought. It will also contain the volumes of water that go waste instead of being conserved for useful purposes (Anuranjan, 2003).

The North Bihar Plain is the play ground of mainly seven living rivers, such as the Gaghra, the Gandak, the Burhi Gandak, the Baghmati, the Kamla-Balan, the Kosi and the Mahananda and numerous tributaries and dead river courses. These rivers have meandering courses and also characterised by frequent shifting of their channels. The major rivers of North Bihar which have been embanked in the last 50 years have shown positive signs of raising their beds and consequently the flood level. The average bed level within the embankments has gone up by 15 to 25 feet (4 to 8 metres) causing its water to spill over the embankments. Thus the protection through embankments now poses a serious challenge to planners. The details of embankments and flood control area are mentioned here :

Table 16.1 : Length of Embankment on the River

Rivers	*Embankments (in kms.)*	*Protected Area (in Lakh Hect.)*	*Un-protected Area (in Lakh Hect.)*
Ghaghra	148.80	0.92	2.34
Gandak	597.20	5.41	8.21
Baghmati	647.54	2.48	3.22
Kamla-Balan	483.96	3.82	5.79
Kosi	357.20	8.38	10.15
Mahananda	438.65	3.26	3.74

Infact, except and, all the major rivers of North Bihar have their sources in Nepal and Tibet. These rivers flow through fertile alluvial plain of North Bihar to join the river Ganga bringing in 20 crore m.cu of water. With nearly 60 per cent of the catchment area of these rivers located in Nepal and Tibet. The rivers are forced to disgorge four times the water that it drains in a normal season. Therefore, the rivers being incapable of draining this excess load, break the embankments, inundating the protected area and causing havoc at the site of breach. Thus the exclusive reliance on embankments for flood control in North Bihar is highly erroneous.

In the light of above problem two measures of water management have been suggested to fightout this hardship :

1. Interlinking of rivers by canals, and
2. Dredging of river courses.

The North Bihar plain is endowed with fertile alluvium. It has rich water resources. Its economy is agrarian. Having two basic components of fertile soil and water the agrarian economy of North Bihar is languishing. In fact, the region faces problems of water mismanagement. There is fluctuation in the volume of water in time and space. The volume of water discharge is maximum during the monsoon season (i.e. in three months from 15th of June to 15th of September) on account of heavy downpour in the catchment of rivers and supplemented by snow melt in the Himalayan zone. It has been observed that all basins do not get flooded at once. While the Kosi is in spate, the Budhi-Gandak and the Gandak may not be flooded. Hence, the water of one river basin can be transferred to other basin by the proposed link canals. This proposal is in tune with the 'Garland Canal Concept' a proposal made by Sri K.L. Rao in 1970 for interlinking country's rivers including much highlighted Ganga-Cauvery link canal (2640 km long). Even currently, the National Water Development Agency (NWDA) has initiated some measures of interlinking rivers in India. Out of four proposed link canals in Bihar, two (Kosi-Ghaghra link canal and Gandak-Ganga link canal) are directly related to North Bihar.

The North Bihar plain stretches more than 410 km from west to east and has a north-south varying width of nearly 120 to 150 km. It has been proposed to dig three major link canals at an interval of 40 to 50 km parallel to Nepal border in east-west direction. These link canals would transfer the water of all major and minor streams from one to another. As the land gradient is not uniform as seen along 26°N latitude (Fig.16.1). The profile drawn along the line 26°N latitude has indicated an imperceptible slope between the two extreme points of west and east. At the western extreme it measures 64 metres above m.s.l. while in eastern extreme it records 44 metres above m.s.l. Hence, in a distance of 370 km along 26°N latitude the variation of altitude is about 20 metres. Therefore, the construction of canals will require locks for transferring water to upper reaches, i.e. towards west. Such measures are required for proper management of water resource of North Bihar. This will definitely remove the flood problem from the scene. The proper distribution of water will also allow the silt-laden water to cover new areas, which will enrich the soil fertility (Mathew, 1996).

The present embankments along the rivers to control flood have definitely disturbed the ecology. The river courses within the embankments are rising. There is always fear of breach in embankments and flood havoc in the adjacent areas. Such incidences

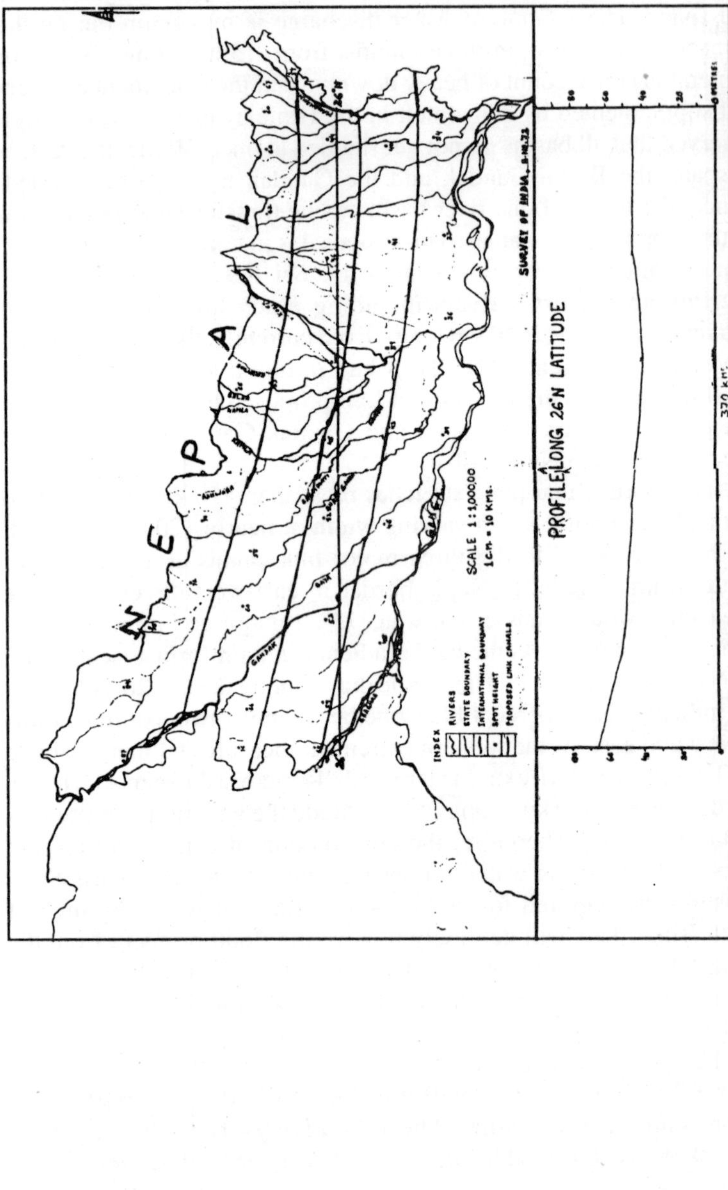

Fig. 16.1 : Rivers of North Bihar

are happening every year and lots of money are spent to control flood and also in relief operations. Ecological imbalances have been such that the railway platform of Jhanjharpur which was built much above the highest of flood level, now gets flooded frequently as the nearby Kamla river has filled up its course abundantly. The level of railway platform is just 2.5 metres above the river bed, which was in the past more than 10 metres above the river bed.

Another proposal is the dredging of river courses of all major streams flowing from north to south, as well as river Ganga flowing west to east need to be dredged properly and regularly, so that their capacity to carry water may not be reduced. The silts which are dredged out of the river courses may be deposited either along the river banks or away from the rivers, which will furnish high level grounds in flood plain. Such raised grounds would be ideal sites for settlements and for plantation of orchards. As all rivers are interlinked by canals and their courses are dredged adequately, properly and regularly, they all will have water in their courses throughout the year. Thus the dependency on rain water and groundwater for irrigation purposes will also be solved. The water in canals and rivers will provide ideal ground for fishing or promote pisciculture. Besides, irrigation and fishing the proposed link canals will provide navigational facilities, which will minimise the cost of transportation. The locks and check dams will also generate a huge quantity of hydro power. Thus, it will give a developmental impetus of unprecedented magnitude.

Regarding the feasibility, technocrats may be invited to examine this proposal. This stupendous task will require huge finance, for which various funding agencies may be approached. If this dream project is brought to reality North Bihar will usher a new life. It would really be a prosperous North Bihar in future.

REFERENCES

Anuranjan : 'Changing Pattern of Land use & Agr. In Flood Prone Area : A Case Study of Biraul (Darbhanga)', Unpublished thesis, Patna University, 2003.

Jha, G.P., *Agriculture in Flood Prone Region : A Geogrpahical Perspective*, Inter India Publication 1989. pp.35-51.

Matthew, Mammen : 'Floods of Fury', *Hindustan Times Monday Extra,* 29 July 1996, p. 1.

Nautiyal, Suresh 'Water Crisis : Agenda For the Century', *Yojana,*Vol. 46, Feb. 2002, pp. 11-15.

Sekar, I., a 'Water at Risk in the 21st Century', *Employment News*, April 2001, p. 1.

17

Water Resource Transfer from Surplus to Deficit Areas

A Case Study of Jharkhand

JANARDAN BHAGAT

Introduction

In the whole world there is serious thinking of inter-linking rivers in order to transfer water from surplus area to deficit areas. The society and the other natural creatures have equal right to water. For human life and other living objects of nature, water is of paramount importance. If the problem of water persists, the day is not far off when the third world war will be fought for water.[1]

In almost every part of the country after the monsoon there is either serious flood or severe drought resulting in scarcity of drinking water and water for irrigation.

In order to solve the problem of water, ambitious project of inter-linking rivers is prepared. In Jharkhand, Damodar River Project, Swarnarekha Project and Koel-Karo Project are important.[2]

In India projects have been prepared to inter-link 26 rivers. 23 years ago the outline of the project was drawn in the name of National Perspective Plan. Recently, the said plan was renamed as "National Water Development Agency".

This state is famous for tribal regions in the world. In this region some tribals are developed, some are developing and some are underdeveloped. In Jharkhand, different river basins are important for water resources, like the Damodar, the Swarnarekha, the Koel, the Ajay, the Ganga etc. At the same time some basins are affected by frequent droughts due to the non-availability of water.[3]

Water is the most important gift of nature not only for human life but also for birds, beasts and entire plants.

Importance of Water

Water is not only an important resource but also an unique gift of nature. All the living objects of the entire creation are dependent upon it. From the mighty trees to the small grass and from the elephants of the forests to the tiniest ants need water. Nature provides water to each according to need. Without water the existence of living objects will be at stake. Water cannot be compared to any other resources.[4]

Man has the basic right to water which cannot be alienated. Not to speak of Jharkhand but in the whole world there is talk of deriving profit from water. In the whole world there is the dialogues of privatisation of water through trade organization. Even in Jharkhand there is hue and cry for water.

In India the idea of inter-linking (uniting) the rivers is gaining ground. Even in Jharkhand there is the thinking of uniting the Damodar, the Swarnarekha and the Kharkai. The idea is to provide water to deficit areas from surplus water areas through canal. To ensure supply of drinking water to water deficit areas and increase in the agricultural production is the purpose of the project. Some such multi-purpose projects have been undertaken in Chotanagpur. We can learn the reality after seeing the development of the projects.

Swarnarekha Project

The Swarnarekha Project is a proposal of three states, Bihar (now Jharkhand), Bengal and Orissa. These three states signed the tripartite agreement for sharing costs and benefits of the same. This project is mainly in tribal and backward region. After completion of the project, the door of development of these regions has opened. The work in Jharkhand can be divided into 4 dams[5] :

(i) Chandil Dam
(ii) Ichhu Dam
(iii) Galudih Barrage
(iv) Kharkai Barrage

Recently on 31st August, 2003, the new Chief Minister—Mr. Arjun Munda has inaugurated the Chandil Dam. The main aim of this dam is to increase irrigated area in these states like Jharkhand, West Bengal and Orissa covering 2,55,000 hectares. It was the target of the government to complete this project in 2001. The Chandil dam would provide irrigation facilities to 29 villages.

Other benefits of the dam are as follows :

(i) Increased Water Supply,
(ii) Generation of farm employment (1,38,000),
(iii) Increased food grain production, and
(iv) Moderation of flood damage.

The Swarnarekha Multi-purpose Project has been given top priority in the Indian agricultural strategy. It is a project where men, minds, machines and materials coalesce to bring prosperity to a region hitherto deprived.

The Swarnarekha river passes through (the middle of) Tata Industrial City. The position of drinking water in different areas is as given below :

Table 17.1 : Need and Supply of Water in Jamshedpur

Area	*Requirement per day*	*Supply per day*
Mango notified area	3.3 million gallon	1.3 million anon
Jugsalai Municipal Area	1.55 million gallon	0.3 million gallon
Adityapur Industrial Area	3.3 million gallon	1.5 million gallon

Apart from this there is increase in population everyday and there is the shortage of rainfall in Jharkhand. And on the other hand, there is scheme to send water to water deficit areas through irrigation projects. And the water-level is going down everyday. All these indicate that there is no proper use of water, it will pose a serious threat.[6]

The Swarnarekha Project was to uproot forests on 3111 hectares of land. It was stipulated that trees will be planted in 4500 hectares of land. How far this has been achieved needs serious consideration.

Koel-Karo Project

The Koel-Karo Project is an important project of Jharkhand. This project will benefit Jharkhand and its neighbouring states of Orissa and Madhya Pradesh. If this project is completed four thousand families of 114 villages will be displaced. Almost 50,000 (fifty thousand) hectares of land will be submerged in water. This project has the target of generating 710 megawatts of electricity. This project is likely to cost Rs. 17,000 crores.[7]

In the coal belt of Jharkhand, Damodar was the only source of drinking water for the local inhabitants from 1940 to 1970. After 1980 there was a tremendous change in this area and the use of water was doubled and there was unprecedented rise in human population. Along with it there was massive felling of trees resulting in shortage of water. The shortage of water is also due to pond projects which maintain the immensity of water in particular areas, where there is greenness and happiness. In other areas where there is poverty there is scarcity of water and loss of forest, the local people have to be dependent for pure drinking water on wells and tubewells and in the summer the whole coal-belt suffers from acute shortage of water.

The irrigation projects which are meant for proper water management proved to be white elephant. The chief aim of these projects is to provide water to water deficit areas. The local people are objecting to these projects because these projects will do more harm than good to them. Many families will be uprooted and displaced and there will be serious problem of rehabilitation. In recent years there has been stiff opposition from the local people. They have resorted to violent agitation. They do not allow the outside engineers and contractors to function and they are driven away. In 1987 the local people staged a stiff demonstration and the administration resorted to firing in which 7 people were killed. In police Lathi-charge many innocent people were wounded. It is due to the stiff opposition followed by massive agitation, the Koel-Karo Project was badly delayed.[8]

The opposition of the local people is not meaningless. The State Government undertake the construction of canals without consulting the local people. Before undertaking such projects the State Government must take the local people into confidence by inviting their view-points and by considering all pros and cons of the project. Water is a natural gift which when stopped will automatically generate dissatisfaction of the local people. The interlinking of one river with another will be meaningless. Now-a-days many companies have started selling water in bottles in the name of mineral water. It is being considered to provide these companies with the task of inter-linking rivers. If this materializes, the people will not be getting drinking water without any cost. Cauvery Water Project may be cited as an example. The Tamil Nadu Government is objecting to this project. The people of Tamil Nadu are siding with the Tamil Nadu Government. The Tamil Nadu Government have filed a case in the Supreme Court so that definite amount of water could be released. The Supreme Court have decided against the Central Government. Such a situation will give rise to a new politics which will fan terrorism and secessionism. There is shortage of pure drinking water in Tamil Nadu since long.

There is large scale sale of pure water in Tamil Nadu. The poor people have to bear the brunt of it while the multinational companies making good profit.

Water Resource in Jharkhand

The following are the details of availability of average pure water in different districts of Jaharkhand till 2003 :

Table 17.2 : Availability of pure water in Jharkhand

District	*Average of Pure Water*
Dhanbad	59.71%
West Singhbhum	49.50%
East Singhbhum	49.32%
Dumka	34.89%
Ranchi	30.73%
Lohardaga	25.23%
Giridih	23.58%
Godda	13.33%

From Fig. 17.1, it is clear that the lowest average of pure water is in Godda whereas the highest average is in Dhanbad. In Dhanbad C.C.L., B.C.C.L. and Water Supply Department of the Government are active in purification of water. It is also a fact that due to the lowering of water level and discharge of wastes from different factories into the river, pure water is being polluted everyday. In such a situation to provide water into the hands of private companies will be definitely harmful and the country and the government cannot escape from its fatal consequences. Its solution has to be sought keeping the interest of the public.

Water is a benevolent gift of nature. It has been available to all living beings and mankind free of cost. But the story of man and the

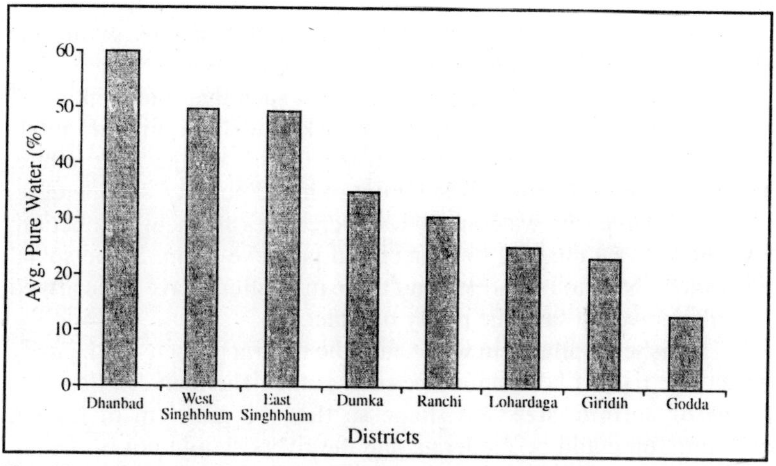

Fig. 17.1 : Water Resource in Jharkhand in Different Districts

development of mankind, rapid industrialization, unreasonable felling of trees, construction of major irrigation projects and scarcity of rain water and man's misuse of water have resulted in the birth of water-crisis.

Conclusion

First of all the government must make projects keeping in mind the judiciary and the welfare of the people so that water disputes like the Koel-Karo dispute do not raise their ugly heads. The State Government and the Central Government must act in unison so that this will eradicate the possibilities of going to the court. Whenever such a project of reaching water to water-scarcity areas from areas where it is in abundance, necessary law has to be enacted and full proprietorship has to be taken by the government so that the public cannot resort to any agitation by making it a local issue.

Water has to be considered as governmental property and it has to be protected from all sorts of pollution by enacting stringent laws so that culprits cannot go unpunished. It should be made a non-bailable offence.

In order to meet the requirements of the local people water reservoirs have to be built on small rivers.

Water has to be kept aloof from the hands of private companies whose only aim is to earn as much profit as they can by giving the allurement to the government in the name of foreign exchange.

In India natural geological situation is such that inter-linking of one river with another is a herculean task. It will require enormous capital which can be procured from levying tax on the poor public. The poor public cannot bear the brunt of it and poverty will increase.

In a bid to purify water many water-creatures are facing extinction; laws have to be enacted to protect and preserve them. Some social institutions have to be formed and these institutions have to be armed with the power to save the purity of water.

The fishes available in water have the natural propensity to purify water. The fishing laws should be such as the fishermen can fish only fishes of definite size and shape so that the problem of human consumption could be moderate and the rivers should not be devoid of fish. The protection of fish is necessary otherwise it will be an object of display, fun and entertainment in acquarium.

The Central Government undertook the Ganga Purification Project. But despite huge expenditure how far it has been successful is for all to conjecture. The pollution instead of lessening will increase.

NOTES

1. *Yojana*, May 2003.
2. Subernarekha Multi-purpose Project.
3. PHD West Singhbhum.
4. *Hindustan Daily News* 18th Nov. 1993.
S. *Prabhat Khabar*, 9 Sept. 2003.
6. *Prabhat Khabar*, 25 Sept. 2003.
7. *Prabhat Khabar*, 24 Sept. 2003.
8. Irrigation Department, Ranchi.

18

Problems of Irrigation in Hazaribag District

PRAWEEN KR. SHARMA AND KAMLA PRASAD

Introduction

Water is an important input for successful agriculture. "The process of supplying water to crops by artificial means such as canals, wells, tube wells, tanks etc. from the source of water such as rivers, tanks, ponds or underground water is called irrigation" (Agarwal, 1980).

Irrigation plays an important role in the agricultural economy of any district. However, in Hazaribag district, due to hilly topography of the area, there is not much scope for exploitation of surface water. The other means of irrigation left are exploitation of groundwater and taking recourse to lift irrigation. Tank irrigation is not very popular. Groundwater exploitation has also its limitations (Ahmed, 1965).

Study Area

It lies between 23°30′ to 24°30′ North latitude and 85°00′ to 86°00′ East latitude and the range of altitude is between 600 m above mean sea level. The district covers an area of 5965.06 km forms the Northern portion of Chotanagpur plateau (North Chotanagpur division) consists of Hazaribag Sadar, Churchu, Barkagaon, Keredari, Katkamsandi, Ichak, Barhi, Bishugarh, Mandu, Gola, Ramgarh, Patratu, Chauparan, Barkatha Blocks. The agriculture is the kingpin of the economy of Hazaribag district.

Need for Irrigation

The major part of Hazaribag district depends upon the monsoon

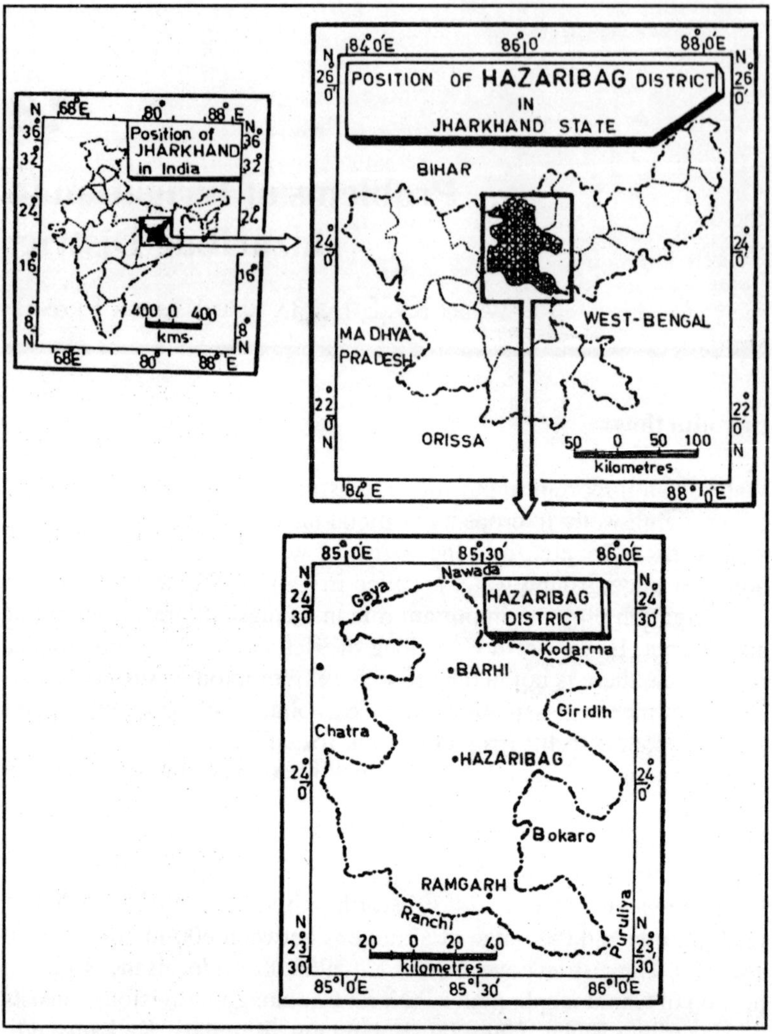

Fig. 18.1 : Hazaribag District—Location of the Study Area

rainfall. Unfortunately, rainfall in India or Hazaribag district is uncertain, unreliable, irregular, variable, seasonal and unevenly distributed. The variability of rainfall is very high in areas of cropped land in Hazaribag. In dry season irrigation is badly needed for successful growth of the crops (Bhatt, 1999).

"Water" being the most important input resources in agricultural farming processes. The source of this water is rainfall. The distribution or rainfall and quantum received are not only inadequate but also completely uncertain. Irrigation is the most important factor of agriculture and farming. Now we shall discuss the present and potential use of irrigation facilities of Hazaribag district. Irrigation facilitics in the district are very meagre. Irrigation in the broadest sense refers to the drainage area of a stream, channel or a river & the source of water being rain. Irrigation in any region is not equally distributed throughout the year, becomes a necessity. As the food is essential for living being similarly irrigation is for sound cultivation. Unreliable and unequal distribution of rain has compelled man to realize the importance of irrigation. Irrigation in Hazaribag district is very limited. Most of the villages carry on the traditional system of irrigation and the extent of irrigation area is also very limited (Bhatt, 1999).

Irrigation plays a dominant role in the agricultural economy of the district. In Hazaribag District uneven and irregular distribution of rainfall during agricultural seasons make the necessity of irrigation. These days production of various crops during different agricultural harvests has further accelerated requirement of irrigation. It may be noted that previously people used to grow a few crops depending upon the natural precipitation and seasons lacking rainfall used to be without farming activities. Presently the production of crops even during seasons having negligible rain has compelled farmers to develop irrigation means. Virtually production of Rabi and garma crops and lot of vegetables to a considerable extent depends upon irrigation and these crops have gained significance because of changing food habits and consumption (Sinha & Singh, 2003, p. 87).

Means of Irrigation

After Independence, considerable attention has been paid to the provision of irrigation facilities in the district. Several major schemes have been taken up by the Damodar Valley Corporation, Konar river, Chharwa Dam and Gonda Dam. Besides, irrational facilities have been extended in the district through a number of medium and major irrigation schemes—Wells, Tanks, Rahat, Nala, Pumps, Electric Pumps, Open Boring, Tube wells and Hand Pumps.

In Hazaribag district about 13,324 hectares of land constituting 13.61 per cent of total agricultural area is irrigated. Irrigation is important for "*Aghani*" crops of rice cultivation but for the cultivation in the dry seasons for rabi crops it is more important in this region. "*Rabi*" crop season always becomes rainless and the important "*Rabi*" crops particularly wheat and vegetables are increasing day by day (Chaudhary, 1957).

There are three major sources of irrigation in the District, i.e. Canal, Tanks and Wells including Tubewells. The following Table 18.1 shows the sourcewise irrigation in Hazaribag district :

Table 18.1 : Irrigated Area in Hazaribagh, 1998

Sources of Irrigation	*Total area irrigated (in hectares)*	*Percentage of the total area irrigated*
Canals	1062	7.97
Tanks	2272	17.08
Tube wells	2825	21.20
Well	7639	34.80
Other sources	2526	18.95
Total	16324	100.00

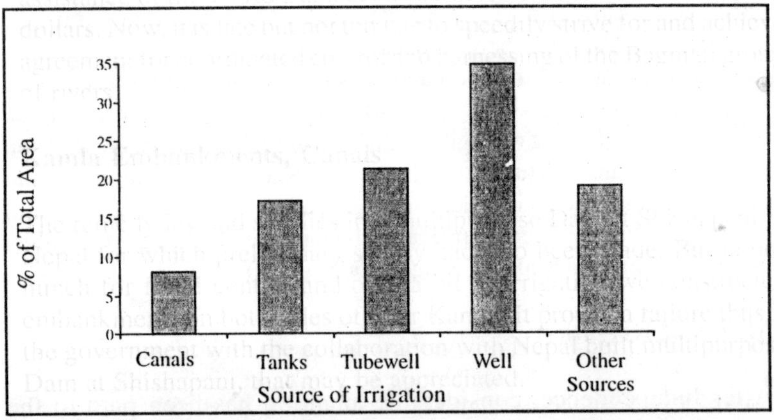

Fig. 18.2 : Sourcewise Net Irrigated Area in Hazaribagh District, 1997-1998

Table 18.1 shows that irrigation facilities is available to 13,324 hectares of land in Hazaribag district by means of canals, about 1,062 hectares constituting 7.97 per cent of the cultivated land has the facilities of canal irrigation in the district. The wells cover about 4,639 hectares constituting 34.80 per cent irrigated area in the district. The tanks cover 2,272 hectares of the irrigated land in the district constituting 17.08 per cent and other sources cover about 7,526 hectares constituting 18.95 per cent of the irrigated lands of Hazaribag district (Hussain, 1999).

Geographical Factors Favouring Irrigation

Hazaribag district is mostly covered by hills and jungles. The soil is rocky and sandy producing jungles and bushes. The cultivable lands are divided into two categories lowland and upland. Many tanks dry up during the dry season and fail to provide irrigation when it is needed most in the event of a drought. The groundwater level fails and enough water is not available in the well when it is needed most. Tubewell can draw a lot of groundwater from neighbouring areas and make the ground dry and unfit. Hazaribag District is a plateau area and the rocks are hard and the surface relief is uneven. Therefore, it is difficult to have canals and wells, tube wells and tanks are used for irrigation (Khullar, 1999).

Problems of Irrigation

Certain geographical factors have helped in developing irrigation in different parts of Hazaribag district. The undulating relief and hard rocks makes it difficult to dig canals and wells. There is little percolation of rainwater due to hard rocky structure and groundwater is not available in large quantity. It is difficult to carry water from the tank to the field through the rocky terrain. The well may dry up and may be rendered useless for irrigation if excessive water is taken out of it. In summer the groundwater level falls and enough water is not available in the well and tube well when it is needed most. Because of rocky structure the development of tubewell becomes difficult. A few rivers have also enabled the facility of canal irrigation. The area is not suitable for the development of canal irrigation due to presence of rough terrain and lack of perennial rivers. At the same time rocky structure beneath the surface unable the development of wells and tube well irrigation. Certainly the area is suitable for the development of minor irrigation schemes and artificial reservoirs which have not been developed as yet (Prasad, 1993).

Suggestions and Conclusion

Hazaribag district is a plateau area with a vast diversity of climate, topography and vegetation. Rainfall distribution is very much erratic and uncertain. The major part of the cropped land depends upon the direct rainfall and is wholly dependent on the monsoon. Irrigation is an important input in terms of its utilization and management to achieve better crop production and productivity (Singh *et al.*, 2003).

Well irrigation is comparatively better developed which irrigates 34.80 per cent of net irrigated area. Well is simplest and cheapest source of irrigation and the poor farmer can easily afford it. Some of the canals provide perennial irrigation and supply water when needed. Canals carry a lot of sediment brought down by the river. Although the initial cost involved in canal irrigation is much higher but it is quite cheap in the long run. Most of the tanks are natural and do not involve heavy cost for their construction. Even an individual farmer constructed on rocky bed and have longer life span. In many tanks, fishing is also carried on. This supplements both the food resources and income of the farmer (Singh, *et al.,* 1999).

Based on the above conditions use of water for irrigation becomes necessary wherever agricultural activities have intensified. Surface and underground water have enabled cultivators to adopt different methods of irrigation. Because of rough terrain natural water bodies are negligible. Certainly the region provides ideal conditions for the development of artificial reservoirs or tanks in Hazaribag district. Most of the rivers in Hazaribag district are seasonal and dry up in summer season. Therefore, they cannot supply water to canals throughout the year. There are several streams which become torrential during rainy seasons. The best use of this water is to impound it by constructing tanks, otherwise this water will go waste.

REFERENCES

Agarwal, A.N. *Indian Agriculture Problems, Progress and Prospects*, Rawat Publication, 1980.

Ahmed, E., Bihar : *A Physical Economic and Regional Geography,* Ranchi, 1965.

Bhatt, S.C., *The District Gazetteer of Jharkhand,* Gyan Publishing House, New Delhi-2, 1999.

Bhatt, S.C., *The District Gazetteer of Jharkhand,* Gyan Publishing House, New Delhi-2, 1999.

Chaudhary, P.C. Ray, *Bihar District Gazetteer, Hazaribag,* Secretariat Press, Bihar, Patna, 1957.

Choudhary, P.E. Roy, *Bihar District Gazetteer's, Hazaribag,* Secretariat Press, Bihar, Patna, 1957.

Hussain Majed, *Systematic Agricultural Geography,* Rawat Publication, New Delhi, 1999.

Khullar, D.R., *A Comprehensive Geography,* India, Kallyani Publication, New Delhi.

Prasad, Basudeo, "Prospects and problem of dry-land farming in Hazaribag district," Unpublished Ph.D. Thesis, Ranchi University, 1993.

Singh, and Sinha, *Land and People,* Jharkhand, p. 92, 2003.

Singh, Jasbir and Dhillon, S.S., *Agriculture Geography,* Tata McGraw-Hill Publication Company Limited, New Delhi, 1999.

19

Kawar Lake Water Resource Management

KUMAR BRAJ NANDAN

Introduction

The Kawar is an inland fresh water lake on the north eastern side of Burhi Gandak river. It spreads over the area under Majhaul, Ekamba, Narayan Pipar, Parora, Kanausi, Manikpur, Rajour, Sakra, Jamangala-garh and Jamangalpur villages of Begusarai district. It is located at 25°38′ N latitude and 86°08′ E longitude. The average elevation of the area is 35 metres above msl. Its water reservoir area is about 24 km^2 which swells over 64 km^2 during the rainy season in flood condition. The ephemeral land around the reservoir is marshy (1971).

The nearest Airport is at Patna, the capital of the State of Bihar and is about 125 kilometre away from the district headquarter. Begusarai is the nearest Railway Station, nearly 22 kilometres away from the lake area. The National Highways (N.H.-31) also starts from Barauni (Zero Mile) and goes up to Assam[2] (Mandal, 1994). Buses run quite frequently in this area. There is a blacktop road reaching up to the lake. The location map of Kawar lake has been shown in Fig. 19.1.

Importance

Kawar lake is one of the biggest freshwater lakes of India. The lake is famous as it provides winter habitat for migratory water birds. It has been identified as one of the sixteen lakes of the country for its conservation and management mainly to protect migratory and non-migratory birds. This area was declared as a prohibited area under section 37 of the Wild-life Protection Act, 1972 (Act 53) by the

Fig. 19.1 : Location and Characteristics of Kawar Lake in Begusarai District (Bihar)

Government of Bihar and National Bird Sanctuary on June 20, 1989 by the Government of India (Chaudhary, 1993) (Fig. 19.1).

Topography

The topography of the Kawar lake has been made by meandering courses of the Burhi Gandak river. At some point of time the river was flowing through this area but slowly it has changed its course leaving the depression formed at the time of flood through sheet wash erosion. The lake, therefore, is made up of depression fed by flood and rain water. The water table varies from one metre to 5 metres in the entire area (1984).

This lake is more or less flat. However, depression upto 2.1 m is found at some places, some area of this lake remain permanently waterlogged throughout the year.

The Kawar lake has been formed probably due to meandering courses of the Burhi-Gandak river.

The meander has occurred in the extensive plains of deep alluvial soil. The ox-bow or brasslet type of meander has occurred in the bend which is sporadically circular with high curvature. This circular bend has two hooked ends which are in line of the main river Burhi Gandak. It also resembles with this type of meander is an advance stage of 'horse-shoe' type. The ox-bow lake dots the lower plain with its name as 'Kawar Tal', leaving the river Burhi Gandak far away. The neck of the brasslet has been gradually filled with sediments, because of clearing action of the flowing stream (Nandan and Mandal, 2002).

The soil of Kawar lake area is sandy loam rich with humus and is also very fertile. As this lake area remains wet and submerged for longer period, it has developed some special type of vegetation and organisms. The emergent, submergent and floating plants present some unique type of representative flora and fauna. Their unique type of association attracts specially water fowl habitat not only for the year round residents but also for the millions of migratory birds. Hence, it is a spectacular wetland habitat and perhaps one of the largest fresh water inland wetlands in the country (Nandan, 2002).

Climatic Condition

The climate around Kawar lake is characterised by hot dry summer (March to mid-June), warm-moist rainy (mid-June to October) and cold-sub-humid winter (November to February). Monsoon rain is the major source of water to the lake. The area experiences a mean annual rainfall of 143.64 cm with highest precipitation around 35 cm in July/ August (Fig. 19.2). The maximum and minimum temperatures range from 21.57°C-35.83°C and 8.61°C-28.17°C respectively. The relative humidity varies between 56.12 to 80.77 per cent recording August/ September as the most humid month of the year.

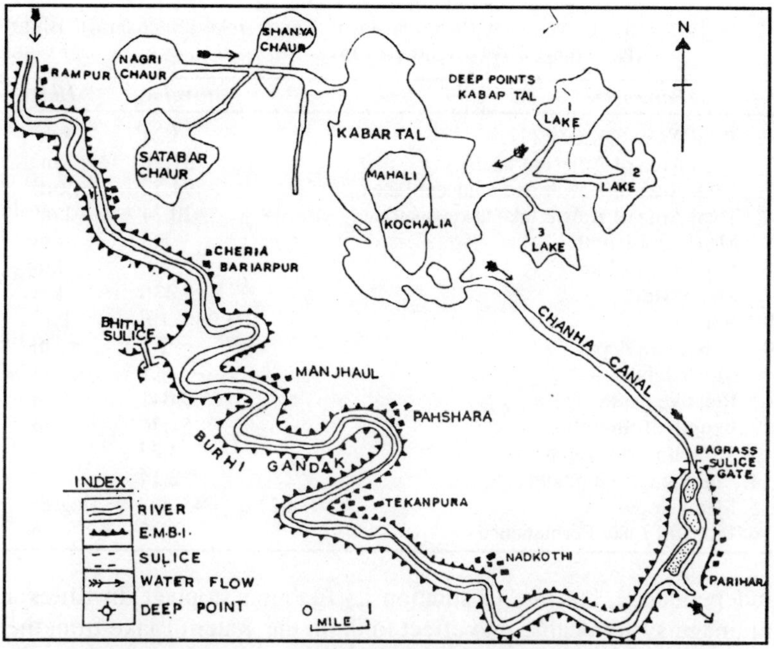

Fig. 19.2 : Catchment Area and Drainage System of Kawar Lake

Catchment Area

Kawar Lake is divided into three major segments, namely Mahalaya, Kochalaya and Sinra. Among these, Mahalaya is the deepest and largest. Its average altitude is 34.5 m above MSL and overspread in an area of 1.85 km^2. In the north-western part of Kawar lake the three feeder chaurs are known as Nagri chaur, Shanya Chaur and Satabar Chaur. On the eastern side of Kawar lake the three artificial chaurs are named as number one, two and three. All these are situated north of Drainage (Chanha) canal which connects Kawar lake with the Burhi Gandak river. On the southern side of Kawar some of the important feeder area Cheria-Bariarpur, Majhaul, Pahshara, Tekanpura and other villages are located. The Drainage (Chanha) canal meets with the Burhi Gandak river with a sluice gate near Bagrass village.

Kawar Lake Drainage System

Kawar lake drainage system existed even much before the

Table 19.1 : Some Relevant Information of Kawar lake (Begusarai), Bihar (November 1991-October 1993)

S.No.	*Parameters*	*Value*	*Unit*
1.	Total Area of Kawar lake	63.24	km^2
2.	Total Area of Adjacent lakes	31.28	km^2
3.	Total Area of Kawar and adjacent lakes	94.52	km^2
4.	Total Area of Kawar lake always submerged	20.24	km^2
5.	Maximum length	8.3	km
6.	Maximum width	4.6	km
7.	Mean width	2.438	km
8.	Volume	$3.036x10^7$	km^2
9.	Maximum depth	2.1	m
10.	Mean depth	1.5	m
11.	Relative depth	0.041	m
12.	Length of Shoreline	51.76	km
13.	Shoreline development	3.25	–
14.	Volume Development	2.14	–
15.	Mean slope	0.0827 or 4°43'46"	Degree
16.	Index of Lake Permanence	1.5	m

independence, but due to siltation its function stopped. In fifties a drainage system came into effect to drain the water of lake from the west of Kawar. Subsequently, the drainage channel meets the river "Burhi Gandak" at a place about 12 km in the east. The lake as well as its drainage system yielded production of fish. Afterwards due to scarcity of water the quantity of fish in the lake dwindles and the fishermen of the area were adversely affected. At the same time fertile land was released for cultivation. Aghani paddy mostly sown in these fields. It gave bumper yield when the area was not flooded. The economic turnover of the lake by the farming was two and half times more than that of fishing.

Due to these benefits land has been settled in the lake either by the *ex-Jamindars* or by the State Government. Thus there seems a line of conflict between two groups of people. However, the disputes have been resolved by giving rights to fishermen for nine months and farmers for three months to exercise economic activities and maintain harmony.

But in the mid-seventies the above drainage system from Kawar lake to the Burhi Gandak river stopped functioning again. The land owners quickly realised the loss. They wanted to have the exclusive rights of fishing and trapping of water birds in and around the lake. This type of demand of right sparked a dispute between the Sahani

Table 19.2 : Seasonal Variations of Water Spreadover Areas of Kawar Lake (Begusarai), Bihar (November 1991—October 1992)

(Approx Values in Acres)

Lake Area	*Seasons*		
Zonal names	*Winter Nov. 91 Feb. 92*	*Summer Mar. 92 June 92*	*Monsoon July 92 Oct. 92*
Jaimangla Garh	12.0	5.0	501.0
Bohara	107.0	92.0	208.0
Bela	621.0	420.0	892.1
Rupai	305.0	203.0	400.2
Bansahi	1172.0	800.0	1404.3
Barda	943.0	407.0	2006.1
Simara	319.0	105.0	411.2
Rajora	211.0	103.0	309.1
Katahi	567.0	350.0	607.0
Surkhuti	93.0	61.0	213.0
Kochlaya	864.0	604.3	1204.0
Kabaila	1549.0	1069.1	1555.0
Bhirokhara	67.0	40.3	98.0
Mahalaya	1069.0	606.2	1402.0
Bahi	103.0	46.1	206.0
Nain	91.0	42.0	203.0
Petua	68.0	36.0	81.0
Larkatia	102.0	89.0	212.0
Gordhua	105.0	80.0	223.0
Amra	1043.0	680.0	1499.0
Chatra	**	**	66.0
Medhua	**	**	104.0
Sopare	**	**	391.0
Daitadih	**	**	19.0
Chatar	**	**	800.0
Gubari	**	**	785.0
Total water spread over areas of Kawar lake including all Zones and sub-zones	9411.0	5839.0	15800.00
Total water spread over areas of Adjacent lakes	5729.0	3111.0	7730.0
Total water spreaded over areas of Kawar lake and its adjacent lakes	15140.0	8950.0	23530.0

** The site became dry. So data could not be recorded.

community (fishermen) and the owners. This matter was sent to the State Government. But its decision is yet to come. However, Sahani community claims that fishing and trapping rights had been vested with them by the order of the Calcutta High Court a century ago during British regime. Up till now Sahani community is enjoying those privileges and rights. The drainage division Irrigation Department. Government of Bihar, located at Manjhaul village had again prepared a scheme in which the water of the lake would be drained into the river Burhi Gandak through another short channel. But due to the interference by the forest department this scheme has been shelved and the people started to look at this national heritage from the conservation, management and tourist point of view.

Inflow-Outflow of Water

For the present the water comes into the Kawar from its catchment area. At the time of flood it comes through drainage canal made amidst-meandering courses of chanha Nala. The depth of the canal is 3.5 metres and width 14 metres only. Therefore, drainage canal helps in the outflow of water from Kawar which rises slowly with the rise of water in the Burhi Gandak and subsides slowly as the level of water in the Burhi Gandak goes down. During flood the water comes into Kawar at the rate of 500 cusecs per second and it goes out of the same rate but during lean months it is not more than 25 cusecs and in May and June water does not go out (Table 19.3).

Table 19.3 : Average monthly inflow and outflow water discharge in Kawar Lake, Begusarai District (1999)

Month	*Inflow in cusecs*	*Outflow in Cusecs*
January	–	–
February	–	–
March	–	–
April	–	–
May	–	–
June	310	90
July	1276	1000
August	1345	1000
September	736	500
October	352	152
November	231	27
December	–	–

Source : Flood Forecasting Dept., Government of Bihar, Patna.

Management of Fresh Water Bodies

The inland water bodies like rivers, lakes, ponds, pools and puddles are of common occurrences all over North Bihar. They are of great economic value to men living therewith. The demand of growing human population for space and food are ever rising. Fresh water bodies are being used increasingly for these purposes. Management of fresh water bodies should aim to maintain them in useful form at a high productive level with provision for removal of plants and animals for human use. Thus a thorough knowledge of drainage, total water and runoff, the biotic communities, the ecological lifecycle of economically important species, etc. rate of water loss through evaporation should be calculated. The management with regard to its economic use such as quantity and periodicity of water removal for irrigation, maintenance of certain fish and plant crops, the extent of carrying capacity of the water body towards pollutants like town refuse, etc. should be undertaken. A well managed river or lake is one which serves in a multipurpose way the human society without itself degenerating whereas in mismanaged fresh water lake the utility is short-term, less efficient and in most cases the system degenerates due to excessive silting, pollution, or rapid drying or due to preponderance of noxious weeds etc.

Fresh water cover in a relatively very small area of earth's surface, but due to their multiple utility, human culture and settlements have developed mostly along rivers. The freshwater bodies like rivers, streams, ponds and puddles are used variously. Rivers are used for (a) irrigation, (b) transport, (c) supply of drinking water, (d) hydro-electric power, (e) aquatic sports and recreation, (f) bathing, (g) for draining out the municipal and industrial refuse, (h) fishing and so on.

There is a range upto which any of these items could be put to use and they are interrelated. For instance excess removal of water for irrigation would affect all other aspects. The pollutants will not be sufficiently diluted due to reduced quantity of water, and may become toxic and injurious for drinking and bathing. It is essential, therefore, that aquatic ecocsystems should be properly studied and management should be done considering the interrelations among multiple items of utility.

Conclusion

The ecosystem found in the Kawar tal and in its watershed should be preserved and protected for the future generation. This is the pride for the state of Bihar and the nation as it comes under the purview of Ramsar Convention. It also attracts very large number of migratory birds, micro-organisms for which this natural eco-system needs conservation. It is said that farmers of the area are trying to cultivate the land which comes under Kawar and machhua society not only to catch fishes but they also trap birds during night hours even it has been considered as illegal. It is happy to note that only recently the Government of India is trying to survey the whole area for the nature conservation.

REFERENCES

Choudhary, U.P., "Geography, Aspects of Wetlands in North Bihar," unpublished Ph.D. Thesis, Bhagalpur University, 1993.

Mandal, R.B. The value of wetlands in North East India, Wetlands Archaeology, (Ed., *Nature Conservation,* M. Cox *et al.*, 1994, p. 30.

Nandan, K.B. & Mandal, R.B., "Ecological Diversities of Kawar Tal," *East West Geographer,* 13 (1), 2002, pp. 16-23.

Nandan, K.B. "Inventory of the Economic Resources and Their Sustenance level in the Kabar Watershed," Begusarai District Ph.D. Thesis (Unpublished); T.M. Bhagalpur Universtiy, Bhagalpur (India), 2002, pp. 232.

Ramsar Convention, UNESCO, Ramsar, Iran, Feb. 1971.

Wetlands Conference in Czechoslovakia; Strategy and Trends, Washington D.C., U.S., 1984, p. 22.

20

Food Security Management During Floods in Bihar State, India*

Girija Nandan Singh and Sudha Kumari Singh

Introduction

Indian subcontinent is one among the world's most disaster prone areas. Flood is an annual feature in the Indo-Gangetic-Brahmaputra plains. The most flood-prone areas in India are the Ganga and Brahmaputra plains in the north and north-east India, which carry 60 per cent of the nation's total river flow (Bhanumurthy, 2004). Nearly 75 per cent of total rainfall is concentrated over a short monsoon period of four months (June-September). The plains have low gradient and the rivers carry huge load of sediments causing erosion of the banks in the upper reaches and over-topping in the lower segments. Thus heavy rainfall (10,000 mm in the north-eastern region and 1000-2000 mm in the central part of northern plains), low slope gradient and vast amount of water coming down the Himalayan Mountains lead to widespread floods. According to Rashtriya Barh Ayog (National Flood Commission) over 40 million hectares of land area in the country experiences periodical floods (Bhadram, 2004). The annual average cropped area affected is approximately 3.7 million hectares (Fig. 20.1) With rampant deforestation, ever increasing population, rapid industrialisation and more and more growth in settlement and construction of roads in the flood plains, flood hazards have become a great natural disaster not only around the world over in general, but also in north India in particular.

The state of Bihar, located in the central part of northern plains of India, has an area of 94,163 sq. km. and a total population of

* Paper presented before the 30th Congress of the International Geographical Union, 15-20 August 2004, Glasgow, U.K.

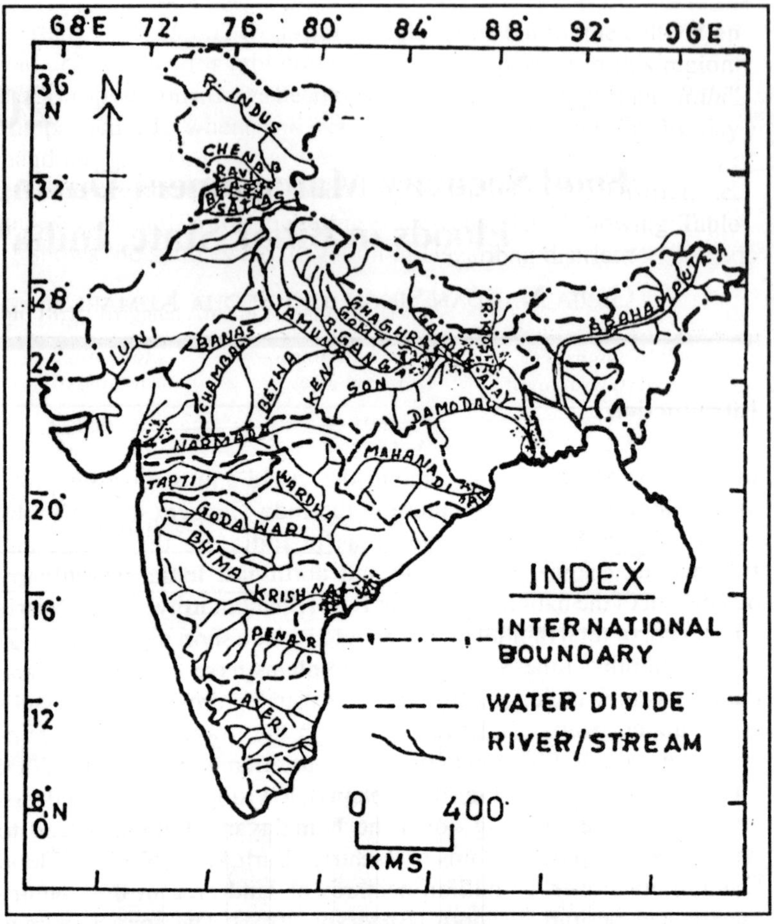

Fig. 20.1 : Flood Affected Area of India.

82,878,796 persons (2001). Bihar is a flood prone state where 19 out of a total number of 37 districts and 119 community development blocks (out of 533 C.D. Blocks) are affected by recurrent floods during rainy season almost every year. During the time of flood thousands of houses collapse, large areas of croplands is destroyed and many of the cattle population either die or are washed away. In the year 2003 alone about 200 persons died in the floods. As per government reports a population of 42.45 lakh had been reeling under flood, standing crop in 3.25 lakh hectares have been damaged and 15,986 houses were destroyed (*Times of India*, Patna, Sept. 12, 2003). Although it is not possible to prevent the occurrence of this natural disaster, yet the suffering of the mankind living in the area may be minimised to a great extent by developing suitable measures.

The worst aspect of the flood disaster is the shortage of food materials for a large number of people marooned in flood waters. In the year 2003, the Government of Bihar took the help of some 4 helicopters and dropped 5000 food packets among the flood affected people, which was quite insufficient (Singh and Singh, 2003).

Objectives of Study

The purpose of this paper is to suggest some ways and means for streamlining food security measures during floods in Bihar. Although, the officials of Bihar Government declare that there is enough foodgrains in godowns located in state capital and elsewhere, but only a little reaches to the needy people during floods. Some of the measures suggested in the paper may help in food security management during floods in this part of India (Bihar State).

Methodology and Sources of Data

The methodology adopted in the present study is based on primary and secondary informations from the following sources :

(a) Ganga Flood Control Commission under the Ministry of Water Resources, Government of India, was set up *vide* Resolution No. FC-47 (2) 72 dated 18th April, 1972. The Commission was entrusted the task of preparing comprehensive plan of flood control of the Ganga basin. The Commission has also to examine all major and medium flood control, drainage, anti-waterlogging and anti-erosion schemes of the Ganga basin states (Annual Report 1994-95 of GFCC). All the data of flood extent and flood damage etc. were collected from the office of Ganga Flood Control Commission, Patna.

(b) The work of preparing the flood maps of Ganga sub-basins with the help of satellite imageries was entrusted to the Space Application Centre, Ahmedabad in August 1978 in association with the Survey of India. At present NRSA (National Remote Sensing Agency, Hyderabad) supplies remote sensing data and satellite imageries of the flood affected area. These data, informations and maps were collected from Bihar Remote Sensing Application Centre, Patna.

(c) India Meteorological Department provides meteorological support in the form quantitative precipitation forecasts (QPF) and heavy rainfall warnings for different river basins. Flood Meteorological Office at Patna provided such data for the Kosi, the Mahananda, the Baghmati, the Kamala, the Gandak, the Burhi Gandak, Upper Son and the Punpun basins of Bihar.

(d) Survey of India topographical sheets (on a scale of 1: 250,000 and 1: 50,000) and road maps provide the minor details of terrain of the flood prone area especially North Bihar.

(e) The author has gathered large amount of data and other information from all above noted sources besides getting a good amount of information from media reports. An intensive fieldwork of the flood prone areas of North and South Bihar has enabled the author to suggest certain measures for food security during floods in Bihar.

Floods in Bihar

Bihar is a flood prone State in the Ganga basin of Indian subcontinent. The Ganga basin covers the States of Haryana, NCT of Delhi, Himachal Pradesh, Rajasthan, Madhya Pradesh, Uttar Pradesh, Uttaranchal, Bihar and West Bengal (Fig. 20.1). Floods are an annual feature in some parts or others of these states. The Ganga basin constitutes 23 river systems (Annual Report, Ganga Flood Control, Commission, Patna—1994-95). In Bihar 1.5 million hectares of land and 7.6 million population were affected by floods (Table 20.1) the damage caused by floods was to the tune of Rs. 963.35 million.

Fig. 20.2 shows the flood affected areas of Bihar state. In the north Bihar there are eight sub-basins of the mightly Ganga basin. From west to east these are the basins of the Ghaghra, the Gandak, the Burhi Gandak, the Bagmati, the Adhwara Group of Rivers, the Kamala-Balan, the Kosi and the Mahananda. In South Bihar, an area elongated along the south bank of the Ganga is also affected by floods every year. The rivers causing flood in their lower reaches in the south are the Son, the Punpun, the Falgu, the Mahane, the Sakri, the Kiul, the Badua and the Chanan. Since the southern levee of the Ganga is high the waters of the above rivers flow parallel to the Ganga from

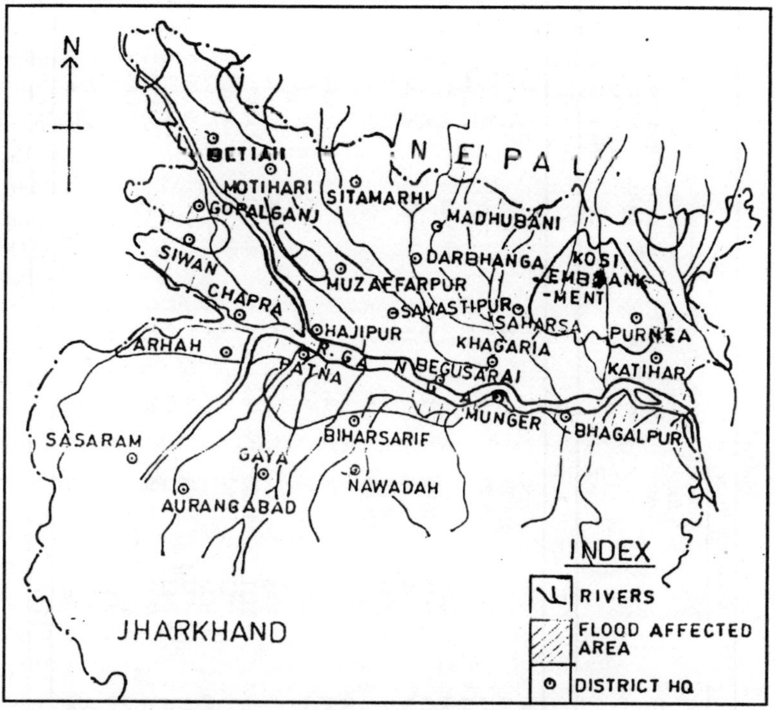

Fig. 20.2 : Flood Map of Bihar

west to east submerging vast area under flood water. It is said that the depression south of the southern bank of Ganga is the abandoned course of the Son. The mouth of this river has now shifted towards west. Now this depression is known as 'Tal' belt extending from Fatuha near Patna in the west to Munger in the east.

Floods in Bihar, as in other parts of the world, are the product of vagaries of climate on the one hand and the relief of land on the other. A great factor causing flood is the human interference with the natural drainage system as has been done in Bihar. Torrential monsoonal downpours in the Himalayan mountain catchment (150-200 cm in four monsoon months) cause high floods (Ahmad, 1965). The slope of the land in the Ganga plains of Bihar is very gentle. The average gradient of the Ganga in Bihar is 6 cm per km (4 inches per mile). Rivers coming down the Himalayas in the north and Chotanagpur Highlands in the south bring vast amount of water and silt with them. Silting of channel brings the beds of the river up and at the time of

Table 20.1 : Districtwise flood damages in Bihar in 2003

Sl. No.	Name of District	Area affected (Lakh ha.)	Population affected in lakh	*Damage fo Crops* Area in lakh ha.	*Damage fo Crops* Value Rs. lakhs	*Damage to House* Nos.	*Damage to House* Value in Rs. lakhs	Cattle lives lost nos.	Human lives lost nos.	Damage to public utilities. (Rs. lakh)	Total damage to crops, houses and public utilities (Col. 6+8+11) (in Rs. lakhs)
1	2	3	4	5	6	7	8	9	10	11	12
1.	Mazaffarpur	0.40	5.60	0.29	773.60	116	19.50	–	26	–	793.1
2.	West Champaran	0.49	3.29	0.17	1135.00	3964	514.72	–	18	1.02	1650.74
3.	East Champaran	0.50	4.07	0.31	220.66	143	28.60	–	9	–	249.26
4.	Sitamarhi	0.80	0.99	0.08	202.84	0	–	–	11	–	202.84
5.	Sheohar	0.33	3.08	0.12	198.00	1205	–	–	22	403.00	601.00
6.	Saran	0.43	6.65	0.28	181.88	375	120.40	2	9	–	302.28
7.	Gopalganj	0.20	1.05	0.90	292.82	30	8.00	1	18	27.62	328.44
8.	Darbhanga	3.04	2.70	0.03	21.66	294	38.80	–	28	–	60.46
9.	Samastipur	0.78	4.74	0.55	1213.33	2652	620.00	8	23	233.50	2066.83
10.	Madhubani	0.13	0.33	–	6.00	249	–	–	3	–	6.00
11.	Saharsa	2.15	3.40	1.38	26.90	1484	55.74	4	6	–	88.64
12.	Supaul	0.39	2.25	–	13.50	1438	28.70	–	2	6.00	48.2
13.	Madhepura	0.003	0.53	0.002	–	0	–	–	3	–	0.0
14.	Purnea	0.00	3.26	–	–	90	–	–	2	0.35	0.35
15.	Araria	0.63	2.03	0.90	6.19	2311	136.00	8	6	180.00	322.19
16.	Katihar	1.13	6.63	0.59	792.80	6162	50.62	–	5	165.87	1009.29
17.	Munger	0.10	2.34	0.02	115.00	125	6.62	–	4	–	121.62
18.	Khagaria	0.20	1.68	0.06	82.56	115	12.44	–	5	–	95.00
19.	Begusarai	0.82	1.84	0.32	346.48	165	2.75	–	9	–	349.23
20.	Bhagalpur	1.13	7.59	0.53	431.68	7297	95.30	80	18	15.40	542.38
21.	Patna	0.30	1.52	0.18	125.55	8362	126.14	–	10	–	251.69
22.	Bhojpur	0.40	4.61	0.27	86.29	6847	–	–	10	–	86.29
23.	Buxar	0.31	1.64	0.15	95.01	473	42.17	–	–	2.40	139.58
24.	Vaishali	1.14	4.21	0.59	198.90	1365	125.60	5	4	–	324.5
	Total	15.083	76.02	6.102	6566.15	45262	2032.10	108	251	1035.16	9633.50

Note : – : Nil or Not available.

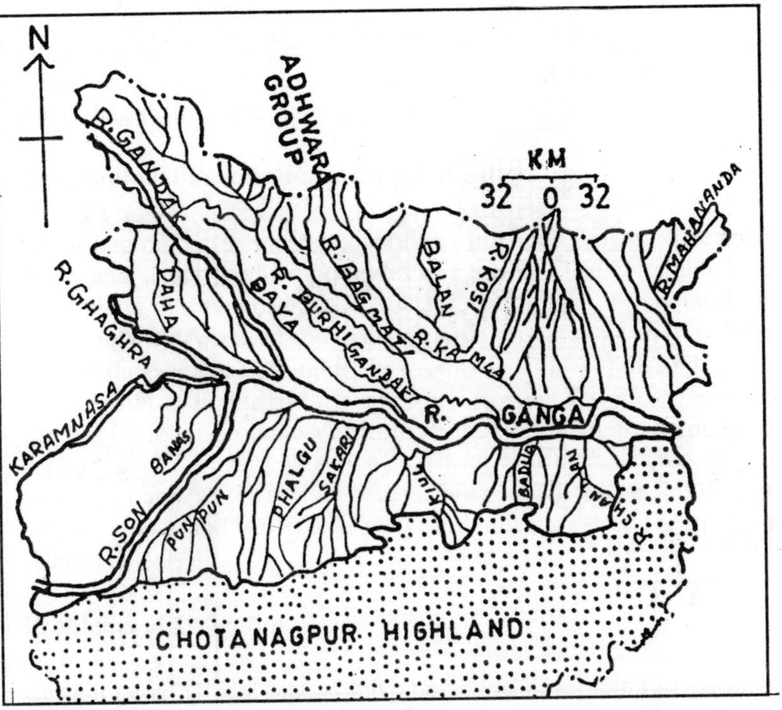

Fig. 20.3 : Bihar : Major Drainage Basins

heavy rain huge amount of water spreads in the flood plains of the rivers breaking the levee or embankment of these streams. On both sides of these streams, there are saucer type depressions known locally as chaurs beyond the levee tract. These are filled up during rains and water remains stagnant for most parts of the year. Deforestation on the hills and catchment of the Himalayas results into sudden rush of water overladen with sediments. The changing course of rivers is a general feature in the Ganga basin. The course of river Kosi has shifted some 150 km west from Purnea in the last 200 years. Artificial or man-made interference such as construction of railways, roads, canals and flood protection embankments without sufficient provision for the escape of natural drainage, bring heavy floods.

In South Bihar plain the floods in the 'Tal' and 'diara' tracts are very common. The 'tal' tract lying south of the Ganga levee is flooded by the waters of south flowing rivers from Chotanagpur highlands. The 'diaras' or the riparian tracts between two stream channels

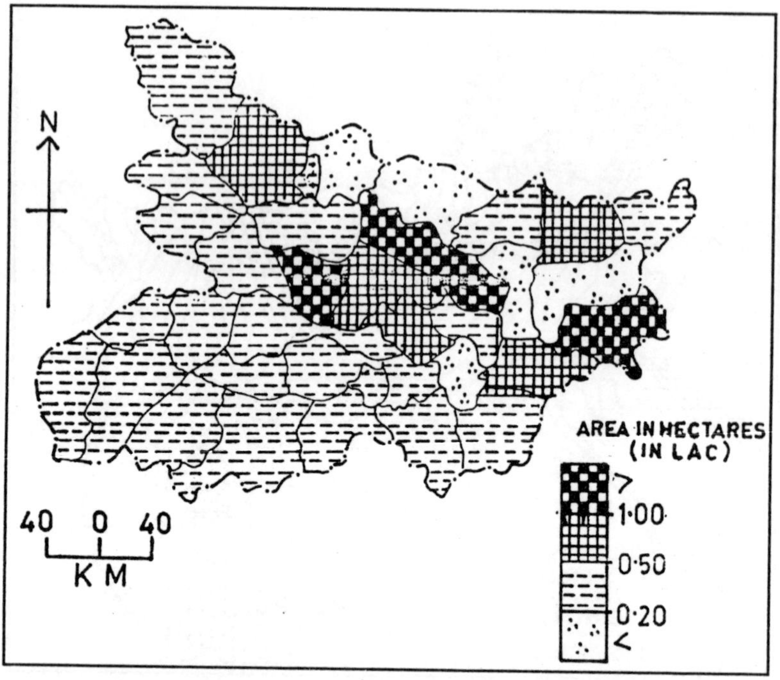

Fig. 20.4 : Flood Affected Area in the Districts of Bihar

experiences erosion. While one diara is formed the another is sometimes completely washed away. The fury of floods in 'tal' and 'diara' tract is a regular feature in this part of the state.

Fig. 20.4 and Fig. 20.5 display the distribution of flood affected areas and population in the districts of Bihar. Altogether 24 districts in Bihar were affected by flood in the year 2003. Out of 24 districts 19 are located in North Bihar and 5 in South Bihar. Over one lakh hectares of land was affected by floods individually in the districts of Vaishali, Darbhanga, Saharsa, Katihar and Bhagalpur. East Champaran, Samastipur, Araria and Begusarai are districts with 0.50 to 0.99 lakh hectares of flood affected area. Of the remaining districts 10 have 0.20 to 0.49 lakh hectares under floods while only five districts of Sitamarhi, Madhubani, Madhepura, Purnea and Munger recorded less than 0.20 lakh hectares of flood affected areas in each one of them.

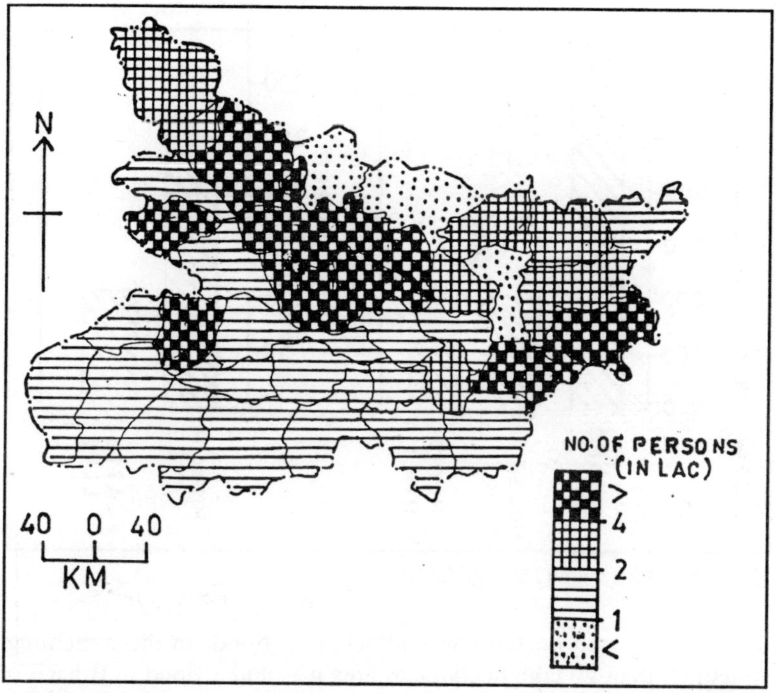

Fig. 20.5 : Number of Population Affected by Floods in the Districts of Bihar

Fig. 20.5 shows the number of population affected by floods in the districts of Bihar. Bhojpur, Bhagalpur, Vaishali, Samastipur, Saran, East Champaran, Muzaffarpur and Katihar are such districts which have over 4 lakh persons affected by flood in everyone of them. Most of these districts are located on both sides of the Ganga in the lower reaches of the tributaries of this river. West Champaran, Sheohar, Darbhanga, Saharsa, Supaul, Purnea, Araria and Munger have 2 to 4 lakh persons affected by flood. In the remaining districts the number of flood affected people seldom exceeds 2 lakh. Sitamarhi, Madhubani and Madhepura are the least affected districts. While Sitamarhi and Madhubani districts lie in the upper reaches of the tributaries of the Ganga, Madhepura lies in between the two embankments of the Kosi.

The temporal analysis of flood affected area and population during 1953 to 2003 shows that there were great fluctuations in flood area. In 1954, 1971, 1975, 1976, 1978, 1984, 1987 and 1998 total flood area in Bihar exceeded 20 lakh hectares of land. During 1987 a total

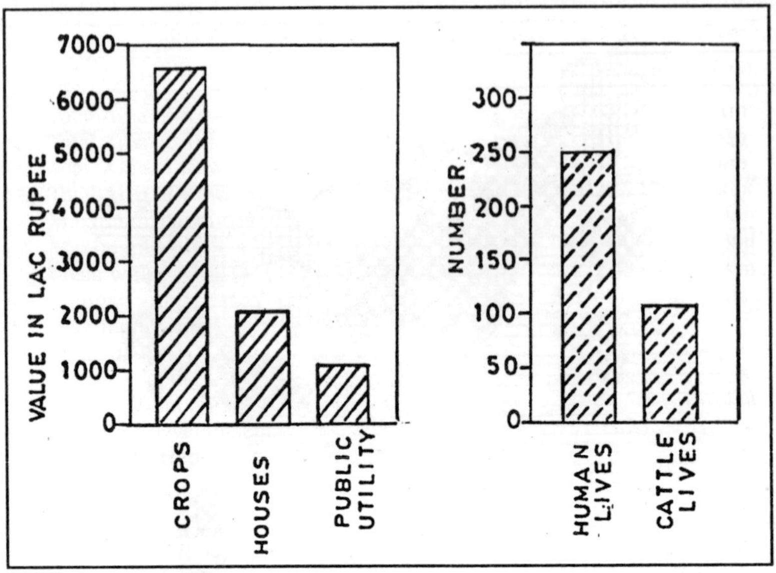

Fig. 20.6 : Bihar Flood Damage (2003)

area of 46.7 lakh hectares was affected by flood. In the remaining years less than 20 lakh hectares of area was under flood in Bihar.

Flood Damage

India experiences severe floods in one or other parts of the country causing loss of life, large scale damage to property and untold misery to millions of people. The loss of life and property due to floods in any drainage basin depend on the density of population, the timing of flood, nature of terrain and basin or basins adjacent to it besides the state of development of the area (Bhadram, 2004). According to the report from UNDP Disaster Risk Management Programme out of 40 million hectares declared flood prone area in the country, 17 per cent lies in Bihar state alone. Table 20.1 shows the districtwise flood damage in Bihar in 2003. The recurrent floods in Bihar cause widespread damage to standing crops. Houses in flood area are destroyed and cattle and human lives are lost. A huge loss to public utilities like roads etc. also occur. The total damage to crops, houses and public utilities were reported to be of Rs. 963.35 million during the year 2003 alone in Bihar (Fig. 20.6).

Damage to Crops

Figure 20.6 shows that the maximum damage by floods is done to standing crops in the flood plains. In the year 2003 crops worth Rs. 656.62 million were damaged. The extent of damage were severe in some districts while it was marginal in others. Maximum damage of crops was registered in the districts of Vaishali, Samastipur, Saharsa, Katihar and Bhagalpur. All these districts recorded a damage of 0.50 to 1.38 lakh hectares of crop area. The district with medium damage of crops (0.20-0.50 lakh hectares) were Muzaffarpur, East Champaran, Begusarai and Bhojpur. In respect of cost maximum damage was recorded in the districts of West Champaran, Samastipur, Muzaffarpur, Katihar and Bhagalpur. All these areas have fertile soils with good croplands. The flood waters, which became stagnant for weeks not only damage standing crops but also delay the time of cultivation of paddy crops.

Damage to House

Bihar is one of the poorest and most backward states of Indian Union. 42.60 per cent people live below poverty line (only above the State of Orissa with 47.15 %) and the per capita income is Rs. 4616 per annum only which is lowest in India (*India Today*, May 19, 2003 pp. 42-43). Most of the people live in villages and about 90 per cent population is rural. These poor people live mostly in mud built and straw or tile thatched houses which are destroyed during the time of floods. The total number of houses destroyed was 45262 in the year 2003, the value of which comes to Rs. 203.21 million. The districts with maximum damage of house property were West Champaran, Katihar, Bhagalpur, Patna, Bhojpur, Araria and Samastipur. In these districts the number of houses destroyed during floods varied from 2000 to 8000 in every one of them. Sitamarhi, Madhepura and Gopalganj districts registered minimum damage of houses (Table 20.1).

Damage to Cattle and Human Lives

Sudden floods usually sweep away many cattle heads and human beings. In the year 2003, as per the government reports, 108 cattle lives and 251 human lives were lost during the floods. In Bhagalpur district alone 80 cattle lives were lost while 8 cattle each in Samastipur and Araria were reported dead. Most precious among all the houses and property is the human life. 15-30 persons died in the districts of Muzaffarpur, West Champaran, Sheohar, Gopalganj, Darbhanga, Samastipur and Bhagalpur. Among all the 24 districts affected by flood there was loss of human life with the only exception of Buxar. Turbulent wave of a sudden flood in the Bagmati river swept away about 50 persons and at least 28 persons had lost their lives in the night of 7th of June 2004 (*Times of India*, Patna, 9 June, 2004). Such flash flood usually occurs taking many human lives.

Damage to Public Utilities

Flood water damages roads, bridges, schools and other public utilities every year. In 2003 alone public utilities worth Rs. 103.52 million were damaged by the flood. Maximum damage occurred in the districts of Sitamarhi, Samastipur, Araria and Katihar. In 17 districts of Bihar damage to public utilities were either nil or negligible.

Overall Damage

An estimate of overall damage due to floods was done by the Government of Bihar (Ganga Flood Control Commission, Patna). It shows (Table 20.1) that Rs. 963.35 million was lost due to damage of cropland, houses and public utilities. Maximum damage was reported in the districts of Samastipur, West Champaran, Katihar, Muzaffarpur and Bhagalpur. Districts lying between the two embankments of the Kosi like Madhepura and Purnea felt minimum damage.

Food Security Management During Floods

If the losses due to flood in terms of lives and property is to be minimised many long term and short term measures are to be taken. Flood control measures adopted to minimise flood damage can be grouped into two major categories—structural and non-structural (CWC, 1991). The structural measures contain the construction of embankments, the improvement of river channel discharge, the construction of bypass and diversion channels to carry excess water, and the construction of reservoirs for the temporary storage of flood waters. The non-structural measures, on the other hand, consist of flood forecasting, flood plain zoning, flood insurance besides rescue, rehabilitation and food security management etc. during floods and after floods.

The worst aspect of the floods in Bihar is the problems of food security during the time when a large number of people are marooned in flood waters. In the year 2003 the government of Bihar took the help of some 4 helicopters and dropped 5,000 food packets among the flood affected people. The scarcity of food supply can well be imagined because a population of 42 lakh had been reeling under floods in the year 2003. While addressing Mithila Association of Geographers at Samastipur in May 2003, Dr. Ram Chandra Purvey, the Primary Education Minister, Government of Bihar, admitted the fact that when flood occurs the readymade food material like crushed rice (*Chura*), *gur* (a crude form of sugar) and bread are in scarce supply in the market of state capital (Patna). The following measures may be adopted for the management of food security during floods in Bihar. The same measures may apply in case of India and other South Asian countries.

Flood Hazard Zone Mapping

Using historic satellite data combined with hydrological data a flood-hazard zone map for each flood prone basin is to be prepared. Hydrological and meteorological information about the basin including landuse/land cover, soil texture, slope of the terrain, drainage network and rainfall etc. have to be incorporated. The use of remote sensing and Geographic Information System will greatly enhance the use of flood hazard zone map. Based on this map a flood risk map for the flood plain of a river basin can be proposed. These maps will certainly give us prior information regarding the incoming of floods in the basin in question.

Food Godowns at District and Block Headquarters

The officials of Bihar Government agree that there is surplus food grains in godowns located at State capital and at some other places like Gaya, Mokameh (in Patna District) etc. It is difficult to lift food materials from Patna or Gaya and to distribute them in the flood affected areas of North Bihar. The author is, therefore, of the view that small food godowns should be constructed at district and sometimes at Block (Community Development Block) headquarters so that distribution of food materials becomes easy in the respective districts.

Road Network above Flood Level

Roads in the flood affected areas must be raised above flood level. Fig. 20.7 provides a framework of roads and godowns in the district headquarters of the flood affected areas. Recently (7th June, 2004) two motor vehicles plying on metalled road at night near Sheohar were swept away by the flash flood of Bagmati. The road was lower than flood level and so this loss of about 30 lives occurred. It is definitely a long term plan. All the roads in flood prone area should be surveyed, the areas below flood level be demarcated and every year some part of the these roads should be raised above flood level, so that even during flood food materials may be transported by roads.

Sufficient Arrangement of Boats

In all the districts of flood prone area some boats are hired on community basis and by the government agency to execute and supervise relief operation. The author came to know that 86 boats were hired in flood area of Supaul district, but due to non-payment of their charges from the government side none of the boatmen is ready to give services in the next flood season. It is, therefore, suggested that in every Panchayat (a group of villages) there should be 10-20 boats constructed with the help of the government or the community itself so that during flood, they may take food materials to the people marooned in flood water.

Construction of Concrete Platforms

The flooded areas present the scene of continuous water covered areas for miles. The person engaged in distributing relief find it difficult to drop food packets, many of which are lost in flood waters. Some people take shelter on roof tops of pucca houses and while the others may be seen sitting on tree tops. The author is of the view that a concrete platform with solid foundation may be constructed phasewise in different Panchayats. It will enable at least 5000 people and their livestock to take shelter there for a few days. It will be easier to drop

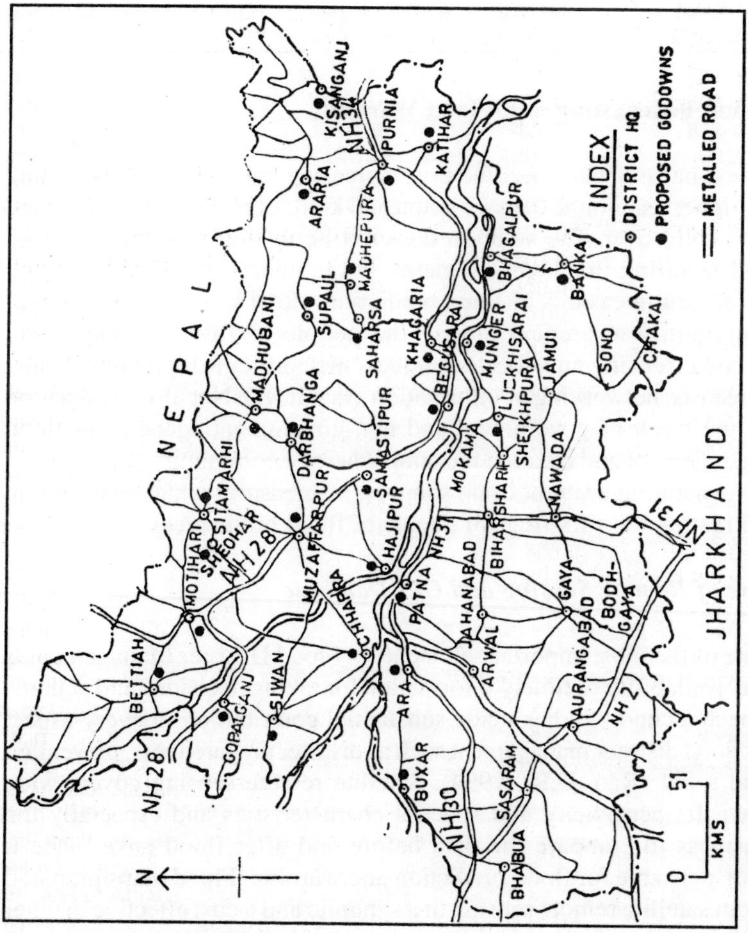

Fig. 20.7 : Bihar : Road with District Headquarters

food packets at those sites and the boats engaged in relief operations may reach these platforms easily. At least some part of the amount allotted for flood relief may be spent annually over the construction of these platforms.

Finally, the awareness created by flood forecasts and flood warnings are essential for planning flood relief measures specially the food security measures well in advance before the actual flood arrives.

Flood Forecasting and Flood Warning

Flood hazards have become ever increasing natural disaster resulting in highest economic damage among all kinds of natural disaster around the world over. The solution does not lie in simply arranging relief and repairing flood embankments, but in undertaking long term and short term measures of flood prediction, flood warning and creating community awareness among the people of flood affected area. Remote sensing and GIS techniques, meteorological predictions and forecasts, networking of information system with Nepal, co-ordination of the work of government and non-government agencies in flood management and creating the atmosphere of community participation by generating awareness are some of the measures which may help in mitigating the sufferings of people of flood prone areas.

Use of Remote Sensing and GIS Database

One of the most important elements in Flood Disaster Management is the availability of timely information for taking decisions and actions. Space technology has made substantial contribution in every aspect of flood disaster management such as disaster preparedness, prevention and relief (Rao, U.R., 1994). Satellite remote sensing covers wide area. Its periodicity and spectral characteristics and especially the easiness to compare the data before and after flood have made it indispensable for flood prediction and warning. Flood maps prepared from satellite remote sensing in a synoptic and a cost effective manner will help in more than one way in the field of flood management.

The development of modern data gathering techniques and computer assisted cartography have given new impetus for the development of Geographical Information System (GIS). In fact GIS is computerised database system for capture, storage, analysis and display of spatial data (Singh, R.B., 1998). In fact, the combined use of GIS and digital image processing provide better prospects of flood monitoring and flood forecasting. Data regarding rainfall in the catchment area of rivers, volume of water flow, sediment load, forest cover, soil texture, land uses and existing embankments may be stored in Geographic Information System of all the sub-basins of the Ganga. Furthermore, the satellite imageries taken at regular intervals during floods and after floods for a long period of time will help in flood prediction and decision making for management of floods.

Meteorological Predictions and Forecasts

Flood forecasting and early warnings for different river basins in India are provided by the Central Water Commission (CWC). Flood Meteorological office at Patna provides meteorological support in the form of Quantitative Precipitation Forecasts, and heavy rainfall warning for the Kosi, the Mahananda, the Bagmati, the Kamla, the Gandak, the Burhi Gandak, the Punpun and the upper Son river basins.

Meteorological offices generally send flood warning to Central Water Commission, Ganga Flood Control Commission and to the Government of Bihar. These warnings are carried out through land line telegrams, telephone, wireless systems and Police W/T. Selective addressing system meant for sending warning directly to concerned districts should be adopted. With the spread of mobile phones, T.V. and Radio it is easy to issue flood forecast and flood warning well in advance.

Networking of Information System with Nepal

All the rivers of North Bihar have large catchment areas in Nepal and some even north of Nepal. Proper co-ordination in the exchange of information system between India (Bihar) and Nepal is essential. Generally, the information regarding high rainfall in the upper reaches of river and high volume of water discharge should be given by Nepal well in advance. The meteorological information from Nepal commences from 15th June but this year there was flash flood in the Bagmati river on 7th June, 2004, causing at least 30 death. The construction of reservoir, canals, dam and embankment are long term measures but augmenting of information system from both India and Nepal side is essential. It should work throughout the year.

Co-ordination Between Government and Non-Government Agencies

Today environmental problems like flood hazard are not only local or regional but a national and global issue. Human induced development activities cause enormous degradation and aggravation in river basins and make our survival questionable (Grewal, Trulio and Singh, 1998). A multi level co-ordination between Central and State Governments, Bihar and Nepal Governments and between different government and non-government agencies is of utmost importance. Poorest Areas Civil Society (PACS) is a seven year joint programme of the Governments of India and the UK and is funded by the UK. While addressing a group of NGOs from different river basins of Bihar, at Patna, the Chairman of PACS Mr. Ajay Kumar Basu, suggested three things for flood control and disaster risk management. These are immediate information of volume of water in river's catchment area, interlinking of the rivers of Bihar and creating awareness at community level among the people.

Community Participation and People's Awareness

NGOs while making delebration for containing flood hazards at Patna (*Times of India*, Patna, June 21, 2004) felt that all the government efforts fail because they do not provide prior information about floods. Participants at the workshop felt that the focus should be shifted from relief and rehabilitation to greater preparedness, including boats, foodgrains and mapping of flood prone areas. A volunteer force of persons between 20-40 age group should be constituted and be given training to remain prepared before the fury of flood actually arrives. These youth groups will not only pass information regarding the breach of embankment etc. but will also make the inhabitant aware regarding the coming of floods.

These measures taken individually and jointly will definitely enhance the effectiveness of flood management in the State of Bihar, India.

Conclusion

Floods are the most common and widespread of all natural disasters.

Indian subcontinent is one among the world's most disaster prone area. The floods are an annual feature in the Ganga-Brahmaputra river basin. About 40 million hectares of land is vulnerable to floods in India out of which 17 per cent lies in the state of Bihar alone. In Bihar state the northern and southern tributaries of the Ganga like the Kosi, the Mahananda, the Gandak, the Burhi Gandak, the Bagmati and the Son etc. bring annual floods in their lower reaches. Heavy rainfall in the catchment area of these rivers coupled with low gredient of slope in the plains are responsible for recurrent floods in Bihar.

The floods in Bihar cause heavy damage by submerging cropland, inundating fields and destroying houses, cattle, lives and properties of the inhabitants. The worst aspect of the floods is the problem of food security to the lakh of population marooned under flood waters. The government godowns are full of food grains in the state capital and elsewhere, but during floods sufficient food materials seldom reach the flood affected people. Important suggestion rendered for food security management during floods in Bihar include the mapping of flood area by remote sensing, construction of godowns with sufficient food stock at district and block headquarters, raising of roads above flood level and constructing concrete platform for sheltering men and cattle during the time of flood. A number of necessary measures like long and short term prediction, prevention, warning, monitoring, relief and participating of local community by generating awareness, are necessary for flood management in the State of Bihar in India.

REFERENCES

Ahmad, E., *Bihar : A Physical, Economic and Regional Geography,* Ranchi University, Ranchi, 1965, p. 32.

Annual Report (1994-95), Ganga Flood Control Commission, Ministry of Water Resources, Govt. of India, Patna.

Bhadram, C.V.V., Role of India Meteorological Department in Mitigating the Flood Disaster, National Workshop on Flood Disaster Management—Space Inputs, 3-4 June, 2004, NRSA, Hyderabad.

Bhanumurthy, V., NRSA Contribution in Flood Management using Satellite Data, National Workshop on Flood Disaster Management—Space Inputs, 3-4 June, 2004, NRSA, Hyderabad, India.

Grewal, V.S., Trulio, L. and Singh, R.B., Status of Environmental Quality and Decision-making in India : Past, Present and Future Trends, in *Ecological Techniques and Approaches to Vulnerable Environment*, (Ed.) R.B. Singh, *op. cit.*

India Today, Special Issue, May 19, 2003, India's Best and Worst States, pp. 40-41, *A Times of India Publication*, New Delhi, Bombay.

Rao, U.R., Floods and Droughts, Presented in TAF—COSPAR Symposium on Space applications for Disaster Prevention, Warning, Mitigation and Relief, Meeting of the Scientific and Technical Committee, UN Committee on Peaceful uses of Outer Space, Vienna, Feb. 21-22, 1994.

Singh, G.N. and Singh, Ramanuj, "Food Security and Disaster Management During Floods in Bihar," Seminar on Water Resources Utilisation and Management, 18-19 Oct., 2003, Bihar Association of Geographers, Patna, pp. 68-69.

Singh, R.B., Geographical Information System as a Tool of Resource Management, in *Ecological Techniques and Approaches to Vulnerable Environment,* (Ed.) R.B. Singh, Oxford & IBH Publishing Co. Pvt. Ltd. New Delhi, 1998, pp. 96-103.

The Times of India, Patna, A Daily Newspaper, Published by Times of India Group, New Delhi (Several Reports cited).

21

Sustainable Management of Land and Water Resources

Problems and Prospects with Special Reference to Barhiya C.D. Block, Bihar

JAYANT KUMAR

Introduction

The study of geography is essentially related to an examination of the relationship between nature and man. In the rural countryside of India, there is an overwhelming dependence of population on natural resources. Prosperity of human beings in relation to social, economic and environmental attributes depend on balanced utilization of natural resources, viz. land, water and bio-diversity. Sustainability is an integral part of development. The two most important and vital natural resources — land and water are very scarce in India and are becoming more and more scarce due to explosive growth of population. The country is affected by the drought-flood-drought syndrome. Thus it becomes, important for us to centralize our focus on sustainable management of land and water resources. It is not possible to study the country as a whole, hence area study is proposed.[1]

This research paper looks into details of the situation pertaining the study area, i.e. Barhiya Block. It vividly shows a deviation in sustainable use of land and water resources.

Study Area

Barhiya Block is situated within the middle Ganga plain of India. Administratively it lies in Lakhisarai district of Bihar State. The Study area exists on the western levee of the river Ganga. Most of the study

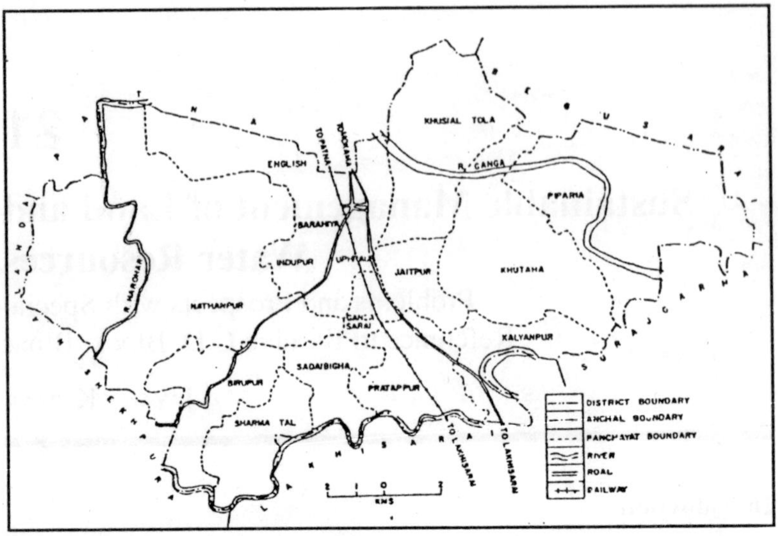

Fig. 21.1 : Barhiya Block Base Map

area constituted a lowlying plain land. This lowland is called 'TAL' area which is severely affected by floods and droughts almost every year. The block extends over an area of 23141.10 hectares and has a population of 153,591 persons, according to the census of 2001. Land and water are the two main physical resources of the Study area (Fig. 21.1). It has basically two types of land, i.e. Diara land (27.97 per cent) and Tal land (39.06 per cent). Diara land is built of sandy soil and Tal land is marked by clay soil or loamy soil[2](Fig. 21.1).

Aims and Objectives

In the contexts of globalization it is often said to think globally but act locally. The present paper is a local area study approach and this kind of approach has also been encourages in the post-modern geographical thought. Considering this new dimensions and direction of geography, this study of Barhiya Block has been taken up.

The scholar conceives this kind of investigation will highlight the problems of land and water resources and such exposures will help in planning and development of a block of Central Bihar where natural hazards like flood and drought are most common yearly phenomena.

Research Methodology

The information has been obtained, both from primary as well as secondary sources. The primary information has been obtained by intensive field study. Empirical and statistical approaches have also been used for explaining the collected information. Personal observation and assessment of the scholar will be an important basis of interpretation and clarification of different kinds of information. Besides them secondary sources would also be used for providing introductory framework and for some comparative work.

Problems and Prospects

Bihar, the land-locked Indian State, presents the most glaring illustration of the drought-flood-drought syndrome. Out of total geographical area of 93.81 lakh ha about 68.8 lakh ha (73 per cent) is flood prone, 16.07 lakh ha. (17 per cent) is drought prone; and 9.43 lakh ha (10 per cent) is waterlogged. The state as well as the study area suffers from flood ravages in one part and drought in the other at the same time; and in extreme cases flood or drought in most part of the study area at the same time and not at distant intervals. It is really paradoxical.[3]

The study area, i.e. *Barhiya Block* forms the core area of agriculture-based economy of the State, where about 70 per cent population gets subsistence from agriculture and allied activities. So far as the present agriculture scenario is concerned, the block has virtually come down to traditional food grain farming. Though agricultural production in the study area has achieved sustainable level but the quality of life of the people has not improved much. The study area has further witnessed that for last fifteen years the production has been fluctuating almost every year. The farming has not been able to generate adequate employment opportunities due to uncertain nature of rainfall, flood, drought, waterlogging, changing courses of the river and periodic inundation (Fig. 21.2).

Barhiya-Mokameh tal area proudly known as pulse bowl of India is which is now-a-days on brink of unsustainable, degenerating and dilapidated condition. While possibility of aquaculture and two/three crops production has available in block by proper use of land and water resources. It is mainly because of improper management of available resources.[4]

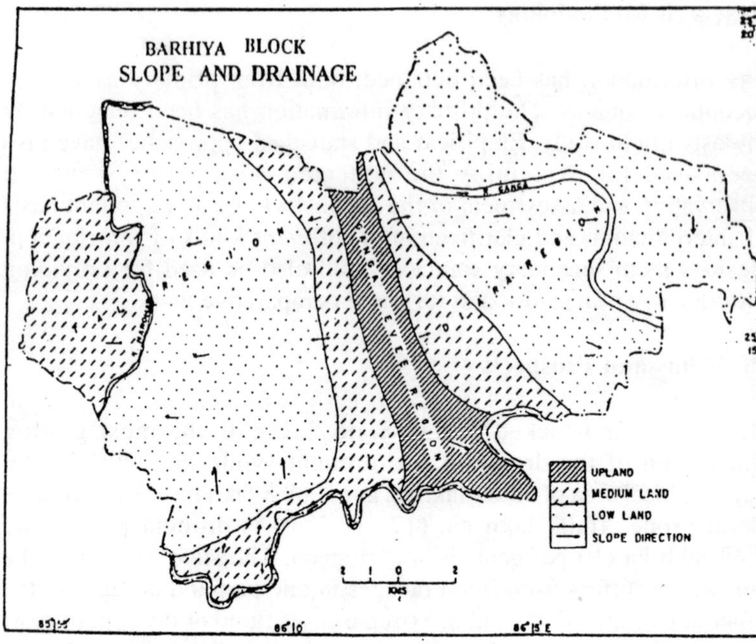

Fig. 21.2 : Barhiya Block Slope and Drainage

In the western part of study area, dozen of rivers, namely the Punpun, the Kiul, the Harohar, the Sakri, the Same, the Jirane, the Mohane, the Joh, and the Falgu drains into tal area almost every year, resulting in flood. In addition, variability in rainfall also degenerates the situation.

Due to breakage of *Zamindari Bandh*, non-clearance of *Gad,* resulting in waterlogging has to lead to erosion of agriculture production.

The tal area which is gifted with four cuts, namely —Phatuha Cut, Bakhtiyarpur Cut, Kanhaipur Cut and Rampur-Dumra-Hemza Cut are now filled up and due to improper management of clearing them the area witnesses long term waterlogging and flood which directly or indirectly leads to land erosion, land pollution, waste of cultivable time and degenerate production. This current year (2003-04), the area went for two to three times cultivation as the crops were laid waste each time. This is remarkable waste in 100 years of history.[5]

Land Use

The land utilization table of any region is a mirror of the economic condition of the region. However, the land use of Barhiya Block has certain peculiarities of its own which can be seen in the following table :

Table 21.1 : Land use in Barhiya Block

Categories of Land Utilization	*Total Area (in hec.)*	*Total area (in per cent)*
Non-Agricultural use	2,998.50	12.38
Forest and Orchards	76.28	0.43
NSA	10,303.78	44.05
Fallow Land for 1 year	6,305.92	26.96
Cultivable Waste land	1,750.98	7.49
Barren and uncultivable waste	2,056.58	8.79
Double Sown Area	1,249.00	–
Total Sown Area	11,552.84	–
Total	23,392.04	100.00

Source : Block Office, Barhiya.

Harvest

It will be seen that rabi is by far the most important harvest and accounts almost 90 per cent of the total sown area in a year. Bhadai comes a long way behind with only 7 per cent. The share of Garma is negligible. No cultivation is possible during the Aghani season owing to waterlogging.

Table 21.2 : Harvest in TSA : Barahiya Block

Type of Harvest	*Percent of Agricultural Land*
Garma	3.18
Bhadai	6.89
Aghani	0.70
Rabi	89.23

Source : Block Office, Barhiya.

Irrigation Means :			
	No. of Govt. Boring	-	34
	No. of Private Boring	-	449
	No. of Private Electric Pump	-	266
	No. of Private Diesel Pump	-	329
	No. of Lift Irrigation	-	27

The diara land lying in the South and South-East is witnessing change in the Ganga river. Around 1500-500 mts. has been shifted (westward) in last fifteen years. This has lead to increased intensity of flooding in the study area.[6]

In same cropping season, diara land witnessed drought and tal land flood and *vice versa.*

Strategy for Solving the Problem

The analysis of the "Problem" suggests a strategy for approaching the sustainable management of the land and water resources of the study area. Through the proper management of land and water resources in the study area, the bane of flood and droughts can be put to boon. It could be done by :

- Clearing the cuts time to time.
- Transferring of flood water to drought area.
- Interlinked the Dhava Soti to Harohar river.
- Construction of embankments, reservoirs, natural detention basin.
- Channel improvements, river diversion, inter-basin transfer, bank stabilization, raising of villages and underground storage.
- Modify flood plain zoning, flood forecasting and warning, disaster mitigation system and preparedness.
- Satellite based remote sensing technology too must be brought to bear upon land and water resources management.
- Integrated steps towards this must have been taken by NNRMS (The National Natural Resource Management System), CWC, CGWB, IMSD (Integrated Mission for Sustainable Development), NLCB (National Landuse and Conservation Board), SLUBs (State Land Use Boards) etc.
- A conceptual integrated plan must be developed for the whole region. This plan could then be used as the basis for long term, bi-lateral and multilateral agreements among the riparian tracts in the block.

Land and water resource management must be considered one of the basic infrastructural needs of study area (Fig. 21.3). It is difficult to achieve sustainable development without implementing long term

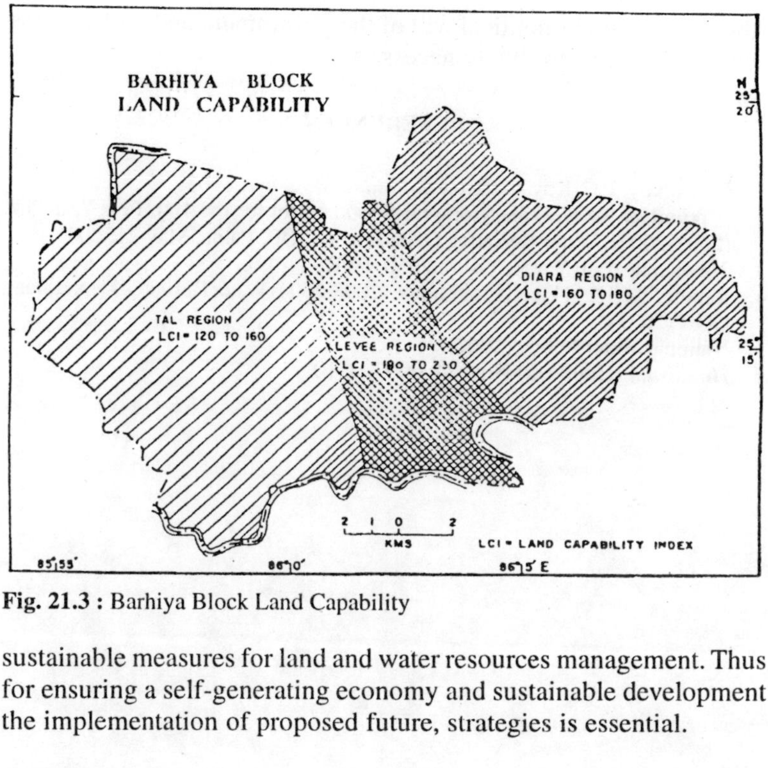

Fig. 21.3 : Barhiya Block Land Capability

sustainable measures for land and water resources management. Thus for ensuring a self-generating economy and sustainable development the implementation of proposed future, strategies is essential.

Conclusion

A scientific approach has to be adopted for providing a long term land and water resource management in Barhiya Block. It has to make use of all types of scientific and technological development for investigation, planning design, implementation and operation of the scheme. Four prong approach, i.e. political force, enlightened and efficient bureaucracy, community participation, competent and capable engineers are recommended for ecological-economic and social sustainability in the study area.

Keeping in view the above mentioned facts, the author proposes practically gained ideas in research orientation. This research paper is oriented towards highlighting the main problems of the study area for better understanding among the learned geographers resource managers, development planners and policy makers for raising the socio-economic situation prevailing in the study area and the state.

Above all, a strong political will of the government and participating beneficiaries are absolutely necessary.

REFERENCES

1. Chaudhary, P.C. Roy, *Gazetteer of India, Monghyr*, 1963.
2. A report of the working group on flood control for the 10th Five Year Plan (2002-2007), Water Resource Department, GOB, Patna, May 21, 2001.
3. Theme paper on Water: Vision 2050, IWRS (1.99).
4. Report (2003-2004) and Programme (2003-2004) Water Resource Department, GOB (2003).
5. National Water Policy (2002) .
6. *Hindustan* (Hindi ed.) Nov. 24, 2003, p. 10.

22

Water Resource Management

Policies and Programmes

MD. NASEEMUDDIN AND SANJAY KUMAR JHA

Water is a limited resource and the efficient use of which is of increasing importance as demand exceeds from agriculture, industry and a water and power using population with rising living standard.

The main prospects for improving the efficiency of water use lie in the continued development of groundwater through sinking traditional open wells and modern tube-wells. The relative importance of well irrigation has increased greatly since independence (Gupta and Singh, 1994).

Already 30 per cent of India's hydroelectric potential has been brought into use. Installed capacity of the power stations is almost equally distributed between the Himalyan rivers and those of the west and east flowing rivers of the Peninsula. Future prospects of the best area is Kerala and Karnataka in the South and in the Eastern Himalaya, all regions with long heavy rainy seasons and steep slopes for power generation.

In several river basins the total volume of water used exceeds the total surface flow, indicating the re-use of water through the exploitation of groundwater reservoirs and recycling of surface drainage through canal and tank systems. Multipurpose river development is the rule, through problems do rise from the competing demands of industry for electric power and process water on the one hand and agriculture for irrigation water always be resolved to every body's satisfaction (Gupta, *et al.*, 1993).

In order to improve the utilization of power and irrigation potential several major rivers have been or are in process of being diverted. At present more than 70 per cent of the population uses groundwater for its domestic needs and more than half of irrigation is provided from this source.

Table 22.1 : Groundwater Resource and Irrigation in India

Sl.No.	*States/UTs*	*Total Replenishable Groundwater Resource*	*Utilisable Ground-water Resource for irrigation in Net Terms*	*Level of Ground-water Development*
1	*2*	*3*	*4*	*5*
1.	Andhara Pradesh	3.52916	2.69981	23.64
2.	Arunachal Pradesh	0.14385	0.11005	–
3.	Assam	2.47192	1.89102	4.48
4.	Bihar	3.35213	2.56439	19.19
5.	Goa	0.02182	0.01670	8.30
6.	Gujarat	2.03767	1.55881	41.45
7.	Haryana	0.85276	0.65236	83.88
8.	Himachal Pradesh	0.03660	0.02637	18.10
9.	Jammu and Kashmir	0.044257	0.33858	1.33
10.	Karnataka	1.61857	1.23821	31.26
11.	Kerala	0.79003	0.59281	15.28
12.	Madhya Pradesh	5.08892	3.89298	16.49
13.	Maharashtra	3.78673	2.29231	30.39
14.	Manipur	0.31540	0.24129	Neg.
15.	Meghalaya	0.05397	0.04128	Neg.
16.	Mizoram	–	–	–
17.	Nagaland	0.07240	0.05535	Neg.
18.	Orissa	2.00014	1.53009	8.42
19.	Punjab	1.86550	1.51109	93.85
20.	Rajasthan	1.27076	0.96418	50.63
21.	Sikkim	–	–	–
22.	Tamil Nadu	2.63912	2.01892	60.44
23.	Tripura	0.06634	0.05076	33.43
24.	Uttar Pradesh	8.38210	6.41233	37.67
25.	West Bengal	2.30923	1.76653	24.18
	Total State	43.14769	32.46621	31.88
Union Territories				
1.	Andaman and Nicobar Islands	–	–	–
2.	Chandigarh	0.002968	–	–
3.	Dadra and N. Haveli	0.004220	0.00323	12.74
4.	Daman and Diu	0.001300	0.00099	–
5.	NCT Delhi	0.029154	–	–
6.	Lakshadweep	0.00243	–	63.79
7.	Pondicherry	0.002877	0.00220	24.34
	Total UTs	0.040760	0.00642	–
	Grand Total	43.18850	32.47264	31.02

Source : India 2000

The total replenishable groundwater in India is estimated to be about 432 billion cubic metres or 4,318,850 million hectare metres per year. About 7.1 million hectare metres per year is used for domestic and industrial uses.

Potential of India

It is estimated that about 3,247,264 million-hectare metres per year is available for irrigation. According to an estimate by Central Ground Water Board 32 per cent of available groundwater resources have so far been developed, there are, some areas in the country, which are facing scarcity of groundwater. The reason for this is that the development of groundwater in different areas of the country has not been uniform. Highly intensive development of groundwater in certain areas in the country has resulted in its over exploitation leading to fall in the level of groundwater and salinity increases in costal areas (Kumari and Rao, 1993).

Water Resources Potential

Average runoff in the river system of the country has been assessed as 1869 $km.^3$ of this, the utilisable portion is estimated as about 690 km^3. In addition, there is substantial replenishable groundwater potential in the country estimated at 432 km^3. The per capita availability of water has reduced from about 5277 m^2 in year 1995 to the present level 1970 m^3.

The situation may aggravate in future due to the growing water scarcity in the river basins.

Irrigation Development

Expansion of irrigation facilities along with consolidation of the existing systems has been the main strategy for increasing production of food grains. Irrigation support is provided through major, medium and minor irrigation projects and command area development with sustained and systematic development of irrigation. Irrigation potential has increased from 22.6 mha in 1951, when the process of planning began in India, to about 89.56 mha.

A large number of irrigation projects have been launched since beginning of the era of planning in India. However, many projects remained incomplete owing to financial constraints of the states.

An Accelerated Irrigation Benefit Programme (AIBP) was launched during 1996-97 to give loan assistance to the states to help them complete their projects.

Command Area Development Programme

A centrally sponsored Command Area Development Programme was launched in 1974-75 with the main objective of improving utilisation of irrigation potential and optimising agricultural productivity and production from the irrigated areas by integrating all functions related with irrigated agriculture (India, 2000).

Flood Management

Flood management is a state subject, Union Government provides central assistance to state for a few specified schemes which are technical promotional in nature such as critical anti-erosion works in the Ganga Basin states. Maintenance of flood protection works of the Kosi and the Gandak projects etc. The Central Water Commission is engaged in the flood-forecasting on inter-state rivers through 21 field divisions throughout the country. Forecasts are being issued at 157 stations are normally issued 24 hours in advance and are found to be useful for civil and engineering authorities for arranging relief and rescue measures and for the protection of engineering structures.

Central Water Commission has developed considerable technical know-how in plan formulation, appraisement, design of major hydrantic structures and projects for development of water resources.

Central Ground Water Board (CGWB)

Central Ground Water Board is responsible for carrying out scientific development and management of groundwater resources from national perspective.

The regional hydrological survey of the country have already been completed and the board is currently conducting reappraisal survey every fifth year to assess the impact of groundwater development and the groundwater resources and water quality under the reappraisal surveys, areas having specific problems like waterlogging, declining groundwater levels and groundwater pollution, etc. These are accorded priority special emphasis is being laid on monitoring of groundwater levels and water quality through a network of about 15,000 observation stations in the country. In order to promote the scientific management of groundwater resources, specially in the problematic areas, the Board is undertaking pilot projects for augmenting recharge of groundwater in the States of Karnataka, Maharashtra, National Capital Territory of Delhi, Union Territory of Chandigarh and some other states studies on the conjunctive use of surface and groundwater are also being undertaken in specific areas to work out the best possible option for optional development of the total water resources with minimum deleterious effects.

The Government of India has been assisting the Royal Government of Bhutan for hydropower development and establishment of hydro-meterological and flood forecasting network on rivers common to India and Bhutan.

India and Bangladesh are jointly conducting scientific studies and field investigations to determine the reasons for the discrepancies in the flows related at Farakka on the Ganga and those arrive at Harding Bridge.

In this way, policies and programmes are being made by the government in order to fulfil the goal.

REFERENCES

Gupta, M.K., Singh, Vibha, Rajvanshi, Poonam, Srivastava, Shalini and Dass, S. 'Fluoride in ground water at Agra'. *Indian J. Environ. Health,* 36 (1), 1994, 43-46.

Gupta, S.C., Rathore, G.S. and Doshi, C.S., Fluoride distribution in ground water of Southern Rajasthan, *Indian J. Environ. Health,* 35 (2) : 1993, 97-109.

India-2000, pp. 429-446.

Kumari, Saral D. and Rao, P.R., Endemic Fluorosis in the Village Ralla Anantapuram in Andhra Pradesh. An Epidemilogical Study. *Fluoride,* 26 (3), 1993, 177-180.

23
The Value of Wetlands

MANJU KUMARI

Wetlands are submerged areas of waterbodies which include both natural and artificial, permanent or temporary, static or flowing, fresh, brackish and saltish lake, ditches and marine water the depth of which at low tide does not exceed six metres for the major portion of the year.

The value of wetland is immense in order to safeguard our environment and maintain ecological balance. It may not be proper to leave out our marshy lands, waterlogged areas, tals and ponds uncared as they have a great potentiality to produce many items which have great utility for human being besides resource generation. The wetlands are also pollution filters along with beautifying the environment, attracting more rainfall and provide living abode for many species of birds, fishes, insects and plants which have very high medicinal value in our day to day life.

Wetlands are among the most productive and most threatened ecosystem. On marshes, Ganga valley, Egypt, Mesopotamia and Indo-China have flourished which continue to support rural and urban communities throughout the world. All these are in jeopardy by drainage reclamation and used as dumping ground of refuse water. Some of the wetlands have been damaged and destroyed in search for short term profit. Many have already been lost their existence.[1]

Most of the wetlands are nature's gift at a place which is neglected but most of them are endowed with an environment of scenic beauty. Since long human beings have not cared about wetlands as they are treated as marginal lands. But with the spurt of population in most countries of the world the wetlands need special attention for the emancipation of people from economic ills. This could be possible as the shallow wetlands are productive of medicinal plants. Wetlands are areas where the source of oxygen supply, develop places of scenic beauty and they are the habitat for local as well as migratory birds. Wetlands serve as suitable niche for fish and aquatic animals, breeding and nursery ground for water fowls and as filters for sediments and other pollutants. Most countries are loosing the wetlands rapidly due to biotic interference and anthropogenic pressure.[2]

Considering the value of wetlands, measures have been initiated for their conservation and management. It is essential to educate people regarding the need for the conservation of wetland as well as their economic utility besides the commencement of scientific and application oriented research on their productivity.

Dimensions of Wetland Development

Wetlands located in the marginal areas of human interactions of tourism, fishing and creating ecological balance between man and

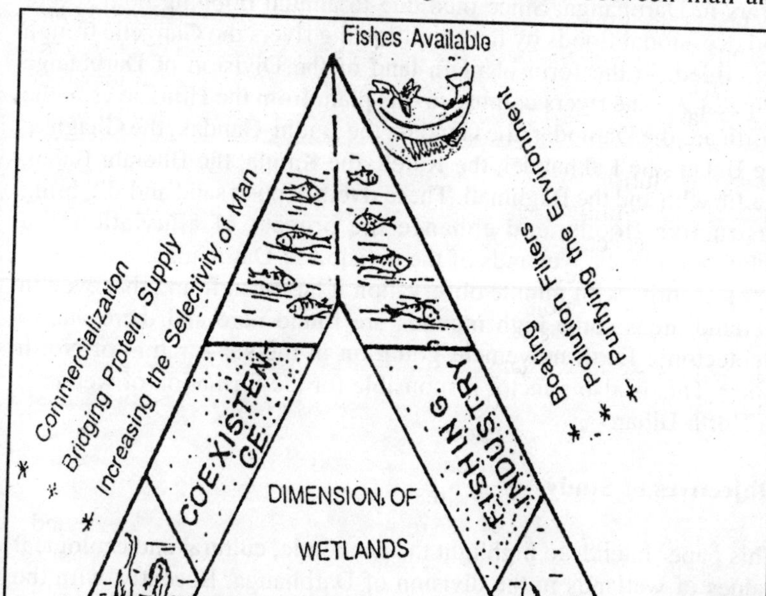

Fig. 23.1 : Highway Development Beautify the Environment Irrigation

the biosphere. Wetland is an area where the availability of varieties of fishes, birds and medicinal plants could be assured from shallow and deep waters. Wetlands act as the highway, beautification of environment, source of irrigation, recreation, bridging the gap of protein supply and increasing the selectivity of man in different types of resources (Fig. 23.1)

Origin and Evolution of Wetland

Wetlands are remnants of the Gangetic trough or the Indo-Braham River formed in course of the rise of Himalayas in three successive periods of Eocene, Miocene and Pliocene. At the end of Pleistocene period when deglaciation took place in the entire northern hemisphere, a vast amount of sand and silt have been deposited by the Himalayan rivers in Darbhanga. Since then due to annual flooding both severe and occasional floods by the southflowing rivers the Gangetic trough gets filled, in the form of plain land of the Division of Darbhanga (Fig. 23.2). The rivers coming to this plain from the Himalayas in the North are the Damodar, the Gandak, the Budhi-Gandak, the Ghaghra, the Balan, the Lakhandei, the Kareh, the Kamla, the Bhutahi Balan, the Jibachh and the Baghmati. These rivers deposit sand and silt, bring destructive floods, and enhance the process of alluviation and deluviation in the wetlands of the division of Darbhanga.

Recently, with minute observation it has been found that even in wetland areas some high mounds are found here and there due to Neotectonic Earth movement going on in the sub-stratum of North Bihar. This is also a factor responsible for the formation of wetlands in North Bihar.

Objectives of Study

This paper intends to highlight the economic, cultural and ecological values of wetlands in the division of Darbhanga. Recently, with the rapid increase of population, and reckless cutting of forests the formation of wetlands is limited. This paper will show how the marshy and waterlogged areas can be utilized in a better way in order to have sound ecological balance and environmental adjustment with various parameters of economic development. Even marginal lands like marshy and waterlogged areas produce a vast amount of fish, singhara, Makhana, Mothi, Purain-leaves, Lotus flower and Jalkumbhi which contains a matter highly suitable for nitrogen fixation in the soil.

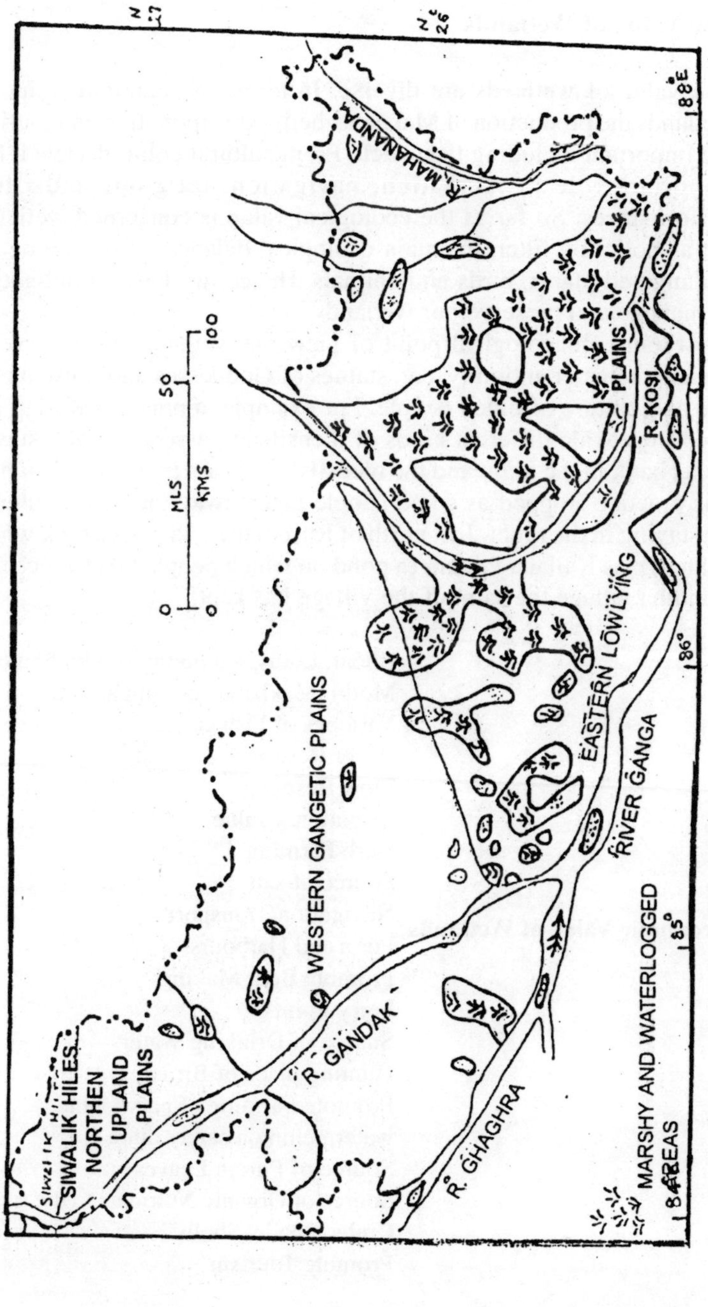

Fig. 23.2 : North Bihar : Distribution of Wetlands

The Value of Wetlands

The value of wetlands are diverse. In terms of economic value of wetlands the production of Makhana, herbs, transportation and tourism are important including fish catch. From cultural point of view it has important role in recreation, navigation, religious and ritual performances. So far as the ecological value is concerned wetlands act as pollution filter, maintain ecological balance, offers abode for endangered plants, birds and animals. Hence, we have to obligation to manage and preserve our wetlands.

From archaeological point of view the wetlands are reserve of various items of antiquity, e.g. statues of Goddesses and presents the life and culture of olden people. For example, a pond on Karian dih used to provide different kinds of utensils to passersbye who stayed on its bank in the night and the utensil disappears in the day. But now this practice stopped as some people taken away the bronze utensil by staying in the night. Just north of Rusera town there is a tank which is known as Kallaua Pokhar (a pond on which people takes lunch). In Bandiha village the saint of the village has kept.

Economic Value of Wetlands

- Bhent, Lotus, Kumudni, production of Mothi, Makhana and Singarhara
- Varieties of Fish catch
- Water Reservoir as Fund Resource
- Flow Resource
- Irrigational value
- Herb Farming
- Source of salt
- Navigation/Transport
- Ports and Harbours
- Promote Boat Making
- Ferry Point
- Source of Drinking Water
- Hunting place of Birds
- Promote Farming of parwal and watermelon on sandy diara.
- Source of Purain Leaves
- Source of Organic Nutrients to the fields.
- Crabs, Snails, Shells
- Promote Tourism

Favours Regional Economic Development
Medicinal Value of Water
Source of Employment to Fishermen and cultivators.

Ornamental fishes and tortoises and this pond has been declared as forbidden ground for fish catch.

The Economic Value of Wetlands

Very little is known about wetland functions such as life-support and pollution assimilation. Equally, the non-use value of wetlands has not been quantified, but environment as resources suggest that their existence values are positive and significant. It can, therefore, be argued that all the remaining wetlands stock ought to be protected, even though not all individual wetlands are considered to be uniformly valuable for the present.[3]

Table 23.1 lists a number of threats to the main wetland types. In terms of market failure there is evidence in the wetlands as there is a lack of incentive to the discloure of information on wetlands.[4] Clearly, the use and non-use value of wetlands are not widely known. In some cases, the precise location and extent of wetlands are not known to public agencies or owners may be unaware of the management programmes that are officially available.

Table 23.1 : Location and Threats to Wetlands Resources in North East India

1.	Flood Plains	Interference with hydrology, dams, river embankments, rehabilitation of flood plains.
2.	River, Lakes and Land Reclamation	Pollution; Industrial development; extraction of water for irrigation; reduction of aquifer supply and surface waterflow; recreation pressure; hunting activities.
3.	Grass lands	Drainage schemes (on- and off-site).
4.	Terai lands	Drainage schemes and agricultural reclamation; resource extraction (Energy and non-energy); forestry.

Externality are also relevant to wetlands, They have suffered external cost damage due to pollution generated by agricultural and industrial activities located outside the wetland boundaries. The economic value of wetland has been summarised in 23.2 and the corresponding chart.

For wetlands that yield recreation opportunities, there is the danger that utilisation levels will result in congestion and subsequent decline in resource quality, as the wetlands carrying capacity is exceeded.

The interface between agricultural development policy and wetland conservation is an appropriate contest in which to analyse such intervention failure. Examples can be drawn from North Bihar (e.g. saline soil marshes in the Kosi river basin of Saharsa and Purnea).[5] In all these cases, high-value wetlands have suffered considerable losses due to conversion into intensive agriculture. Wetlands are also source of varieties of fishes, snails, crabs, tortoise, prawn, snake skin, frogs, mothi, makhana, situa shell, medicinal plants and bird's meat (Table 23.2).

In this way, it could be said that the economic value of wetlands are very many and on any cost it should be saved from dwindling.

Ecological Value of Wetlands

In order to maintain ecological balance the chief aim is to analyse, classify and to map the various types of wetlands in their correct position and examine the mutual relationship for assessing their physical properties and economic potentialities in relation to wetlands.

(a) The division of Darbhanga is an alluvial plain. Most of the diversities seen on the surface are those due to river action and a series of raised riverside uplands known as levees, dotted with wetlands in the form of alternating depressions (chaurs) of streams.

(b) A sub-terai belt of marshy land in the north with intervening tracts of uplands along rivers is succeeded in the south by a wide belt of marshy lowlands, characterised by permanent depressions and lakes besides tanks which are man-made features of wetlands.

(c) In the riparian tracts of the Ganges the land is high due to which wetlands are found slight away from levee in the form of intervening depressions. Due to the presence of natural levee on the northern bank of the Ganges, all rivers flowing along the gravity of slope from north to south turn towards

Table 23.2 : Production of Various Resources from Wetlands in Darbhanga Division Production in M.T. (1997)

S.No.	*Districts*	*Fishes*	*Snails*	*Crabs*	*Tortoise*	*Prawns*	*Snake skin*	*Frogs*	*Mothi*	*Makhana*	*Situa shells*	*Medicinal Plants*	*Birds' Meat*	*Total*
1.	Darbhanga	23,000	1100	295	1650	1200	190	270	205	220	275	145	205	28755
2.	Samastipur	3,300	320	105	451	315	85	101	95	110	100	51	75	5108
3.	Madhubani	3,100	295	102	405	285	75	100	92	105	95	45	65	4764

Source : Fisheries Department, Government of Bihar, Patna (1990-91) and Estimates made by the author, 1991.

east and run parallel along the Ganges river for a few kilometres before they finally make confluence.

(d) In the extreme south the delta is known as Moribund Ganga delta Sunderban which covers 360 square kilometre area. The whole country is dotted with tributaries of Ganges chiefly known as Ganga Sagar. Here the wetland is characterised by mangrove forest and governed by tidal waves.

The conservation of wetland focuses attention on the ecological disturbance caused by the impoundment of water in dams and reservoirs. The ecological effects of water impoundment have been summarized and certain measures for the conservation of fish, flora, vertebrate and invertebrate fauna in the affected areas have been suggested. Udhwa Birds Sanctuary in Rajmahal presents a model of nature conservation under wetland environment.

The development of Kabar lake and Gogabeel as birds sanctuary have been planned to attract tourist flow in order to save our nature and develop these marginal lands which are neglected since long. The major factors responsible for the depletion of the rich fish wealth of the river Ganges, namely over exploitation and pollution should be stopped. The declining fisheries of the region can only be saved through proper management and balanced exploitation of the resource on the basis of sound ecological principles.

The dangers to the sensitive ecosystem of the beautiful flowering valley of the Gandak near Balmikinagar posed by the tourist boom resulting may be considered although the area is infested with criminals. They plead that the valley should be declared restricted area till the time of effective measures for its protection could be planned and enforced.

Ox-Bow Lakes and Bayous

As meanders grow, it frequently happens that a narrow neck of land is cut through from two sides thus allowing the stream to straighten its course. The two ends of the meander so separated from the channel, are likely to be filled up by sand. The best example of an ox-bow lake on the bank of river Burhi-Gandak in Vaishali district. These water-bodies form excellent settlement sites. The whole face of the country is dotted with rural settlements besides small ox-bow lakes or elongated water bodies and chaurs (long semi-circular marshes) which lie in between the rivers making the old abandoned courses of the streams Fig. 23.3). Though found extensively in all parts of this region, the

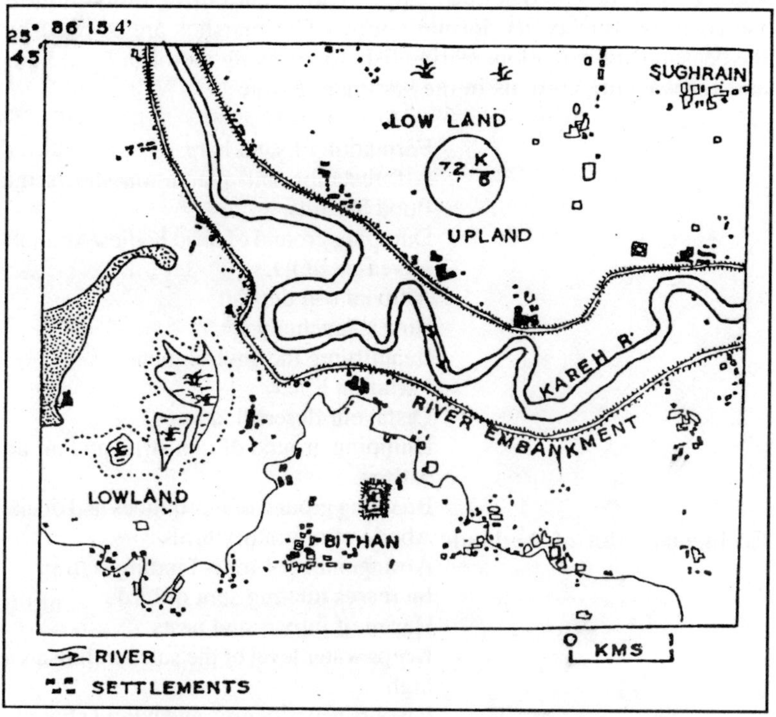

Fig. 23.3 : Riverside uplands and alternating depressions in the division of Darbhanga

abandoned courses are more prolific in Madhubani, Samastipur and Darbhanga districts of North Bihar.

Marshes

The abandoned channel of a stream on a flood plain may become partially filled with vegetation, thus forming a marsh. They may also occur in any depression on the flood plains especially in areas of waterlogging. Marshes are numerous towards the south-eastern part of Samastipur district.

Some of these marshy lands dry up during the summer season. There are some marshes which exist throughout the year like a *tand* (man-made square shaped wetland). Marshes are also found in the beds of rivers like the Mahananda, the Panar, the Kosi, the old Kosi, the Bhutahi Balan, the Kamla, the Jibachh, the Kareh, the Burhi

Gandak and the Gandak during hot weather but during rainy months the river establishes its normal course. The marshes are utilised by the peasants for irrigation, rearing fish, for growing mothi and makhana and for washing animals in the summer season.

Ecological Value of Wetlands

- Formation of sand bars
- Afforestation and plantation shows the flood hazards.
- Dumping ground of dead bodies/Animals increases BOD.
- Alluvial soil deposit
- Bird's Sanctuary
- Beautifying the environment
- Pollution Filter
- Disfavour desertification
- Dumping ground of industrial and urban wastes
- Breeding ground of mosquitoes and ducks
- Abode of migratory birds
- Arrangement of birds binding station
- Increases hunting spot of birds
- Haven of insects and pests
- Keeps water level of the surrounding area high
- Favours waterlogging and humid climatic condition
- Favours luxurious growth of vegetation
- Maintain ecological balance.
- Saviour of flora and fauna wealth
- Marshy areas are dispersed type.

The ecological value of wetland has been summarised in a Table given below. But is quite unfortunate that during the recent fury of floods many wetlands of North Bihar suffer from sedimentation and some of them have completely lossed their existence especially in Manigachhi Anchal of Darbhanga district.

Cultural Value of Wetlands

The cultural value of wetlands include religious performance along its shores, recreation by navigation, cradle land for civilizations, cremation ground for dead bodies and provide beautiful site for human settlements.

Distribution of Tanks

Tank is an artificial square shaped water body constructed near settlement site for bathing of human beings and animals. Its construction by the owner also attaches religious sentiments due to welfare of people.

Cultural Value of Wetlands

- Bathing place for men and beasts
- Marriage ritual
- Den of criminals
- Shradh/Tarpan/Nagpanchmi
- Emersion of Goddess—Saraswati, Bihula, Durga and Kali
- Bathing on Purnimas, Sankranti and Sun and the Moon Eclipses.
- Natural boundary
- Quarrel ground
- Embankment provides site for human settlements
- Abode of Goddess Kamla (Goddess of Water)
- Sama-Chakwa
- Sun Worship (Chhat)
- Marriage of pond with mango orchard
- Cremation ground of dead body
- Centre of civilization—the Cachar and the Ganga Valley
- Recreation/Sports
- Promote isolation
- Temple site of Lord Shiva
- Working place for fishermen
- Favourable area for ghosts
- Favours rice and fish culture
- Flood hazards—damage roads and disrupt boundary of agricultural holdings.

In North Bihar the total number of tanks are 8509 which are distributed unevenly in different parts of the area and determined by the presence and absence of river in the area. It is quite discernible that river embankments of the Ganges, the Kosi, the Mahananda, the Gandak and others have very few number of tanks near them but away from river banks their number increases. In the districts of Saharsa, Madhubani, Darbhanga and the northern parts of Samastipur, Sitamarhi and Muzaffarpur the number of tanks are very high because these are the areas of "rice and fish culture". The highest number of tanks are available in Madhubani district (2421) and Darbhanga district (1435) in 1991.

In Pokharvinda village of Manigachhi anchal, there are 75 tanks and in Narayanpur village of the same anchal there are 32 tanks which are not only a lowlying wetlands but economically they are highly potential. For example, Rajokhar pond of Narayanpur which has an expanse of over 21 hectares of land is annually producing makhana of Rs. 3 lakhs and fish of Rs. 3 lakhs respectively. It has a powerful tool to make ecological balance, beautify the environment, providing recreation ground of boats, bathing place for human beings and cattle. Besides irrigating the land through pumping sets over more than 5000 hectares of land in the surrounding area.

In the division of Darbhanga there is a close correlation between ponds as artificial wetlands and planted mango orchards as vegetation cover, because people have a belief to marry tank with mango orchard as these two are the assets for making the ecological balance, checking flood hazards besides increasing the water holding capacity of the land in tank to use it for irrigation and provide a bathing place for buffaloes in each and every village.

Conclusion

Wetlands are waterlogged and flood affected marshy low-lying areas of Darbhanga division whose investigation is rightly directed because the rapid increase of population and livestock wealth have endangered the ecological balance due to over-exploitation of forest, by reckless cutting of trees for fuel and building materials since ancient period. In North East India most of the lakes, old tanks and dried river beds are almost filled up by the agent of weathering and erosion due to human activity and floods. For example, Motihari was surrounded by 43 lakes in 1800 A.D. but now most of them have filled up by deritus and silt from the surrounding area and nowadays only the remnants of some of them have left. This clarifies the point that wetlands should be saved to beautify the environment, maintain the ecological balance, producing Singhara (a fruit produced in shallow water) and Makhana (a black bead produced in thorny plant of shallow water) rearing varieties of fishes and providing place of surrounding higher embankment of ponds, canals and river embankment for the plantation of trees. A national and international wetland development committee should be constituted comprising the experts of various disciplines related to wetlands for nature conservation and search of archaeological evidences.

Wetlands are not wastelands rather they are among the most fertile and productive ecosystems in the world. They are essential life support systems and play a vital role in controlling water-cycles, and help to clean up our environment. They make many commercial fisheries possible and protect coasts from floods and strong surges wetlands are pollution filter, water reservoirs, offering homes for endangered plants, birds and animals and hence we have an obligation to maintain and preserve them.

REFERENCES

1. Gopal, B., Turner, R.E., Wetzel, R.G. and Whigham, D.F., *Wetlands Ecology and Management,* National Institute of Ecology and International Scientific Publication, Jaipur, 1982.
2. Wetlands Conference in Czechoslovakia, *Nature and Resources,* UNESCO, Vol. XX, No. 2, 1984, p. 22.
3. U.S. Fish and Wildlife Service, Wetlands States and Trends, Washington D.C., U.S. Department of the Interior, Fish and Wildlife Service, 1991.
4. *White House Press Release, "Presidential Address 15th Plan for Wetlands",* An Action Agenda (Washington D.C., The Conservation Foundation, 1988).
5. Sklar, F.H., Costanza, R. and Day, J.W., Dynamic, Spatial Simulation Modelling of Coastal Wetland Habitat Succession, *Ecology Mod.* 1985, 29, pp. 261-281.

24

Strategy of Development Through Dams

R.B. MANDAL

Introduction

A dam constitutes about the most important device for development, management and multipurpose utilization of nature's water resources. It has comprehensively transformed the socio-economic scenario of various regions of the world and has been universally regarded to be a powerful tool for development. Nations have put in inordinate resources, have adopted extraordinary legislations and have been even gone to wars in order to be able to construct dams and get enormous consequential benefits. In the post-independence surge for economic emancipation from centuries of impoverishment of our country, dams were accorded a high priority and pedestal in the scheme of harnessing our natural resources to production, so much so that dams symbolized development and Pandit Nehru, the first Prime Minister of free India termed them as "temples of modern India".

As a dam is essentially a measure of intervention in the natural regime of water resources in order to regulate their behaviour and make them yield diverse benefits to mankind, it necessarily has to contend with certain adverse consequences, such as displacement of people and impacts on environment and ecology. In recent years and decades, these consequences have been launched for ensuring adequate compensation for, and safeguards against them. Due to these concerns and agitations, dams appear to have become 'controversial' and there is a danger of 'throwing away the baby with the bath tub'. The Report of the World Commission on Dams constituted in the midst of this controversy has itself become controversial. Some have hailed this Report titled "Dams and Development" as a verdict against dams, others have severely criticized and even rejected it as being irrational and lopsided in its recommendations. Thus, it is high time that the civil society engages in a serious and enlightening dialogue and deliberations on the topic of dams and development.

It is in this context under India Water Partnership (IWP), a forum for diverse stakeholders in water resources in India, a series of workshops are being held in different regions of India, for which the Institute of Resource Management and Economic Development, Delhi has taken the leading role and responsibility. Apart from the general and common issues, each regional workshop will discuss the issues specific to, or dominant for the region concerned. The first workshop in the series was held at Delhi in February, 2002, participated by Government of India officials, multi-disciplinary experts and other stakeholders. Another workshop is being planned to be held at Kolkata. A workshop on the topic was held at Patna in June, 2002 covering the region of Bihar, Jharkhand and U.P.

Dams are considered as strategic point of regional economic development. Hence, they should be regarded as the base of modernity, ushering new dimensions in flood control, checking soil erosion, rise of multipurpose projects besides creation of employment and give morale booster to the cause of nationalism. It is true that dams have displaced poor people. It creates waterlogging and people of diverse nature are struggling for have and have-nots.

Hence, in order to get something better one has to sacrifice to some extent without which we cannot think of any progress. Dynamicity in development is progress oriented whereas traditional is static and having no likelihood of progress. Hence, the strategy of development through dams could be viewed in Fig. 24.1(a).

Purpose of Study

(a) To assess the benefit of dams in the makeup of modern India.
(b) People's agitations against big dams are due to lack of farsightedness.
(c) Big dams should be constructed only on stable landmass of Peninsular India because North India is earthquake prone, and they may create disaster at the time of earthquake and eruption of volcanoes [Fig. 24.1(b)].

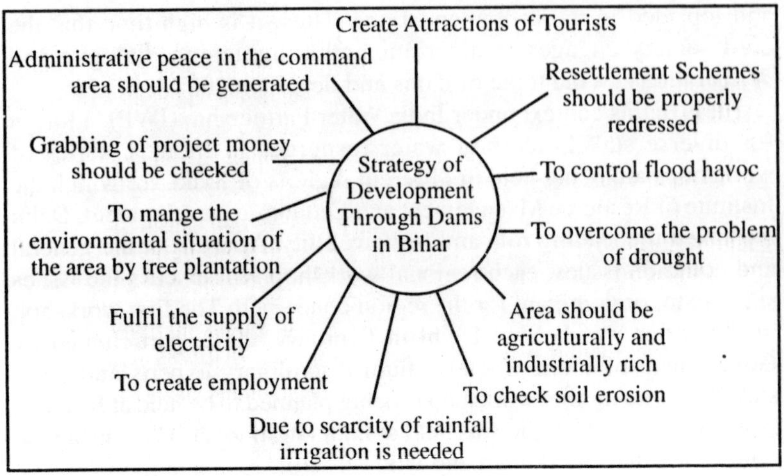

Fig. 24.1(a) : Strategy of Development Through Dams

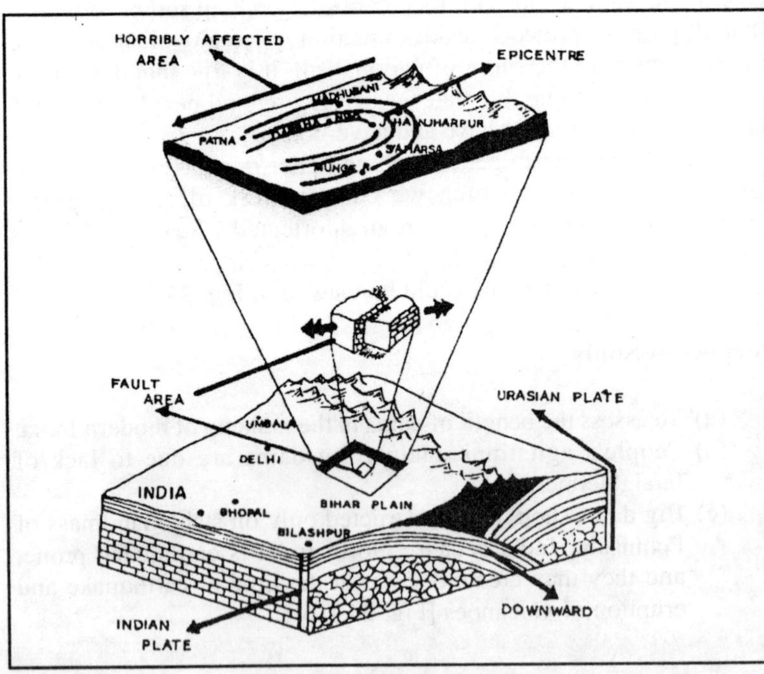

Fig. 24.1(b) : Effect of 1988 Earthquake on Darbhanga Division

Sustaining Rivers and Livelihood

The Himalayan rivers are not only problem oriented but they are sustaining the livelihood of people residing in the area. Rivers :

- help in collecting gold in Dun hills of West Champaran especially by Tharus.
- provide newer alluvium soil on the cultivated land.
- the rivers act as fishing ground and seat of human activities through boating and recreation.

Sharing Rivers for Peace, Development and Society

The countries like India and Nepal have agreed to use the dams and rivers not as quarrelling ground but as source of friendly relations, development of electricity production, irrigation on dry land and agricultural development through hydro-electric power stations and construction of canals. Ultimately, the benefit of all these go to the society and people of India and Nepal both.

Addressing Existing Dams

On the northern border of North Bihar and Nepal at present there are two dams: One on the Kosi river. It helps in collecting the water coming from Sapt Kosi of Nepal. In this river the total discharge of water is more than 30 lakh cusecs (Fig. 24.2).

On the other hand, in the north-western side in Champaran district the dam on the Gandak river at Valmikinagar helps in channelising the flood water of this river. Its total discharge is not more than 5 lakh cusecs of water per second. Two canals have been taken out from this dam: one Tribeni Canal towards east and the other western canal towards Gorakhpur through Nepal.

The Case of North Bihar

The Central Government has decided to construct high dam on the Kamla and the Bagmati rivers. The directive has been given to make extensive project proposal (DPR) these two rivers along with the Kosi river. The joint committee on water resource of India and Nepal agreed

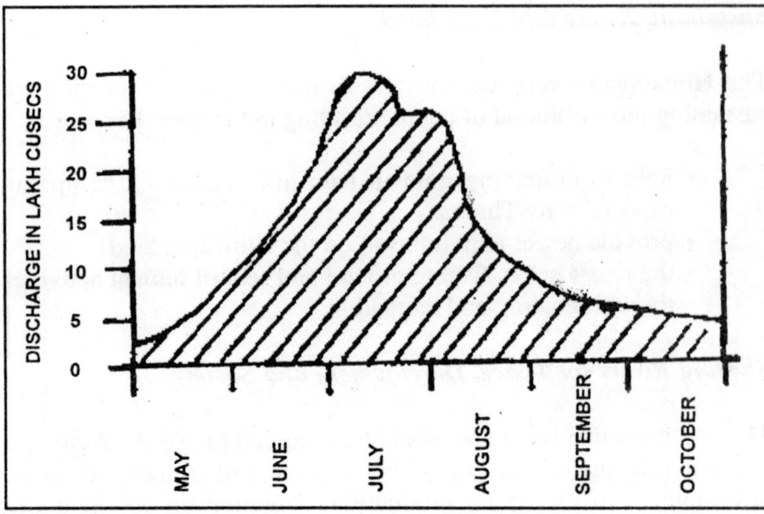

Fig. 24.2 : Water Discharge Level in the Kosi River

for this. It has been said that it is difficult to fight with nature but with the proper management of water resource the protection from flood could be ensured. On Sapt Kosi a high dam of 269 metres high would be constructed. This will help in producing 3300 megawatt electricity. It will help in irrigating 5.4 lakh hectares of land in Nepal and 9.7 lakh hectares in India. It will help in managing 5 to 15 lakh cusecs of water.

With the construction of these dams the permanent solution of flood in North Bihar could be possible. In order to have immediate flood forecast five offices have been opened at Kathmandu, Viratnagar, Janakpur, Dhahran and Kurle. Now all hurdles for the construction of high dam have been cleared.

Analysis of the Problem

Generally dams are designed in accordance with the need and demand of people in the area. Therefore, in the initiation of any dam the people of the area should be taken into confidence by dissemination of proper message to the society. This is considered as local participation. In this regard greater good of the society should be considered as positive factor because it is not possible to make happy the entire masses.

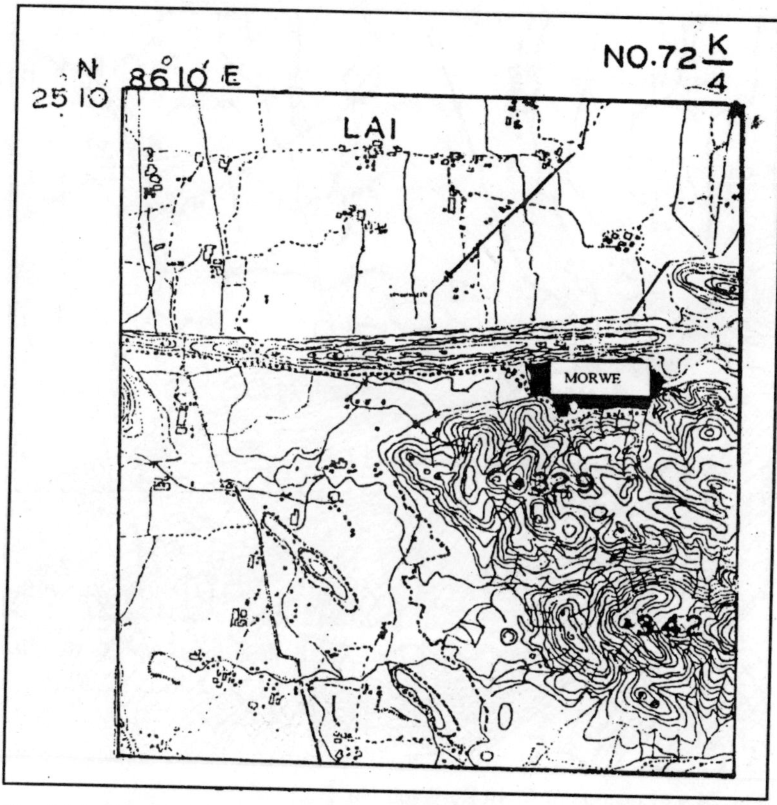

Fig. 24.3 : Location of Morwe Reservoir Project

Because in any developmental process some one has to suffer and hence, we should not run our business by the whims of the society.

In fact, water, electricity, roads and afforestation are needed everywhere for crop production, for running the factory, for drinking purpose, for utilisation of livestock and for beautifying the environment. In North Bihar the construction and timely repair of flood protective embankments are essential but in South Bihar plain where drought is almost certain in most of the years, the people are aware of the doubtful completion of the projects based on dams and benefit derived from them, e.g. Dakranala, Naktidam, Morwe dam, Amrit reservoir and the completion of Upper and Lower Kiul projects are doubtful due to lack of fund for the repair of canal, culvert, cleaning

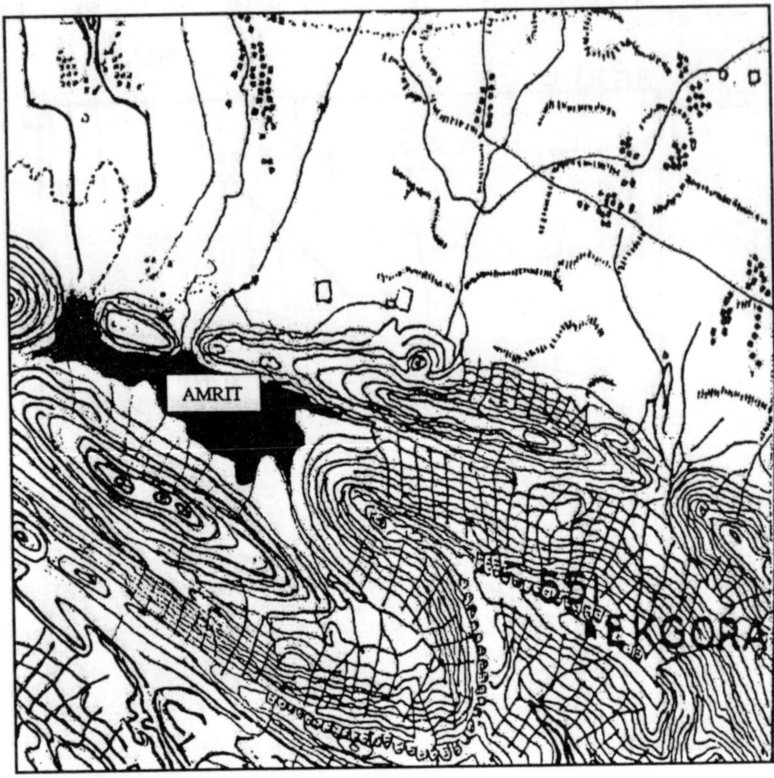

Fig. 24.4 : Location of Amrit Reservoir No. 7

of pynes, ahar, start of a fresh project due to menace of rangdars and the demand of ransom by several groups of people.

Thus our discussion should also focus as to:

1. Why different irrigation schemes operating in Bihar are failing to irrigate the required amount of land in their command areas ?
2. Any dam should be designed by considering the need and desire of people.
3. Such schemes should also incorporate the integrated development of watershed, planning of wastelands for the better and fostering irrigation management.
4. In order to construct the dam the deforestation is inevitable but on the other hand, the water reservoir constructed also

Table 24.1 : Irrigation Schemes Based on Dams in Munger District

Sl. No.	*Name of the Scheme*	*Amount Invested (Rs. in lakhs)*
1.	Gideshwar Beer	17.50
2.	Anjan River Project	5.08
3.	Kaurihari Project	58.00
4.	Kharagpur Lake Scheme	24.00
5.	Nagi Dam Project	40.17
6.	Kundhit Project	4.80
7.	Ganli Project	0.98
Second Five Year Plan		
8.	Morwe Dam Project	126.00
9.	Tanti Irrigation Project	4.08
10.	Bajan Irrigation Project	6.40
11.	Bagra Irrigation Project	2.46
12.	Mohane Beer Project	8.50
13.	Jalkund Reservoir Project	8.62
14.	Firangi Dam Project	4.38
15.	Lower Kiul Project	115.00
16.	Badua Reservoir Project	628.00
Third Five Year Plan		
17.	Sirkhandi Project	7.10
18.	Amrit Reservoir Project	5.08
19.	Khand Bihari Project	2.00
20.	Dorma Beer Project	—
21.	Nagi Dam Project	9.75
22.	Nakti Dam Project	288.00
23.	Kiul Dam Scheme	100.00

Source : D.P. Yadav, *Munger of My Dreams,* 1996.

act as pollution filter as does the wetland and this has nullified the '*Chipco Movement*' of S. Bhuguna.

Morwe Dam Project

This dam and reservoir is located in Lakhisarai district. It was completed in 1969 at the cost of Rs. 1.26 crores. It irrigates 4532 hectares of land. The height of the dam is 52.3 metres and the length is 56 metres (Fig 24.3).

Amrit Dam Reservoir

Amrit Dam reservoir (Fig. 24.4) is located in Sikandra Block whose command area is 4484 hectares.

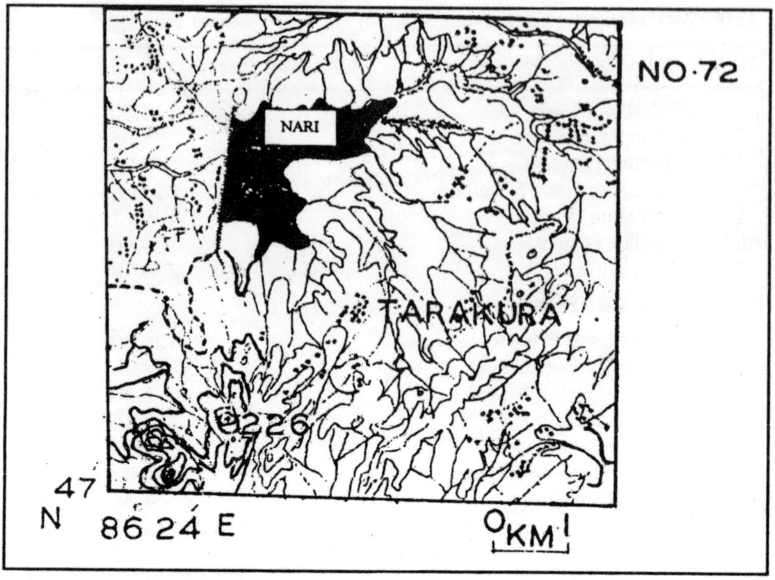

Fig. 24.5 : Location of Nagi Reservoir

Nagi Dam Reservoir

Nagi dam reservoir scheme is situated in Jhajha and Lakshmipur blocks in Jamui district. The total command area of this irrigation scheme is 2428 hectares (Fig 24.5).

Now coming to the above Table 24.1 it could be said that it is a sheer wastage of resource. Primarily, 6.20 lakh rupees have been allocated for the completion of Belharna Project. Second time this amount has been raised to Rs. 12 crores out of this Rs. 5 crores have already been spent but only 20 per cent work has been done as yet. Similarly, in Anjan Scheme the initial allocation was Rs. 1.41 crores but later on it has raised to Rs. 16 crores out of this Rs. 7 crores have already been spent but unfortunately even 20 per cent work has not been done uptil now.

On the basis of above Table 24.1 it could be concluded that in First, Second and Third Five Year Plans the completion of irrigation projects were very quick, the expenses were low and completion was 100 per cent. But during Fifth, Sixth and Seventh Five Year Plans the progress of the Projects were nil but the number of engineers have increased manifold. The construction work have progressed well but the irrigation works have not been up to its mark.

Uptil now more than Rs. 60 crores have been spent but due to administrative slackness the coordination in the work has not been possible. Engineers are not fearful to the administration. Politicians are giving protection to the contractors. All these factors are responsible for the failure of irrigation projects in Munger and now it would be useless to start a fresh project.

In Dakranala Scheme Rs. 16 crores allocated in 1976. Now this amount has been raised to Rs. 50 crores. Out of this Rs. 7 crores has already been spent but only 70 per cent work has been done as yet. It is a sheer chit and wastage of public money. But it is unfortunate that no one look after these schemes as all engineers, ministers and contractors are grabbing the money. I don't know who is to blame.

REFERENCES

Ahmad, O.K. *et al.* (eds), *Ganges, Brahamputra, Meghna Region: A Framework for sustainable Development,* The Dhacca Univercity Press, 2001.

Bandopadhyay, J., "A critical look at the World Commission on Dams (WCD) in the context of the Debate on Large Dams on the Himalaya River, *Indian Journal of Landscape Systems and Ecological Studies*, Vol. 27, No.A. June 2004.

Bandopadhyay, J. and B. Mallick, *Book Review in Water International* 26 (4), 2001.

Bandopadhyay, J. and D. Gyawali, Himalayan Water Resources: Ecological and Political Aspects of Management, *Mountain Research and Development*, (14). 1-24-1994.

Bandopadhyay, J., Dams for the Third Millennium, Himalayas, *the South Asian Magazine* 11 (3), 1998.

Bandopadhyay, J.; Sustainability of Big Dams in the Himalaya, *Economic and Political Weekly*, 30(38) September 23, 1995.

Bandopadhyay, J., 'Water Management in the Ganga Brahamputra Basin: Changes for the 21st century", *International Journal of Water Resource Development*, 11(4), 1995.

Biswas, A.K., *Systems Approach to Water Management*, Tokyo, McGraw Hill, 1976.

Dixit, A., (2001), *Basic Water Science*, Nepal Water Conservation Foundation, Kathmandu, 2001.

Falkenmark, M., Fresh water : Time for a modified Approach, *AMBIO* 15(4), 1986.

Gaur, V.K., *Earthquake Hazards and Large Dams on the Himalaya*, New Delhi, INTACH, 1993.

Gupta, H.K., Seismicity in the Vicinity of dams in the Himalayan Rivers, *Journal of the Geological Society of India*, 1984.

Gyawali, D. and A. Dixit, Mahakali Impasse and Indo-Nepal Water Conflict; *Economic and Political Weekly*, Feb.27, 1999.

Limaye, S.D. To Dam or not to Dam? A water resource overview from Developed Countries, Stockholm Water front, No.2, June 2001.

Lundduist, J., *et al., Sustaining our Water into 21st Century : Comprehensive Assessment of the Fresh Water Resources of the World*; Stockholm Environmental Institute, 1997.

Mowr, Major River Basins of India—An overview, Ministry of Water Resources, New Delhi, 1989.

Nawalawala, B.N., World Commission on Dams, *Ecomomic Political Weekly*, 2004.

Rangachari, R. and R.G. Verghese, Making water work to translate poverty into prosperity. The Ganga Brahmaputra Barak Region in O.K. Ahmad (Ed), p.87.

Rao, K.L., *India's Water Wealth*, Orient Longmans, New Delhi, p.219,1975.

Shiklomanov, LA., World Fresh Water Resource: in P.H. Glick (Ed) *Water in Crisis*, Oxford University Press, 1993, p.16.

Verhshes, B.G. *et al., Converting Water into Wealth,* Konark Publishers, Delhi, 1994.

World Commission on Dams, *Dams and Development. A New Framework for Decision Making,* London, 2000.

25

Impact of Floods on Land Use in Muzaffarpur District

SHOBHA KUMARI

Introduction

Floods are one of the most dramatic interactions between man and his environment, emphasising both the sheer force of natural events and man's inadequate efforts to control them. Floods are natural events but when men put themselves at risk by developing floodplains for settlement, agriculture and industry, they become disaster. Construction of roads, bridges and railway lines has further aggravated the intensity of flood devastation. Among all the disasters that occur in India, river floods are the most frequent and often the most devastating. "River flood is relatively high flow of water which overtakes the natural channel provided for the runoff" (Ven Te Chow, 1956).[1] Rostvedt and others (1968) viewed it "as a high stream flow which overtops natural banks of a stream."[2] There are clear evidences that despite massive expenditure on flood control, flood losses continue to rise in many countries of the world. River floods are very common in most of the humid region of the world.

The peculiarities of rainfall are the major causes of river floods in India. 75 per cent of the annual rain of India, falls during short monsoon season of 3 to 4 months. The heavy discharge from the river during monsoon months causes widespread floods in the Ganga, the Brahmaputra and the Meghana basins.

The Study Area

Muzaffarpur district is located in Tirhut division of Bihar. Its present territory extends from 25° 45′N Longitude. Being a part of the North Bihar plain, Muzaffarpur district is an aggravational plain with even skyline. The general height of the area varies between 49 metres and 58 metres from the M.S.L. The district is divisible into three phsyiographic units. These are (1) The Trans-Bagmati region, (2) The Bagmati-Burhi Gandak Doab and (3) The Burhi Gandak-Gandak Doab. Muzaffarpur district is drained by the Great Gandak, the Burhi Gandak and the Bagmati rivers. All these rivers are notorious for shifting their courses and rivers evulsions. They usually flow on alluvial ridges. Beds of rivers are relatively higher than their adjoining flood plains. These conditions lead to frequent flooding in the flood plains during rainy season when the study area receives 76.47 per cent of its annual rainfall.

Floods : Unwelcome Guests for the Study Area

Floods are unwelcome guests for Muzaffarpur district. They wash away the standing crops from more than one lakh hectare and take many lives each year. Even the movement of people and commodities, to a large extent, is constricted during floods. Floods are boon for soil but a curse for the crops and people. Floods have been the major influents of agriculture in Muzaffarpur district since long but its effect has been felt more profoundly since the beginning of the 20th century due to rapid increase in population to huge pressure on precious but fixed land resource.

Causes of Floods

Flooding in the rivers of Muzaffarpur district has been caused by :

- Inadequate capacity within the banks of the river to contain high flows.
- River bank erosion and silting of river beds.
- Synchronization of flood in main and tributary rivers.
- Poor natural drainage.
- Unique coincidence of the snow melting in the Himalayan ranges and heavy downpour in the area during summer.
- Frequent changes in the course of the Bagmati and other rivers of the area together with river evulsions.

- Compounding of the flood problems due to the construction of bandhs, embankments along river sides, canal bandhs, roads and railway lines obstructing the free flow of water.

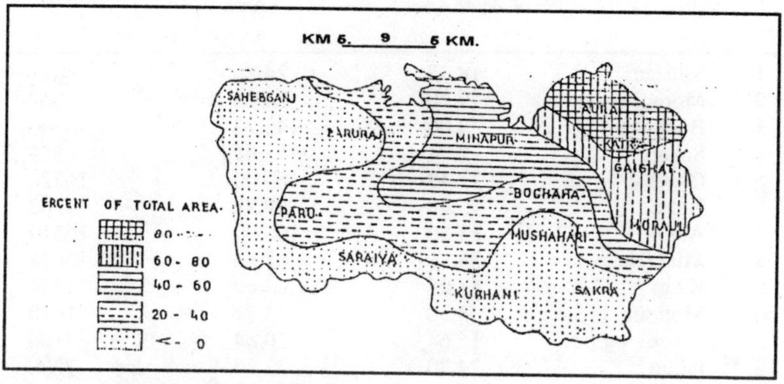

Fig. 25.1 : Muzaffarpur District Flood Prone Area Scale

Flood Prone Area

A total of 100,899 hectare of land in Muzaffarpur district is classed as flood prone area. Out of the total flood prone area of the district 54.24 per cent is affected occasionally while 45.76 per cent is affected every year. The flood prone area accounts for 31.98 per cent of the total geographical area and 39.13 per cent of the cultivable land of the district (Table 25.1). The proportion of flood prone area in the district varies from 2.94 per cent in Sakara Anchal to 84.80 per cent in Aurai Anchal. It is found highly concentrated in the Bagmati-Gandak-Doab and trans-Bagmati Area.

All the Anchals located in the Bagmati riparian belt have more than 75 per cent of their area is classed as flood prone.

During floods the entire Bagmati riparian belt turns into a vast sea dotted with settlements on higher sites as islands.

Impact of Floods on Land Use

Methodology

In the present study ecological, physiognomic and statistical approaches have been adopted. The former was employed to study

Table 25.1 : Flood Prone Area in Muzaffarpur District

S.No.	*Flood Prone Area in Muzaffarpur District*			*Total Flood Prone Area in Hectares*
	Anchals	*Flood Prone Area % of Total Area*	*% of Cultivable Area*	
1.	Mushari	18.47	24.85	3621
2.	Moraul	79.78	94.25	5747
3.	Bochaha	38.00	45.23	10790
4.	Sakara	2.94	3.81	515
5.	Gaighat	77.43	100.00	16526
6.	Katra	75.40	99.98	14262
7.	Aurai	84.80	100.00	16519
8.	Minapur	53.36	65.89	12625
9.	Kanti	51.05	64.69	1340
10.	Motipur	3.36	3.77	1010
11.	Sahebganj	15.64	20.54	3140
12.	Paroo	24.70	33.80	7200
13.	Saraiya	9.52	11.30	2407
14.	Kurhani	19.90	25.18	5304
	Muzaffarpur District	31.98	39.13	100899

Source : Kharif Report 2000-2001, Department of Agriculture, Muzaffarpur, District.

the crop pattern. The impact of flood, land use, cropping patterns and intensity of cropping have been evaluated through statistical methods. Both observational descriptive and observational rational methods have been employed in the present study. The study is based on secondary data collected from the District Statistical Office, Muzaffarpur.

The purpose of the present study is to examine the economic impact of floods in Muzaffarpur district. It intends to examine that how far flood has led to decrease in the cropping intensity and changes in the crop pattern and land use in the study area.

For this purpose the economic impact of irrigation in Muzaffarpur district has been discussed with reference to land use, cropping intensity and crop pattern at two points of time is 1988-89 and 1998-99. The former represents relatively flood immune conditions while the latter period when flood was very severe. Table 25.2 shows the changes that have occurred in the land use pattern due to floods. Floods have affected directly on three categories of land use, i.e. area put to non-agricultural uses, current fallow and net area sown.

The area put to non-agricultural uses has increased from 15.76

Table 25.2 : Muzaffarpur District : Impact of Flood on General Land Use

S.No.	*Anchals*	*Area put to non-agriculture Uses (% of total area)*		*Current Fallows (% of total area)*		*Net Sown Area (% of total area)*	
		1988-89	*1998-99*	*1988-89*	*1998-99*	*1988-89*	*1998-99*
1.	Minapur	20.27	21.38	6.86	4.10	67.12	60.16
2.	Bochaha	17.19	18.04	4.70	2.82	73.38	68.26
3.	Mushari	27.27	26.25	5.20	12.18	58.24	50.33
4.	Katra	17.82	35.23	11.48	11.63	68.85	47.79
5.	Aurai	15.89	15.90	2.99	4.99	77.70	76.11
6.	Sakara	21.05	15.44	0.23	6.08	73.61	69.35
7.	Moraul	16.43	17.69	8.92	15.12	61.03	61.51
8.	Gaighat	17.56	17.14	9.56	32.20	68.35	46.12
9.	Kanti	24.53	26.53	–	1.03	70.53	66.67
10.	Kurhani	14.46	16.37	13.42	10.26	67.63	68.83
11.	Paroo	18.86	25.94	6.49	5.60	64.72	63.81
12.	Sahebganj	10.02	9.43	8.18	5.84	78.54	78.46
13.	Motipur	16.53	14.53	–	5.48	72.44	68.86
14.	Saraiya	15.76	21.99	5.53	4.79	67.53	66.70
	Muzaffarpur District	15.76	21.99	5.89	7.83	69.25	63.85

Source : Jinswars 1988-89 and 1998-99

The area put to non-agricultural uses has increased from 15.76 per cent of the total area of the district in 1988-89 to 21.99 per cent in 1998-98. The increase is more pronounced in flood prone area, i.e. Minapur, Katra, Moraul, Paroo and Saraiya anchals. The maximum increase has been registered in Katra, the worst flood affected anchals of the district. In Katra anchal the area put to non-agriculture has increased from 17.82 per cent to 35.23 per cent.

Floods have led to increase in the current fallows. In 1988-89 current fallows covered 5.89 per cent of total area of the district which increased to 7.83 per cent in 1998-99. Gaighat, Moraul, and Mushari anchals located in the Bagmati-Burhi Gandak-Doab witnessed phenomenal increase in the extent of current fallows. In Gaighat anchal it has increased from 9.56 per cent in 1988-89 to 32.20 per cent in 1998-99 while in Moraul and Mushari anchals an increase of 6.20 per cent and 8.98 per cent respectively was recorded during the same period due to waterlogging throughout the year.

Floods, on the other hand, have played negative role on the N.S.A. In Muzaffarpur district, the N.S.A. accounted for 69.25 per cent of the total area in 1988-89 which decreased to 63.85 per cent in 1998-99 due to flood and post flood waterlogging. The maximum decrease was recorded in Gaighat anchal (22.13%) followed by Katra anchal (20.94%). Other worst affected anchals of the district were Minapur, Bochaha and Mushari. All these anchals lie in the flood prone belt of the district.

Impact of Flood on Crop Pattern and Cropping Intensity

Floods, not only affect the land use pattern but they also affect badly the crop pattern and cropping intensity. It is evident from Table 25.3 that both Bhadai and Aghani harvests are the worst sufferers in the flood prone area. Bhadai crops are sown with the early monsoon rains in the month of June and are harvested in August and September. This is the period of heavy rain associated with flood. In 1988-89 Bhadai harvest covered 13.74 per cent of the total cultivated area of Muzaffarpur district which decreased to 11.28 per cent in 1998-99. The decrease is more pronounced in Katra, Gaighat, Kanti, Paroo and Saraiya anchals either due to flood or due to waterlogging.

Tables 25.3 : Muzaffarpur District : Impact of Flood on Crop Land Use

S. No.	*Anchals*	*Bhadai Harvest (% of total crop land)*		*Aghani Harvest (% of total crop land)*		*Paddy (% of total crop land)*		*Wheat (% of total crop land)*	
		1988-89	*1998-99*	*1988-89*	*1998-99*	*1988-89*	*1998-99*	*1988-89*	*1998-99*
1.	Mushahri	15.92	15.76	26.13	32.02	32.99	38.10	17.99	16.39
2.	Minapur	13.68	15.76	37.30	29.45	47.99	38.51	12.95	34.15
3.	Bochaha	12.97	15.83	35.82	19.62	42.12	24.82	16.62	28.37
4.	Aurai	10.51	14.73	39.24	29.63	46.88	44.69	18.81	18.27
5.	Muraul	11.94	24.62	36.42	21.97	45.13	45.68	15.96	29.26
6.	Gaighat	11.60	1.17	40.22	8.66	49.20	9.82	24.64	45.86
7.	Sakara	14.42	12.27	28.16	36.07	36.68	41.96	20.84	32.22
8.	Kanti	15.34	6.51	29.17	37.74	30.99	34.26	14.37	29.49
9.	Motipur	16.40	11.51	48.79	37.69	37.59	42.42	14.61	24.80
10.	Sahebganj	11.74	20.10	39.67	52.22	44.84	67.43	19.27	8.63
11.	Kurhani	11.16	13.86	35.19	30.45	37.59	42.42	332.51	35.86
12.	Paroo	10.64	4.01	42.05	44.11	59.75	49.27	244.06	33.37
13.	Saraiya	14.34	8.13	42.60	39.85	52.76	42.52	18.60	24.49
	Muzaffarpur District	13.74	11.28	38.10	33.17	44.89	40.38	19.01	27.99

Source : Jinswars 1988-89 and 1998-99

It is the most dominant harvest in Muzaffarpur district. In 1988-89 Bhadai crops were raised on 38.10 per cent of the total cultivated land which decreased to 33.17 per cent in 1998-99. Paddy is the principal crop of the season. It is a water-loving crop but excess of water due to flood causes great damage to paddy. Both broadcast and transplantation paddy are grown in the district. The former occupies the flood prone areas while the latter prefers the flood free zones. During 1988-89 and 1998-99 period Bhadai harvest suffered great loss due to floods. The loss is more prominent in Katra, Gaighat, Bochaha, Minapur and Moraul anchals due to high incidence of flood and post flood waterlogging. Due to high incidence of flood and waterlogging the farmers of the riparian anchals prefer to leave their land fallow during the season than to transplant paddy and passively watch the consequences as crop failure.

Impact of Flood on Cropping Pattern

Somewhat drastic change has occurred in cropping intensity in Muzaffarpur district between 1988-89 and 1998-99 period. The main cause of this negative change is assigned to flood and waterlogging. The overall cropping intensity in the district has fallen from 164.46 per cent to 152.67 per cent during the period. All anchals except Minapur, Mushari, Moraul and Saraiya have noticed decrease in cropping intensity but Kanti, Gaighat, Sakra, Aurai, Katra and Bochaha anchals are the prominent losers due to high incidence of flood and waterlogging retarding multiple cropping. The maximum decrease has been registered in the Kanti anchal. The flood prone anchals, i.e. Katra and Mushari have low cropping intensity in both the years.

Floods have also affected the cropping pattern in Muzaffarpur district. Paddy is the most dominant cropping in the district followed by wheat occupying 40.38 per cent and 27.99 per cent of the total cultivated land respectively. But flood has different impact on paddy and wheat. Paddy is badly affected by flood while wheat gains its strength because vast extent of land becomes available for cropping which remain fallow during Bhadai and Aghani harvests due to flood.

Muzaffarpur district has registered 4.51 per cent of decrease in the strength of paddy during 1988-89 to 1998-99 decade. 9 out of 14 anchals have recorded decrease ranking between 2.2 to 39.8 per cent. But the decrease has been more pronounced in Gaighat, Katra and Bochaha anchals due to their hydrographic conditions.

But the decrease has been more pronounced in Gaighat, Katra and Bochaha anchals due to their hydrographic conditions.

On the other hand, there has been a general intensification of wheat cultivation. The spectacular increase in wheat cultivation in riparion anchals, i.e. Katra (25.98%), Gaighat (21.22%) and Minapur (21.20%) is related more to decrease in the total cropped land due to flood than to increase in the hectareage under wheat.

Conclusion

It is evident from the above discussion that flood is the worst natural hazard that adversely affects the land use and agriculture in Muzaffarpur district. So the economic development in the district has to be geared up by controlling the menacing flood. Floods in the district have international implication which involves the Bihar Government, Central Government of India along with the Government of Nepal.

Flood Mitigation

Various measures adopted for flood mitigation in the district which may be categorised into two groups :

1. Pre-Flood Measures

- "Pre-Monsoon Inspection" of all railway tracks, canals and drains by the respective department, which could include silt and detail clearance from the seasonal rivulets.
- Regular clearance of the drains from silt and weeds to make the drainage system fully functional and restoration of natural drainage blocked by roads, railway tracks and canals.
- Regular maintenance of embankments of rivers, canals distributaries etc. and regular check of the canals and siphons and clearing them from silt.
- Clearing of storm water and sewerage drains in towns before monsoon.
- Constitution of committees comprising of heads of all emergency services, medical, police, transportation and the district administration to ensure proper coordination during the crisis.

Post-Flood Management

Post-disaster management could *inter alia* include the following essential requirements :

- Speedy restoration of roads and the postal services.
- Normal water supply in the affected areas either by arranging tankers or fire tenders.
- Repair of the power, telephone and sewerage lines on priority basis so that normalcy is restored.
- Proper arrangements for the supply of food, shelter and clothing to marooned people.
- Ensuring adequate supply of POL and kerosene oil and keeping the supply line moving.
- Constitution of a survey team to assess the loss and compensation to be given to the affected population.
- Assistance for repair/rebuilding of the inundated areas.
- Taking up appropriate measures according to contingency plan for the agriculture sector.

REFERENCES

1. Chow, V.T. (1956), *Hydrologic Study of Floods in the United States*, Ins. Ass. Scient Hydrol Publ. 42, 134-70.
2. Rostvedt, J.O. *et al.* (1968), *Summary of Floods in the United States during 1963,* U.S. Geol. Survey Wat-sup pap 1830-20.

26

Pattern of Irrigation in Katkamsandi Anchal, Hazaribag

RAJENDRA KUMAR DAS

Introduction

Water is an important input for successful agriculture. Water may be available to crops in the natural course by rainfall or it may be supplied to the agricultural fields artificially by human efforts. The process of supplying water to crops by artificial means such as canals, wells, tube-wells, tanks, etc. from the sources of water such as rivers, tanks, ponds or underground water is called irrigation.

Study Area

Katkamsandi Anchal lies between 23°52′ to 24°14′ north latitudes and 85°8′ to 85°22′ east longitude, covering an area about 464 sq. kms in the district of Hazaribag. This Anchal is bounded by six Anchals of Hazaribag and Chatra districts. In the northern side, there is only one Anchal, i.e. Itkhori of Chatra district. In the southern side it is bounded by Barkagoan Anchal of Hazaribag district. Hazaribag Sadar, Ichak and Barhi Anchals are found in the eastern side of Katkamsandi Anchal. Simria (Chatra district) is the main boundary of the western side of this Anchal. Itkhori Anchal is also situated in the north western side (Fig. 26.1).

Aims and Objectives

The main objectives of the present paper are to highlight the pattern of irrigation in Katkamsandi Anchal, Hazaribag district, Jharkhand.

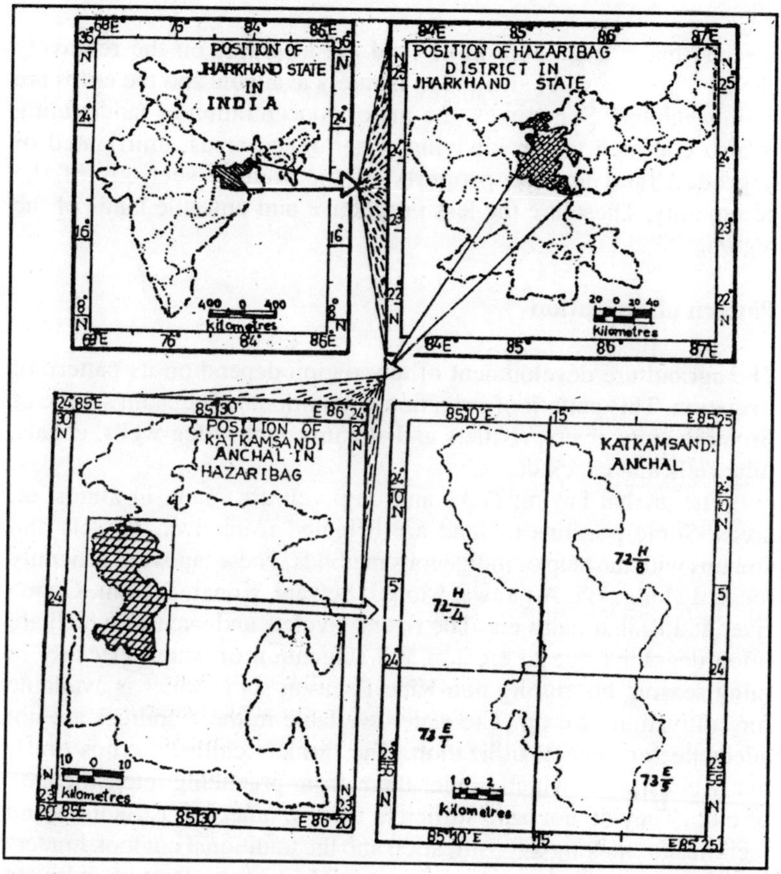

Fig. 26.1 : Location of the Study Area

Expansion at irrigation facilities along with consolidation of the existing systems has been the main strategy for increasing production of foodgrains. Irrigation support is provided through major, medium and minor irrigation projects and command area development.

Importance of Irrigation

Irrigation is the main technology that is used in agriculture. The crops which get adequate irrigation are also supposed to be served by other technology inputs. So, amount of irrigated area plays a vital role to indicate cultural development of the region. The Katkamsandi Anchal reveals that a large portion of land are available on the relatively elevated portion where irrigation is rarely available and the crops are mainly rainfed. Sometimes, the major concentration of landholding is also confined to the lowlying waterlogged areas, unirrigated or degraded land are the property of the weaker sections of the community. These are the less productive and unfertile lands of the region.

Pattern of Irrigation

The agriculture development of any region depend on its pattern of irrigation. This pattern of irrigation is traditional. The main source of irrgation from rivers, rivulets and streams, tanks, dug wells, canals, tubewells and check dams.

The anchal having tanks and dug well are found in almost all areas. Some portions of land are irrigated from river, rivulets and streams with the help of indigenous methods. These lands are generally located along, viz. Anjanwa, Mohni, Sewani, Konar, Piprahi, Gonda river and Rajhar nalas etc. The rivers, rivulets and streams which are often degraded due to erosion and stagnation of water specially in rainy season, but during non-Kharif season some water is available for cultivation of crop. The water available in these sources are not adequate for general utilization. The farmers cultivate crops under many constraints which hinder them from practicing intensification of crop. They do not have sufficient money, other infrastructures and facilities for making intensification and the traditional out look hinders them to go for further intensification. Most of the farmers cultivate only paddy in a year. Very few farmers cultivate rabi and pre-kharif crops due to lack of proper sources of irrigation. Whatever they produce i.e., for their own home consumption and not for trade.

Table 26.1 : Source of Irrigation in Hazaribag District

Sl. No.	*Sources of irrigation*	*% of total irrigated area*
1.	Ponds	60
2.	Wells	12
3.	Rivers	10
4.	Check Dams	8
5.	Canals	4
6.	Others	6
	Total	100

Problems of Irrigation

It has been mentioned that the Katkamsandi anchal has great topographical inequalities in general which have rendered quick run-off in the anchal. The rivers of this anchal are rain-fed which are not able to supply water throughout the year or whenever needed. We should not forget the past experiences in the area in terms of water availability from the monsoon rain. Hence, it is essential to say that the need of irrigation in the area under study for agricultural operations and development is essential for increasing agricultural production. The quantity of irrigation water to be applied for certain area depends on the annual rainfall and its utilization along with type of soil, existing irrigation facilities, irrigation practices followed by cropping patterns.

The anchal under study, tanks and dug wells are prevalent in almost all areas. Here Jharkhand Hill Area Lift Irrigation Corporation have not been implemented honestly and successfully. Due to this every season the area has negligible number of intake wells. The scheme of water reservoirs has been still in the pen and paper. The area also lacks canal irrigation facility except Gonda Dam from here about 1 km. The canal has not become successful in so many places of Hazaribag district because canals do not supply irrigation regularly rather haphazardly which often damages crops. This indicates that a large amount of land is rainfed. Check dams have been constructed at few places on the river keeping in view of the benefit of tribal people.

Suggestion and Conclusion

The sourcewise irrigated area reveals that some land are irrigated from river and rivulets with the help of indigenous methods. These lands are located along the rivers and rivulets which often degraded due to erosion and stagnation of water specially in rainy season but during non-kharif seems to be inadequate for the cultivation of crops. Some of the lands are irrigated by tanks. These are mostly derelict that the villagers of this Anchal receive irrigation from those sources which suffer from several socio-economic and technical problems and very small proportion of their land is irrigated by deep and shallow tubewells where irrigation can be regular.

REFERENCES

Agarwal, A.N., *Indian Agriculture : Problems, Progress & Prospects*, Rawat Publication, 1980.

Ahmad, E., *Bihar : A Physical, Economic and Regional Geography*, Ranchi, 1965.

Bhatt, S.C., *The District Gazetteer of Jharkhand*, Gyan Publishing House, New Delhi, 1999.

Bhatia, S.S., Pattern of Crop Combination and Diversification in India, 1965, *Bihar Distict Gazetteer, Hazaribag*, Secretariat Press, Patna, Bihar, 1957.

Dayal, P., *Bihar in Maps*, Kusum Prakashan, Patna, 1953.

Devi, P., "Scarps of Chotanagpur : A Study in Physiography and Human Geography," Ph.D. Thesis, Ranchi University, Gupta, S.N.P. 1967.

Hussain, Majid, *Systematic Agriculture Geography*, Rawat Publication, New Delhi, 1999.

Prasad, A., Agriculture in Chotanagpur, *Geographical Outlook*, Vol. V, 1968.

Sahu, S., Geomorphology Assessment of the Konar Irrigation Project, *Geographical Outlook*, Vol. XV, 1979.

Singh and Sinha, *Land and People*, Jharkhand, 2003.

27

An Approach for Sustainable Water Resource Management

Interlinking of Rivers

SATYA RAJ

Introduction

The river networking concept is based on the theory of transfer of water from surplus to deficit river basins. It is one of the geographical quirks of the huge Indian subcontinent that when one part of it is submerged in floods other parts are parched. Delayed monsoons in the north and central India and floods in the eastern parts have hardened "babus" scurrying to the boardrooms trying to draw out familiar relief packages for both areas. According to a World Bank report there is going to be a huge water crisis in developing countries. Another report says that one-third of thirsty population across the world resides in India. It is amazing that in spite of the fact that we have so many rivers even then this situation has arisen. The problem basically lies in the uneven distribution of run-offs and precipitation rates during the monsoon season. The very famous agricultural scientist M.S. Swaminathan has remarked that the time is now ripe for careful planning of water resources which includes water harvesting and of course successful interlinking of rivers.

Objectives

The main objective of this paper is to highlight the problems of water distribution in India. Water resource is not only specially uneven but has rapidly becoming a scarce resource. It is leading to river water disputes in many parts of the country. The scholar intends to study the scenario of India in general and Darbhanga division of Bihar in particular. Meso and Macro area studies have got momentum in post-modern geography and the present work is directed to meet the new priorities and challenges of geography.

Methodology

Every research work provides some conclusion on the basis of some standard methodological approaches. Present work is based on imperical investigation. Most of the information is collected from Government Reports, Journals and Newspapers. System approach is adopted to present the facts and figures in a systematic way. Waterflow linkages may bring rationalised distribution and use of water. The phenomenon is investigated in geographical perspective. The work is taken up at 2 levels—National level and Meso level. National level is for general reference while meso level study is exclusively on personal field investigation.

Inter-linking of Rivers : A National Target

The two proposals put forth for this in 1970s which attracted considerable attention were National Water Grid by Dr. K.L. Rao (1972) and Garland Canal by Captain Dustur (1977). Dr. Rao's proposal involved 2,640 km long Ganga-Cauvery link which essentially envisaged the withdrawal) of 60,000 cusecs of flood flows of the the Ganga near Patna for about 150 days a year. But this proposal involved large scale pumping over a head of 549 m. The power required for lifting water was 5000-7000 MW for irrigating only 4 million hectares. So the scheme was technically not feasible.

Captain Dastur's proposal envisaged the construction of 2 canals—the first 4,200 km long Himalayan canal at the foot of Himalayan slopes running from Ravi in the west to Brahmaputra and beyond in the east. The second 9300 km long Garland canal covering the central and southern parts and both the canals integrated with numerous lakes interconnected with pipelines at 2 points Delhi and Patna. The cost estimated by Captain Dastur was Rs. 24,095 crores which would come to Rs. 70 million crores at 2002 price level. The proposal was examined by various committees of experts from CWC, State Governments, Professors from IIT, Delhi and Roorkee University

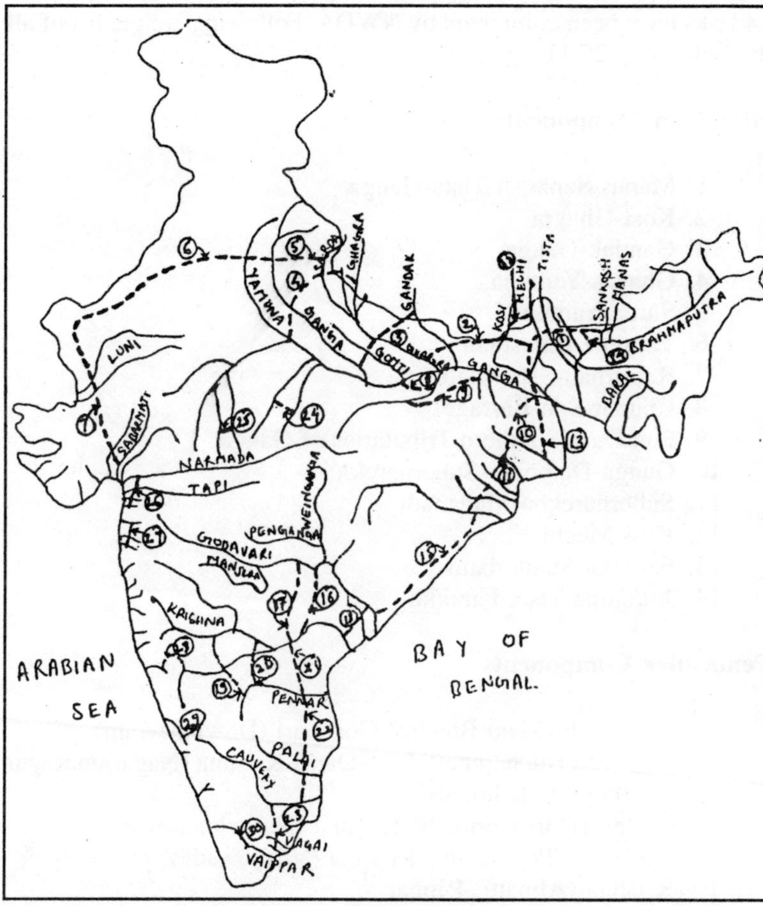

Fig. 27.1 : *NWDA's* Concept of Potential Interbasin Water Transfer Links

and scientists from Indian Meteorological Department and GSI. They found the proposal technically infeasible.

But since the scourge of flood continues so the Supreme Court on October 31st, 2003 directed the Union Government to consider interlinking of rivers within 10 years. Now the proposal involes 30 links but Himalayan Component is separated from Peninsular Component. In Peninsular component the studies indicate that while Mahanadi and Godavari basins are water surplus other basins like the Krishna, the Pennar, the Cauvery and the Vaigai are water deficit. 16 links have been proposed and feasibility of 7 links out of 16 have been compeleted. In Himalayan component feasibility studies of 14 links have been completed by NWDA. Following are the list of all the links (Fig. 27.1):

Himalyan Components

1. Manas-Sankosh-Tista-Ganga
2. Kosi-Ghagra
3. Gandak-Ganga
4. Ghagra-Yamuna
5. Sarda-Yamuna
6. Yamuna-Rajasthan
7. Rajasthan-Sabarmati
8. Chunar-Son Barrage
9. Son Dam-Southern Tributaries of Ganga
10. Ganga-Damodar-Subernarekha
11. Subernarekha-Mahanadi
12. Kosi-Mechi
13. Farakka-Sunderbans
14. Jogigopa-Tista-Farakka

Peninsular Components

15. Mahanadi (Mani Bhadra)-Godavari (Dowlaiswram)
16. Godavari (Inchampalli Low Dam)-Krishna (Nagarjunasagar Tail Pond/Pulichintala)
17. Godavari (Inchampalli)-Krishna (Nagarjunasagar)
18. Godavari (Polavaram)-Krishna (Vijayawada)
19. Krishna (Almatti)-Pennar
20. Krishna (Srisailam)-Pennar
21. Krishna (Nagarjunasagar)-Pennar (Somasila)
22. Pennar (Somasila)-Cauvery (Grand Anicut)
23. Cauvery (Kattalai)-Vaigai-Gundar
24. Ken-Betwa
25. Parbati-Kalisindh-Chambal
26. Par-Tapti-Narmada
27. Damanganga-Pinjal
28. Bedti-Varda
29. Netravati-Hemavati
30. Pamba-Achankovil-Vaippar

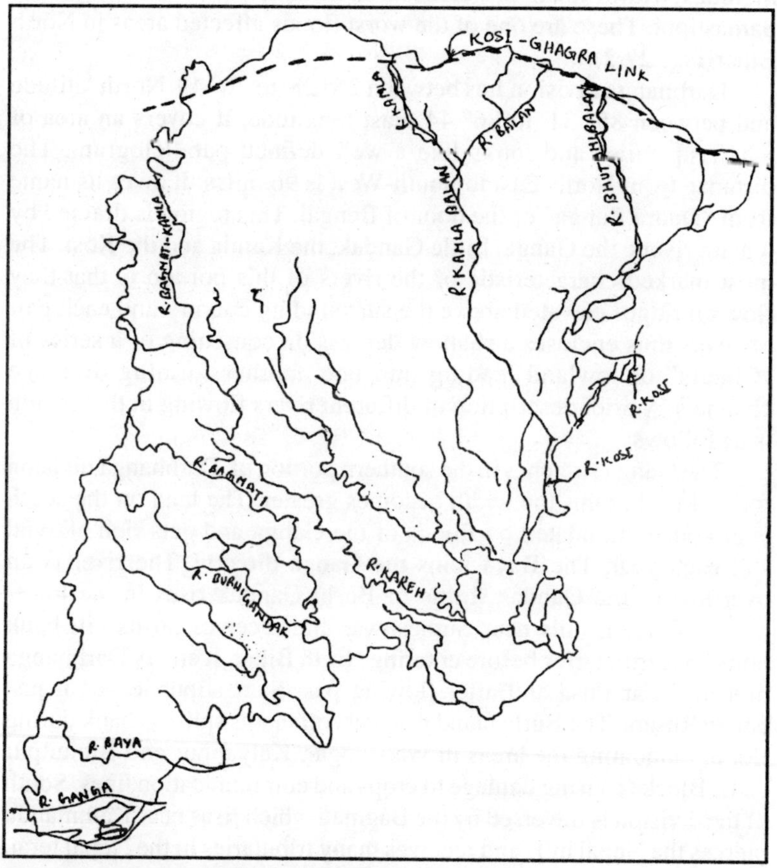

Fig. 27.2 : Darbhanga Division : Drainage

The entire river linking involves the construction of 32 new dams which would reduce the floods by 30 per cent. About 5 lakh people are to be displaced. So different task forces have been constituted to look into different aspects of interlinking of rivers, like environmental aspects, rehabilitation aspects and also negotiations with the neighbouring countries like Nepal, Bhutan and Bangladesh with respect to rivers in the Ganga-Brahmaputra-Meghna basin.

The Study Area

The study area of this research article is Darbhanga division which includes within itself the districts of Madhubani, Darbhanga and Samastipur. These are one of the worst floods affected areas in North Bihar(Fig. 27.2).

Darbhanga division lies between 25° 28′ to 26° 40′ North latitude and between 85° 31′ to 86° 44′ East longitude. It covers an area of 3,510 sq. miles and looks like a well defined parallelogram. The distance from North-East to South-West is 96 miles. It owes its name from "Duara Banga" or the door of Bengal. This region is drained by 4 main rivers the Ganga, Little Gandak, the Kamla and the Kosi. The most marked characteristic of the rivers of this portion is that they flow on ridges elevated above the surrounding country and each pair of rivers thus encloses a shallow depression consisting of a series of "Chaurs" or lowland leading into one another forming drainage channels. A brief description of different rivers flowing in this region is as follows.

The Ganga stretches in the southern portion of Darbhanga division for 32 km. In rains the width becomes greater. The land on the south is of course inundated by floods of the Ganga and gets rich alluvial soil each year. The Baya joins the Ganga directly. The river is an overflow of the Gandak. Little or Burhi Gandak rises in the lower range of Nepal hills near Sumeshwar and receives on its left bank numerous tributaries before entering North Bihar. It enters Darbhanga division near Pusa and after flowing past Samastipur leaves it just below Rusera. The Burhi Gandak and its offshoots spill the bank during flood, inundating the areas in Warisnagar, Kalyanpur and Bibhutpur C. D. Blocks causing damage to crops and communication lines. South of the division is traversed by the Bagmati which risas near Kathmandu pierces the Nepal hills and receives many tributaries in the Nepal terai. It enters Darbhanga division near Kalanjar Ghat. It flows in south easterly direction parallel to the Burhi Gandak and enters Samastipur district at the village Gangaura and passing through the boundary of the district. It moves southward between Warisnagar and Rusera and joins the Burhi Gandak west of Rusera. Shanti enters Darbhanga south of the Bagmati and runs parallel traversing through Warisnagar and joins the old course of the Bagmati and flows into the Burhi Gandak near Rusera. Little Bagmati finds its way to the Kareh near Hayaghat. Chief tributary 'Dhaus' runs through north-west of Benipatti. Kareh, prior to its junction with the Bagmati is an unimportant stream and after joining it flows south-east to Tilkeshwar and ultimately falls into the river Kosi. In flood season it overflows. The Kamla enters

Darbhanga east of Jaynagar town in the north and flow southwards and in south-easterly direction to Tilkeshwar and falls into Tiljuga and ultimately into Kosi by various tortuous routes. This river changes its course from year to year and its beds are found all over North of Madhubani district. In floods Madhubani and Jaynagar towns are threatened every year and the Ryam area becomes a vast sheet of flood. East of Kamla is Little Balan, a deep narrow river with well defined beds which runs south through the eastern part of Khajauli and Madhubani and joins Tiljuga near Rusera. The Balan proper known as Bhali Balan is a river with wide sandy beds also liable to heavy floods but practically dry during greater part of the year. The Kosi is a major river and flows through Saharsa, Darbhanga, north Monghyr, and Purnea districts and meets with the Ganga. As it shifts westward a number of villages in Darbhanga gets affected (Fig. 27.2).

So it is evident that this area is intersected by numerous rivers and streams, many of which rise in Nepal hills and are subject to violent floods.The beds of the rivers are further raised above the surrounding country due to siltation.Thus a sudden heavy rain in the northern Tirhut, Nepal terai and the range of hills to the north of it may easily cause these narrow drainage channels to overflow their banks. When this happens inundation inevitably follows and the lower reaches one goes more evil is aggravated not only by the converging of streams towards the same point but also by the network of private 'bandhs' or embankments that have been made year after year. This year (2004) has seen the worst flood ever in history breaking all records in terms of loss of life and property. In Bihar itself about 1 crore population of 17 districts have been badly affected. In Darbhanga division all the rivers have been flowing above the red mark. All important rail-road link have been disturbed. Almost 65 per cent of cultivable area have been inundated 52 per cent of population affected and 74 per cent of villages affected. (Radar image of Darbhanga town and the adjoining areas to the west highlights the amount of inundation) (Fig. 27.3). Bihar Water Resources Minister Jagdanand Singh admitted that all major embankments made to control the flow of water proved useless and once again the people have fallen victim to this natural calamity. Interlinking of rivers seem to be the only solution to this end the grim situation that takes place each year.

The two links, viz. the Kosi-Mechi and the Kosi-Ghagra involves three rivers originating or passing through Nepal. Their source being in the Tibetan region of China. They are the Kosi, the Mechi and the

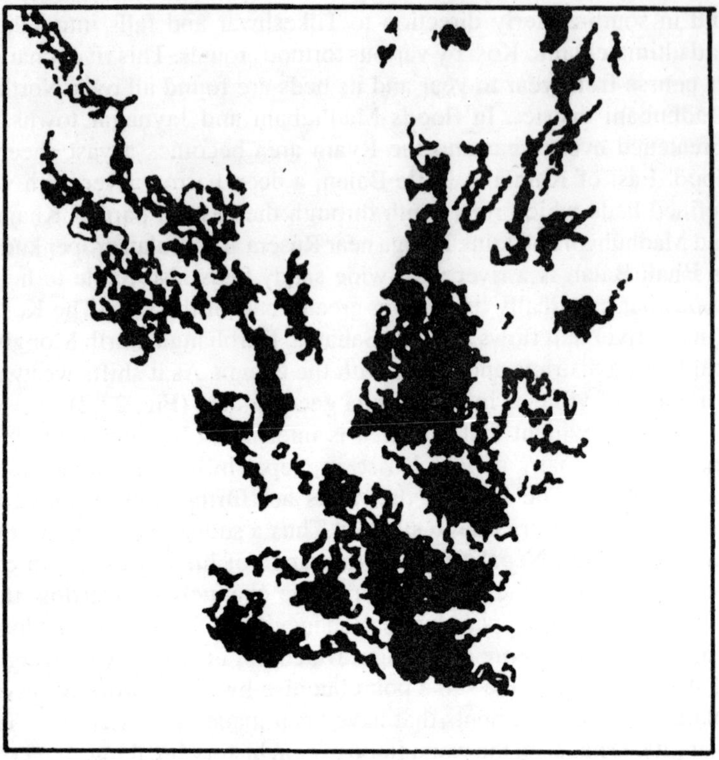

Fig. 27.3 : Radar Image of Darbhanga Town and Adjoining Areas to the West of it (courtsey : Planetorium, Patna) 'D' => indicates Darbhanga Town Black portion => indicates incidation.

Ghagra. Mechi determines the eastern border of Nepal with India. Our study area is related with these 2 links and if they become reality then the scourage of floods can be reduced and agricultural loss as well as loss of life and property can be igńored. River Ganga has no surplus water above Allahabad. However, a large number of rivers, viz. the Ghagra, the Kosi, the Mechi etc. originating in Nepal joins it. Surplus water of these rivers will be taken towards west to join the Yamuna and a part of this supply will be provided for Rajasthan-Gujarat link.

The main problem of our study area is the stagnation of rain and flood waters which prevents agricultural operations during the Kharif season. If this accumulated water is drained off the area then we have good Kharif crop along with winter maize and wheat during the Rabi season.

Major Constraints

These are discussed considering the river networking of entire country in general which are also applicable to the study region :

(i) *Financial Crunch*—The project involves Rs. 5.6 lakh crores and the figure is liable to increase. So it is a pretty good amount. This constraint is also applicable to our study region which is in Bihar a poor state so the financial resources will have to be generated.

(ii) There is an apprehension of the states regarding the project's impact on the already implemented interstate river dispute tribunal rulings on sharing of water. Bihar is also reluctant to provide waters of Ganga to the proposed scheme. The study region gets fresh deposition of clay and silt every year. Diaraland produces good rabi crops after the flood water recedes without spending a penny. People of diaraland are opposing this scheme.

(iii) Since a number of canals would have to pass through national parks and sanctuaries, clearance would have to be sought from Union Ministry of Environment and Forests.

(iv) Relief and rehabilitation measures for huge populations displaced by canals.

(v) *Ecological Impact*—It has been feared that interlinking of rivers would create ecological imbalance to the natural drainage of the river basins and entire hydrological cycle would get disrupted by preventing rivers from draining into the oceans.

(vi) *Bangladesh Protests :* Under the India Bangladesh Treaty of December 1996, on sharing of the Ganga water. India had undertaken to protect the flows arriving at Farakka barrage. Now the question arises how will a diversion of water from Ganga to southern rivers be consistent.

Benefits of the Project

The advocates of the project pointed out that it will be a phenomenal project to unite all people of country and give a developmental impetus. The ultimate aim of inter-basin transfer is to ensure that India produces about 450 million tonnes of food grains by 2050 when the population would be stabilises to 160 crores. The project will provide irrigation to about 35 million hectares of additional land. It would avoid losses of the type that occurred during 2002 to the extent of Rs. 25000 crores by loss of crops due to drought conditions and flooding in many parts like our study area. It would save Rs. 3000 crore a year in foreign exchange by avoiding importing of oil because of alternative navigation provided along coastline and national waterways which would become a reality. It would provide employment to 10 lakh people for the next 10 years. It would further encourage fishing which could provide alternative means of livelihood to the people. Slow release of stored water will not only produce hydroelectricity (34000 MW) but also help large scale plantation of trees on the canal embankment of which would compensate several times the loss of trees during the construction phase. NEERI, Nagpur and other institutes are looking into this aspect. Drinking water problem would get solved in many villages and towns.

Other countries like Canada and USA have implemented many large scale water transfer schemes. In Canada 16 inter-basin water transfer schemes have been implemented for hydropower development. Similarly, in USA California State Water Project envisages transfer of water from Sacramento river in North California to the south. Now China is also planning for transfer of 48 BCM of water from South to North through Grand canal 3500 kms long close to eastern coast. So the project can be implemented in India too.

REFERENCES

Chronicle Year Book, River Interlinking Mega Project sans viability, 2004.

Competition Wizard, Interlinking of River : Some Facts (Sources : High Level Task Force : Interlinking of Rivers) March 2004.

District Census Hand Books, Darbhanga, Madhubani and Samastipur, 1991, 2001.

Ghose, Arbinda., Inter-Basin Transfer of River Water : Key to Prosperous India, *Yojana,* January 2004.

Jha, G.P., *Agricultural Land use and Population in Kamla-Balan Plain,* North Bihar, 1979.

Sahara Times, Hell and High Water, Water Woes, 24th July, 2004.

Singh, Brajanand, *Samastipur—A Study in Urban Geography,* 1991.

28

Irrigation Planning and Sustainable Development of Wastelands

R.B. MANDAL

Wasteland is a land not suitable for cultivation by the current technological abilities of society. It could be properly harnessed by the availability of irrigation facilities besides proper management of afforestation, soil conservation, tillage practice, systematic management of pasture lands besides use of improved technology to reclaim wastelands for the emancipation of poverty.

In 1993 more than 50 million hectares of land was under wasteland category. In case this vast chunk of land could be reclaimed by improving the technological know how of people only than one should hope for a prosperous agricultural society in India.

Irrigation Planning

It could be possible by considering the various facets of land and management of water supply in the land for better crop production. It is needed only in those areas where the normal rainfall fails to supply required amount of water for cultivation.

Sustainable Development

It means the most suitable way of irrigational management by harnessing local resources so that it may judge the progress of fishery, deplete the underground sources of water and the systematic management of land and water conservation for effective success of irrigation.

Wasteland is a land not suitable for cultivation, afforestation or any other full utilization by the society at the current technological level. In the district of Munger the continued deforestation has brought people to ecological and socio-economic crisis. This has caused in the establishment of "Association for wasteland development in 1986" by D.P. Yadava in New Delhi. In mid-1987 the Government of West Bengal has established "Wasteland Corporation" based on "the model of the corporation for forest lands". In the district of Munger about one lakh hectare of land is wasteland, due to lack of irrigation and proper water supply.

Wasteland has recently attracted the attention of both government and public, because the land which is not suitable for agriculture can be utilised in a judicious manner for environmental protection and giving sustenance to the ever increasing population by the progress of land reclamation, soil conservation, watershed management and afforestation.

Purpose of Study

1. It will examine why different irrigation schemes operating in the district of Munger fails to irrigate the required amount of land in their command areas.
2. Irrigation deficiency in soils during the growing season so as to ensure proper and sustained growth of crops.
3. In addition, second and third crops may be produced on the land having irrigation facilities.
4. The productive aspect of irrigation helps in establishing a surplus agriculture production against drought.
5. Irrigation may help in changing soil sterelity caused by drought, i.e. overcoming low productivity due to dryness.
6. The optimum agricultural production potential may be attained in rural areas by reinforcing measure connected with the development of local land and water resources.

Overview of Literature

R.J. Chorley in his book on 'Water, Earth and Man' considered integrated planning of wastelands as interrelated system in which soil, vegetation and hydrological balance are involved and with the recognition of the need to solve problems like flood control, irrigation, sedimentation, soil erosion, hydro-electric production, and even nature conservation and stream pollution.

Small scale and mixed type of piecemeal irrigation is possible within parts of a drainage basin and early operation in Western Europe and Peru of this kind. In coastal Peru, for example early piecemeal irrigation was soon replaced by canal system incorporating the irrigable area of a drainage basin as watershed below the Andean foothills.

So far as the current problem of irrigation, wasteland reclamation and integrated irrigational planning is a quite new problem at hand which needs the identification of watersheds on the basis of catchment area of rivers and 10 metre contour lines depicted on one mile topographical sheets.

Ram Mohan Rao and S. Sinha conducted field investigation and collected data of command area of Sriramsagar Irrigation Project in Telengana region of Andhra Pradesh. They have presented in depth study of the socio-economic transformation of the above project area since 1971. This analysis provides an insight into the changes observed in land use, cropping pattern, demographic aspects, agricultural system, pattern of distribution of settlements and levels of development. They are more realistic and able suggestion for formulation of development strategy of the command areas.

Irrigation Project Cycle

There are five phases in a project cycle.

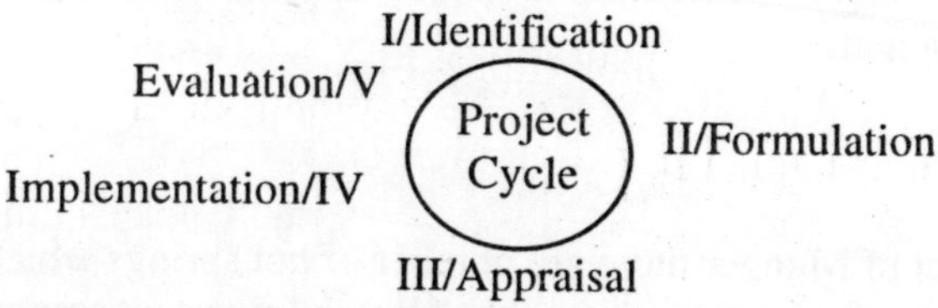

The reason why it is considered as a cycle is that each phase not only grows out of the preceding one, but leads into the self-renewing cycle so that new projects grow out of old ones in a continuous process.

Methods of Irrigation

There are various methods of irrigation which may be classified as follows :

1. Surface irrigation method,
2. Sprinkler irrigation method, and
3. Sub-surface irrigation method.

Surface Irrigation Method

Surface irrigation is accomplished by allowing water to flow over the surface. There are two criteria for supplying water in the form of surface irrigation. Summary of the conditions through which the various surface irrigation methods suited is given in Fig. 28.1.

Sprinkler Irrigation Method

The area where surface irrigation methods are not applied due to uneven topography, sprinkler method is widely used. In this method water is supplied in the form of driplets rain, as it is done in the gardening. There are various systems of sprinkler methods also.

Sub-Surface Irrigation Method

Water is drawn from sub-surface layer either directly from wells or from tubewells. A great amount of energy is needed to draw such water. This system of irrigation is mostly applied where the aquifer layer is sufficient.

Hot Springs

In the district of Munger there are number of hot springs which form good example of sub-surface sources of water. Important among these are Bhimbandh, Sitakund, Rishikund, Makdum Kund etc.

The origin of these hot springs may be due to the deep rooted thermodynamic action and the existence of active volcano in this region during different geological periods. In the South-Western fringe of Khargpur hill, Shringirishi Kund is a sacred place which is associated with Shringirishi.

State Tubewells

Due to sacrsity of rainfall sufficient number of state tubewells have

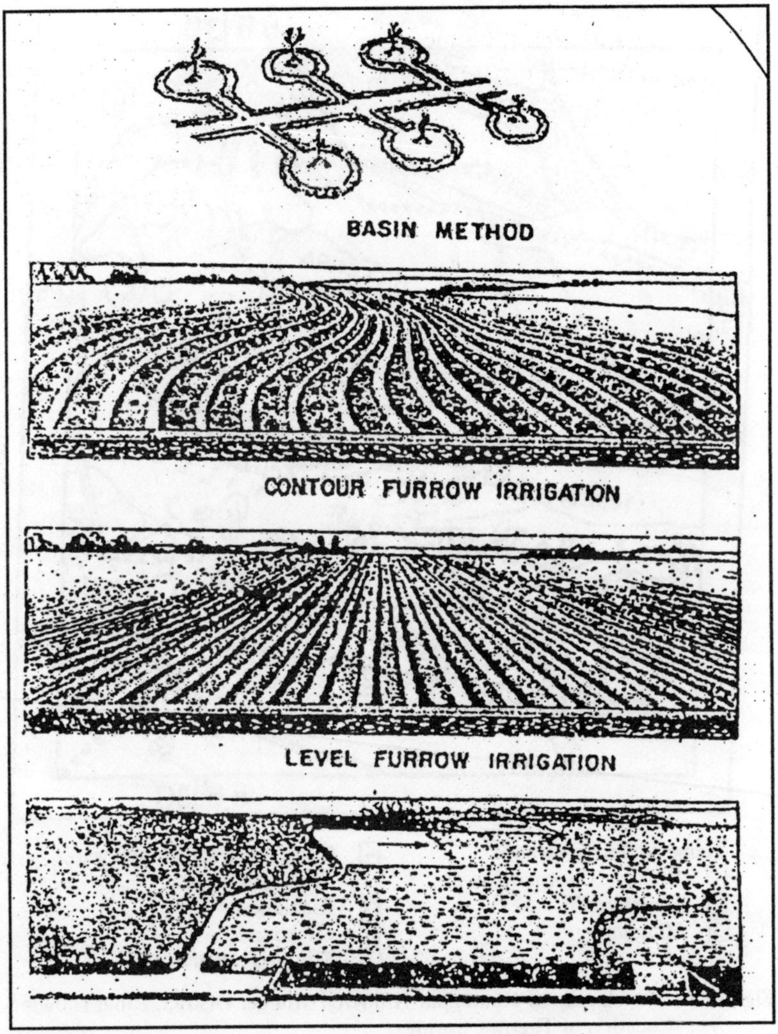

Fig. 28.1 : Modes of Irrigation in Munger and Jamui Districts

been installed so that farmers having small holdings may be able to grow double or treble crops. The schemes of sinking state tubewells in the form of rig boring has proved very successful.

Information regarding sub-surface water was received from State Tubewells Department, Munger. The Strata charts of six tubewells in

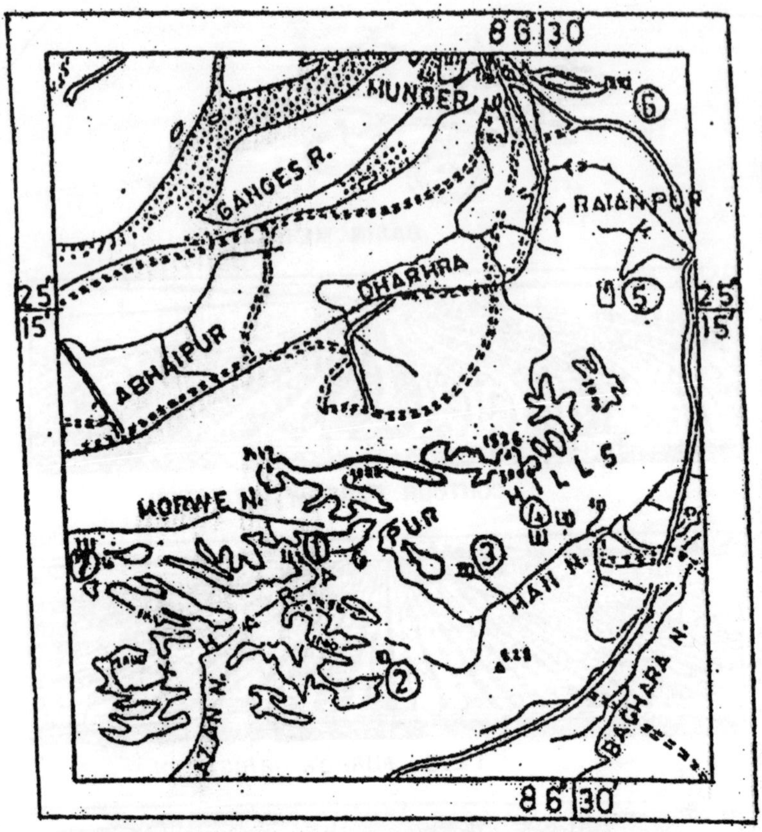

Name of Spring Groups

1. Bharari (Chormara)
2. Bhimbandh
3. Hingania
4. Rameshwar Lakchmishwar Bhowrah Kund
5. Rishikund
6. Sitakund
7. Sringirishi Kund

Fig. 28.2 : Sketch map of Kharagpur Hill Area Munger District, Bihar showing Location of Thermal Springs

the Jamalpur Anchal show that in almost all cases at the depth of 8 metres and below sub-surface water is available in fine to medium and coarse sandy layer. In upper part at the depth of 3 metres the layers of sand, silt and clay are found. Below this layer there is layer of clay with silt. This is followed by yellow to red calcareous nodular beds, found as the sub-surface aquifer zone. Table 28.2 shows the details of sub-surface conditions of tubewells (Fig. 28.2).

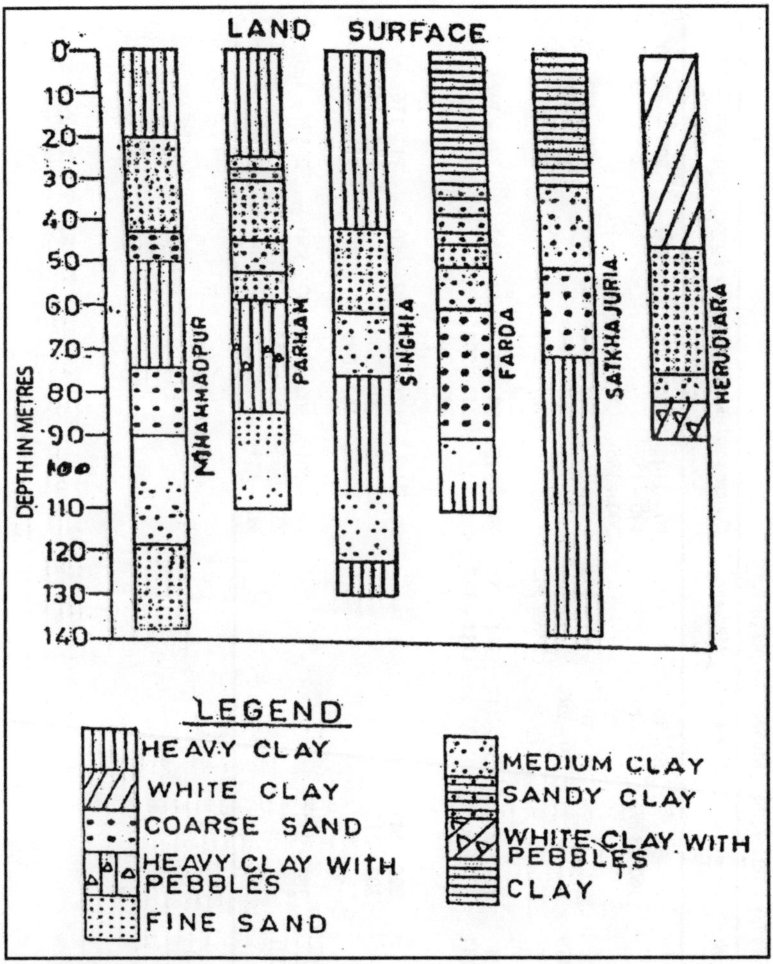

Fig. 28.3 : Strata Chart

While dealing with the watershed management the idea of drainage basin is an appropriate areal unit for the organization of irrigation and for integrated planning of wastelands which has recently been revived with the recognition of the basin as an interrelated system in which soil and vegetation cover as well as hydrological balance are involved and with the recognition of the need for integrated plans and policies to deal with problems posed by flood control, irrigation, sedimentation, soil erosion, hydro-electric power generation, navigation, and even nature conservation and stream pollution.

Table 28.1 : Lithological Data Obtained from Tubewells in Munger District (in feet)

	Silt clay	*Clay with Kankar*	*Sandy clay*	*Fine sand*	*Medium sand*	*Coarse sand*	*Sand with Graod*	*Discharge GPH*	*Screen Depth in Feet*
Mehus (Sheikhpura)	0 – 12	–	21 – 36 162 – 179	20 – 80 110 – 140	–	80 – 110 140 – 150 200 – 330	150 – 200	40 – 800	99'7" – 113'10" 209'5" – 302'3"
Pratappur (Barahya)	0 – 12	21 – 36 162 – 179	–	36 – 104 179 – 207	147 – 153 243 – 264 283 – 302	–	104 – 147 153 – 162 207 – 243 264 – 283	47 – 850	105' – 146' 155' – 167' 208'4" – 242'
Manikpur (Surajgarha)	0 – 78 147 – 213	93 – 121 213 – 247	121 – 131	131 – 147	341 – 354 131 – 147	293 – 325	78 – 93 243 – 293 325 – 341 354 – 405	47 – 850	278 – 392
Rampur (Surajgarha)	0 – 84 116 – 134 147 – 220		220 – 240 302 – 312	84 – 90		90 – 116	134 – 147 240 – 302 312 – 345	49 – 900	91 – 116 132 – 147 247 – 302 319 – 339
Mustafapur (Surajgarha)	0 – 21 71 – 119	21 – 71 201 – 221	221 – 232			199 – 201 232 – 302 313 – 345	302 – 313 345 – 353	47 – 850	233'3" – 333'

In the context of drainage basin, the most important types of irrigation are those which involve some degree of community action for their construction, operation, and maintenance of these the chief are those which use water from a stream network and have more or less elaborate systems of canals for the distribution of water to individual fields. Irrigation of this type has been characteristic of the great hydraulic societies of India, China and Peru. Limits are set to the extension of irrigation systems of this type by the availability or suitable terrain for cultivation or for the distribution of water, usually within the context of a single drainage basin, by the volume and seasonal regime of water supply by the technology available, and not least by the sole and nature of social and political organization within which the construction, maintenance, and administration of water control must be carried out. Small scale and piecemeal irrigation is possible within parts of a drainage basin, and early operations in Western Europe and Peru were of this kind. But the competition for water supply and the pressure of population leading to demands for the extension of irrigation to new land frequently sum to have lead at an early stage to the integration of piecemeal systems within the drainage basin as a whole. In coastal Peru, for example early piecemeal irrigation was soon replaced by canal system incorporating the whole of the irrigable area of a drainage basin below the Andean foothills.

Pattern of Irrigational Development

For the present Harohar river, Sakri river and Lower Kiul rivers help in irrigating the anchals of Barahiya, Sheikhpura, Barbigha and Lakhisarai. Morwe irrigation scheme and lower project help in the irrigation of southern Lakhisarai, Dharhara and Kharagpur anchals. The command area of Upper Kiul, Barnar, Nakti dam, Nagi dam, Gidheshwar Project and Belharna Weir scheme irrigate south and eastern parts of Jamui and Munger districts. On the northern part of diara tract near the Ganges riparian tract bamboo boring, cavity boring and lift irrigations are preferred, because diaras are under flood during rainy season and only hope rely on rabi and summer crops. Hence, irrigation is quite essential in these marginal lands. Similar situation prevails in *tal* lands which comes under annual flood during rainy season and need assured irrigation for rabi and summer crops. Without irrigation the production will be 4000 kg. per hectare but with irrigation it could be raised to 8000 kg. per hectare. In southern part of

Table 28.2 : Main Rivers and Irrigation Projects in Munger District, 2004

Rivers	*Anchal*	*Project*	*Anchal*
Kathia	Kharagpur	Chora	Tarapur
Tajpur	Kharagpur	Belharue	Sangrampur
Mani	Kharagpur	Garkhe	Surajgarha
Mahane	Kharagpur	Rishikund	Jamalpur
Daugri	Kharagpur	Jalkund	Kharagpur
Jokia	Kharagpur	Khand Bihair	Kharagpur
Kharra	Kharagpur	Kharagpur Lake	Kharagpur
Kauria	Kharagpur	Chanken Scheme	Kharagpur
Bagra	Kharagpur	Udwah	Kharagpur
Koriari	Kharagpur	Sangot	Lakhisarai
Ratauna	Kharagpur	Sindh Barni	Kharagpur
Mafi	Lakhisarai	Gaight Scheme	Kharagpur
Manna	Lakhisarai	Kaurihari	Ariari
Harohar	Barahiya	Kukurjhap	Lakhisarai
Manki	Lakhisarai	Baskund	Lakhisarai
Son	Lakhisarai	Shringi Rishi	Surajgarha
Kiul	Lakhisarai	Uppersakri	Sheikhpura
Nati	Lakhisarai	Chanken Scheme	Tarapur
Bahua	Lakhisarai	Ajgaibinath Pump	Tarapur
Hasaura	Lakhisarai	Utrao Ganga	Tarapur
Kaljugwa	Lakhisarai	Pump Canal Scheme	Tarapur
Kohrin	Lakhisarai	Surajgarha Pump Canal Scheme	Tarapur
Bhurha	Lakhisarai	Amrapani Prijulia Water Fall	Tarapur
Rati	Sheikhpura	Morwe Dam Scheme	Tarapur
Tati	Sheikhpura		
Channail	Sheikhpura		
Kaurihari	Sheikhpura		
Sakri	Barbigha		

Source : Compiled by R.B. Mandal.

mountainous areas rig boring preferred along with the construction of minidams, reservoirs and the construction of canals and pynes.

River System

The rivers of Munger and Jamui districts are the Kiul, the Man, the Omi, the Harohar and the number of hill streams which came down in freshets during the rains, but subside as rapidly as they rise for the greater part of the year. They are sandy water course with little or no current and exhausted by the demand for irrigation before they reach the Ganges. The following is a brief account of the major rivers and

Table 28.3 : Irrigation in the District of Munger 2003

Anchal	*Area in Km²*	*No. of Villages*	*No. of Tubewells*	*Area Irrigated in acres*
1. Munger Sadar	224.5	51	220	6753
2. Jamalpur	207.1	57	296	2078
3. Dharhara	282.8	84	514	1429
4. Khargpur	373.8	112	115	35522
5. Tarapur	130.5	97	35	33418
6. Sangrampur	143.2	100	21	16644
7. Lakhisarai	321.1	123	617	39207
8. Barahiya	235.0	43	125	3238
9. Surajgarha	418.4	115	118	7205
10. Halsi	275.1	93	132	41096
11. Sheikhpura	228.7	86	38	18207
12. Barbigha	139.9	73	308	383554
13. Ariari	204.6	79	10	37298
Total	3184.7	1113	2589	281759

Source : Dept. of Statistics and Evaluation, Fort, Munger, 2003.

different irrigation projects found in different anchals of Munger district.

On the basis of Table 28.3 it could be said that there are 2,589 tubewells in the district of Munger which irrigates 140,000 hectares of land. This clearly presents that tubewells are most frequently found in the district of Munger where the water borne disease is much in comparison with South Munger and Jamui where the rocky sub-stratum disfavours normal tubewells. It is possible only with the rig boring.

Table 28.4 : Source of Irrigation in the District of Munger, 2003

Source	*No.*	*Irrigated Area in Acre*	*Per cent*
Canal	33	141,027	55.86
Tank	255	29,851	11.65
Tubewell	1,544	54,545	21.29
Otherwell	704	12,614	4.92
Other Sources	349	15,085	5.88
Total	2,915	256,122	100

Source : Dept. of Statistics and Evaluation, Fort, Munger, (2003)

Table 28.4 shows that total sources of irrigation are 2,915 in the district of Munger which irrigates 55 per cent land by canal,

12 per cent land by tank, 21 per cent by tubewell, 5 per cent by other well and 6 per cent land by other sources. This clarifies the need of irrigation in this drought prone area where the rainfall is deficient for crop production.

Strata chart of some tubewells in Munger and Jamui Districts

The data regarding strata chart of borings have been collected for 19 places in both these districts. Altogether 7 layers have been detected upto a depth of 150 metres. Different layers of soil detected are silt clay, clay mixed with kankar, sandy clay, fine sand, medium sand, coarse sand, sand with gravel. The sandy layer in the form of aquifer zone have been found at varying depth, i.e. 7 metres, 15 metres, 20 metres and 30 metres but in some cases it starts at depth of 33, 66, 100 and 112 metres as well. This happens especially in Kharagpur hills and the plateau region of Jamui district where the rocky sub-stratum favours rig boring. Most of these charts have been meant for Barahya, Sheikhpura, Surajgarha, Jamalpur and Kharagpur blocks. In northern Munger the aquifer zone starts at a depth of just 4 metres due to formation of diaras along the courses of the river.

Anticipated Impact

1. Irrigation channels help in navigation, rearing fishes and recreation as well. Irrigation will raise production of different crops.
2. Irrigation will enrich the natural fertility of the soil and enrich the natural eco-system.
3. Irrigation will arrest soil erosion, flood control, check sedimentation and change the total environment of the region for betterment.
4. Irrigation projects help in proper utilization and conservation of water resource for judicious use of the future.
5. It will help in harnessing surface runoff, underground reserve of water along with hot springs and lift of water from lowland to fields and farms.

Conclusion

Irrigation is an artificial act of applying water in the land where the rainfall is deficient for the crop production. Irrigation planning requires the watershed management and basinwise conservation of water for better utilization of available land with the help of current technological level. It is essential in order to safeguard the land by conservation of moisture and check aridity for the best utilization of land water resources.

REFERENCES

Chorley, R.J., *Water, Earth and Man,* Methuen & Co. Ltd., London, 1969, p. 109.

Forbes, R.J., *Irrigation and Power Studies an Ancient Technology,* Vol. 2, 1965, p. 220.

Mandal, R.B., "Spatial Variations of Wasteland Development in Bihar", *East-West Geographer,* Vol. 3, No. 1, March 1992.

Sinha, U.P., *Planned Development of Resources in a Development Region,* Inter-India Publications, New Delhi, 1985.

Willey, G.R., Prehistoric Settlement Patterns in the Viru Valley, Bureau of American Ethnology, *Smithsonian Institute Bulletin,* 155, 1953, p. 453.

29

Meandering Courses of the River and Its Impact of Socio-Economic Life of People in North Eastern Bihar

R.B. MANDAL

Introduction

Meandering courses of the river comes under alluvial geomorphology. As North Eastern Bihar lies in the alluvial plain and hence, soil of the area have been quite vulnerable to erosion and deposition by recurrence of flood each and every year especially during the rainy season. This has been caused due to the processes of alluviation and diluviation formed by spill way of water from the loose detritus and the formation of alluvial cone.

The sole purpose of this paper is to judge frequent change in courses of the river, disruption of rural settlements, damage to the standing crops in the field, loss of livestock wealth due to the paucity of fodder and the availability of polluted drinking water locally. In fact, meandering of the river course, recurring flood and breach of embankment are recurrent issues of the area. In this, all these aspects have been delineated in between Baryahighat to Dharampur villages which lie on the southern levee of the Kareh river. The impact could be seen as :

(a) Deepening of erosional site of embankment in the form of deep gorge even in the alluvial plain.
(b) Heavy pressure of flood water gives way to the water pilferage through dams.
(c) Destruction of standing houses of mud wall and thatch roof in most of the cases.

(d) Ravage to the standing kharif crops in the field, i.e. paddy, ragi, cheena, maize, sama and kauni.
(e) Loss of valuable properties from the houses as the flood water takes away the belongings of poor people specially in areas of its severity.
(f) Erosion on one side of the embankment and deposition on the other led to the formation of destructional and constructional shore lines.
(g) The meandering courses of the river need redressal by cutting the paleolithic boulder clay in the middle course of the river near Lalpur, Kharsam, Ghibahi and Shankarpur villages.
(h) The meandering course makes such bend that in case one stands on high trees on the southern side of Kharsam village and an areal view towards the south gives a synoptic view of 8 flood protective embankments.
(i) West of Ghibahi village now the Kareh river has excavated a new channel by partly deserting (75%) the old course in which the breach of embankment has caused south of Mahdewa village in Shankarpur panchayat.
(j) The breach (July, 2002) has washed away even the pucca houses and filled the rivulets, tanks and fields with micaceous sand about one kilometre away from the breach site and so on.

Objectives

The purpose is to analyse the causes of flood, suffering of people and better management of water resource and the flood for the emancipation of people from economic ills.

Analysis of the Problem

The meandering courses of the river help in the concentration of greater volume of water in a small area which leads to flooding and breach of flood protective embankment along the rivers. This has caused extensive flood in the entire north eastern region of Bihar in the year 1987 and 2004 as well.

The flood scenario of different districts could be seen below:

Floods in Katihar

In Kathihar city, station and medical college all come under flood water. Besides, this the government quarter, offices, officer's colony, Sahebpara, O.T. Para, Hridayanganj, Budhchak, Barmasia, Laliyahi, Teja Tola and Mirchaibari all come under knee deep to neck deep water.

Floods in Begusarai

The embankment erosion continued on the southern bank of the Budhi Gandak river near Sikarhulla. The gunny bags full of sand and trees are used to plug the point of soil erosion in nylon crate. The problem has heightened on 14th of September when due to breach of southern embankment of the Kareh river east of Rosra has flooded the entire area of Begusarai and Khagaria districts. The management of Barauni Oil Refinery kept themselves alert to save the factory area from the incoming floods (Fig. 29.1).

Damage of Standing Crops due to Flood and Rain

On 11th of September, 1998 it has been reported from Bhagalpur that in different districts of north-eastern Bihar, the standing crops worth Rs.19 crores have been destroyed due to torrential rain and incoming of floods.

In order to overcome this damage, the agriculture department has made a crash programme. This has estimated that the damage was of worth Rs.19,57,75,000. In Munger division the damage of crop was reported worth Rs.8,21,49,000 only.

According to the report received from flood forecasting department in Bhagalpur district the rice crop over 7135 hectares have been destroyed. In Munger district this damage occur in 1902 hectare and in Lakhisarai 240 hectares (Table 29.1). The damage of Maize crop has been reported as follows :

Besides these in Bhagalpur and Munger divisions pulse crop worth 2,358 and 2,456 hectares have been destroyed respectively.

On 6th September, 1998 it has been reported from Katihar that due to cutting of *Jamindari* dam by the unsocial elements several panchayats of Manihari anchal and Katihar town become flooded.

Table 29.1 : The Damage of Maize Crop in the Flood of 1998

Sl. No.	*District*	*Damage in Hectare*
1.	Bhagalpur	9,447
2.	Banka	925
3.	Munger	3,040
4.	Jamui	3,322
5.	Lakhisarai	2,127
6.	Sheikhpura	1,782

Due to this the water of the Ganga river enters forcefully into Mednipur Panchayat, Mirjapur, Azampur Gola, Simudih, Tanti tola, Paswan tola, Manihari notified area, Majbartal, Nima, Mahuar, Rajemadhe,

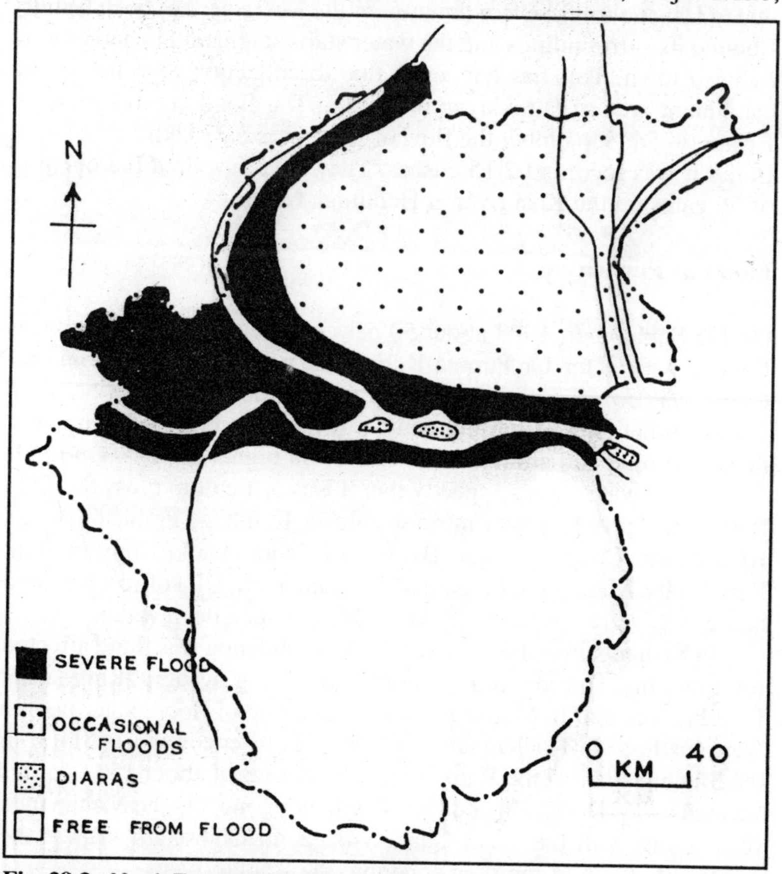

Fig. 29.2 : North Eastern Bihar Flood Affected Area (2003)

Rajbiraj, and from Simlapara towards the urban area. In Katihar district the rise of flood water of the Ganga, the Kosi and the Mahananda continued. All these rivers flow one to 1.5 metres above the point of danger. The flood position of Amdabad anchal is more accute in comparison with Manihari. Here people of several villages are residing on the branches of trees. In Bhagodia village five persons died with the flood. In Katihar district near Kursela on National Highway No.31 in between 4 to 5 kilometres at 9 kms distance of one km both the Kosi and the Ganga water was flowing which disrupted the road link from north-eastern India (Fig. 29.2).

On 5th September, 1998 it has been reported from Saharsa that due to last one week severe down-pour the Kosi river has been heavily flooded its surroundings and the water starts stagnating in and around Saharsa town. This has happened due to collection of water in the catchment area of Himalayan mountain. The flood control room of Birpur on 5th September the flow of water was 2.37 lakh cusec but in Barah it was recorded 2.15 cusecs. They have favoured the opening of 56 gates on the Kosi river at Hanuman Nagar.

Flood in Purnea

On 5th September, 1998 about 50 per cent area of Purnea town was flooded with water. On Purnea-Kasba road near Rambag 5 kilometres length was covered with knee deep to neck deep water. In between Purnea Junction and Purnea court rail line had been submerged at places. People and animals took shelter on higher ground. On roads the flow of water was so speedy that it was difficult to cross them. In Purnea the problem was more accute in Rambag, Prabhat colony, Khairuganj, Chimney bajar, Baghmara, Janta chauk, Court station, Purnea clty, Mahopara, Lalganj Milki, Tatma toli, DIG office, Remand home area were covered with knee deep to neck deep water.

In Kishanganj district about 1.5 lakh population was flood affected for 2 months. The southern part of the town, e.g. Khagra, Ruighasha, Bachhia toli, and in Modia Juli due to entering of flood water people were restless. In Kochadhamin anchal due to encoming of flood in the Mahananda and the Kanki rivers the houses of about 150 families washed away. Dangatoli and Patkoli villages gone into the Mahananda river along with the Chak-Chaki village. In Churakatti village the houses of about 25 families gone into the Kantai river.

Table 29.2 : Damage due to Flood in Khagaria District, 1987

Sl. No.	*Description of Damage*	*Damage in Rupees*
1.	National Highway No.31	1,775,000
2.	PWD Roads	11,200,000
3.	REO Roads	3,510,000
4.	Rural Roads	5,223,000
5.	Government Machinery and Materials	978,000
6.	Udwah Irrigation Project	725,000
7.	Water Supply and Tubewells	1,854,000
8.	Flood Control and Embankment	2,760,000
9.	Hospital	1,900,000
10.	Social Forestry	4,500,000
11.	Damage of Standing Crops	30,000,000
12.	Industry and Planning	8,500,000

Source : Collected from Different Sources, 1987.

Khagaria District

Cause

In Khagaria the main cause of incoming of flood is the extensive rise of water level in the Kosi, the Bagmati, the Kareh, the Kali Kosi, the Amni river and the Chatar river. This has been also caused due to weak embankment and improper care of the flood protective embankment.

River Group : The Ganga, the Kosi, Kali Kosi, Chatar river and the breach of the embankment of Amni river causes flood.

Suggestion to Solve the Problem

The height of flood protective embankment should be raised and it should be cemented upto the height of 4 metres.

Sufferings of People

1. Loss of life and property.
2. Loss of standing crops.
3. People suffers from Diarrhoea, Fileria and Cholera.

Table 29.3 : Water level of Flood in Khagaria and Munger

Year	*Ganga (Munger)*	*Budhi Gandak (Khagaria)*
1970	39.275	38.016
1971	40.805	38.891
1972	38.547	36.875
1973	39.527	38.110
1974	39.657	38.395
1975	40.397	38.555
1976	40.998	39.220
1977	40.080	38.240
1978		
01.07.78	36.212	34.645
01.08.78	30.712	37.260
19.08.78	40.792	39.160
04.09.78	38.982	38.670
07.09.78	39.707	38.140
09.09.78	40.032	38.365
10.09.78	40.182	38.530
14.09.78	40.537	38.890
18.09.78	39.327	38.920
20.09.78	38.612	37.280
23.09.78	38.222	36.920

4. Childrens and oldmen lost life in the flood water due to drowning.
5. More than one hundred people died due to turning of boat.
6. Even property in the houses washed away during flood.
7. Market route disconnected.

Immediate Relief Measures

1. Construction of houses on the highland near railway.
2. Problem of food, clean water and cloth should be solved.
3. The arrangement of boat should be made in the village.
4. The arrangement of medicine to fight with the disease.

Long Term Solution

1. Small rivers should be interlinked with the big river.
2. Demanded dredging of the courses of rivers.

Table 29.4 : Flood affected Villages and Suggestion to Solve the Problem in Beldaur Block, Khagaria District

Sl.No.	*Village*	*Affected by the Flood of River*	*Suggestion to solve the Problem*
1.	Mali	Kali Kosi	
2.	Mahinathnagar	Kali Kosi	
3.	Pirnagra	Kali Kosi	
4.	Murasi	Kali Kosi	
5.	Gawas	Kosi	
6.	Kanji	Kali Kosi	1. Construction of Sulice Gate near Telihar on the Kosi embankment. 2.Reclamation of waterlogged 52 chaurs and lakes in Beldaur Block at the end of flood.
7.	Telihar	Kosi	
8.	Ramnagar	Kosi	
9.	Bira	Kosi	
10.	Bela Nawbad	Kosi	
11.	Kumbraili	Kosi	
12.	Bobil	Kosi	
13.	Pachrasi	Kosi	
14.	Sakrohar	Kosi	
15.	Dumri	Kosi	
16.	Pachath	Kosi	
17.	Dhadhi	Kosi	
18.	Chodhli	Kosi	
19.	Itmadi	Kosi	
20.	Barun	Kosi	
21.	Rohiama	Kosi	
22.	Balaitha	Kosi	
23.	Beldaur	Kosi	
24.	Pachaut	Kosi	
25.	Kurwan	Kosi	
26.	Gendharsan	Kosi	
27.	Sathma	Kosi	
28.	Dadroja	Kosi	
29.	Dighaun	Kosi	

Demand from the Government

1. Subsidy for the repair of houses.
2. Safety latrines should be made.
3. The arrangement of clean drinking water should be made.
4. The breach point should be plugged.
5. The repair of roads, schools and electricity lines should be done.

Flood Ravages in Araria

In 1998 due to the ravages of flood 72 roads and all bridges have been damaged in the district of Araria. According to the survey done by the PWD of Araria the damaged roads are as follows :

1. Araria-Bahadurganj 16 kilometres
2. Jokihat-Palasi Road 19 kilometres
3. Palasi-Terhagachhi Road 15 kilometres
4. Araria-Sikti Roads 40 kilometres
5. Purnea-Forbesganj Road 10 kilometres
6. Bathnaha-Birpur Road 14 kilometres
7. Jogbani-Kala Balua Road 40 kilometres
8. Forbesganj-Narpatganj Road 16 kilometres
9. Araria-Raniganj Road 12 kilometres
10. Araria-Chandradei Road 4 kilometres
11. Araria-Railway Stations 3 kilometres
12. JBC to Bhargama Road, 5.5 kilometres

The construction all these roads need Rs. 4 crores for which the estimate has been sent to the State government.

The destruction of bridge in the flood could be seen as follows : Araria-Bahadurganj—9 R.C.C. bridge; Araria-Palasi Raod—6 wooden bridges; Palasi-Tedhagachhi—1 wooden bridge; Araria-Sikti—6 H.P. culvert; 3 bridges; Purnea-Forbesganj—1HP culvert, 1 R.C.C. bridge; Bathnaha-Birpur 2 R.C.C. bridges; Jogbani-Balua—3 H.P. bridges; Forbesganj-Narpatganj Road—6 wooden bridges; Araria-Raniganj—8 wooden bridges and Araria to Chandradei Raod—4 Bridges destroyed.

Table 29.5 : The Damage of Cropped area in Araria District

Blocks	*Cropped Area in Hectare*	*Damage in Lakh Hectares*
Araria	0.14	0.11
Forbesganj	0.09	0.08
Jokihat	0.19	0.17
Palasi	0.15	0.13
Sikti	0.15	0.14
Kursakata	0.11	0.09
Raniganj	0.36	0.28

Conclusions

On the basis of above it could be said that the saucer shaped basin of north-eastern Bihar help in the concentration of rivers as well as flood water in the area. Sometimes the situation cropped up is so alarming or disastrous that houses get washed away, standing crops damaged, roads, culverts and embankments give way to the flood and what to talk of sufferings of human being and livestock. Therefore, the north-eastern Bihar needs special care for management and control of flood.

REFERENCES

Mandal, R.B., *Planned Development of Rural Settlements in North Bihar.* Unpublished D. Litt. Thesis, Patna University, 1976.

Pandey, M.N., *Patterns of Land use in the Environs of Samastipur,* Unpublished Ph.D. Thesis, LNM University, Darbhanga, 1982.

30

Watershed Management

KAUSHALENDRA PRAKASH GOSWAMI

The management of water, land, livestock, forest for population and society is known as watershed management. It is related with *Jal, Jamin, Jangal, Janwar avam Jansankhya* because all these need proper use of water for overall development of a river basin.

1. Water help in irrigation of dryland.
2. Water help in afforestation and maintaining the ecological balance.
3. Livestock rearing is not possible without water.
4. Human being need water for drinking purposes.

Hence, watershed management is the basin-wise conservation and proper utilization of water through different means of irrigation. It is a sort of irrigational management which considers different facets of land and different modes of irrigation. Thus watershed management is an integrated irrigational planning measure. It considered that water is a precious resource in the form of fund and flow resources and it is our duty to use it judiciously either for drinking purposes or establishment of industry or raising crops.

Watershed Development Projects have been taken up under different programmes launched by the Government of India. The Drought Prone Area Programme (DPAP) and Desert Development Programme (DDP) adopted the approach of watershed management in the year 1987 (Ministry of Rural Development, 1994). The Integrated Wasteland Development Project (IWDP) taken up by the National Wasteland Development Board in the year 1989 and also considered the Development of Wasteland on watershed basis. At present watershed management comes under the Ministry of Rural Development. Fourth is the National Watershed Development

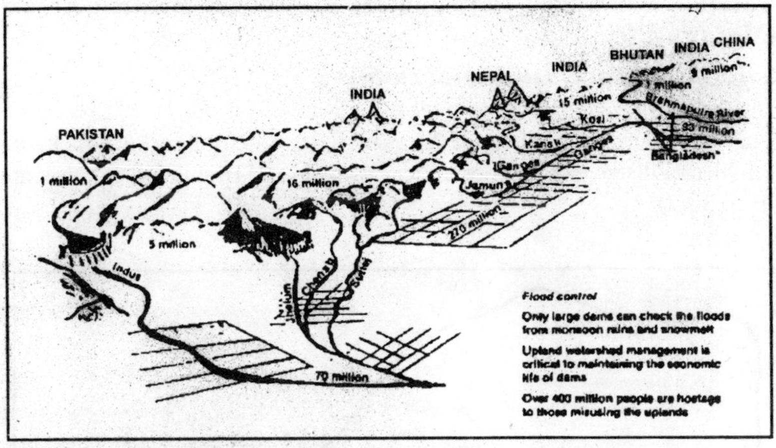

Fig. 30.1 : Himalayan Watershed

Programme especially for rainfed areas in the Ministry of Agriculture (UNDP).

"Watershed is an area bounded by the divide line of water flow so that a distinct drainage basin of any small or big water course or stream can be identified. The rain falling over this area will flow through only one point of the whole watershed or the area will be drained by only one stream. In this way, we have a definite amount of water resource which could be assessed and analysed for making plans for the optimum utilization through groundwater wells, tubewells, small farm ponds, bigger tanks, reservoirs and diversion of lift irrigation schemes" (Bali, 1984).

The problem is vast in extent and magnitude and delineation has to be done in manageable watershed units on a priority basis. In India, the government has identified 214 priority areas of watersheds of the flood prone rivers (MOA, 1984). It has also proposed dryland development through water harvesting technology on the basis of micro-watersheds and in India 4246 such watersheds have been identified in 1983. The Himalayan states like Uttar Pradesh, Himachal Pradesh and Jammu and Kashmir have several watershed catchments (Fig. 30.1) delineated on the basis of erosional hazards, Gujarat on rainfed area, Orissa and Tamil Nadu adopted integrated approach of mini-watersheds for implementing programmes.

National Watershed Development Project for Rainfed Areas (Morawa Utry)

Surajgarha Block, Lakhisarai District

This is Mircro-watershed of Morawa Utry in Surajgarha Block of Lakhisarai district and comes under Dwarsen and Brania hill catchment (Fig. 30.2).

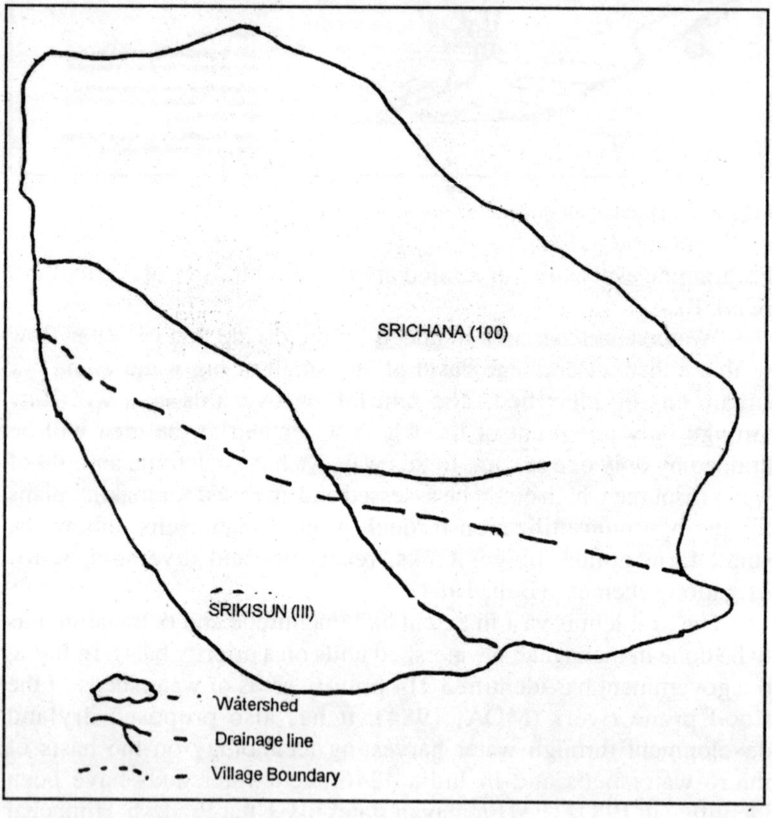

Fig. 30.2 : Morawa Utry Watershed Surajgarha Block (Lakhisarai District)

The total geographical area of the Micro-watershed is 504.16 hectares comprising of 466.08 hectares of arable land. Arable land constituted 92.4 per cent area of the Micro-watershed. Area under habitation and road is about 4 hectares. The length of drainage lines is 8 km.

This Micro-watershed area has no irrigated land at all. The topography of watershed is predominantly undulating where valley lines are well defined. The only structure constructed and maintained by farmers are paddy terraces. The upland slopes vary from place to place and cannot be put under a thumb rule may be classified as gently to moderately shopy ground.

Poor managed watershed sources and lack of potential the farm income generating activities has affected along with socio-economic backwardness of the watershed community (Khosho).

Background

This geographic hydrological unit has been name as 'Micro-watershed'. 'Morawa is a river in the southern side of Brania and Dwarsen hill. The project has initiated from the north side of this river. Brania and Dwarsen hill are in between this Micro-watershed and Morwa river. There are two villages near the foothill of this hill and they are known as Shreegona and Shree Kisan from where the 'NWDPRA' is initiating. A small seasonal river 'Kusamva' started from the Brania hill that runs off east-side of Shreegona village. Second river that is called 'Gogala Nala'. Mr. Gogala starts from Gogala Kol and meets in the Kelay river. Gonary meets with Dakranala and Dakranala meets with the Ganga nçar west of Munger city. The 'Kusumva' and Gogala rivers become dry during summer but flash floods are very frequent in Gogala during rainy season.

Location of Watershed in the District and its Approach

This Micro-watershed is located in Surajgarha Block under Lakhisarai district. This Micro-watershed is situated at a distance of about 17 kilometres from Surajgarha block headquaters via Kajara Railway Station. This Watershed area starts at a distance of 1 kilometre from Kajara Station by a short-cut *(Kacha)* road. There is 12 km. metalled *(Pacca)* road Surajgarha to Kajara and rest 5 km is *Kacha* road.

Size of the Watershed and its Shape

The average length of this Micro-watershed is 3 km (North-South) and average width is 24 km. The length and width ratio is (3:2). The total geographical area is 504.16 hectare covering two villages of Surajgarha Block, namely Shree Ghana and Shree Kisun. Project area is 500.16 hectare. Its shape is irregularly oval.

Problem in the Watersheds

Over grazing and trampling by animals are major problems for depletion and soil erosion. Animals graze freely and destroyed the grasses, legumes, bushes and shrubs. Plants are selling for his livelihood. For this reason almost every type of soil cover is being destroyed. Landscape is deemed to deteriorate day by day. Soil erosion and water loss is the urgent problem for delimitation of the area and biomass production under existing condition. Monocrop production system has added as measures of the watershed community.

Integrated Watershed Development

This watershed consists of three sectors, namely :

1. Arable and cultivated land privately owned,
2. Non-arable land including pasture and grazing ground culturable waste land and other barren and unculturable land, and,
3. A network of natural drainage lines.

These three *sub-sectors* would be treated as one organic geo-hydrological entity for this project planning and implementation to ensure sustainable use of land and water resources.

Drainage

The area drains into Goghala and Kusumva river are rainy and seasonal rivers. Surface and sub-surface soil drains clearly and fastely from upland water run-off very rapidly to terraced paddy land where water drained plot to plot but water did not stand in paddy field for long time. Permeability, infiltration and precipitation rate of water is very high and this has affected again and again for poor yield of paddy upland which is called (Tanr land) in this locality due to high slope and land is not terraced, therefore, water drain rapidly from this type of land so without moisture and rapid erosion. Soil loses their fertility hence these types of soil in this area are infertile land. This can be changed by the action of a good water and soil management technology.

Ground Water Level

Depth of water table in different seasons are given below:

Season	*Depth*
Summer	30″-35″
Rainy	10″-15″
Winter	15″-20″

Runoff Surface Flow

The critical runoff in this Micro-watershed indicates them that quite a substantial quantity of water is harvested by the streams. This high rate of water yield is due to heavy rainfall. Due to the lack of any permanent reservoir the water is not harvested by streams. This loss of natural resources of water could be minimize by constructing water harvesting structure and can be utilized for crop production by recycling the stored water.

Location, Length and Courses of Drainage Lines

There is 8 km length of this drainage lines including main nala (Kusumva and Goghala river). The main river 'Goghala' flows north to west and meets with others. So subsidiary line is from west to north. The total area of drainage lines is question of intensive survey. But after a dense observation and measuring the total length of this drainage line is 8 km approximately. More than 90 per cent water is lost as runoff and goes to the Ganges river.

Treatment of Drainage Line

Stabilization of Nala Banks with Vegetation

Nala bank erosion is problem in the area. It has been proposed to stabilize the Nala banks 475 metres with vegetative measures. The cost RMT will be Rs. 1000.

Treatment of Upper Reaches

Live Check Dams

The treatment of upper reaches by raising 50 dams has been proposed. The cost per dam will be of 100 working days.

Brush Wood Dams

35 such dams have been proposed to be constructed at the cost of Rs. 175.00 each.

Loose Boulder Check Dam with Vegetable Support

Ten such structures have been proposed at a cost of Rs. 750 on an average. These structures will be provided with vegetative support.

Treatment of Middle reaches of drainage

Treatment of middle reaches of drainage lines has been proposed by constructing eastern structures reinforced with vegetation. The number of such structures would be 6 and the cost of per structure is Rs. 1500 workings days.

These loose boulder structures have been proposed. The cost per structure will be Rs. 3000 including provision for vegetative support.

Research Support

A team has visited the watershed area and suggested some of the trials included under this programme and some other trials have been proposed as described below:

To determine Micro-nutrient level of soils and for this four trials have been proposed to be taken—One on every village for 3 years. The total cost comes to Rs. 6000.

Vital Statistics

Item	*Amount Rs.*
1. Watershed as a whole	2,507.80
2. Employment potential likely to be generated	50,000.00
3. After saturation of the watershed	11,993.00

Conclusion

It has been learnt that Bali (1984) has extended the concept of watershed management to agro-industrial watersheds which is more comprehensive and considers this as cognate element of watershed management. Hence, it is a concept which bring people, land, forest and water resources based on local materials in an integrated manner on cooperative basis in between two water divides of a river basin.

Therefore, the programme like the Himalayan watershed project in upper Ganga catchment of Uttranchal with the help of World Bank need to be intensified. The people should be ensured about the benefit of this project. There is an urgent need to consider similar comprehensive programmes need to be taken up in the entire country covering the major watersheds of India.

REFERENCES

Bali, J.S.: 'Agro-Industrial Watersheds, XXI'. Convention of Indian Society of Agricultural Engineers, 1984.

Khosho, T.N.: Environmental Priorities in India. Indian Science Congress Association. New Delhi. pp. 15-17.

Ministry of Rural Development : 'Guidelines for Watershed Development', Government of India, 1994, p. 1.

MOA: 'Soil and Water Conservation and Watershed Management in India', Ministry of Agriculture. GOI. New Delhi. 1984.

UNDP : 'Forestry Development and Watershed Development in the Upland Region'. Food and Agriculture Organization of the UNO, p. 21.

31

Water Harvesting

A Need of Hour

KAUSHALENDRA PRAKASH GOSWAMI

Sources of Water Resource

India receives 75 to 90 per cent of its rainfall from the advancing monsoon. This rainfall is concentrated over four months—June to September. Rivers overflow during this period in both the regions—Himalayan and peninsula (Planning Commission, 1972). A general graph provided by the Ministry of Water Resource and published in the fortnightly *India Today* in the month of June 2003 clears that how much water is available in our country.

Table 31.1 : Availability of Water in India

Items	*Amount of Water*
1. Rainfall and Snow	400 Arab cubic metres.
2. Available Water Resource	1869 Arab cubic metres.
3. Used by the Nation	690 Arab cubic metres.

The above noted date clears that about 1179 ACM Water goes every year into the sea. And we are not in a position to harvest them for our needful. India is the land of monsoon. It lies in the tropical and warm temperate zone. Rapid run-off and quick evaporation is the root cause of the depletion of water in the nation while India faces long intervals of rainless weeks (Naegambala, 1973).

On the other hand, the water distribution is very uneven. Cherrapunji (1240 cm) and leg (8 cm) are the two points which clear the statement. Our nation uses water in different forms. These are as follows :

Table 31.2 : Distribution of Water Use

1.	Agriculture	90%
2.	Industries	06%
3.	Domestic	04%

How much water is being wasted everyday in our country is given in this statement. 'In the urban areas of Delhi everyday about 80 crore litre fresh water is leaked through the old network of pipelines made by iron'. On the other hand, in old Mysore about 1500 tanks and man made lakes 25000 go dry (*Source : India Today*, June 2003).

Water Budget

By water budget is meant balance between the potential water resource available and developed. On this account even though substantial ground water resources are utilised. India is a deficit country on account of water resources. It means that our needs are far more than even the potential water resources. India's total surface water resources are 187 million hectare metres and it has also 43 million hectare metres of groundwater potential. Only about 69 million hectare metres can be used by conventional storage and diversion methods like check dams, canals, ponds and roof top water use. Of the total groundwater potential about one-third of this potential is being currently utilised. Though these groundwater resources are replenishable, there are heavy costs involved because of deep depth at which water is available. On the other side, the irrigation potential has increased from 22.60 million hectares in 1951 A.D. to about 85 million hectares in 2000 A.D.

Bihar

Bihar is also the part of warm temperate region where extreme hot conditions during summer are experienced. *Loo* is the local wind moves fastly in the plain area which causes rapid evaporation from (i) the Himalayan rivers—the Ganga, the Gandak, the Kosi and the rivers of Adhwara ground and (ii) Peninsular rivers the Son, the Phalgu, the Punpun, the Mahane, the Jamuna, the Sobh, the Morhar, the Sorhar and other small seasonal rivers. The rapid run-off is the another problem of water depletion. Bihar gets 10 cm annual rainfall by the advancing monsoon while it gets 2-4 cm rainfalls by winter cyclones.

Steps are being taken by the State Government with the help of the Central Government (Ministry of Water Resource) to harvest the rain water of Bihar. Since Bihar is mostly an agricultural state with few urban centres which are located in the lap of Gangetic plain, so water harvesting technique is being a need of hour in this state for making Bihar strong agriculturally and industrially.

Water Harvesting

Water harvesting is now being popularised as a measure to augment of replenish ground water supplies particularly in areas facing the problem of lowering the level of water table. The process is nothing new. Only the ancient wisdom has been put to practice in the present circumstances of water scarcity particularly the ground water. Presently two chief practices of water harvesting are being followed (i) Root Top Water Harvesting and (ii) Check Dams.

REFERENCES

Michael, A.M. Water Resource Utilization in India, *Journal of Planters and Agriculture,* August, 1970. pp. 321-324

Naegambala, J.P. "Development of Water Resources in India for Irrigation and Hydel Power", *Souvenir: U.N. Seminar on Water Resources Administration*, Jan. 22 to Feb. 2. New Delhi, 1973.

Planning Commission, Government of India: "Report of the Task Force on Ground-water Resources." 1972, p. 131.

32

Susceptibility of Water Resources

R.B. MANDAL

Water at all the places is contaminated to some extent. But the level of contamination vary from one place to another based on the local environmental condition as in agricultural belt the mix of insecticides and pesticides, in industrial belt lead, zinc, sulphur etc. are important. In this way, this paper will examine that what level of impurities in water is tolerable for human being in our society. In almost all sectors of our society people use groundwater for drinking purposes but millions of rural and urban families do not know that whether the water is potable or not (Kumar and Shah 2004). According to an estimate, it accounts for 80 per cent domestic needs of rural families and 50 per cent in urban areas of India. This is because the level of contamination is relatively low in underground water in comparison with surface water bodies. This is because when the rain water is infiltrating through the strata of soil inside the earth its natural impurities become replenished (Alam, 2004).

In India, the groundwater is extensively used for irrigation of dry fields, industrial use and hence, the variety of land and water based activities of human beings are responsible for pollution of water resource. Its over extraction is causing aquifer contamination at some places, while at others the less knowledgeable person engaged in water extraction, the flow dynamics and geo-hydrochemical processes has led to its mineralization and chemical transformation.

Objectives of Study

The sole purpose of this paper is to analyse the effect of fluoride, salinity, arsenic and other pollutants found in the water in different parts of India and assess their impact on the human health. In terms of these intoxicants the sustainability of water may be judged.

Regional Distribution

The fluoride above permissible level of 1.5 ppm is found in 14 states of India, e.g. Bihar, Andhra Pradesh, Gujarat, Haryana, Karnataka, Kerala, Madhya Pradesh, Maharashtra, Orissa, Punjab, Rajasthan, Tamil Nadu, Uttar Pradesh and West Bengal. According to an estimate altogether 69 districts are affected with excessive fluoride content in the water. Another estimate shows that 65 per cent villages in India has been affected with fluoride risk. High levels of salinity have been recorded in almost all the states of India except West Bengal (Dasgupta, 2004). In Delhi salinity affects 73 districts and 3 blocks only. It has also been reported that iron content above permissible level of 0.3 ppm is found in 23 districts of India especially in Bihar, Rajasthan, Tripura, West Bangal and Orissa.

The high amount of arsenic above the permissible level of 50 parts per billion (ppb) is found in the Ganges valley especially in six districts of West Bengal. So far as the heavy metals are concerned it is found in the groundwater of 49 districts in the states of Andhra Pradesh, Assam, Bihar, Haryana, Himachal Pradesh, Karnataka, Madhya Pradesh, Orissa, Punjab, Rajasthan, Tamil Nadu, Uttar Pradesh, West Bengal and in some parts of Delhi. (Dakshinamurati *et al.* 1973).

The pollution caused by fertilizers and pesticides used in crop raising often disseminate over large area put a threat to the underground water sources. The use of chemical fertilizers by the agricultural farmers along with the indiscriminate disposal of human and animal carcasses on the land and water cause heavy nitrate concentration in the water. Its permissible level is 45 ppm found in 11 states of India. The most common pesticides used in India are DDT, BHC, cardamate, endosulfan and others. All these are making the groundwater poisonous. The bad effect of chemical fertilizers and pesticides are governed by soil texture, and their degradation produces organic matter in the soil. The pollution of groundwater has also been caused by industrial effluents and municipal wastes in the water bodies found in urban areas. In the year 1995, the Central Pollution Control Board has identified 22 sites in 16 states as a critical point for groundwater pollution caused due to industrial effluents. In a recent survey conducted by the Centre of Science and Environment reported the traces of heavy metals from Gujarat, Andhra Pradesh and Haryana along with cadmium, zinc and mercury. A shallow aquifer zone in the city of Ludhiana is polluted by a stream which receives effluents from 1300 industries. It has also been recorded that due to excessive extraction of underground water from the aquifer of coastal zone has led to the intrusion of saline sea water in the aquifer of Kutch, Saurashtra in Gujarat, Chennai in Tamil Nadu and in the city of Kozhikode in Kerala along with some other areas here and there.

Impact of Contamination

Due to above mentioned pollution in water the sustainable level of contamination depends on the typology of pollutants present in the groundwater. It has been reported that mercury cause impairment in the functioning of brain along with neurological disorders, retard the growth of children, induce abortion and disruption of endocrine gland. Pesticides damage the liver, nervous disorder and the formation of tumour as well. The presence of fluoride and arsenic could be known only after testing the quality of water with the help of an equipment named Atomic absorption spectrometer for arsenic fluoride ion activity meter. But the presence of fluoride in water could be judged as yellow colour of teeth, damages of joints, bone deformations due to use of fluoride containing water for a longer period. Hence, by the time this menace gets detected several people in the society gets affected. A survey done by International Water Management Institute has detected in north Gujarat that 28,425 people were affected by dental fluorosis (25.7%), skeletal fluorosis (6.2%) and others. It has been indicated that fluoride might have genotoxio effect. It has the capacity to cause depressions in DNA and RNA synthesis in cultured cells. Fluoride is also associated with cancer, arteriosclerosis and disrepair of DNA. Long exposure of water containing salt may cause the formation of kidney stone especially reported from coastal areas of India.

Increasing Sustainability

With the reversal of osmosis one can get rid of all the impurities found in drinking water. It also includes ion organisms and residues of pesticides and fertilizers. In the system of reversal of osmosis water has to pass through a number of membrane having a pore size of 0.0001 micron under high pressure and in this process only 10 per cent ions are able to slip through the membrane which is acceptable as per World Health Organization. Other pollutants found in dissolved form in the water can also suitably removed as the residues of fluoride, pesticides, fertilizer and heavy metals and other impurities found in water.

The presence of arsenic could be treated in a household and the method of treatment is the ferric chloride coagulation system. With the precipitation of arsenic by adding a packet of coagulant in 25 litres of water in a tubewell and filtration of such water with sand filter will clean the water. In treated water the presence of arsenic is 1/20th and the cost of ferric chloride is just Rs. 0.09 per litre of raw water. Another method of removing arsenic is 'sorptive filteration based on iron coated sand bed'. Water should be put into a bucket and sometimes to accelerate precipitation of excess iron. Now allow it to pass through a sand filter which will filter out the iron. Now this water should pass through an iron coated sand filter but stop the crossing of water when the permissible arsenic level reached the limit of 50 ppb. The arsenic may also be cleaned from raw water after passing through a gravel media containing iron sludge.

The methods of water treatment require some knowledge of Physics and Chemistry. Hence, qualified technical man-power is needed to regulate the system and do maintenance as well. The Gujarat Water Supply and Sewerage Board had set up 28 desalination systems in 1989. The Government of India has established 117 desalination plants in different States but unfortunately all are non-functional due to lack of technical man-power.

The water treatment plant may be tried out at community level in order to make it cost effective and affordable. The treated water should be supplied to almost all sections of the society because it is essential for the survival of human being at minimum cost. It is difficult for the monitoring agencies to establish a network of WQM centre due to involvement of high cost and the use of technical manpower. Therefore, only the private agency and the non-governmental organization can play a big role in managing the database of groundwater quality of different places and manage better the ill-effects of using polluted water and suggest possible preventive measures.

Control of Groundwater Pollution

The presence of arsenic in drinking water can cause arsenicosis for which there is no treatment in India. Arsenic mix water is so poisonous that it has affected 20 million people in West Bengal and Bangladesh.

In order to control groundwater quality deterioration is to get correct information regarding water quality monitoring to assure the cause, source, type and level of water pollution. Measurement of water quality is a difficult process to operate the sophisticated machineries and expensive in collecting, analysing and managing the data available. It favours artificial recharge of groundwater and reducing the level of fluoride, arsenic and salinity in the aquifer zone following the principle of dilution.

Industrial zone requires the pumping out of polluted water, needs proper treatment and replenishing of depleted aquifer with input of fresh water. Sometimes it is difficult as in Rajasthan.

Agencies Working in the Field of Water

According to the Central Groundwater Board the available ground water in India is 210 billion m^3. This estimate is based on different hydro-geological and related studies along with taking into account irrigation, seepage and evapotranspiration in the recharge of groundwater.

In order to deal with water resources there are Central and State organizations for considering specific aspects of water resource management and some of them are as follows :—

1. The Central Pollution Control Board (CPCB)
2. The State Pollution Control Board (SPCB)
3. Central Groundwater Commission—Surface Water
4. Central Groundwater Board—Ground Water
5. Indian Meteorological Department—Precipitation
6. Central Board for Prevention and Control of Water Pollution—Water Quality
7. Ministry of Agriculture and ICAR—Water use for Agriculture
8. Department of Environment—Environmental Impact Assessment
9. Central Public Health and Environmental Engineering Organization (Ministry of Urban Development)—water supplies, sanitation and sewage disposal
10. Department of Power—Hydro-electric Power
11. Department of Forest-–Watershed Management

The sulfuric acid plant has contaminated the underground sources of water at 22 places and it is difficult to replenish them with fresh water.

These are considered as the nations watchdog to control the pollution in India. Monitoring of underground water and quality of the water of rivers come under the purview of these agencies. The performance of Gujarat State Pollution Control Board (GPCB) reveal that in Sabarmati basin four priority areas has been identified which were facing severe pollution, but due to lack of adequate facilities it has failed to control pollution. Actually, groundwater pollution occurs due to geo-hydro-chemical processes activated by pumping. Once pollution starts nothing could be done to check it except ban on pumping.

On the other hand nitrate pollution could be controlled by applying prescribe dose of fertilizers, crops rotation and use of organic manure.

Conclusion

At the end it could be said that the government should continue the preventive and curative measures to control pollution. Reverse Osmosis (RO) system can remove hazardous elements for drinking water especially nitrate, fluoride and arsenic wherever it is present beyond permissible level. As the technology used in Saudi-Arabia, the cost of desalination has been considered cheaper. Similarly, low cost technology may help in removing arsenic from groundwater which we use for drinking purposes. Hence, the treatment of water properly and the supply of quality of water is a general issue of our society and for proper water management this should be tackled in a right earnest manner.

REFERENCES

Alam, A.; Andhra Pradesh : Fluoride in Water; in Survey of the Environment, *The Hindu,* 2004.

Dakshinamurti, C. *et al., Water Resources of India and Their Utilization in Agriculture,* Water Technology Centre, IARI; New Delhi, 1973.

Dasgupta, R., West Bengal : Arsenic in Water; in Survey of the Environment, *The Hindu,* 2004.

Kumar, M.D. and Shah, T., Ground Water Contamination, in Survey of the Environment, *The Hindu,* 2004, pp. 1-6.

33

Urban Water Supply

R.B. MANDAL AND NAVIN KUMAR

Water is one of the three basic needs of man. In urban areas the concentration of population is so high that the timely and regulated supply of water is considered necessary. In India the supply of clean drinking water and sanitation are State subject, but the Government of India provides technical assistance to the State Governments and the Union Territories for formulation, implementation and maintenance of urban water supply and sanitation programmes through the Ministry of Urban Development. This Ministry organizes conference, seminars, provides training, research and management of the Information System through technical personnel (MUD, 1988-89).

Need for Water Supply and Sanitation

1. The water in wells, ponds and rivers are contaminated and for this fact, the supply of safe drinking water is essential.
2. The garbage and night-soil are dangerous, hence their proper management is essential in order to usher an era of cleanliness in our cities and towns.
3. In urban areas due to congregation of population, huge rush of traffic especially during day time ejects such a huge amount of carbon monoxide, obnoxious gases and solid wastes that they are polluting the sources of groundwater and giving rise to slums in urban areas where the maintenance of sanitation is quite essential.
4. The congregation of large number of people require quick and timely supply of water because they cannot move too far away places to fetch water for safety reasons and convenience of work.

2005 Conference on Water in Stockholm

On August 22, 2005, participants from more than 100 countries gathered at the Swedish capital, Stockholm, to deliberate development of water resource infrastructure, water supply and sanitation, and pollution management. The occasion : the Stockholm Water Week. Organised by the Stockholm International Water Institute (SIWI) since 1991. This annual event has become a common platform for experience-sharing among water professionals, decision-makers and activists form all over the world.

The opening ceremony witnessed rich deliberations on water management. Inaugurating the symposium, Lena Sommestad, the Swedish Minister of Environment, called for greater democracy to manage water in a sustainable manner. In her keynote address, Buyelwa Patience Sonjica, the South African Minister for Water Affairs and Forestry, emphasised that African countries require large infrastructure to store and distribute water. "But mere infrastructure development won't be enough," retorted Mariela Garcia Varga, a Columbian delegate. "The involvement of communities holds the key to sustainable water management," she added. Garcia Varcia Vargas held up a women's group-run water treatment system in the Coli region of her country as an example of sustainable water management. Sunita Narain, Director of the Delhi based Centre for Science and Environment (CSE), this year's Stockholm Water Prize winner, opined : "If the hold of the high-level bureaucracy is not broken, spending on water resources will become unsustainable."

The symposium reached fever pitch when 1,400 people debated large water infrastructure projects. Not surprisingly, there was no consensus. Asit K. Biswas, of the Mexico-based Third World Centre for Water Management, tried to strike one by suggesting, "A judicious mix of small and large hydro insfrastructure projects."

How could the water week go by without discussions on water supply and sanitation in the context of the UN's millennium development goals (MDGs)? And indeed, the trady progress over the attainment of this MDG was cause for concern at the *UN water seminar*—one of the side events at the concern at the conference—on August 24, 2005. There were anxious calls for country-level coordination to integrate water and sanitation issues in poverty reduction strategies.

Indian Situation

The provision of safe and adequate water supply for the ever increasing population and hygienic disposal of wastes is a basic necessity for the healthy living of the urban community. The urgency for water supply and sanitation measures assume special importance in a tropical country like India which is a subject of periodic wars with water and filth borne diseases, viz., cholera, dysentery, typhoid and gastro-enteric fevers. An organized water supply system also provides an opportunity for speedy removal of human excreta and other offensive wastes through water flushed sewers. Unfortunately, in the subcontinent of India—no one cares to discuss the methods of fecal disposal. This task has been entrusted to sweepers whose job throughout his life is to remove night-soil—has earned him the ultimate epithet of social degradation. The sweepers are considered here as untouchables. This is a very sad state of affairs in the way of social development (Lee and Burton, 1965).

The science of environmental hygiene is of recent origin. It gained importance with the shifting of emphasis from the curative to the preventive aspects of public health. This again was result of the growing industrialization and urbanization in the more advanced countries in the West which pin-point problems relating to environmental hygiene—which deals with town and country planning, housing, safe water supply, collection and disposal of community wastes, prevention of water and air pollution, control of industrial wastes, food, sanitation, etc. Hence, water supply and sanitation measures got priority in their nation building programme as an essential prerequisites. It has been emphasized by the Bhore Committee and the Environmental Hygiene Committee (1948-49) which aims to supply safe water upto 90 per cent population of urban areas within 40 years. The programme also carried out 100 per cent grant for rural investigations and Public Health Engineering Training Programme, based on urban centres.

During the Seventh Five-Year Plan an outlay of Rs. 2,935.64 crores under the state sector and Rs. 30.11 crores under the Central Sector have been provided for urban water supply and sanitation as against the projected requirement of Rs. 5,797.7 crores. Keeping in view the outlay provided, the decade targets in respect of urban water supply and urban sanitation were scaled down to 90 per cent and 50 per cent respectively and these revised targets are expected to be achieved by March 1991. It has been envisaged that the progress during the Seventh Plan period in the Urban Water Supply and sanitation sector would be as follows :

Table 33.1 : Population Coverage *(in millions)*

	Water Supply and Sanitation	*As on 31.3.1985*		*As on 31.3.1990 (Envisaged)*	
		Population	*%*	*Population*	*%*
1.	Urban Water Supply	127.23	72.88	169.96	86.40
2.	Urban Sanitation	49.56	28.40	87.91	44.70

The working group formulating the Eighth Five-Year Plan (1992-1997) has envisaged a requirement of Rs. 14,094 crore for water supply, sanitation and solid waste management. This includes a provision of Rs. 44 crore as central sector outlay for the support programmes. It has been decided by the working group of Eighth Plan to provide water supply facilities to 100 per cent and sewerage and sanitation facilities to 75 per cent of the urban population by the end of the Eighth Plan. The government has introduced use of Micro-Computer for planning and designing of water supply distribution and sewage systems besides imparting training to public health engineers.

The Urban Development Ministry has developed a Management Information System (MIS) which has been disseminated to State Public Health Engineering Departments and Water Supply and Sewage Boards for application. It gives technical advises and clearance of urban water supply and sanitation schemes for external assistance. It has helped in completing six World Bank Aided Development Projects in Maharashtra, Uttar Pradesh, Punjab and Rajasthan. It has recently taken up the programme of liberation of scavengers in collaboration with the Ministry of Welfare in 500 towns in the first phase within a period of two to three years. It is also responsible for monitoring progress besides improvement of sanitation, roads, drainage, street lights, slaughter houses and community facilities under the Sri Nagar Core Area Development Project.

In the State of Bihar upto 1947 only 8 urban centres, e.g., Patna, Gaya, Ara, Munger, Bhagalpur, Muzaffarpur, Sultanganj and Jamshedpur had piped clean water supplies. Up to 1966 about 60 per cent urban population of the State of Bihar enjoyed this facility in more than 30 urban centres. A sum of Rs. 2,500 crore has been estimated to fulfil the task but during Fourth Five-Year Plan of the State of Bihar only Rs. 4.86 crore has been given for the purpose. This clearly points out that the problems of safe water supply will stay for a longer time not only in the State of Bihar but throughout the Third World countries.

Urban Water Supply and Sanitation in Karachi

The shortcoming of sanitation and water supply have been highly felt by the urban poor who are living specially in slums, shanty towns and squatter settlements which are mushrooming all over the developing world.

Out of Karachi's six million population, two million live in the slums. Their houses are known as *Karachi Abadi* (temporary dwellings). These settlements have no drainage, no water supply and they are over-crowded insanitary and unhygienic, and sometimes they lack even the legal right to exist.

One out of five children born in the slums dies before the age of five—due to poor arrangement of human waste disposal and a lack of health consciousness. The problem is common in most of the Third World big cities. It is very difficult to deal with Flush, toilets and water taps are out of question. Even if there is no shortage of water in Karachi, the costs of laying sewers connection to every house would be prohibitive.

In the city of Karachi, the Baldia project aims to install soak-pit latrines. The starting point was the design by a Dutch Advisory Mission of low-cost household latrine. It consists of a soak-pit 14 feet deep and 5 feet in diameter connected to a squatting plate by a four-inch pipe with a water seal. The cost per soak-pit is Rs. 600 ($ 12) and it has a life of 20 years for nine people.

Initially, the Karanchi Municipal Corporation was not interested with water supply and sewerage on a mass scale. The project of Baldia will take at least ten years to supply water. The slums of Baldia are not at all uniform in layout, buildings and inhabitants—and hence, for the time being it is futile to think about the supply of safe drinking water and avail the facility of soak-pit latrines in the near future. The migrants people of Sind and Punjab adopt rural life-style even if they reside in urban areas.

In urban areas rivers and pools used for drinking water can be polluted by industry, or by washing and bathing. Urban water pipes are also contaminated by sewage, especially when the pressure drops, like dirty water, the inadequate sanitation causes disease. In too many developing countries the municipalities still have to wash inner drains contaminated with sewage. Therefore, it has been felt that safe latrines are an essential for basic health.

Situation of Water Supply in Bangkok

The provision of safe water to the inhabitants of a metropolitan city of Bangkok—which has a population of 8.5 million spread over an area of 6,400 km^2 is really a gigantic task. The authorities of Thailand's capital have been working on it for the last 75 years. The huge immigrant population to achieve economic book and industrial development itself also have to provide the clean water.

Today about 68 per cent population of Bangkok have access to piped water, and some 700,000 households are connected to a metred and charged for the supply of safe water.

The expansion of such services has been recognized to be of utmost priority for health and to facilitate continuous development. The Asian Development Bank has lent the Metropolitan Water Works Authority $ 130 million for the third phase of water treatment plant construction and this project has completed at the end of the International Drinking Water Supply and Sanitation Decade, 1990.

Water Woe's in Kanpur

River Ganga supplies most of Kanpur's water needs. At many places in its Kanpur stretch, the river is an open sewer that carries toxic materials spewed out by the numerous tanneries and chemical industries along its banks. Moreover, adds Rakesh K. Jaiswal of Ecofriends, a Kanpur based non-governmental organisation, "People come from all over India to bathe in the Ganga, to offer ritual oblation to the holy river, or even to die along its left bank. They do not realise that their religious zeal pollutes the river."

Of course, the Ganga wasters are decontaminated at but they are polluted again during supply to the households. Engineers associated with the Kanpur Municipal Corporation say that pipe leakage is a common problem; so is the inflow of sewage and other affluents into the water distribution network that dates back to 1892.

Rapid depletion of underground water coupled with groundwater pollution has compounded the city's water woes. Chemicals such as manganese, chromium, nitrate and fluoride have been detected in the groundwater on the banks of the Ganga. Recently, a team from the National Environmental Engineering Research Institute, Nagpur, has found that wastes from bleaching and electroplating units contaminate groundwater sources, rendering them unfit for domestic consumption. Kanpur's groundwater has also been sullied by sewage inflow.

Mismanagement of Water Resource in Mumbai

September 9, 2005, panic gripped Mumbai, again. Within 24 hours the city received more than 200 mm rain. It started pouring heavily in the morning. By 11 am the unrelenting downpour caused traffic jams. Not leaving anything to chance, the state government issued a rain alert. With Terrible Tuesday (July 26) fresh in mind, people left offices. Schools were shut down. As everyone came on to the roads, or headed towards local train stations, the Bandra-Mahim highway, a major intersection joining suburbs with the island city, was chock-e-block with traffic. Within an hour or so of rain, lowlying areas like Kurla, Sion, Mahim, Dadar, Andheri, Goregaon and Bandra East were flooded. To avoid another public baklash, the state government evacuated close to 300 families. The infamous Air India colony of Kalina once again went under water. Services on Central Railway were suspended for about 3 hours. It is September 10 today, and the rain has still not relented. Most low-lying areas remain flooded and trains are running late.

The flood was foretold. The disaster, in all is dimensionless. Perhaps not the scale already mapped. For years now, Mumbai's politicians of all hues have ignored the signs; the crumbling drainage system; the built-over natural drainage; the poisonous landfills where garbage stands 8-10 metres high, exuding poison; the untreated sewage, shamelessly dumped into the Arabian Sea.

Groundwater Conditions in Bangalore

The latest groundwater report of Karnataka, brought out by the Department of Mines and Geology (DMG), shows that entire Bangalore is an overexploited zone. The 2004 study puts 55 *talukas* in the overexploited category. The situation is worst in Kolar and

Tumkur, apart from Bangalore's rural and urban areas. Besides the quantum of the resource, the quality of groundwater in Bangalore city is also slarming due to contamination with sewage and industrial affluents. Groundwater meets 40 per cent of the city's domestic potable water needs.

An analysis of 918 water samples collected from 735 locations shows that at 370 locations, the groundwater is not suitable for domestic use as per the specifications of the groundwater quality report of Bangalore city, 2003. Iron content in the groundwater was over 1 milligramme per liter (mg/1) in many places; the permissible limit is 0.3 mg/1. Of the 918 samples, 116 had iron content over 1 mg/1; at a few locations, it was over 6 mg/1. "High iron content is due to rusting pipes and industrial contamination," says Shashi Rekha, chief chemist, DMG. Regarding nitrate concentration of over 50 mg 1 in 262 samples, she says it indicates heavy sewage contamination and domestic pollution. Also, hardness exceeds the permissible limit of 600 mg/l in 51 samples— a result of sewage contamination. The pH value is below the permissible range of 6.5 to 8.5 in 106 samples, another result of industrial pollution.

To determine bacteriological pollution, 100 samples were collected from areas without underground drainage systems to test for total coliforms and faecal coliforms. Bacteriological pollution of upto 23 most probable number per 100 millilitres (MPN/100 ml) was found in 74 samples; the permissible limit for drinking water (without chlorination) is 0 MPN/100 ml. The report urges checking sewage and industrial waste pollution and stresses on the need for rainwater harvesting.

Water Management in Delhi

The State Government of Delhi is concerned over the declining per capita availability of water in the National Capital Territory of Delhi. The Planning Commission has called for better water management and conservation to tackle water scarcity on a sustained basis.

At an internal meeting of the Planning Commission presided over by the Deputy Chairman, the then Mr. Pranab Mukherjee, recently the Commission felt that while tackling the present water shortage problems of Delhi on a sustainable basis, the demand for management including conservation measures were necessary than turning merely to supply side of the problem.

> "It is estimated that with the technological innovations available today, water consumption for cities could be curtailed by at least one- third with no sacrifice of economic output or quality of life," the meeting felt.

The installed capacity of Municipal Water Supply of Delhi is 600 million gallons per day (MGD); out of which 15 per cent of transmission losses are excluded, leaving the net quantity of water available to be about 450-475 MGD, the Commission observed.

With this level of water availability, per capita water in Delhi may be about 56 gallons per day (GPD) as against about 55 GPD in Mumbai, 30.5 GPD in Kolkata and 15.5 GPD in Chennai.

The Commission noted that there was substantial variation in the availability of municipal water supply in different areas in Delhi which at times created law and order issue.

The long-term strategy to fulfil the ever-growing water needs of Delhi was through few multi-purpose projects like Tehri Dam (U.P.), Kishau Dam (U.P.) and Renuka Dam (H.P.), whose estimated costs are Rs. 5,058 crore, Rs. 1,054 crore and Rs. 372 crore respectively.

"Going by the present experience, these projects may take quite long time and benefit from these may not be expected at least in this century" the Commission felt.

The Commission also suggested few "action points" as part of demand management of the water supply problems in the national capital.

A vigorous and extensive mass information campaign through airing radio and television spots should be taken up to enhance public awareness about city's water plight and to let people know how they can conserve water, it said.

The water pricing structure should have adequate built-in financial penalty to act as an effective restraint on consumer to remain within the allotted quotas, it said adding that the restructuring of water pricing as recommended in the study report was very much needed inasmuch as only about one-tenth of one per cent of the annual expenditure of an average family was spent on water.

Commercial establishments particularly big hotels and automobile service stations should be compelled to meet most of their water demands for various uses other than drinking.

Ills of Mega Cities and Water Supply

In the Mega city of Mumbai the Flimi shacks of the one million homeless poor living on the coast of Arabian sea always hug the water mains. The tiny pipes hidden in the dust and rubble provide precious trickles of drinking water. Taking potable water from an illicit source, in a city where the daytime temperature rise above 40ºC.

In Africa, the population of Nairobi, Dar es Salaam and Lusaka and the mega cities of Mumbai, Mexico city, Cairo, Lagos, Rio de Janeiro and Bangkok have all increased seven fold in the last 30 years are all facing famine and drought like situation due to the paucity of drinking water. About 140 mega cities of Africa, Asia and Latin America are facing the pressure of overpopulation and inadequate services especially the provision of fresh water, disposal of human waste, shortage of housing and transportation.

With the funding of IDRC Canada, the Municipal Corporation of Bhopal had to deal with a severe shortage of fresh water, but it has decided to look at the possibilities of improving the utilization of drinking water resources. Construction of low cost overhead tanks with tube wells for example, resulted in a better water distribution system as well as a higher overall level of supply (McNicoll, 1985). Therefore, the subject of water management and its catastrophic mismanagement has been a topic of perennial interest.

International Drinking Water Supply and Sanitation Decade

The United Nations declared the period 1981-90 as the International Drinking Water Supply and Sanitation Decade and 2003 as International Year of Fresh Water under U.N. Programme with a view to provide safe drinking water supply and adequate sanitation facilities in all the member countries by 2005. The Decade Programme was launched in India on 1st April 1981 with the objective of increasing the urban population coverage with water supply facilities upto 72.25 per cent.

Remedies of the Problem

1. The remedies of the water supply and sanitation lie in the hands of the State Government and the residents of the town. The regular cleaning of roads and timely supply of water are quite essential.
2. On community basis it could be decided to throw the garbage

at a definite point so that the Municipal Van could collect it easily.

3. The other way is that the residents of the area could clean their surroundings as this system is practiced in Tanzania.
4. The construction of water tanks, laying of pipes, regular cleaning and maintenance of tanks and pipes are essential to supply clean drinking water.
5. The town administration should restrict themselves in throwing used dirty water through regulated channels to the nearby rivers and wetland areas as this can also pollute our water and environment as well.

REFERENCES

Lee, T., and Burton, J. "Future Water Supply for Indian Cities", *Deccan Geographer,* 1965, pp. 3-4.

McNicoll, A. "The Ills of Urbanization : India looks for a solution", *The IDRC Reports,* Vol. No. 3, October, 1985, p. 39.

"Water Supply and Sanitation", Ministry of Urban Development, New Delhi, Government of India Report 1988-89, pp. 12-14.

34

Multi-Purpose River Valley Projects

R.B. Mandal

Nature and Scope

Since India got independence several river valley projects have been undertaken in the country in order to utilize waters of the rivers more efficiently. The success of these projects involve the construction of dams, reservoirs and canals, and fulfil number of objectives at the same time. Most of them have been designed for integrated development in the area concerned and hence, they are known as multi-purpose river valley projects (Bose, 1948).

The purpose of these projects are to fulfil the need of irrigation, flood control and generation of hydro-electricity along with fishing and recreation through navigation. Hydro-electricity is generated by allowing water of the reservoir to fall through huge heights below dams constructed purposely. Such projects also have afforestation programmes on barren and wastelands which check soil erosion and conserve water received from rainfall and flowing rivers in the area (Das, 1969). Fisheries have been developed in the reservoirs. The bigger size canals are often used for navigation and water gets distributed in the nearby rural settlements and urban centres. Due to generation of electricity and availability of clean water, these projects also encourage growth of industries in the surrounding area. Hence, a multi-purpose project can usher development in the surrounding region. For this fact, the first Prime Minister of India called these projects 'the new temple of modern India'. Major multi-purpose river valley projects of India are discussed as follows (Fig. 34.1) :

Bhakra-Nangal Project

This has been considered as the biggest multi-purpose river valley

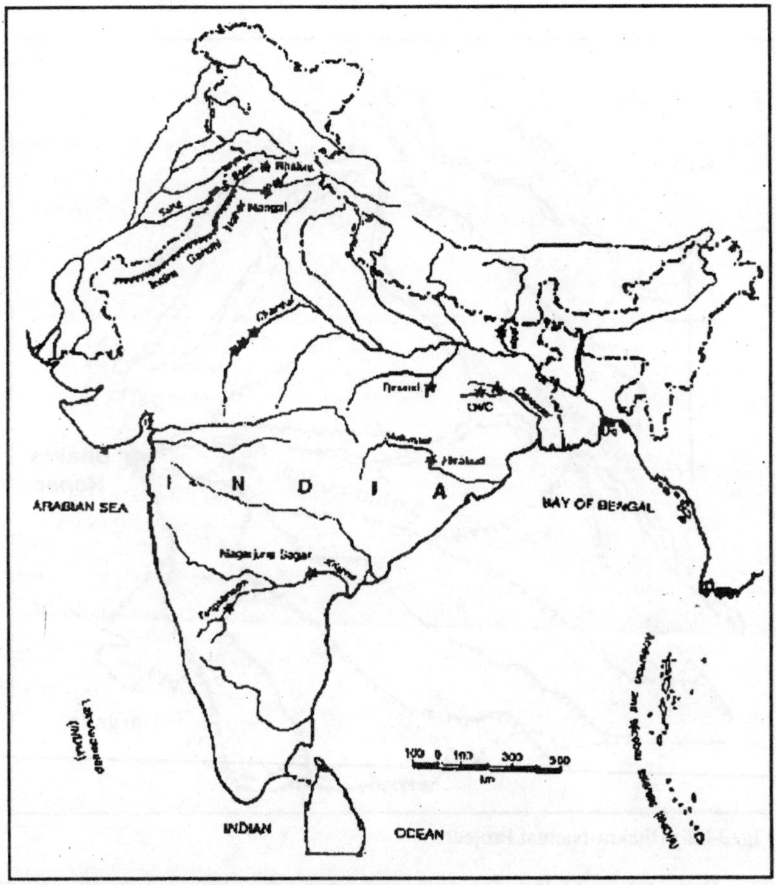

Fig. 34.1 : Sites of Major River Valley Projects of India

project in India. It has been constructed on river Sutlej and irrigate the semi-arid region of north-western India and made it agriculturally productive. Several dams have been constructed including Bhakra and Nangal. Bhakra has been considered as the highest dam in India and the reservoir constructed for this lake is known as Govind Sagar Lake. Its jurisdiction is on the Punjab, Haryana and the State of Rajasthan. Besides these three, it supplied hydro-electricity to Himachal Pradesh and the metropolis of Delhi as well (Fig. 34.2).

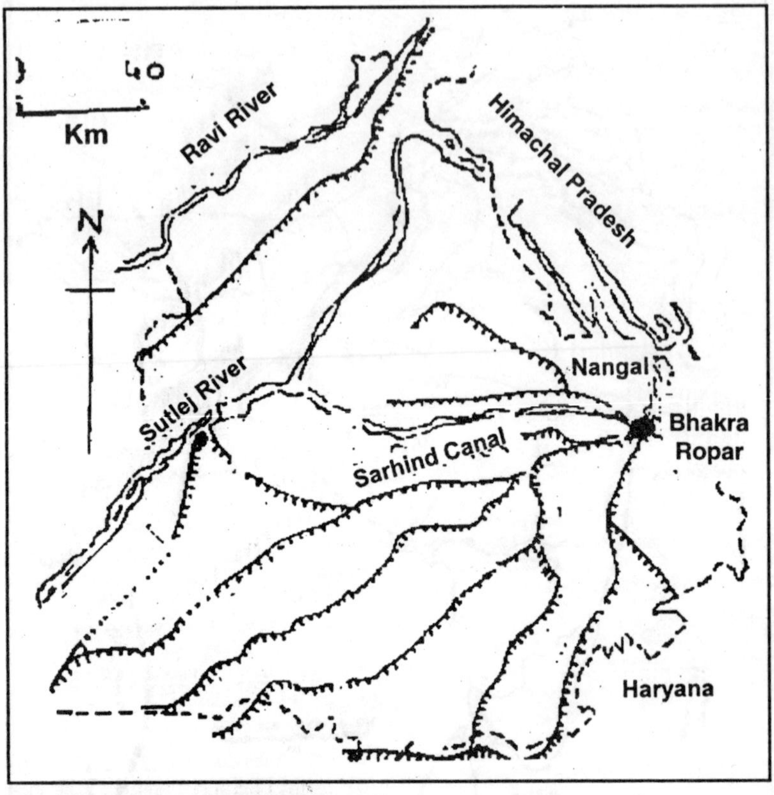

Fig. 34.2 : Bhakra-Nangal Project

The Beas River Valley Project

It has also been constructed under the joint venture of the Punjab, Haryana and Rajasthan. The Beas dam has been constructed at Pong near the border area of the Punjab and Himachal Pradesh. This area also consists of Beas-Sutlej link canals. The purposes of this canal are irrigation, electricity generation and navigation as well.

The Hirakud Project

The Hirakud dam has been constructed on the Mahanadi river in Orissa. This has a length of 4.80 km and considered as the longest dam in the world. The purpose of this project is to accomplish the task of hydel power generation, flood control, irrigation and the development of water transport. It has also helped in the growth of industries on the basis of minerals available locally and crop production.

The Chambal Valley Project

It consists of three dams constructed on the Chambal river in Madhya Pradesh. It is a joint project of M.P. and Rajashthan. This project irrigates the dry land and supplies electricity to these two states (Fig. 34.3).

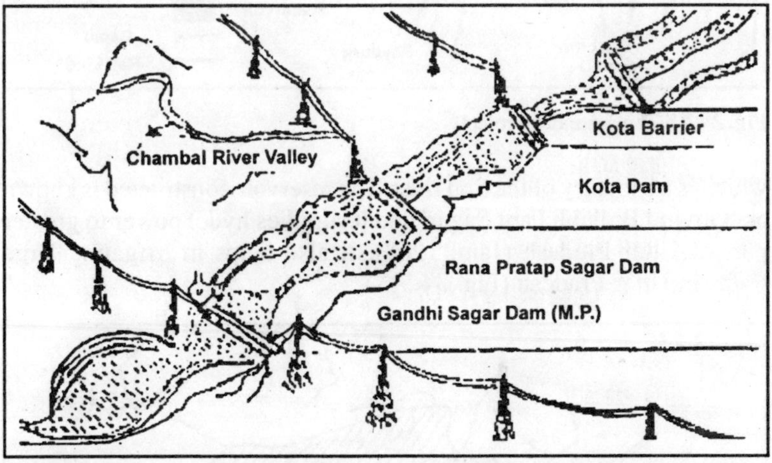

Fig. 34.3 : Chambal Valley Project

The Tungabhadra Project

This has been constructed under the joint venture of Andhra Pradesh and Karnataka. A dam has been constructed across Tungabhadra river for irrigation of dry fields and generation of hydro-electricity (Fig. 34.4).

The Rihand Project

A dam has been constructed in Uttar Pradesh on the Rihand river

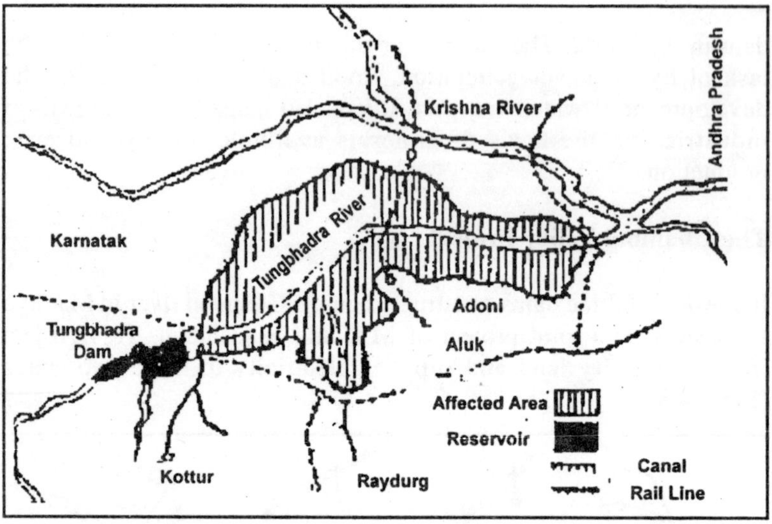

Fig. 34.4 : Tungabhadra Project

which is a tributary of the Son river. The reservoir constructed is known as 'Govind Ballabh Pant Sagar' and it supplies hydel power to greater part of Uttar Pradesh (Jain, 1968). It also helps in irrigating large tracts in Uttar Pradesh (Fig. 34.5).

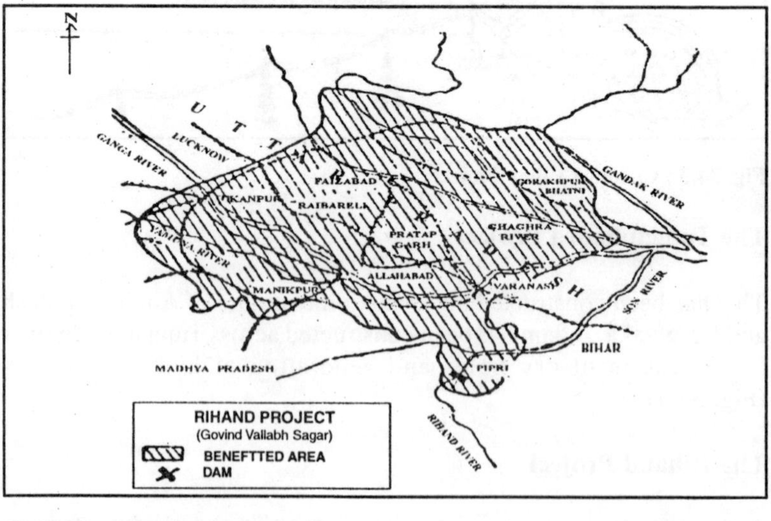

Fig. 34.5 : Rihand Project (U.P.)

The Nagarjun Sagar Project

The dam has been constructed across the Krishna river. It generates electricity and provides water for irrigation to the drought stricken areas of Andhra Pradesh.

The Gandak Valley Project

A dam has been constructed at Valmikinagar in Bihar and two canals western and eastern have been constructed to irrigate fields in Champaran district of Bihar and Gorakhpur district of U.P. (Fig.34.6).

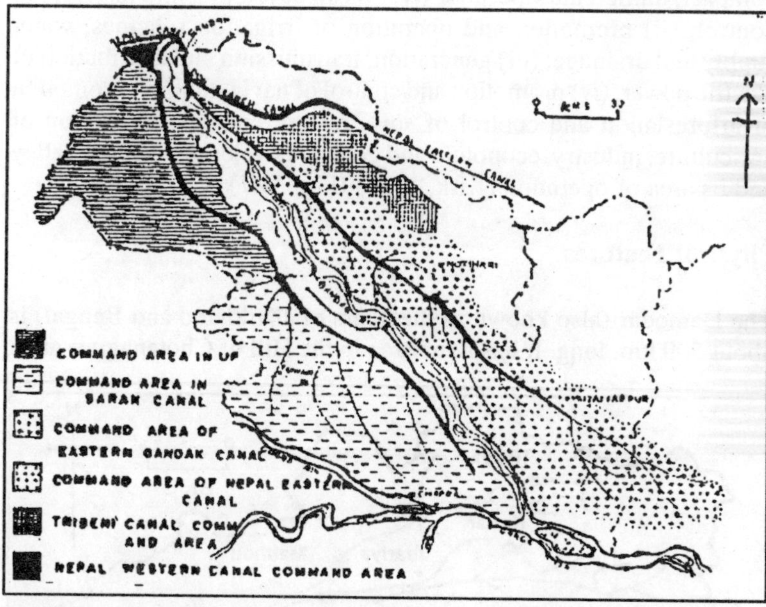

Fig. 34.6 : The Gandak River Valley Project

Hence, in Champaran district, about 90 per cent irrigation has been done from Dhaka (Lal Bakya) and Tribeni (from the Gandak) canals which together irrigate about 150 hectares of land. The Gandak Project has been originally designed to irrigate 13 lakh hectares in Bihar, 3.24 lakh hectares in Uttar Pradesh and more than 40,000 hectares in Nepal. Area mainly benefited would be west and east Champaran, Gopalganj, Siwan, Saran, Sitamarhi, Muzaffarpur,

Vaishali and Samastipur districts. The Gandak Project includes Tirhut main canal, Western main canal, Saran canal, Eastern Nepal canal, Western Nepal canal, besides generating hydro-electricity and providing the facility of navigation. The hydel power station of 15 Megawatt is situated at Surajpura in Nepal.

DAMODAR RIVER VALLEY PROJECT

Introduction

The basic feature of the Damodar Valley Project is that it constitutes a compact, unified multipurpose river basin development, viz. (i) flood control; (ii) promotion and operation of irrigation schemes, water supply and drainage; (iii) generation, transmission and distribution of electric power; (iv) promotion and control of navigation; (v) promotion of afforestation and control of soil erosion; and (vi) promotion of agriculture, industry, economic and general development of the valley and its area of operation (Kirk, 1950) (Fig. 34.7).

Physical Features

The Damodar (also known as the Tears of Jharkhand and Bengal) is about 500 km. long. It has its source in the Hill of Chotanagpur at an

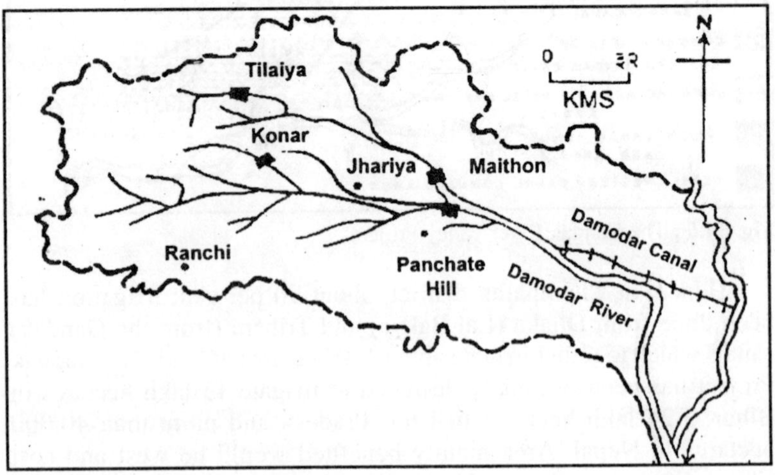

Fig. 34.7 : The Damodar Valley Project

elevation of 2000 feet. After flowing 240 km in Bihar it enters West Bengal and ultimately joins the Hooghly. In its upper valley lie parts of Hazaribagh, Palamu, Ranchi, Manbhum and Santhal Parganas in Bihar. The rainfall is about 47 inches annually. The lower portions of the valley lie in West Bengal, where the flooded Damodar overflows its banks destroys crop and carried away men and cattle dislocating temporarily the economic life of the valley. The Damodar Valley has a catchment area of about 12,000 sq. km.

The Dams

The project comprises four storage dams with hydro-electricity installation. They are as follows :

The Tilaiya Dam is an all concrete dam on the river Barakar, about 208 km above its confluence with the Damodar. It is 30 m high and 366 m long and has a gross storage capacity of 394.7 m. cu.m. There are two power houses of 2000 k each with a provision for third unit.

The Konar Dam has been built across the Konar river in Hazaribagh. It is 49 m high and 3546 m long with a gross storage capacity of 337 m.cu.m.

The Maithan Dam is an eastern dam on the river Barakar. It is 94 m high above the river bed and 144 m long and has a gross storage capacity of 1357 m.cu.m. It is mainly designed for flood control. It has 3 units of 20,000 kW each.

The Panchet Hill Dam has been completed in 1959, across the river Damodar in Dhanbad district. It is 45 m high above river bed, 2545 m long with a gross storage capacity of 1497 m.cu.m. It has one unit of 40,000 kW.

Thermal Power Station

The thermal power stations have been installed to meet the increasing demands for power. They are as follows :

The Bokaro thermal power station has an installed capacity of 225 mW. Damodar Valley and the adjoining areas in Bihar and West Bengal are benefited by it.

Durgapur thermal power station has two units of 75 mW each and one unit of 140 mW. The power is used in the valley and adjoining parts of Bihar and Bengal.

Chandrapura thermal power station has 3 units of 140 mW. each and 2 units of 120 mW.

The DVP has an installed capacity of 1181 mW. It is distributed along the industrial belt of Bihar and West Bengal and also over the adjoining districts of Patna, Gaya, Rohtas and Bhojpur in Bihar and Mednapur in West Bengal.

Industries

The Damodar Valley with its surrounding area is the highly developed industrial region in India. The main industries are as follows :

Industry		*Location*
1. Iron & Steel Industry	-	Jamshedpur, Bokaro, Durgapur, Kulti and Asansol.
2. Fertilizer Plant	-	Sindri, Durgapur.
3. Cement Industry	-	Sindri, Durgapur, Dalmianagar.
4. Glass Factory	-	Patratu, Jamshedpur.
5. Agro Industry (Bidi, Honey, Lac & Silk)	-	Ranchi.
6. Engineering goods, automobiles, steel goods, spun pipes, fire engines etc.	-	Ranchi

Minerals

The Damodar Valley contains the largest coal deposits of India and considerable quantities of bauxite and aluminium. The Valley has also fire clay, china clay, lime-stone, mica, lead, silver, antimony and quartz. It produces nearly 38 per cent of the total mineral production of India.

Minerals	*Country's % Production*
Mica	57
Coal	41
Copper	38
Graphite	33
Bauxite	32
Iron Ore	18

Agriculture

Due to rugged terrain and continuous soil erosion agriculture is not properly practised. Rice, Maize and Gram are grown in Palamu district; Rice-Fruits and Vegetables in Ranchi district; Rice, Maize and Millets in Hazaribagh district; Rice, Maize, Fruits and Vegetables in Dhanbad district and Rice, Maize and Gram in Singhbhum district.

Population

Physical, economic and cultural factors play an important role in the growth and distributional pattern of population in any region of the world. The districts of the Damodar Valley can be divided into 3 groups :

Districts of High Growth Rate : It includes the districts of Palamu, Hazaribagh, Lohardaga, Midnapur, Asansol and Durgapur with a growth rate above 25 per cent.

Districts of Moderate Growth Rate (20-25%) : It includes the districts of Ranchi, Singhbhum and Burdwan.

Districts of Low Growth Rate : It includes Singhbhum, Gumla and Santal Pargana.

Benefits

This region is blessed with a number of benefits as follows :

(a) A number of erosion-resisting structures have been built in the catchment area. The Adivasi Dam, Deochanda Dam, Bachhi Dam and Gauria Karma Dam hold back main water, prevent gully erosion and supply water for irrigation.
(b) Reforestation and large scale plantation of timber, mulberry and other fast growing trees has been undertaken in the denuded forests.
(c) Lac culture has been started.
(d) The D.V.C. produces 800 tonnes of fish every year.
(e) The D.V.C. accounts for nearly 10 per cent of the country's total power output. The major industries located are Tata, Durgapur, Burnpur and Kulti and the coal mines of Jharia and Raniganj operate with D.V.C.
(f) Electric traction of trains on D.V.C. have electrified the railway track between Howrah and Mughalsarai.
(g) Recreational facilities for swimming and boating in the lakes,

drinking water supply and control of malaria and reclamation of marshy lands are other benefits.

Source of the Total Irrigated Area

	Source of Irrigation	*Per cent of irrigated area from the source to the total irrigated area in the State.*
1.	Government Canals	22
2.	Private Canals	7
3.	Tanks	20
4.	Wells	13
5.	Other Sources (aharas, rivers etc.)	38
	Total	100

KOSI RIVER VALLEY PROJECT

Introduction

The Kosi is the Hwang Ho of Bihar and the wildest and most uncertain among the Indian rivers. Among the Himalayan rivers the catchment area of river Kosi is the biggest (130,000 km). It passes through deep defile in Himalayas which has 7 branches in Nepal, viz., Doodh Kosi, Arun Kosi, Saryu Kosi, Bhote Kosi and Indravati. All these rivers come into the north Indian Plain along Great Boundary Fault known as Hanuman Nagar. Here a big dam has been constructed as a reservoir and water is thrown into the canal through big dam which help in electricity generation and irrigating the rice fields (Das, 1970).

Need of the Kosi Project

The Kosi river brings a lot of sand, pebbles and boulders from Himalaya upto down stream and the velocity of water is so speedy that it cannot be checked. In the districts of Saharsa, Katihar, Purnea and Madhepura the Kosi river brings such a devastating flood that it is known as "the sorrow of Bihar". Hence, to save the area around Kosi from devastating flood, the Kosi Project has been started (Fig. 34.8).

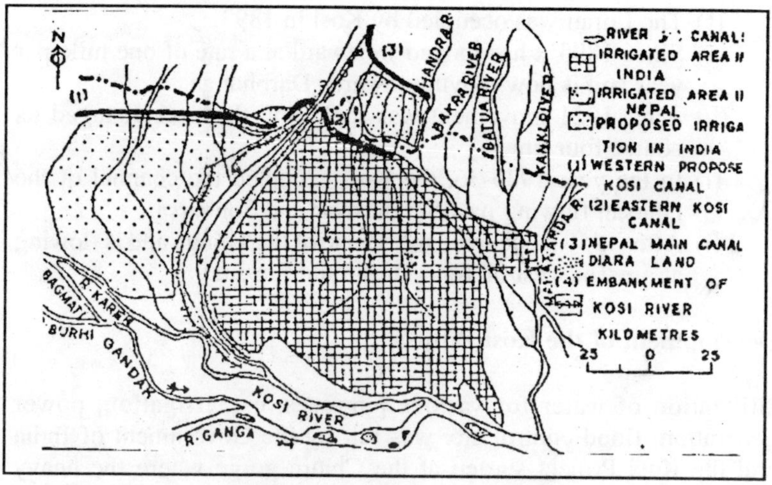

Fig. 34.8 : The Kosi River Valley Project

Changes in the Course of the Kosi

"कभी हँसाती, कभी रुलाती, कभी इठलाती, कभी बलखाती,
पल–पल में राह बदलती, ये है कोसी की गाथा।"

Each and every year the Kosi river changes its course and it converts a big chunk of agricultural land into its fold. With the help of Kosi River Valley Project, we have overcome on this great problem. Within the last 100 years the courses of river Kosi has changed 174 km towards east which makes its course meandering. This helps in protecting the area from devastating floods and flows sluggishly in the plains of Sharasa and Purnea. While changing its course it deposits vast amount of sand and silt. Within the last two hundred years the shifting former courses of the Kosi towards west could be seen as follows :

(a) The Kalakosi flowing a mile west of the Purnea town. This was the Kosi before and during the year 1731, joining the Ganga near Maniharighat.
(b) From 1731 to 1807 the Livasi was the course of the Kosi.
(c) Kosi occupied the Dhamadaha Kosi during 1808-1811.
(d) The Hiran was the main Kosi during 1840-47.
(e) The Dams was the Kosi of 1873-93 flowing into the Ghugri river.

(f) The Loran was occupied by Kosi in 1893.
(g) Since 1893 it has moved westward at a rate of one mile per year and is now moving towards Darbhanga.
(h) After 1921 movement was rapid and the river changed its course four times.
(i) In the year 1935-36, the Kosi occupied the channel of the Dhusan flowing past Singheswar and Sonbarsa.
(j) After 1950 it occupied the course of the Tiljuga and is flowing at present west of Tehri Bazar and Supaul.

Development of the Kosi Project

Utilization of water for various purposes, e.g. irrigation, power generation, flood control etc. was felt by the Government of India and the Kosi Project started at the Chatra gorge where the heavy discharge of the sand could be arrested by building a high dam. The following features can be observed on the Kosi River Project :

1. The construction of a dam across the Kosi river at Hanuman Nagar near the Geart Boundary Fault in between Nepal and India.
2. Construction of 240 km long embankment for flood production on both sides of the Kosi river.
3. Digging of eastern and western main Kosi canals along with the distributaries.
4. Construction of a Power House to generate 20,000 kW electricity.
5. To irrigate 3.15 lakh hectare in the districts of Madhubani, Darbhanga and Samastipur and 1.4 lakh hectare in the districts of Saharsa and Madhepura.

Hanuman Nagar and Bhimnagar Dams

The Kosi Project was started in the year 1955 and under this scheme 1132 m. dam has been constructed at Bhimnagar which has 56 gates. It also includes the construction of metalled road from Bhimnagar to Bathnaha railway station. Its purpose is to obstruct the river from westward movement.

With the construction of Kosi Dam the problem has been lessened upto substantial degree. But the problem of soil erosion is still continuing. The government has constructed 120 km of river embankment in order to protect the area from the engrace of flood. On the right side this embankment extends from Bharda upto Gyanda and on the left side from Daljhora to Myna. Due to the construction of these embankments, the water level of the river has gone up due to sedimentation which is a serious problem.

Flood Control

For the success of crop production and integrated development of the area, the control of flood is quite essential. In the year 1967 and 1987, the flow of water was 9.13 lakh cusec in the Kosi river. This area suffers a lot in terms of damage to the standing crops and livestock wealth. This has also created a problem of unemployment, supply of medicines, poor economic condition and disturbance in the study of children.

Canals

In its eastern and western part of the Kosi canal Saharsa, Purnea, Katihar, Madhepura, Madhubani, Samastipur and Saptri district of Nepal about 10 lakh hectare land is irrigated.

East Kosi Canal

In the east Kosi canal, there are four branch canals and several tributaries. It irrigates 580567 hectares of land every year. The length of the canals are as follows :—

Canal	*Length (in km.)*
1. Main canal	43
2. Murliganj Branch canal	64
3. Janki Branch canal	82
4. Purnea Branch canal	64
5. Araria Branch canal	48

The digging of Kosi canal started in the year 1957 and the irrigation in 1964 which is still continuing.

Rajpur Canal

Rajpur canal has a capacity to flow 5000 cusec of water per second in between Menga Dhar and Kosi river. The water flows in the name of Rajpur canal which has 4 sub-branches and distributaries as follows :

	Name	*Length*
1.	Rajpur Branch canal	10 km
2.	Small Branch canal	325 km
3.	Total Command Area	176.113 hectare
4.	Culturable Command Area	117.409 hectare
5.	Annual Irrigated Area	140.891 hectare

Rajpur Canal was built in 1975 and the irrigation is going fluently.

Arrangement of the West Kosi Canal

The Kosi river has commanded 1.13 lakh hectare of land for irrigation through 113 km long canal in its western part. The Hanuman Nagar and Chatra Dam irrigates 27,000 hec. of land in Saptri district of Nepal. 86,000 hectare land is irrigated in Morang district.

Generation of Hydro-Electricity

In Kosi Dam and its canal the turbines have been established by the Electricity Board of the Government of Bihar. It provides electricity to Viratnagar and Rajbiraj of Nepal. But the supply is intermittent due to deposition of sand on the turbines and the work is suspended quite often.

Development of Irrigation

With the help of East Kosi Canal about 3.5 lakh hectares of land got irrigated in 1992. In between 1981-1991 the irrigated area by the Kosi and Rajpur canal, is as follows :

Total Irrigated Area

Year	*Kosi Canal (in hundred hectares)*	*Rajpur Canal*
1980-81	91	12
1981-82	114	12
1982-83	211	31
1983-84	120	26
1984-85	152	22
1985-86	172	30
1986-87	116	18
1990-91	150	27
2000-01	152	29

Conclusion

In the year 1947, when India got independence the Kosi was known as "The sorrow of Bihar". But with the construction of dam at Chatra and Hanuman Nagar, it is not considered as a curse but a boon which has freed the area from matarious climate. The generation of hydro-electricity has transformed the economy of the area into a prosperous one.

The Kosi Project aims at flood control, soil conservation, water supply, malaria control, fishery development and power production. Nepal is receiving the facilities of electricity and irrigation from this project. Stability of cultivation, increased agricultural output due to irrigation, growth of tobacco, sugar and jute and oil industries as a result of improved and secure and cheap power, stability to railways and roads, increase in pasturage, navigation from resulted discharge, growth of population following a healthier environment and improved economy are a result of this project.

REFERENCES

Bose, N.K.; 'Future of Multi-purpose River Valley Projects', *Indian Journal of Power and River Valley Development,* 1948, 8 (4), pp. 1-2.

Das, K.N.; 'The Changing Pattern of Land Use and Population in the Kosi Region of Bihar' : Unpublished Ph.D. Thesis, Bhagalpur University, 1970.

Das, K.N. & Lal, S.N.; "Major River Valley Projects of North Bihar" *Essays on Geography,* Bhagalpur 1969, pp. 155-167.

Jain, P.K.; "Development of Water Resources of Western Rivers of U.P.", *Indian Journal of Power and River Valley Development,* 1968, 17 (12).

Kirk, W.; The Damodar Valley "Valles Opima", *Geographical Review,* 1950, pp. 415-443.

35

Formulation of Project Proposal

Management of Flood Disaster in North Bihar

R.B. MANDAL

The entire North Bihar has been filled by alluvium and micaceous sand brought by the rivers flowing in the area during pleistocene period. At present as many as eleven major rivers, e.g. the Ganga, the Kosi, the Bagmati, the Gandak, the Budhi Gandak, the Kareh, the Kamla, the Mahananda and the Bhuthi Balan flow through this densely populated area (800 persons per km^2). These rivers have to channelise 2500 mm of rain water falling in 42,000 km^2 of Nepal Terai through a narrow plain of 52836 square kilometre area of North Bihar. In addition it has to carry 1300mm of rainfall in North Bihar itself. The onrush of such a huge accumulation of water flowing to leave behind sufferings of ailing millions of people year after year. Taming of rivers are the real problem. Because in 1954 when the total length of embankment along the courses of rivers was only 150 km and the flood ravaged area was just 25 lakh hectares but now in the year 2004 the length of embankment along the rivers have increased to 3000 kilometres and the flood ravaged area has increased to 35 lakh hectares. Hence, to much interference by the local people and the governmental agencies have also created acute problem and several task force and commission report have also not been successful in solving the problem.

Objectives of the Project

1. It will search the causes of flood.
2. Which group of rivers are causing flood in which area.
3. Some suggestions will be investigated to lessen the ravages of flood.
4. What were the impact of flood on the economy of the area?

5. What should be the short term and long term solutions of the problem ?
6. It will include the peoples mandate for solution of the problem.
7. Assessment of damage to the standing crops, houses, roads and pasture lands.
8. Assessment of death toll of people and livestock wealth.
9. Assessment of erosional hazards and area of the deposit of micaceous sand.

Geographical Personality of the Study Areas

The geophysical character of North Bihar has peculiar features of land. It is a saucer shaped basin dotted with more than 250 lakes and dozens of rivers.

The meandering course of the Ganga has 8 km, whereas the Kosi has 140 km, the Budhi-Gandak over 250 km and the Kareh over 175 km. All these forced the flood water to stagnate in the area for a longer period causing flood havoc. Along with these the huge inflow of sand and silt by the Terai rivers is a boon and bane in itself. North Bihar has an area of 52836 square kilometre and population of 8.20 crore in 2001. Its latitudinal extent is 23°N to 27°N and longitudinal extent of 84°E to 87°E. It means North Bihar lies in subtropical monsoon climate which receives torrential rain during the rainy season when it faces the problem of flood.

Statement of Problem

1. Protection from flood in North Bihar is quite essential in order to safeguard our environment and maintain ecological balance.
2. To enhance the resource base in the flood prone areas of North Bihar.
3. The enhancement of economic order is not possible unless we produce such crops which could resist flood water for longer period.
4. The construction of flood protective embankment, prevention of diseases and search of the ways and means of raising livelihood, house plans and measures of the checking and

minimization of the incoming of flood would be included in this investigation.

5. People's opinion regarding the flood protection will be considered along with the lessons obtained from the sample studies for each and every district.

Theoretical Background

North Bihar is the remnant of Gangetic trough and Indo-Braham river formed in course of the rise of Himalaya. The stagnation of water along the saucer shaped basin is inevitable to bring devastating flood. The cause may be the accumulation of vast amount of rain water and melt of snow on the Himalaya along with its own vast amount of heavy downpour which lead to flooding in North Bihar each and every year. The basic fact is that due to deposit of sand and silt the courses of the river get raised their channel and now they have no space to accommodate any amount of extra water. This leads to breach of river embankment and the criminals are also active in this area to cut the embankment of other side in order to save the embankment of their own side.

The River Systems

The rivers flowing through North Bihar come to this flood plain from the Himalaya in the north. They are the Gandak, the Budhi-Gandak, the Ghaghra, the Balan, the Lakhandei, the Kareh, the Kamla, the Bhuthi-Balan, the Jibachh, the Bagmati, the Kosi, the Panar and the Mahananda. These rivers deposit sand and silt, brings devastating flood and goads the process of alluviation and deluviation in the marshy and lowlands of North Bihar Plain (Fig. 35.1).

Review of Past Literature

Within last one crore years since pleistocene period when deglaciation took place on the Himalaya the North Bihar got filled with sand and silt. It must have experienced thousands of floods. Hence, several conferences, seminars and reports have been prepared on the issue of flood but due to lack of enthusiasm on the side of government to solve this problem, the problem for the people living with natures

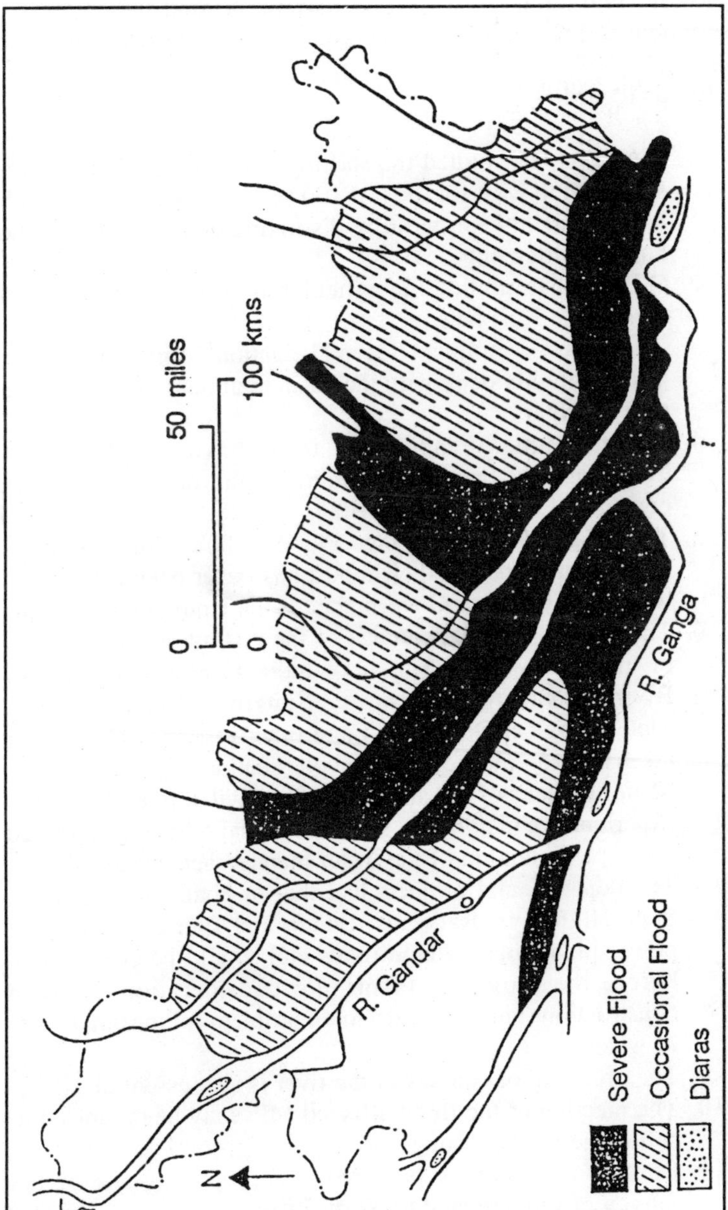

Fig. 35.1 : North Bihar Flood Affected Areas (1954-91)

malady is continuing since long. It may be beyond the control of government and mightyness of the issue which cannot be tackled so easily.

In this regard—

1. K.N. Das has studied the shifting courses of the Kosi river from east to west for the last 100 years and concluded that it has shifted 114 km west by disrupting cultivated lands and human settlements.
2. G.P. Jha has studied the agricultural development in flood area of the Kosi belt.
3. The Bihar Government Second Irrigation Commission report has thoroughly dealt with the basin treatment of flood prone area of Bihar.
4. There are many aspects of flood havoc in Bihar, but unfortunately these recommendations have never been considered as problems of Bihar.
5. The Headquarters of Ganga Flood Control Commission is situated at Patna but their report has never been considered whether it be Bihar Government or the Union Government.
6. The technological advantage of the institutions like Survey of India, Geological Survey of India, Central Groundwater Board, National Remote Sensing Agency, IITs, Meteorological Department and other institutes have never taken into confidence and their coordination is extremely poor.
7. Senior citizens of the area should be invited to express their experiences and opinions so that practical schemes be drafted for implementation of the water management system.
8. The departmental projects like that of National Highways, State Highways, Railways, Bandh and spur constructions, power plant sites, village roads etc. should be coordinated before the project is taken into consideration. Earthen constructions have created a lot of problems of the quick flow of water.
9. The dredging of courses of the river is also essential.
10. The meeting of the flood affected MPs may be organised to solicit their valued suggestions.
11. Contour map may be prepared at appropriate scale by the Survey of India related to North Bihar.
12. The presence of chaurs, beels, and ponds have severally

damaged the agriculture of the area. Hence the Indian Council of Agriculture Research should be invited for the process of agricultural planning of the area.

13. The socio-economic problem of the study area can be well imagined by the fact that mass exodus of unemployed labour to Delhi, Punjab, Haryana etc. is from the districts of North Bihar. The study of this aspect should be made by the National Disaster Management Agency, Government of India to ameliorate the situation.

Methods of Study

1. It has been tried to complete this investigation through field study and analysing the causes of flood in different parts of North Bihar.
2. The data will also be collected through cartographic analysis of toposheets, geological memories, aerial photographs and satellite imageries available for North Bihar.
3. Regional analysis of flood cannot be ruled out in terms of spatio-temporal dimensions because the area was covered with a lot of lowlying marshy lands during ancient period, but now-a-days due to flash flood most of the water bodies lost their character due to over siltation.
4. At some places the use of statistical techniques may be adopted to draw inferences for the intensity of flood in North Bihar.
5. The impact studies which explain the regional variations of flood in terms of damage of houses, flood affected population, damage of crops, transport network and the ecological imbalances in the area concerned.

Hypothesis

Hypothesis shows the relationship between observed real these world situation with different probable factors responsible for the event in order to search the most appropriate variable.

1. Floods in North Bihar are the outcome of heavy rainfall in the catchment area of river and stagnation of water for a longer period in the meandering courses.

2. The flood plains of North Bihar is also responsible for high mounds and lowlying areas caused by neotectonic earth movement going on in the area.
3. The investigation about conservation of resources necessitates the management of flood affected areas of North Bihar.
4. The process of deforestation in almost all areas of North Bihar has accelerated the incoming of floods.
5. At present the measures of relief to the flood victim is a boon for people of the area and it is an apathy for the flood victims as they are the real sufferers.

Research Design

1. One can adopt watershed management for flood control but partial management of the river course will not solve the problem unless we do it for the whole river basin.
2. One can construct flood protective embankment on the side of all the rivers but it may aggravate the problem further by rats and unsocial elements of our society.
3. All the rivers and chaurs of North Bihar should be interlinked for quick discharge of flood water as there are numerous chaurs and wetlands found in the area.
4. One may also suggests the digging of river channels to accommodate more volume of water and for the quick disposal of flood water.
5. The construction of water reservoirs with the help of dam in the Terai area of Nepal may reduce the problem of flood but as the border zone is an earthquake prone area, and hence at the time of earthquake the flood problem may be more disastrous.
6. The construction of interlinking canal of rivers and chaurs west of Khagaria towards the Ganga river in the south by connecting Dasin chaur and Kabar lake may solve the problem partially in the year when the Ganga river is not in spate.
7. Generally, this has been heard that when the North Bihar is reeling with disastrous flood, the South Bihar suffers from drought. Hence, after through interlinking canals, from this junction water should be lifted through wider diametre pipe or high level steel canal to the drought prone area of South Bihar Plain especially covering the districts of Banka, Jamui,

Nawada, Aurangabad and Rohtas. It should be considered essential in order to divert the problem for the betterment of our society.

8. It has also been suggested to make high mound after digging tank in each and every village, where the high mound will serve the purpose of flood protective platform and tank will serve the purpose of water reservoir. As an immediate relief measure it should be considered essential.
9. In order to control the flood in true to the sense people's mandate must be considered and I shall try my best to collect data through questionnaire along with sample study taken from each and every district.

Evaluation and Monitoring

This project will evaluate the expenditure encurred on flood control as the government is trying to expend crores of rupees for the imancipation from flood in North Bihar. The procedure of evaluation will be cost-benefit analysis. The cost benefit analysis well work in per cent besides judging the social value and environmental quality needed for people of the area.

The monitoring of flood control is quite essential in order to :

1. The incoming of flood in the form of disaster is not a new natural phenomenon and hence concerted effort is needed to control the flood.
2. Judging the nature of slope of the terrain, types and patterns of courses of the river, intensity and density of drainage lines and the volume and speed of water found in the rivers are quite essential in order to control the flood.
3. The flood planning alone is meaningless because in North Bihar it is a regional problem and hence it should be tackled under integrated planning scheme.
4. The annual flood is a menace in managing the affairs of wetlands because it hampers afforestation work, plugging the breach point is bit difficult, scare away the fishes and birds and disrupts the whole economy of the area.
5. Monitoring of flood is quite essential because it damages the living abode of people, standing crops in the field, roads,

railway tracks, educational institutions and intensity of soil erosion and deposition as well.

Flood Affected Regions

In North Bihar, there are several flood affected regions of intense nature. Some of them are as follows :

(a) Panar-Mahananda Belt of Purnea.
(b) Kosi Belt of Saharsa-Purnea.
(c) Kamla Jibachh and Bhuthi Balan Belt of Darbhanga.
(d) Adhwara Group of Rivers of Sitamarhi Darbhanga.
(e) Benua-Farkia Belt of Gogri-Jamalpur.
(f) Gogabeel and Kosban Jalkar Belt of Katihar.
(g) Dasin Chaur and Kabartal Belt of Khagaria-Begusarai.
(h) Phulhara-Simri and Kuleshwar Asthan Belt of Darbhanga-Samastipur.
(e) Chakia chaur Hardia chaur and Tal Baraila of western Bihar.

Sources of Data

(a) Data will be collected from Flood Forecasting Office, Patna.
(b) Primary data will be collected from each panchayat of North Bihar with the help of questionnaire.
(c) Waterlogged and marshyland data will be collected from topographical sheet, aerial photographs and satellite imageries.
(d) The data regrading intensity of flood will be collected from different newspapers published from various places.
(e) Photography and slide making for the relevant problem will be done.
(f) Preparation of plan to construct flood protective embankment, approach roads, regulation of excess water available during rains and floods.

Tentatively this investigation may be done on the following sub-heads through proper data collection and analysis:

Introduction

Definition, statement of problem, purpose of study, pilot survey and inventory analysis, review of past literature, methods of study, sources of data, hypothesis testing, geographical personality of the study area, references.

Geographical Framework

Phyical : Geology, Relief Feature, Drainage, Soil, Climate, Vegetation.

Economic : Landuse, Agriculture, Irrigation, Mineral, Transportation, Industries, Settlements.

Demographic : Growth, Distribution, Occupational Structure, Population Projection.

Factors Affecting Flood

Topography, Climatic Hazards, Accumulation or stagnation of rainwater, Breach of embankment, Problem of rats.

Distribution of Flood Affected Areas

(a) Panchayat affected
(b) Village affected
(c) Population affected
(d) Animals affected
(e) House damaged

Impact of Flood

On houses, on crops, on transportation lines, on industries, on wetlands, on embankments.

Problems of Flood Disaster

- Catchment area in waterlogging areas.
- Branch of embankment.
- Distribution of flood affected areas.
- Problems of soil erosion.

Flood Disaster Management

- Interlinking of rivers.
- Watershed management.
- Transfer of flood water to south Bihar plain.
- Flood protection embankment and construction of water reservoirs.
- Construction of high dam.

Flood Relief Measures

- Relief camps
- Ration, supply of ready made food
- Food for work
- Cloth/Blanket
- Roofing material
- Medicine/control of diseases
- Match box, drinking water
- Immediate repair of bridges

Sample Study

- One village in each disdrict.

Flood Control Measures and Management

(a) Short term planning
(b) Long term planning

Summary and Conclusion

Table 35.1 : Total Flood Affected Area of North Bihar, 2004

District	*Total Area in Hectares*	*Flood Affected Area in Hectares*
(1)	*(2)*	*(3)*
Saran	266,480	94,800
Siwan	226,780	81,200
Gopalganj	201,890	99,700
E. Champaran	398,000	290,600

(Contd.)

Table 35.1 *(Contd.)*

(1)	*(2)*	*(3)*
W. Champaran	444,750	96,020
Muzaffarpur	315,000	223,200
Sitamarhi	2638,840	260,000
Vaishali	203,670	87,100
Darbhanga	226,910	216,000
Madhubani	349,030	329,000
Samastipur	282,290	121,600
Khagaria	196,060	156,000
Begusarai	190,390	103,400
Bhagalpur	8,890	87,090
Saharsa	119,230	105,700
Supaul	233,440	217,560
Madhepura	178,810	87,881
Purnea	323,450	229,800
Araria	280,240	230,400
Kishanganj	194,070	84,706
Katihar	302,070	265,300
Total	5,283,690	3,467,150

Note : Average 65% area flooded in North Bihar.

QUESTIONNAIRE RELATED TO FLOOD PROBLEMS

Name of the District....................	*Name of Block...........................*
Name of Panchayat.....................	*Village/Mohalla.......................*
Post Office.......................................	*Person giving Answer................*

1. What are the causes of flood in your area?
2. Which river or group of rivers bring flood in your area?
3. What should be the way to control flood?
4. What difficulties people of your area faces at the time of flood?
5. What are the losses due to flood?
6. What should be the immediate relief measures at the time of flood?
7. What should be the long term solution of the problem of flood?
8. What are your demands from the state and the Central Government to control flood?

REFERENCES

Anuranjan, Changing pattern of land use and agriculture in flood prone area : A case study of Biraul, Darbhanga, Unpublished Ph.D. Thesis, Patna University, 2003.

Centre for Science and Environment, Floods, Flood plains and Environmental Myths, State of India's Environment. *A Citizen's Report,* No. 3, New Delhi, CSE, 1991.

Choudhary, S.N., *Geography of floods in North Bihar,* LNMU Press, Darbhanga, 1993, p. 8.

Flood Report, Central Flood Control Department, Government of Bihar, Patna, 1996.

Jha, G.P., *Agriculture in Flood Prone Region : A Geographical Perspective,* Inter India Publication, 1989, pp. 35-51.

Mathew Mammeri, 'Floods of Fury,' *Hindustan Times,* Monday, 29th July, 1996, p. 1.

36

Flood Disaster in Bhagalpur District

Cause and Effect

U.S. PANDIT

Introduction

Bhagalpur District is the easternmost part of the Anga Plain, hemmed between the geographical co-ordinates of 25° 05′ N to 25° 30′ N of latitudes and 86° 39′ E to 87° 32′ E of longitudes, consisting of three subdivisions (Bhagalpur Sadar, Kahalgaon and Naugachhia), 16 Anchals, 237 Gram Panchayats and 1536 villages (Chiragi and Bechiragi), spreaded over 2569.50 km^2 or 2,55,822 hectare of lands, population of 24,30,331 persons (12,94,192 Males and 11,36,136 Females), a literacy of 50.28 per cent, S.C. 1,88,234 persons and S.T. 44,984 persons during 2001 census year. Bhagalpur city, district H.Q. is a Municipal Corporation in status with 38 wards. It is delimited by the districts of Madhepura, Purnea and Katihar in the north; Banka in the south; Sahibganj and Godda (Jharkhand state) in the east and Munger and Khagaria in the west (Figure 36.1). Table 36.1 shows the above facts.

Review of Past Literature

Edward Suess states that the whole Ganga plain is the outcome of bed soil of Tethysea. Geologically, Bhagalpur district consists of alluvium—Bhangar and Khadar. Orographically, it can be divided into two parts—(i) The alluvial plains in the north (Naugachhia Sub-division) and (ii) The highland plain in the south (Kahalgaon and Bhagalpur Sub-divisions). The entire region is dotted with chaur lands (10 miles in length). The average height is less than 50 m above MSL. Spot height of Bhawanipur and Nagarpara (Naugachhia) is 37

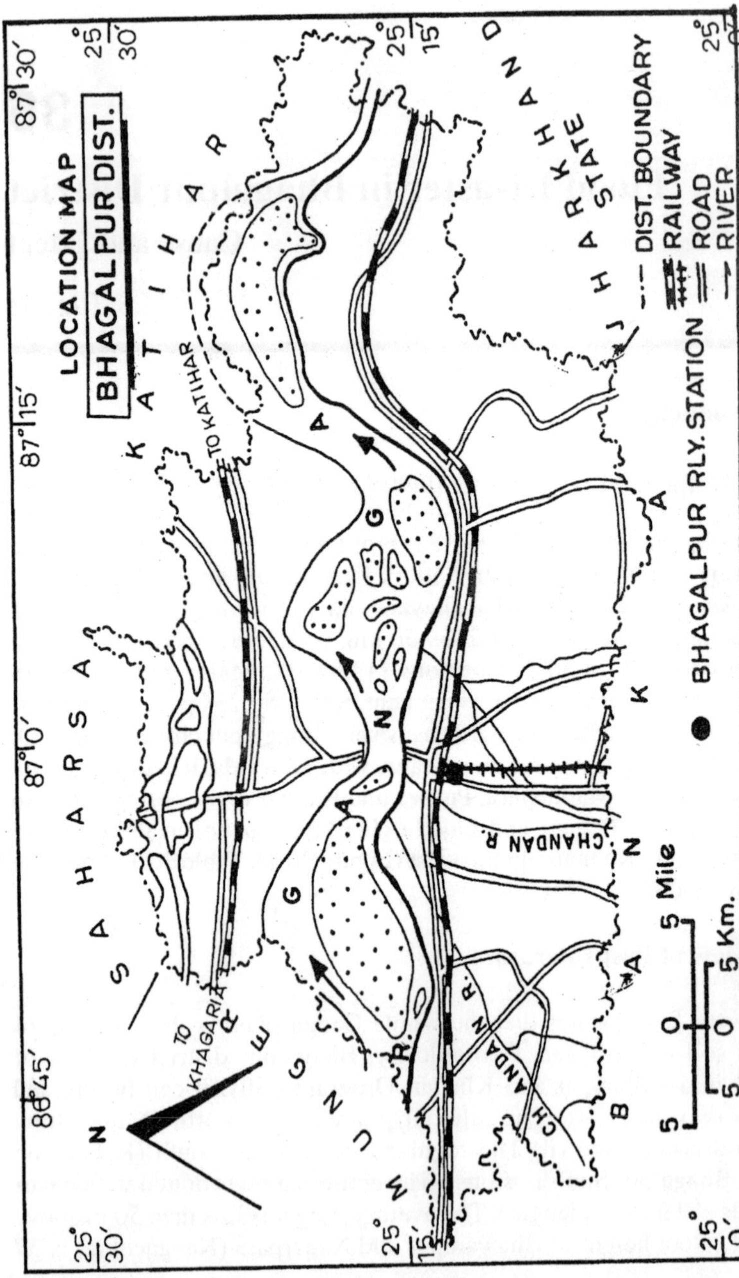

Fig. 36.1 : Bhagalpur District

Table 36.1 : Bhagalpur District 2003

S.No.	*Anchal*	*No. of G.P.*	*No. of villages*	*Area in hect.*
1.	Bihpur	15	42	15,365
2.	Gopalpur	9	20	10,973
3.	Goradih	5	119	10,875
4.	Ismailpur	9	15	9,945
5.	Jagdishpur	2	168	9,160
6.	Kahalgaon	25	212	33,521
7.	Kharik Bazar	12	35	5,856
8.	Narainpur	12	31	14,271
9.	Nathnagar	15	157	12,608
10.	Naugachhia	11	27	20,051
11.	Pirpainty	25	113	35,006
12.	Rangra chowk	8	11	15,399
13.	Sabour	14	84	14,159
14.	Sanhaula	17	177	174,420
15.	Shahkund	20	170	16,818
16.	Sultanganj	18	155	20,695
	Total	217	1536	2,55,822

m., whereas, Bhagalpur city 48, Jagdishpur 40, Akbarnagar 36.8, Nathnagar 42.2, Shahkund 60 and Shahkund hill 148 m (Topographical sheet No. 72 K/15 and 16).[1]

The Kosi, called as Sapt Kosi, (Sat Kosi, Bhote Kosi, Tamara Kosi, Zikhan Kosi, Dudh Kosi, Arun Kosi and Indravati), washes Naugachhia subdivision in the north and the Ganges sacred and perennial river flows in the core of this district. The district receives an annual rainfall of 1136 mm.

India is a par excellent a tropical monsoon country and so is the climate of this district. Koppen (1922), Hann (1932) and Angot (1943) state "The monsoons represent simply a land breeze and a sea breeze on a large scale and the annual period of the monsoon corresponds to the diurnal period of the breeze." [2] According to A. A. Ramashastri[3] "Monsoons are large scale seasonal wind systems flowing over vast areas of the globe, persistently in the same direction, only to be reversal with the change of season."

India has two types of monsoon :

(i) S.W. monsoon or the advancing monsoon, and
(ii) N.E. monsoon or the retreating monsoon.

When the monsoon fails to shower, it causes deficient rains

resulting droughts and famines. Sometimes, the monsoon has heavy rains causing flood disasters. Droughts and floods result in crop failure. Flood is a state of high water level along a river channel or on coast that leads to inundation of land which is not normally submerged. The danger mark of the Kosi river water level is 47.75 m at Supaul, 33.85 m. at Baltara (Khagaria) and 30 m. at Katihar. Whereas, the danger marks of the Ganges river water level is 33.68 m at Bhagalpur and 31.09 m at Kahalgaon. The highest water level of the Ganges was recorded 62.09 m at Buxar in the year 1948; 52.52 m at Dighaghat (Patna) in 1975; 40.99 m at Munger in 1976; 34.18 m at Bhagalpur in 1978 and 32.84 m at Kahalgaon in 1998; whereas, the highest water level of the Kosi was 36.40 m at Baltara (Khagaria) in 1987 and 32.04 m at Katihar in 1998 (Central Water Commission).[4] The above facts flash the flood disasters of the Kosi as well as the Ganges.

Flood is an attribute of physical phenomena and hence, it is important component of hydrological cycle of drainage basin. "Flood simply means inundation of extensive land area with waterlogging for several days in continuation. Generally, floods are considered being associated with rivers and people conceive floods as the outcome of accumulation of huge volume of water coming out of rivers through over topping of river banks during the peak discharge period." [5] Flood hazards are both natural and man-made. They are still severe environmental hazards which are related to the atmospheric processes. The Middle Ganga Plain is frequented by severe flood hazards. In India, total Flood affected areas have increased 6.48 mha during 1950; 9 mha in 1970 and 1980. The Rastriya Barh Ayog (RBA) or National Commission of Floods was set up by the government in 1976. According to RBA (1980), 16.5 per cent of the entire flood prone area within the country is located in Bihar, while 22.5 per cent of the flood affected population dwells in the flood plains of the state. It is, usually, the poor who are extremely affected, as they settle on the periphery of the human habitats. One disaster makes the poor more vulnerable to the next and in this way, converts a disaster into a disaster process. Most of the flood regions lie in the Basins of the Ganga, the Tsangpo, the Kosi, the Baitarni, the Brahmini, and the Subarnrekha in the states of Assam, Bihar, Orissa, U.P. and W.B. Even in the chronically flood prone area of U.P. and Bihar, the flood affected areas have been increasing in nature. The Ganges and the Kosi are notorious rivers in Bhagalpur resulting devastating floods. The Kosi, often, shifts its course causing floods in new areas and converting once fertile lands into wastelands. The Kosi was flowing east of Purnea over 200 years ago, has shifted westward by about 130 km. It is not the rainfall, but the sediments which are responsible for it.

Rivers were called as the mother of the world due to abundance of water and fertile soil and hence, attracted the early men to reside in that region. There is narration of floods in the *Nardiya Purana.* It says that a river does not spill beyond its boundaries which it defines as the river bed. Around 70 m (450 ft) beyond the river bed is the river bank and upto 5 km (One *Yojan*) beyond the river bank is the river belt. Again, it forbid the people to settle within the river bed and the river banks and recommends dwelling only in the river belts and beyond 5 km away from the river bed. Chanakya in his "Chanakya Niti" has pitied a person who has his house located on a river bank, facing threats of erosion and devastating.

The settlement in flood prone areas of Bihar is as early as 700 B.C. It emerged as the first Kingdom of the Magadh, the Vijis, the Mauryan Empire etc. During the British period, Bihar experienced the worst form of exploitative imperialism. The poor peasants were pushed into agriculture of flood plains.

Sources of Data

The flood data has been collected from Kendriya Jal Ayog, the Branch Office, Barari, Bhagalpur and compiled by the Kendriya Jal Ayog, Middle Ganga Division-5, 148, Anandpuri, West Boring Canal Road, Patna-800 001. The spot heights have been collected from the Soil Survey Division (Topographical Sheet), Agriculture College, Sabour, Bhagalpur (Bihar). The population, area etc. data (2001) have been obtained from Statistical Department of Bhagalpur District and Block Development H.Q. Offices.

Purpose of the Study

The main purpose of the study is to highlight the flood disaster—cause and effect in Bhagalpur district. The people awareness of flood is also the main aim of this study, so that the people may take protection during the flood peak period from different problems.

Causes of the Flood

Floods are chiefly caused by heavy rainfall, cyclone, silting, shifting courses of rivers, deforestation etc. Thus, floods are caused by three main factors—meteorological, physical and human interactions.

Meteorological Factors

1. *Run off :* July-August-September are noted months which causes surplus water into the river through streams and tributaries. These excess water causes river bed to swell and to spread over vast areas via broken natural levies or embankment or tributary channels forming the flood scenario.

2. *Cloud Bursts :* Cloud burst means the heavy rainfall during a very short period. In 1979, Saurastra received 37-50 cms. rainfall within 24 hours. It broke Machhu Dam and flooded Morvi town.

3. *Cyclones :* Cyclonic rainfall is received mainly in the coastal region. These violent storms have huge tidal waves, heavy shower and speedy wind causing damages in the coastal and inner areas. In 1982 and 1983 storms caused overflowing of 27 dams by more than 2 metres.

Physical Factors

1. *Large catchment area :* Many tributaries meet the Kosi and the Ganges. Hence, their catchment areas are the Himalayan and the Peninsular drainages. A large volume of water causes damages by these two rivers during the rainy season.

2. *Inadequate Drainage System*

(a) *Less developed drainage channel*—The Punjab has less developed drainage. So, floods area caused.

(b) *Less carrying capacity of rivers*—Due to silting the carrying capacity of bigger rivers is low. So, excess water causes floods. The Kosi and the Ganges carry soil and sediments into their beds every year.

(c) *Landslides*—Landslides cause blocking of river course (constructing temporary dam) and after brushing the temporary natural dams cause floods in the lower regions. In 1981, Tinnau river (Nepal) killed 200 persons after bursting.

(d) *Ox-bow-lakes*—In the lower Ganga and the Brahmaputra regions rivers meandering cause overflow on the bank area. Ox-bow lakes are flooded during the heavy shower year.

Table 36.2 : Level of Ganga Water at Bhagalpur, 2003 (in metres)

Month	*Years*				*Month*	*Years*			
	2000	*2001*	*2002*	*2003*		*2000*	*2001*	*2002*	*2003*
July					*September*				
25	31.20	32.00	29.00	31.19	1	31.53	–	31.19	32.74
26	31.67	32.13	29.39	31.30	2	31.78	–	30.97	32.68
27	32.37	32.20	29.82	33.68	3	32.10	–	30.75	32.64
28	32.70	32.38	30.30	31.23	4	32.40	32.25	30.59	32.64
29	32.91	32.41	30.58	31.19	5	33.40	–	30.43	32.92
30	32.96	32.52	–	31.16	6	33.20	32.42	30.31	33.23
31	32.83	31.25	–	31.11	7	33.20	32.34	30.34	33.35
August					8	33.30	32.25	30.46	33.46
1	32.59	32.81	–	31.23	9	–	32.24	–	33.53
2	32.30	32.89	–	31.35	10	33.36	32.16	–	33.59
3	32.23	32.93	–	31.61	11	33.32	32.06	–	33.74
4	32.16	32.90	30.19	31.84	12	33.27	32.01	–	32.68
5	32.16	32.81	30.10	32.07	13	33.23	31.90	31.71	23.03
6	32.19	32.72	30.00	32.17	14	33.20	31.80	32.03	34.10
7	32.21	32.65	29.94	32.23	15	33.17	–	32.15	34.16
8	32.24	32.46	29.85	32.13	16	33.11	31.57	32.27	34.16
9	32.19	32.24	29.77	31.95	17	33.00	31.34	32.34	34.17
10	32.17	32.01	29.76	31.78	18	32.90	31.30	32.31	34.02
11	32.03	31.68	29.76	31.69	19	32.01	31.14	32.16	33.82
12	31.87	31.37	29.83	31.62	20	32.85	31.03	31.88	32.75
13	31.79	31.17	30.18	31.52	21	32.80	–	31.56	33.60
14	31.73	31.05	30.39	31.51	22	32.71	–	31.28	33.45
15	31.72	30.95	–	31.61	23	33.59	–	31.04	33.55
16	31.66	30.87	–	31.86	24	33.21	–	30.87	33.48
17	31.53	30.81	31.28	32.03	25	32.95	–	30.77	33.43
18	31.49	–	31.43	32.13	26	32.65	–	30.67	33.42
19	31.47	20.86	31.48	32.26	27	32.24	–	30.77	33.42
20	31.55	31.01	31.41	32.38	28	31.93	–	30.86	33.40
21	31.71	31.35	31.30	32.50	29	31.63	–	30.88	33.33
22	31.88	32.03	31.32	32.73	30	–	–	30.90	33.27
23	32.03	32.47	31.58	32.79					
24	32.08	–	31.90	33.12					
25	32.07	32.88	32.19	33.19					
26	32.00	32.91	32.36	33.17					
27	31.88	32.82	32.37	33.05					
28	31.76	32.79	32.22	32.93					
29	31.64	32.79	32.03	32.84					
30	31.52	32.70	31.79	32.79					
31	31.53	32.55	31.48	32.76					

(e) *Sand bars*—In the coastal areas of W.B. and Orissa rivers from sand bars and delta areas. Due to heavy shower lowlands are submerged.

Table 36.3 : Water Level of the Kosi at Baltara (Khagaria) 2003 (in metres)

	July 2003	*August 2003*	*September 2003*
1	33.86	–	34.65
2	33.60	34.73	–
3	–	34.73	34.59
4	–	34.70	–
5	–	34.73	–
6	33.86	34.62	–
7	33.90	33.85	–
8	–	34.46	–
9	33.89	34.37	34.55
10	–	34.52	34.45
11	34.69	34.59	–
12	–	34.42	34.18
13	34.78	34.39	–
14	34.73	34.35	–
15	–	–	–
16	34.73	–	34.29
17	34.61	–	–
18	34.56	–	–
19	34.62	34.42	–
20	–	–	34.18
21	–	–	–
22	34.89	34.87	–
23	–	–	34.29
24	34.79	–	34.30
25	–	–	–
26	34.62	34.72	–
27	34.47	34.68	34.21
28	34.30	–	
29	–	–	
30	34.19	–	
31	34.15	34.70	

Source : Central Water Commission (Middle Ganga Div. 5) 148, Anandapani, West Boring Canal Rd, Patna-800001.

Human Impacts

1. *Deforestation*—The natural vegetations have a violent control over runoff. Forest affects the hydraulic cycle in many ways. The country has lost 86 per cent of its forest. So, deforestation has caused increase in flood phenomena and has affected rainfall.

2. *Silting*—Indirectly, deforestation has caused soil erosion and sediments in V-shaped valley. The Kosi river bed is higher than the flood plain and hence, the floods are caused on a vast area.
3. *Mal-agricultural practices*—Valley sides are tilled rabi crops. This causes loose soil. River water carries away these loosen soil into river V-shaped bed. After silting V-shaped bed is changed into U-shaped and causes floods during the rainy season.
4. *Mal-practices of irrigation*—Canals are prepared in the alluvial and black soil. The heavy shower changes canals into rivers and overflow.
5. *The reservoir water*— The big rivers have been dammed and canals have been constructed. Due to heavy shower dam bed is full of water or overflow from its mark of danger. The excess water is allowed to flow or leave out through gates. Suddenly water is discharged. Hence, the lower and bank areas are flood-damaged.
6. *Urbanisation*—Increasing urbanization have increased the quantity of pucca buildings, metalled roads, pucca drains etc. and hence, have reduced infiltration capacity of water. Surface runoff has been affected causing floods. Besides these, embankment consequently, has been reduced the drainage capacity of rivers.

In short, the geographers, the scientists, the economists, the politicians etc. are of the same opinion that the above discussed causes are responsible for floods.

Causes of Flood in the Study Area

In Bhagalpur district flood disaster has been caused by the above mentioned factors. It has gradual sloping towards east. It has many lowland areas in the form of chaur and diara land. The longest river in India, the Ganges and the shifting course of the Kosi cause flood disaster every year. N.E. and Eastern railway, metalled roads (NH 31 and NH 80 under construction) run along the river banks. The Farakka barrage on the Ganges causes flood disaster for Bhagalpur district by accumulating water and for W.B. and Bangladesh by discharging sudden water.

Table 36.2 reveals the daily water level of the Ganges during rainy season in 2000, 2001, 2002 and 2003. It shows that the water level increases from July to September and decreases from second half of September every year. Hence, the flood regions during these periods. Again, the maximum height of water level is experienced from the last week of July to the first half of September every year. It shows that flood damages during theses periods are high. In 2000, the highest water level (33.59 m) on the 23rd September, i.e. a little less danger mark of water level at Bhagalpur. From the 5th September to 25 September 2000 water levels are approaching the danger mark. It means that comparatively lesser flood damage was found in 2000. When water level is higher than the danger mark, then the area is affected with heavy loss. More or less the same case is remarkable in the year 2003. The water level crossed the danger mark on the 27 November 2003. It caused the sudden flood damages.

Table 36.3 shows the water level of the Kosi in the year 2003. It reveals that the water level remained higher than the danger mark almost all the months. Hence, the Kosi has damaged a lot. Really, it is "the sorrow of Bihar". The author visited Khagaria to Rangra Anchal via Narainpur, Bihpur, Naugachhia and saw the natural calamities. In a few minutes Milki Panama village turned into main Kosi current meandering before my naked eye. The populated village vanished in the lap of the Kosi. It shift even today towards the west.

Flood Impact in the Study Area

Flood impact on the people, agricultural activities, livestocks, flora-fauna etc. are seen per year in this district, 80,762 hectare lands is affected per annum. 15000 partially and 28000 completely mud-built houses are affected yearly. Naugachhia, Gopalpur; Kharik, Ismailpur, Rangra, Jagdishpur and Sonhaula anchals were affected in 2001. 192,000 persons and 304 villages are affected by the Kosi per year and more than lakh people are affected by the Ganges. Between 1953 and 1987 about 50,374 persons and average of 1500 deaths annually have been remarked. In 1987, due to heavy rainfall for several days caused floods. The Kosi river damaged the railway and road at Kahalgaon and caused obstacle for several days. The pillars of the bridges were washed away. After three months they were repaired for the plying of bus and trains.

The areas lying in Naugachhia Sub-division are less than 37 m hith from msl. The danger mark of the Ganga water level is 33.68 m at Bhagalpur and the Kosi is 33.85 m at Khagaria and 30 m at Katihar. Water level of both rivers exceeds the danger mark every year during the rainy season. The high lands and the natural levee areas are little safe from flood. The railway lines run from Mansi in the west to Purnea in the east via Narainpur, Bihpur and Naugachhia stations. Parallel to railway lines NH 31 also runs from Mansi to Purnea. Except some of these highlands, most of these areas are flood affected. The people stay and spend their evil days along these roads and railway lines. Sometimes this NH is under water for 6 to 12 hours disconnecting the neighbouring regions.

Flood prone area by the Kosi is 1.015 mha, the Ganges 1.127 mha and Chandan 0.113 mha in Bihar. *Navbharat Times* journalist, Mr. Mukul Sharma has indicated the case of hundreds of displaced families from Shankarpur-Dildarpur diara. They kept wandering from 1971 to 1985. In 1986, 300 families were settled on 1.3 hectare by the government far away from the town. Laloo Nagar in T.M. Bhagalpur University, Bhagalpur campus was settled by the displaced persons of the flood prone areas for several years. The rich persons buy land in the town and shift during the rainy season. The poor persons are compelled to stay there, because they are unable to pay high rate of land sale. During the flood, they have to sit under knee or waist deep water and even on their roof. They live on the mercy of God, government and local voluntary organizations for food. According to *Dainik Jagran*, 25 September 2003, Mr. K.P. Ramaih, D.M. of Bhagalpur stated that 7,59,575 persons and 1,52,550 animals of 291 villages of 117 G.P. under 15 anchals have been flood affected. 15 animals and 26 men health centres have been opened in the flood prone areas. 336 boats are working and 8252 families have been helped. 211.30 quintals beaten rice, 195 quintal gur, 346 quintal salt, 88166 match pkts., 51726 pkts. candles, 11000 quintal foodgrains etc. have been distributed. He has demanded Rs. 2 crore, but the State Government has allotted Rs. 55 lakh only. Thus, the above statements show that the flood impact on the people is very severe directly or indirectly. The impact of the Kosi was greater than the Ganges in 2003 due to severe flood damages.

The flood impact on other activities in the areas is also intolerable. Soil erosion by the rivers are very fearful. Ismailpur, Gopalpur, Kamlakund, Saidpur agricultural lands were eroded by the Ganges. The agricultural tracts under Buhland were merged into flood water for 3 months. Rani diara, Athania, Choania, Bakharpur Bairia-Mohanpur, Akbarnagar chaur etc. are noteworthy. Villages after villages are disconnected and men and animals led their miserable lives.

Conclusion

The flood disaster in Bhagalpur district has been threatening during the advancement of the S.W. Monsoon every year. Soil erosion, croplands under water for several days, silting in fertile lands, dampness, problem of food, fodder, clothing, shelter, transportation etc. are common phenomena directly. Indirectly, the people face epidemics, economic indebtness etc. which worsens the situation much more. The impact of flood disaster is severe on the people, livestock, agriculture, transport, flora-fauna, etc. The people of the flood prone areas must get lesson from the Kosi and the Ganges. They must vacate the areas before the good advancing monsoon showers and come back after the peak periods. Neither the government nor the public organizations can save their natural damages during the flood. The lowland area cannot be converted into highland in such a vast region. Some people have built their houses in the neighbouring highlands and shift during the flood periods. Again, they have built *pucca* buildings double and triple floor to protect them. By removing the silting materials of the river bed one can lessen a little, but cannot end it. No permanent solution can be done to check this natural calamities—flood.

REFERENCES

1. Topographical Sheet, GSI, New Delhi.
2. Khullar, D.R. (2002) : *India a Comprehensive Geography,* Kalyani Publishers, p. 74.
3. *Ibid.*
4. Kendriya Jal Ayog (Middle Ganga Division - 5) 148, Anandpuri, West Boring Canal Road, Patna-800 001 & Branch Office, Barari, Bhagalpur.
5. Singh, S., Environmental Geography, p. 391.

37

Summary and Conclusion

R.B. MANDAL

Water is such a precious gift of nature to the humanity that no life can survive without water. It is a vital input to agriculture which is the basic requirement not only of human being but also of plants and animals. The water management and strategy for the development of irrigation has to be formulated for each region taking into account its agro potential and temporal need of water resources. Management approach should include better use of existing water supply, development of tanks and other measures for storing and retaining rain water. Since, there is good availability of groundwater, its judicious use will minimise the drought. Measures of surface water conservation such as creation of surface water storage etc. has also to be adopted.

A.K. Sinha and Tulika Sinha have discussed water, its importance, uses, problems and management in terms of its vitality for the maintenance of all forms of life and on the other hand, it helps in movement in the biosphere.

Sumit Dhanuka analyses the use of GIS and remote sensing in water resource development in India. He said that GIS approach is playing a vital role in the field of hydrology and water resource development. It has helped in the preparation of hydrological modelling in spatial and temporal dimension. All these help in checking water pollution, water utilization, flood control, surface and sub-surface water management, river basin development and sustainable development of water resources.

Deepak Kumar is of the opinion that remote sensing utilizes the interaction between electromagnetic radiation for water, water vapour, ice, snow and waterbodies appear in the satellite imagines as dark regions. In their paper Naseemuddin and S.K. Jha emphasized that water is a limited resource and the efficient use of it is increasing due to more and more demand from agriculture, industry and power generation. Rashmi Prakash in her paper discussed that the development of river water resource involved combined efforts of various agencies under different state governments which creates inter-state water disputes. A. Mishra was of the opinion that watershed management is essentially management of rain water, surface water and groundwater resources.

M.N. Pandey in his paper on management and utilization of water resources said that the whole world is under stress due to lack of fresh drinking water which is a life sustaining resource. Today about 2 billion people living in 80 countries of the world suffer from chronic water shortage. A.K. Gupta analyses water crisis emerging hazards and management in order to save, conserve and strengthen this scarce resource without fail. Rana Pratap discussed about the Ganga water pollution that 80 per cent pollution of the Ganga water is only due to urban disposals in the peripheral areas. Devendra Prasad discussed about the challenges of water pollution and suggested measures for their remedies. Anil Kumar Choudhary analyses the polluted lakes in the heart of the city of Darbhanga. Namita Pattnaik discussed about the levels of water pollution in the Mahanadi river with special reference to Sambalpur industrial complex.

S.N. Choudhary analyses the river management of flood, drought and power shortage which are the playground of several rivers. Similarly, V.N. Jha highlighted the water resource use and conservation in North Bihar plain. Here the use of water vary in spatio-temporal dimensions. Anuranjan delineated about the water crisis and integration of river systems in North Bihar in relation to perennial rivers and extensive groundwater aquifer.

J. Bhagat discussed water resource transfer from surplus to deficit areas in terms of interlinking of rivers. K. Prasad analysed the problems of irrigation in Hazaribag district. Here the main sources of irrigation are canals, well, tubewells and tank, etc. Kumar Braj Nandan analyses the Kawar Lake water resource management in terms of fresh water reservoir which provides winter habitat for migratory birds. G.N. Singh and Sudha Kumari talked about food security management during floods in Bihar. Flood is an annual feature in the Indo-Gangetic Plains of India.

Jayant Kumar has discussed about sustainable management of land and water resources with special reference to Barahiya C.D. Block of Bihar. M. Kumari has considered the value of wetlands in terms of ecology, economy, society and nature's paradise of North Bihar where more than 250 wetlands are found, Shobha Kumari in her paper on impact of floods on land use in Muzaffarpur district discussed about the changing nature of land use from season to season. R.B. Mandal discussed about the management of wetlands in North Bihar, because in this flood affected riverine plains wetland governs the economy and regional development. Satya Raj in her paper has discussed about interlinking of rivers : an approach for sustainable water resource management as they have the capacity to save us from the furry of floods.

R.B. Mandal discussed about the importance of basin-wise conservation and proper utilization of water through different means of irrigation for better crop production which is known as watershed management. In this chapter R.B. Mandal contended that a dam constitutes about the most important device for development, management and multi-purpose utilization of water resources.

While delineating irrigation planning and sustainable development of wasteland he emphasised that water resource should be properly harnessed for wasteland management. The paper on meandering courses of the river and its impact on socio-economic life of the people and flood damages in north-eastern Bihar has been discussed which is located in a saucer shaped basin.

CONCLUSION

The availability of water resource both for agricultural use and drinking purpose is scarce. It is abundant at a wrong place of chaurs where its utilization for the human society is very low. Water resource is available differently on different terrain conditions. For example, diaras need proper treatment and planning. Tal land need timely withdrawal of waterlogging for wheat and gram cultivation, upland plain needs irrigational management as drought is the regular feature and the hilly area need terracing, contour bunding, reservoir formation in order to channelise and better utilization of the available water resource.

The following conclusions may be drawn:

Ground Water Utilization

Only with the groundwater utilization the maximization of produce in diara land may be possible. For example, in the diara tract of Munger district in Bihar, it would be necessary to sink at least 3000 more tube wells to assist diara farming. It is essential to develop suitable groundwater use project in consultation with the Ministry of Water Resources, Government of India.

Establishment of Diara Land Development Authority

In order to exploit underground water for integrated diara development it is quite essential to have Command Area Authority of irrigation projects. In spite of several difficulties including the need for moving long distances during floods, diara farmers are seem to be more enterprising as they use bamboo tube wells to tap underground water. The setting up of an Authority may develop water use plans and promote fisheries in the area.

Flood Prone Area Programme

The Ministry of Water Resource at the Centre should develop a flood prone area programme in order to mitigate the adverse effects of floods on human, animal and crop production.

Energy Generation

In case the groundwater potential is to be tapped effectively for making the flood-free season, it will be necessary to provide adequate source of energy for pumping water, wind energy or solar pans may be used for pumping water in diara areas.

R.B. Mandal also discussed about sustainability of the use of water wherever fluoride, arsenic and other pollutants are found above permissible level in the underground water. He has also analysed the problems of water supply in urban areas. Because, either the source of availability of drinking water is located at far off places, the drains are old and in dilapidated condition or it is so polluted that in no case it could be used for drinking purposes.

At the end R.B. Mandal discussed about the management of flood disaster in North Bihar, because it is an area of changing courses of the river and menace of flood disaster.

Water is Precious Gift of Nature

The two-third of our earth is covered with water. The water which sustains all living organisms is the precious gift of nature. Human being is the source of all types of pollution who has endangered the whole environment including the life sustaining water bodies. The unfettered industrial activity poisoned the water bodies with its waste products. This has created water borne diseases and hence, we are living in an age of water crisis. It needs safety and proper conservation for the healthy growth of future generation.

The Value of Water

For almost all creatures water is the most indispensable element of nature. Hence, no human being can survive without water. About 60 per cent of human body is made up of water. As body fluids are needed for digestion, urination, and in the form of sweat and hence, water needs to be replaced regularly with pure drinking water. On the earth surface there is nothing as refreshing as a gushing stream of crystal clear water. Rain, rivers, springs and lakes are the grand resource of nature that sustain life.

The Problem of Drinking Water

Nowadays what to talk of surface water but underground source of water also got polluted. Hence, water resources are strained by unchecked pollution and ill-planned development. Drinking water is scarce and the quality is deteriorating day-by-day. The available water is contaminated by sewage and industrial waste. People in urban and rural areas are forced to drink impure water which resulted into widespread disease and rise in death toll.

As per United Nations 40,000 children die worldwide everyday, many of them are the victims of diarrhoea and suffer from side effects of water crisis. Quite often we put our safe drinking water resources in jeopardy. For short term interests, we have destroyed our traditional water harvesting systems and ignored village ponds in favour of other infrastructure facilities.

Solving Drinking Water Crisis

Some people have planted trees around the tank and water reservoirs, while others have laid pipelines from the sweet water well to their homes ensuring daily supply of pure water. The water used for drinking must be boiled and filtered before its use. In some villages wells are regularly cleaned and chlorinated with bleaching powder. One should avoid wasting our stock of safe drinking water.

The Ministry of Rural Development, Government of India has started "Swa Jal Dhara Yojna" by providing 90 per cent financial help to the village community, Panchayat Bhawan and Schools.

The Use of Water for Irrigation

In India, the food production is entirely dependent on availability of water. Hence, water directly influences the quality as well as the quantity of crop production. About 73 per cent of the entire fresh water used by human being goes to agriculture sector in the form of irrigation. Rainfall is the major source of irrigation in India which is directly dependent on the amount of forest cover. The deficiency of rainfall causes drought and famine. Hence, we should conserve forest as well because rainfall and forest cover has close relationship.

We are Victims of our own Device

Most of our industries use water in the process of manufacturing but they ignore the effect of effluents on the environment. Some of the factories have effluent treatment plants which purify and recycle the used water. However, this is an expensive process and quite often contaminated water containing caustic soda, mercury and other harmful chemicals are drained into the open fields. All these poses severe threat to health and hygiene and pollutes clean sources of water. The leather tanneries turn out their waste right back into the Ganga river in Mokameh without any consideration. We are still not opting for micro hydel power project even after knowing how large dams upset the ecological balance especially the Himalayan zone which is an earthquake prone area.

Our Contributors

A. Mishra
H.O.D. Geography, C.N. College Ramgarh Cantonment,
Jharkhand.

Anil Kumar Chaudhary
Department of History, M.L.S.M. College,
Darbhanga, Bihar.

Anil Kumar Gupta
H.O.D. Geography, Nalanda Mahila College,
Biharsharif, Bihar.

Anuranjan
Lecturer in Geography, C.M.J. College,
Khutauna, Bihar.

Ashok Kumar Sinha
Department of Geography, Magadh University,
Bodh Gaya, Bihar.

Deepak Kumar
H.O.D. Geology, Giridih College,
Giridih, Jharkhand.

Devendra Kumar
Reader in Geography, R.D. & D.J. College,
Munger, Bihar.

Girija Nandan Singh
H.O.D. Geography, R.D. & D.J. College,
Munger, Bihar.

Janardan Bhagat
Reader in Geography, Vinoba Bhave University,
Hazaribag, Jharkhand.

Jayant Kumar
Research Scholar, Department of Geography,
Patna University,
Patna, Bihar.

Kamla Prasad
H.O.D. Geography, Vinoba Bhave University,
Hazaribag, Jharkhand.

Kaushalendra Prakash Goswami
P.G. Geography, Magadh University,
Bodh-Gaya, Bihar.

Kumar Braj Nandan
Research Scholar, T.M. Bhagalpur University,
Bhagalpur.

M.N. Pandey
Principal, R.N.A.R. College,
Samastipur, Bihar.

Manju Kumari
Research Scholar, T.M. Bhagalpur University,
Bhagalpur, Bihar.

Md. Naseemuddin
Reader in Geography, T.M. Bhagalpur University,
Bhagalpur, Bihar.

Namita Pattnaik
Lecturer in Geography, Government Women's College,
Sambalpur, Orissa.

Navin Kumar
Lecturer in Geography, V.K.S. University,
Ara, Bihar.

Prakhar Prakash
Government School of Dharhara Block,
Munger, Bihar.

Praween Kumar Sharma
Department of Geography, Vinoba Bhave University,
Hazaribag.

R.B. Mandal
University Professor of Geography
T.M. Bhagalpur University, Bhagalpur, Bihar.

Rajendra Kumar Das
Research Scholar in Geography,
Vinoba Bhave University,
Hazaribag, Jharkhand.

Rana Pratap
H.O.D. Geography, Magadh University,
Bodh-Gaya, Bihar.

Rashmi Prakash
Reader in Geography, T.M. Bhagalpur University,
Bhagalpur, Bihar.

Sanjay Kumar Jha
Lecturer in Geography, Sabour College,
Sabour, Bihar.

Satya Raj
Research Scholar in Geography, Patna University,
Patna, Bihar.

Sharda Nand Choudhary
Reader in Geography, M.K. College, Laheriasarai,
Darbhanga, Bihar.

Shobha Kumari
Research Scholar, B.R.A. Bihar University,
Muzaffarpur, Bihar.

Sudha Kumari Singh
Asstt. Teacher, S.D.S. High School,
Munger.

Sumit Dhanuka
Research Scholar, P.O. Kasba,
Distt. Purnea, Bihar

Tulika Sinha
Research Scholar, Magadh University,
Bodh Gaya, Bihar.

U.S. Pandit
Reader in Geography,
T.N.B. College, Bhagalpur, Bihar.

Vinay Nath Jha
Lecturer in Geography, M.L.S.M. College,
Darbhanga, Bihar.

Bibliography

Agarwal, A. *Ganga Action Plan—An Assessment,* Delhi Book Depot, Delhi. 1999.

Agarwal, D.K., Gaur, S.D., Tiwari, T.C., Narayanswami, M.S. and Marwah, S.M. "Physio-chemical characteristics of Ganga water at Varanasi", *Indian Journal of Environment and Health,* Vol. 18, 1976, pp. 201-205.

Ahmad, Q.K. *et al: Ganges, Brahamaputra, Meghna Region: A Framework for Sustainable Development,* the Dhaka University Press, 2001.

Alam, A. 'Fluoride in water.' In survey of the Environment, *The Hindu,* 2004, pp. 25-28.

Annual Report (1994-95) *Ganga Flood Control Commission,* Ministry of Water Resources, Govt. of India, Patna.

Arun, K. Saraf and Arun Kumar, GIS in Small Hydro Planning Resource Management; *GIS Development,* Sep.-Oct. 1997.

Bandopadhyay, J., 'Water Management in the Ganges, Brahamputra Basin : Challenges for the 21st Century', *International Journal of Water Resource Development,* 11 (4), 1995.

Bandopadhyay, J., Sustainability of Big Dams in the Himalaya, *Economic and Political Weekly,* 30 (38) September 23, 1995.

Bansil, P.C., *Water Management in India,* Concept Publishing Company, New Delhi, 2004.

Bavadam, Lyla; 'Fluoride in water, in Survey of the Environment', *The Hindu,* 2004, pp. 29-32.

Bhargave, D.S., "Purification Power of the Ganga Unmatches", *L.S.T. Bulletin,* No. 34, 1982, pp. 50-56.

Bilgrami, K.S. and Dutta, Munshi J.S., "Effects of Industrial Water on the Hydrobiological Status of the River Ganges", *The Indian Journal of Zoology,* Vol. 20, No. 2, 1979, pp. 95-102.

Bilgrami, K.S. and Dutta, Munshi J.S., "Ecology of River Ganga

Impact of human activities and conservation of aquatic biota", Final Report (May 1982 to April 1985), Post-Graduate Department of Botany, Bhagalpur University, 1985.

Bilgrami, K.S., *The Living Ganga : Ganga Down the Ages,* Narendra Publishing House, New Delhi, 1991, p. 3.

Biswas, A.K.; *Systems Approach to Water Management,* Tokyo McGraw Hill, 1976.

B.J., Dams for the Third Millonium, Himalaya, *The South Asian Magazine,* 11 (3), 1998.

B.J. and B. Mallick, *Book Review in Water International,* 26 (4), 2001.

B.J. and D. Gyawali, Himalayan Water Resources : Ecological and Political Aspects of Management, *Mountain Research and Development,* (14) 1-24, 1994.

Bhadram, C.V.V., Role of Indian Meteorological Department in Mitigating the Flood Disaster, National Workshop on Flood Disaster Management Space Inputs, 3-4 June, NRSA, Hyderabad, 2004.

Bhanumurthy, V., NRSA Contribution in Flood Management using Satellite Data, National Workshop on Flood Disaster Management—Space Inputs, 3-4 June, 2004, NRSA, Hyderabad India.

Burns, B.R. and Dick, R.M., *Negotiating Water Rights,* Sage Publications, New Delhi, 2000.

Chopra, K. *et al., Water Resources, Sustainable Livelihood and Ecosystem Services,* Concept Publishing Company, New Delhi, 2003.

Chorley, R.J., *Water, Earth and Man,* Methuen & Co. Ltd., London, 1969, p. 109.

Dasgupta, R., 'Arsenic in Water', in Survey of the Environment, *The Hindu,* 2004, pp. 33-38.

Dastane, N.G., Water Supply to Crops. *Indian Farming,* Vol. XXII. No. 2, 1972, pp. 18-23.

Dakshinamurti, C., Michael, A.M. and Mohan, S., *Water Resources of India and Their Utilization in Agriculture,* Water Technology Center, New Delhi, 1973.

Dakshinamurti, C. *et al.,* 'Soil Management for efficient water use', *Indian Farming,* Vol. XXII, No. 2, 1972, pp. 9-11.

Dutta, S.K., 'Geohydrological Reporting on Thermal Springs of Munger', Rural Electrification Corporation of India Undertaking, 1973, pp. 2-3.

Dixit, A., *Basic Water Science,* Nepal water Conservation Foundation, Kathmandu, 2001.

Falkenmark, M., Freshwater : Time for a Modified Approach, *AMBIO* 15 (4), 1986.

Forbes, Rej., *Irrigation and Power Studies in Ancient Technology,* Vol. 2, 1965, p. 220.

Gadgil, D.R., *Economic Effects of Irrigation,* 1945, p. 173.

Gandhi, R.T. *et al., 'Handbook on Irrigation Water Management; Water Management Division,* MOA, GOI, 1971, pp. 7-17.

Gaur, V.K., Earthquake Hazards and Large Dams on the Himalaya, New Delhi, INTACH, 1993.

Gopal, B., *et al., Wetland Ecology and Management,* National Institute of Ecology and International Scientific Publications, Jaipur, 1982.

Grover, Swati, Perspectives of GIS Modelling in Hydrology GIS Development; Nov.-Dec. 1999.

Gupta, H.K., Sciesmocity in the vicinity of dams in the Himalayan Rivers, *Journal of the Geological Society of India,* 1984.

Gyawali, D. and A. Dixit, Mahakali Impasse and Indo-Nepal Water Conflict; *Economic and Political Weekly,* Feb. 27, 1999.

Guha, S.K. and Nag, P., *'Studies on Hot Springs of Munger District,* 1971.

IARI, "Water Requirement and Irrigation Management of Crops in India", Water Technology Centre, IARI, New Delhi, 1977.

Jain, S.N. *et al.* Inter-state Water Disputes in India : Suggestions for Reform in Law; The Indian Law Institute, New Delhi, 1971.

Jairath, J.; *Water User's Association in Andhra Pradesh,* Concept Publishing Company, New Delhi, 2001.

Jagadeesha, C.J. *Water Resources Development and Management GIS Development,* Nov.-Dec. 1999.

Jayanta Bandopadhyay, "A Critical Look at the World Commission on Dams (WCD) in the Context of the Debate on Large Dams on the Himalayan Rivers", *Indian Journal of Landscape Systems and Ecological Studies,* Vol. 27, No. 1, June 2004.

Johnson, I.N.C, *Ground Water and Wells,* Edward E. Johnson Inc., Minnesota, 1966, p. 440.

Kathpalia, G.N., "Water Policy in Agriculture", *Indian Farming,* Vol. XXII, No. 2, 1972, pp. 17-18.

Kayastha, S.L. and Kumra, V.K., "Ganga Water Pollution in Kanpur City : A Geographical Analysis", *Transactions of the Institute of Indian Geographers,* Vol. 4, No. 1, 1982, pp. 5-6.

Kumar, De and Shah, Tushaar, 'Groundwater contamination'; in Survey of the Environment, *The Hindu,* 2004, pp. 1-6.

Kumar, S.; *Agricultural Utilization of Water Resources in Munger and Jamui Districts, (Bihar),* Ph.D. Thesis, 2003.

Laskhminarayan, J.S.S., "Phytoplankton of the River Ganga", Unpublished Ph.D. Thesis, B.H.U., Varanasi, 1959.

Lee, T. and Burton, J., 'Future Water Supply for Indian Cities', *Deccan Geographer,* 1965, pp. 3-4.

Limaya, S.D., To Dam or Not to Dam ? A Water Resource Overview from Developed Countries, Stockholm Water Front, No. 2, June, 2001.

Lundquist, J. *et al.,* Sustaining our Water into 21st Century : Comprehensive Assessment of the Freshwater Resources of the World; Stockholm Environmental Institute, 1997.

Mandal, R.B., *Urban Water Supply in Urban Geography : A Text Book,* Concept Publishing Company, New Delhi, 2000, pp. 389-395.

Mandal, R.B.; '*Water Resource Utilization and Management',* Abstract Volume, University Department of Geography, Bhagalpur, 2003.

Mandal, R.B., '*Wetlands Management in North Bihar',* Concept Publishing Company, New Delhi, 2004.

Mamoria, C.B., *Irrigation and Floods : Agricultural Problems of India,* Kitab Mahal, Allahabad, 1973, p. 161.

Mithal, R.S., 'Geotectonic Evaluation for Development of Water Resources in India', Presidential Address at the 66th Session, Indian Science Congress Association, Calcutta, 1979, pp. 1-2.

Mirthy, *Irrigation Research,* Publication Division, Patiala House, New Delhi, 1970, p. 13.

MOA, Soil and Water Conservation and Watershed Management in India. Ministry of Agriculture, GOI, New Delhi, 1984.

Mollinga, P., *Water for Food and Rural Development,* Sage Publication, New Delhi, 2000.

MOWR, Major River Basins of India : An Overview, Ministry of Water Resource, New Delhi, 1989.

Nag, B.S. and Kathoplia, G.N., Water Resources of India; Proceedings of Second World Congress on Water Resources, 1975, pp. 373-382.

Nawalawala, B.N., World Commission on Dams, *Economic and Political Weekly,* 2001.

Navalawala, B.N., Water Resources Development in India : Shift in Polio Paradigm; Water & Energy International, Jan.-Mar. 2002.

Pahwa, D.V. and Mahrotra, S.N., "Observation on fluctuation on the abundance of Plankton in relation to certain hydro biological condition of river Ganga", Proceeding of National Academic, Science of India, Section B, 36 (2), 1966, pp. 157-187.

Pandey, G.N., Bharti, A. and Saxena, R.P. "Role of Microflora in the Assessment of Pollution Level of River Ganga at Kanpur", *Journal Inst. Engn. India,* Vol. 61, 1980, pp. 27-34.

Prasad, M., *Water Resource Utilization : A Case Study of Gaya District (Bihar),* Abstract Water Resource Utilization and Management, Bhagalpur, 2003, p. 26.

Pratap, R. "Pollution in River Ganga in Bihar—A Geographical Analysis", in B. Thakur (ed.) *Research Management in Developing Countries,* Vol. 6 (Water Supply and Quality), Concept Publishing Co., New Delhi, 1993.

Pratap, R., "The Main Pollutants in the Water of River Ganga in and around Patna : A Geographical Study", *Magadh Geographical Review,* Bodh-Gaya, Vol. I, No. 1, 1998, pp. 33-38.

Pratap, R. and Pratap. D., "Waste Water Management for Controlling the Ganga Pollution : A Case Study of Patna", Proceedings of Bihar Vigyan Congress, Patna, February 28, 2003, p. 25.

Pratap, R., "Water Pollution in Bihar", *Geographical Review of India,* Vol. 47, No. 4,1985, pp. 75-78.

Pratap, R., "Action Plan and the Control of Pollution in Ganga Water in Bihar", Paper presented at the Earth System Sciences Section of the 78th ISCA, Calcutta, 1990, pp. 1-5.

Punmia, B. & Pandey, B.B., '*Irrigation and Water Power Engineering,* Standard Publishers and Distsributors, Delhi, 1992, pp. 59-60.

Rama; Underground Reservoirs Intensive Irrigation and Flood Control, *Science Today,* 1971.

Ramana, M.V.V., *Inter-state River Water Disputes in India,* Orient Longman Ltd., 1990.

Rangachari, R. and R.G. Verghese, "Making water work to translate Poverty into Prosperity." *The Ganga Brahamputra Barak Region* in Q.K. Ahmad (Ed.), 1987, p. 87.

Rao, K.L., *India Water Wealth,* Orient Longman Ltd., New Delhi, 1979.

Rao, K.L., *India's Water Wealth;* Orient Longman, New Delhi, 1975, p. 219.

Rao, U.R., Floods and Droughts, Presented in TAF-COSPAR Symposium on Space Application for Disaster Prevention,

Warning Mitigation and Relief, Meeting of the Scientific and Technical Committee, UN Committee on Peaceful uses of Outer Space, Vienna, Feb. 21-22, 1994.

Rautela, P., *Water Resources in the Himalayas : Harvesting Technology and Change,* Concept Publishing Company, New Delhi, 2000.

Ray, P. and David, A., "Effects of Industrial Water and Sewage upon the Chemical and Biological Composition and Fisheries of the River Ganga at Kanpur", *Indian Journal of Environment and Health,* Vol. 8, 1966, pp. 307-338.

Report of the Kiul Badua Chandan Command Area Development Project, Agricultural Finance Consultants Limited, Bombay, 1990.

Riyar, R., *Water, Perspectives : Issues and Concerns,* Sage Publications, New Delhi, 2003.

Saxena, K.L., Chakravarty, R.N. Khan, A.Q. and Chattopadhya, S.N. "Pollution Studies of the River Ganges Near Kanpur", *Indian Journal of Environment and Health,* Vol. 8, 1966, pp. 270-286.

Seth, S.M., *Physically Based Hydrological Modelling*; GIS Development, Nov.-Dec. 1999.

Shanker, V., Sangu, R.S.P. and Joshi, G.C., "A Report on Integrated Study of the Ganga," Dept. of Botany, Gurukul Kangri University, Haridwar, 1986.

Shankar, G. Jai, B.S. Prakasa Rao, M. Jagannadha Rao and D.K. Jugrar; Hydromorphogeology and Remote Sensing Applications for Groundwater Exploration in Agnigundala Mineralised Belt, Andhra Pradesh, India; *Journal of Indian Society of Remote Sensing;* Sept. 2001.

Sharan, R.K. and Sinha, R.K., "Ganga Basin Research Project (Buxar-barh)" Final Technical Report, Dept. of Zoology, Patna University, 1988, p. 7.

Sharma, K.M., "Ganga Action Plan in Bihar", The Institute of Engineers, India (Souvenir, All India Council Meet), Patna, 1992, pp. 25-29.

Sklar, F.H. *et al.,* 'Dynamic Spatial Simulation Modelling of Coastal Wetland-Habitat Succession", *Ecology,* Vol. 29, 1985, pp. 261-281.

Saswati, Palk, The Saraswati, Where Lies the Mystery; *GIS Development,* Feb. 2000.

Shiklomanov, I.A.; World Freshwater Resources; in P.H. Gleick (Ed) *Water in Crises;* Oxford Uni. Press, 1993, p. 16.

Sinha, R.C. and Dayal, P., "Comprehensive Pollution Survey and Dry Studies of the Ganga River Basin in Bihar". A Project Report, Centre for Development Studies, Patna University, Patna, 1982.

Sinha, U.P., *Ganga-Pollution and Health Hazard*, Inter India Publication, New Delhi, 1986.

Singh, G.N. and Singh, Ramanuj—Food Security and Disaster Management During Floods in Bihar, Seminar on Water Resources Utilisation and Management, 18-19 Oct. 2003, Bihar Association of Geographers, Patna, pp. 68-69.

Singh, L. and Sinha, B.P., *Dynamics of Peoples Participation in Doon Valley Watershed Projects,* Concept Publishing Company, New Delhi, 2002.

Singh, R.S. (1989), "An Approach to Ganga Action Plan" in *Water Pollution 'Conservation and Management'* A.K. Sinha & others (eds.), Gyanodaya Prakashan, Nainital, pp. 7-12.

Srivastava, M. (2000), *Pollution of Ganga Water : A Limnological Study at Hardwar,* Shree Publishers, New Delhi, 2000.

Tejwani, K.G., *'Reservoir Sedimentation in India—Its causes, Control and Future Course of Action'*, Water International, 1984, pp. 150-154.

The Conservation Foundation, *'Protecting Americans Wetlands'*, An Action Agenda, 1988.

The Inter-state Water Disputes Act, 1956 (Act XXXIII of 1956).

The United State Army Corps of Engineers in Oregon, "Water Resource Development," North Pacific Division, Customs House, Protland, 1975, p. 37.

U.S. Fish and Wildlife Service, Wetlands Stratas and Trends Washington, D.C., U.S. Department of the Interior, 1991.

Verghese, B.G. *et al., Converting Water Into Wealth,* Konark Publishers, Delhi, 1994.

Vora, B.B., *A Policy for Land and Water,* Dept. of Environment, GOI, New Delhi, 1980.

'Water Supply and Sanitation', Ministry of Urban Development, New Delhi, Government of India Report 1988-89, pp. 12-14.

Wetland Conference in Czechoslovakia, *Nature and Resources, UNESCO,* Vol. XX. No. 2, 1984, p. 22.

World Commission on Dams, Dams and Development : A New Framework for Decision Making, London, 2000.

Index